Corel®

WordPerfect® 8

Illustrated Standard Edition

Corel® WordPerfect® 8

Illustrated Standard Edition

Rachel Biheller Bunin
Mary-Terese Cozzola
Pam Conrad

COURSE TECHNOLOGY

ONE MAIN STREET, CAMBRIDGE, MA 02142

an International Thomson Publishing company I(T)P®

Cambridge • Albany • Bonn • Boston • Cincinnati • London • Madrid • Melbourne • Mexico City
New York • Paris • San Francisco • Singapore • Tokyo • Toronto • Washington

Corel WordPerfect 8—Illustrated Standard Edition is published by Course Technology

Managing Editor: Nicole Jones Pinard
Product Manager: Jennifer Thompson
Production Editor: Melissa Lima
Development Editors: Maxine Effenson Chuck, David C. Crocco
Composition House: GEX, Inc.
QA Manuscript Reviewer: Heather McKinstry, Jessica Sisak, Alex White
Text Designer: Joseph Lee
Cover Designer: Joseph Lee

For more information contact:

Course Technology
One Main Street
Cambridge, MA 02142

ITP Europe
Berkshire House 168-173
High Holborn
London WC1V 7AA
England

Nelson ITP, Australia
102 Dodds Street
South Melbourne, 3205
Victoria, Australia

ITP Nelson Canada
1120 Birchmount Road
Scarborough, Ontario
Canada M1K 5G4

International Thomson Editores
Seneca, 53
Colonia Polanco
11560 Mexico D.F. Mexico

ITP GmbH
Königswinterer Strasse 418
53277 Bonn
Germany

ITP Asia
60 Albert Street, #15-01
Albert Complex
Singapore 189969

ITP Japan
Hirakawacho Kyowa Building, 3F
2-2-1 Hirakawacho
Chiyoda-ku, Tokyo 102
Japan

Trademarks

Disclaimer

ISBN 0-7600-5948-9

Printed in the United States of America

1 2 3 4 5 6 7 8 9 BM 01 00 99 98 97

Exciting New Illustrated Products

The Illustrated Projects™ Series: The Quick, Visual Way to Apply Computer Skills

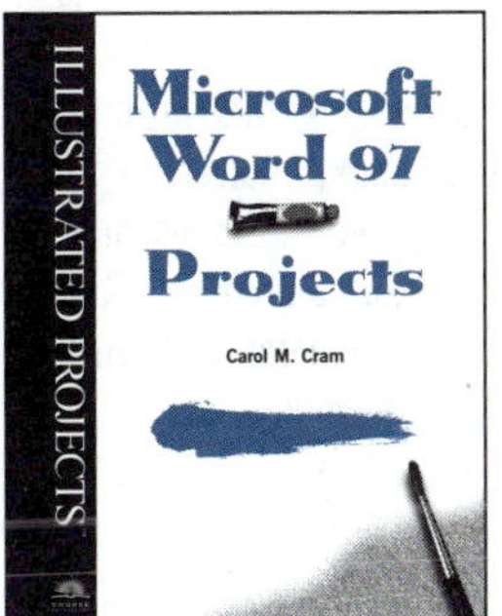

Looking for an inexpensive, easy way to supplement almost any application text and give your students the practice and tools they'll need to compete in today's competitive marketplace? Each text includes more than 50 real-world, useful projects—like creating a resume and setting up a loan worksheet—that let students hone their computer skills. These two-color texts have the same great two-page layout as the Illustrated Series.

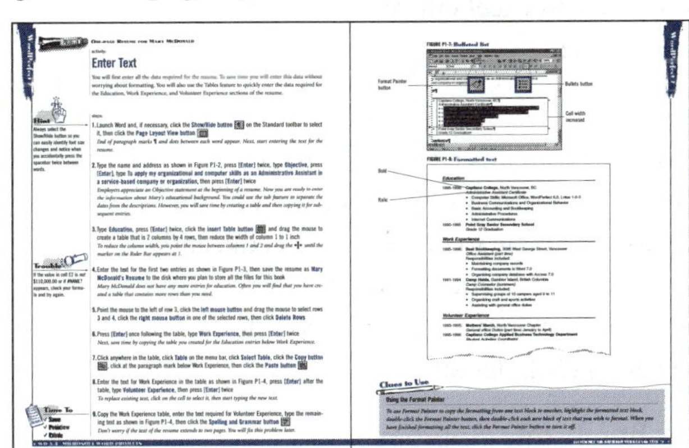

Illustrated Projects titles are available for the following:

- Microsoft Access
- Microsoft Excel
- Microsoft Office Professional
- Microsoft Publisher
- Microsoft Word
- Creating Web Sites
- World Wide Web
- Adobe PageMaker
- Corel WordPerfect

Illustrated Interactive™ Series: The Safe, Simulated Way to Learn Computer Skills

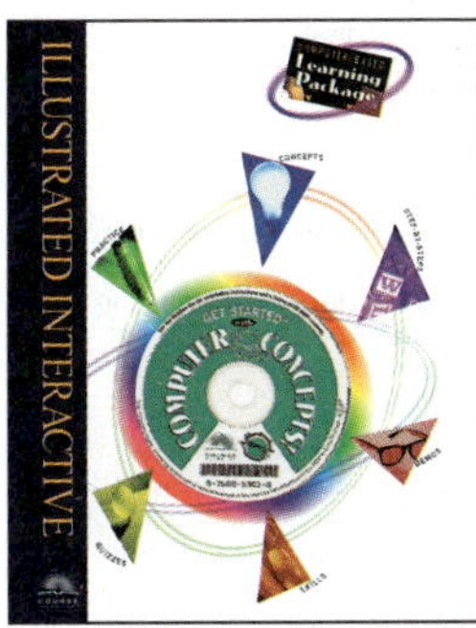

The Ilustrated Interactive Series uses multimedia technology to teach computer concepts and application skills. Students learn via a CD-ROM that simulates the actual software and provides a controlled learning environment in which every keystroke is monitored. Plus, all products in this series feature the same step-by-step instructions as the Illustrated Series. An accompanying workbook reinforces the skills that students learn on the CD.

Illustrated Interactive titles are available for the following applications:*

- Microsoft Office 97
- Microsoft Word 97
- Microsoft Excel 97
- Microsoft Access 97
- Microsoft PowerPoint 97
- Computer Concepts

***Standalone & networked versions available. Runs on Windows 3.1, 95, and NT. CD-only version available for Computer Concepts and Office 97.**

CourseKits™: Offering You the Freedom to Choose

Balance your course curriculum with Course Technology's mix-and-match approach to selecting texts. CourseKits provide you with the freedom to make choices from more than one series. When you choose any two or more Course Technology products for one course, we'll discount the price and package them together so your students pick up one convenient bundle at the bookstore.

Contact your sales representative to find out more about these Illustrated products.

Preface

Welcome to *Corel WordPerfect 8 – Illustrated Standard Edition*! This highly visual book offers new users a hands-on introduction to WordPerfect 8 and also serves as an excellent reference for future use.

► Organization and Coverage

This text contains eight units that cover basic WordPerfect skills. In these units students learn how to design, create, edit, and enhance WordPerfect documents. The last unit focuses on using WordPerfect to create an HTML document.

► About this Approach

What makes the Illustrated approach so effective at teaching software skills? It's quite simple. Each skill is presented on two facing pages, with the step-by-step instructions on the left page, and large screen illustrations on the right. Students can focus on a single skill without having to turn the page. This unique design makes information extremely accessible and easy to absorb, and provides a great reference for after the course is over. This hands-on approach also makes it ideal for both self-paced or instructor-led classes.

Each lesson, or "information display," contains the following elements:

Each 2-page spread focuses on a single skill.

Concise text that introduces the basic principles discussed in the lesson. Procedures are easier to learn when concepts fit into a framework.

Deleting and Inserting Text

You often need to edit a document by deleting text or inserting new text. WordPerfect's correcting tools save you time and energy by deleting portions of text, adding new text, or correcting text. Different modes in WordPerfect allow you to add and delete text as well. Table B-3 lists methods of changing or correcting text. Emily Caitlin reviewed your first draft and marked a few words that you need to change. Figure B-6 shows the changes she wants you to make.

Trouble? If the pointer changes to , click outside the selected text, then try again.

1. Click before the **D** in **Diner** in the first paragraph of text, then press **[Delete]** six times
   The Delete key is a **destructive movement key**; it deletes characters to the right of the insertion point. The word "Diner" is deleted. The correct name is actually "Frazzle's Restaurant."
2. Type **Restaurant**, then press **[Spacebar]**
   The text is entered at the insertion point. The General Status button on the Application Bar indicates that WordPerfect is in **Insert** mode, as shown in Figure B-7. Insert mode allows you to type additional text without deleting or writing over the existing text. The existing text moves to the right as you type and automatically wraps to the next line. Next, you'll use the Delete key again.
3. Double-click the word **block**, then press **[Delete]**
   The word "block" is deleted.
4. Press **[Spacebar]**, type **road**, click after the word **so** in the first line, then press **[Backspace]** three times
   The [Backspace] key is also a destructive movement key; it deletes characters to the left of the insertion point. You deleted the two letters and the extra space between the words "are" and "happy." Now you need to correct the Corel product name.

QuickTip Whenever you select text, release the mouse button after you reach the end of the text you need to select.

5. Scroll down and click after the word **Core**, then type **l**
   The word Corel is now spelled correctly. This correction highlights the importance of reading through your work before you print it. The Spell-As-You-Go feature only flags words not in WordPerfect's dictionary. A word such as "Core" may be contained in the dictionary, yet still be a misspelling in the context of a particular sentence. Next, Emily wants you to include a note about recycling paper.
6. Scroll down and click after the word **creatively**, press **[Enter]**, then type **Recycle all scrap paper**
   The letter is coming along nicely. As you continue working, remember to save your changes.
7. Click the **Save button** on the Toolbar

Clues to Use

Typeover and Insert Modes

Double-click Insert on the Status bar or press the Insert key to display "Typeover" in place of "Insert" on the Application bar. Double-click Typeover on the Status bar or press the Insert key to display "Insert." This Status bar item is called a **toggle button** because it switches WordPerfect back and forth between two modes: Insert and Typeover. In Insert mode, as each character is added, the text shifts to the right to make room for the inserted text. In Typeover mode, you "type over" or replace existing text when making a correction.

► WP B-8 CREATING A DOCUMENT

Clues to Use boxes provide concise information that either expands on one component of the major lesson skill or describes an independent task that is in some way related to the major lesson skill.

Tips as well as trouble-shooting advice right where you need it – next to the step itself.

Clear step-by-step directions explain how to complete the specific task, with what students are to type in red. When students follow the numbered steps, they quickly learn how each procedure is performed and what the results will be.

Other Features

The two-page lesson format featured in this book provides the new user with a powerful learning experience. Additionally, this book contains the following features:

► Real-World Skills

The skills used throughout the textbook are designed to be "real-world" in nature and representative of the kinds of activities that students encounter when working with WordPerfect 8. With a real-world case, the process of solving problems will be more meaningful to students.

► End of Unit Material

Each unit concludes with a Concepts Review that tests students' understanding of what they learned in the unit. The Concepts Review is followed by a Skills Review, which provides students with additional hands-on practice of the skills they learned in the unit. The Skills Review is followed by Independent Challenges, which pose case problems for students to solve. The Visual Workshops allow students to learn by exploring and to develop critical thinking skills.

Every lesson features large-size, full-color representations of what the students' screen should look like after completing the numbered steps.

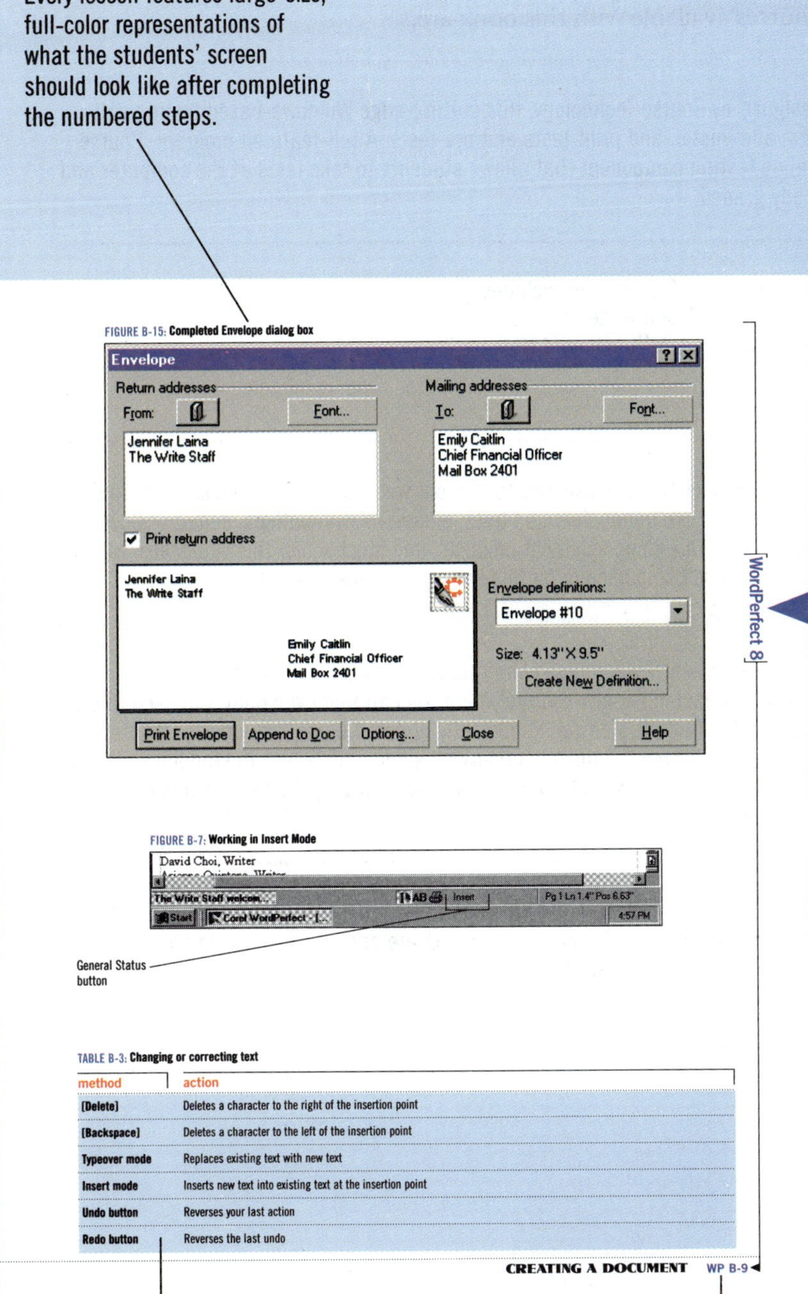

FIGURE B-15: Completed Envelope dialog box

FIGURE B-7: Working in Insert Mode

General Status button

TABLE B-3: Changing or correcting text

method	action
[Delete]	Deletes a character to the right of the insertion point
[Backspace]	Deletes a character to the left of the insertion point
Typeover mode	Replaces existing text with new text
Insert mode	Inserts new text into existing text at the insertion point
Undo button	Reverses your last action
Redo button	Reverses the last undo

CREATING A DOCUMENT WP B-9

WordPerfect 8

Quickly accessible summaries of key terms, toolbar buttons, or keyboard alternatives connected with the lesson material. Students can refer easily to this information when working on their own projects at a later time.

The page numbers are designed like a road map. WP indicates the WordPerfect section, B indicates the second unit, and 9 indicates the page within the unit.

Instructor's Resource Kit

The Instructor's Resource Kit is Course Technology's way of putting the resources and information needed to teach and learn effectively into your hands. With an integrated array of teaching and learning tools that offer you and your students a broad range of technology-based instructional options, we believe this kit represents the highest quality and most cutting edge resources available to instructors today. Many of these resources are available at www.course.com. The resources available with this book are:

Course Test Manager Designed by Course Technology, this cutting-edge Windows-based testing software helps instructors design, administer, and print tests and pre-tests. A full-featured program, Course Test Manager also has an online testing component that allows students to take tests at the computer and have their exams automatically graded.

Instructor's Manual Quality assurance tested and includes:

- Solutions to all lessons and end-of-unit material
- Detailed lecture topics for each unit with teaching tips
- Extra Independent Challenges
- Student Files

www.course.com We encourage students and instructors to visit our web site at www.course.com to find articles about current teaching and software trends, featured texts, interviews with authors, demos of Course Technology's software, Frequently Asked Questions about our products, and much more. This site is also where you can gain access to the Faculty Online Companion or for this text – see below for more information.

Faculty Online Companion Available at www.course.com, this World Wide Web site offers Course Technology customers a password-protected Faculty Lounge where you can find everything you need to prepare for class including the online Instructor's Manual. Periodically updated items include any updates and revisions to the text and Instructor's Manual, links to other Web sites, and access to student and solution files. This site will continue to evolve throughout the semester. Contact your Customer Service Representative for the site address and password.

Student Files To use this book students must have the Student Files. See the inside front or inside back cover for more information on the Student Files. Adopters of this text are granted the right to post the Student Files on any stand-alone computer or network.

Brief Contents

Contents

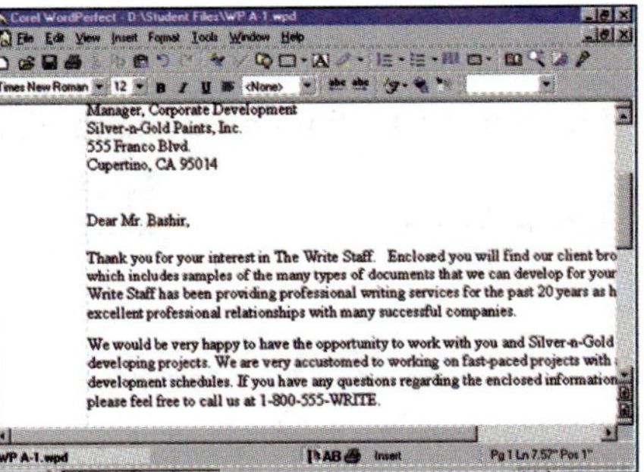

Manager, Corporate Development
Silver-n-Gold Paints, Inc.
555 Franco Blvd.
Cupertino, CA 95014
Dear Mr. Bashir,

Contents

Creating a Document WP B-1

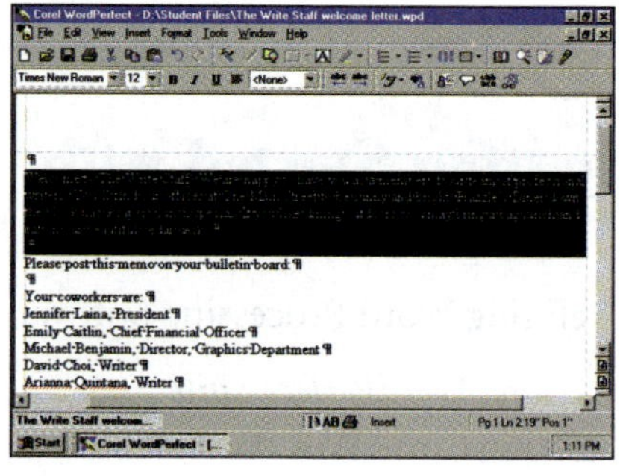

Editing a Document WP C-1

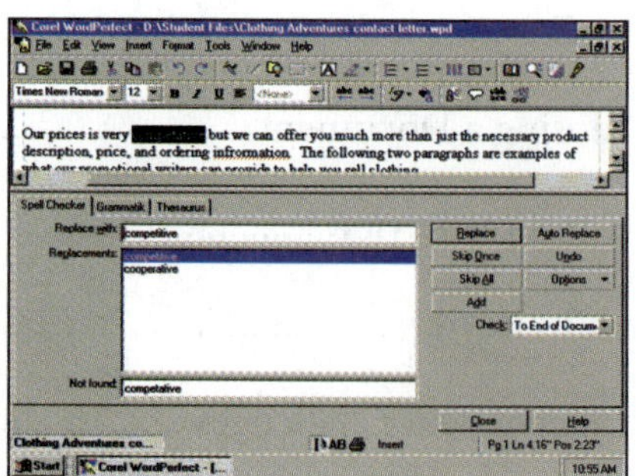

Formatting a Document WP D-1

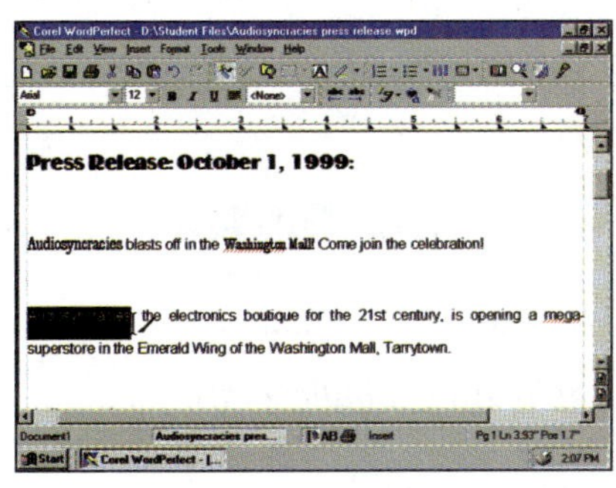

Working with Multiple-Page Documents and Graphic Images WP E-1

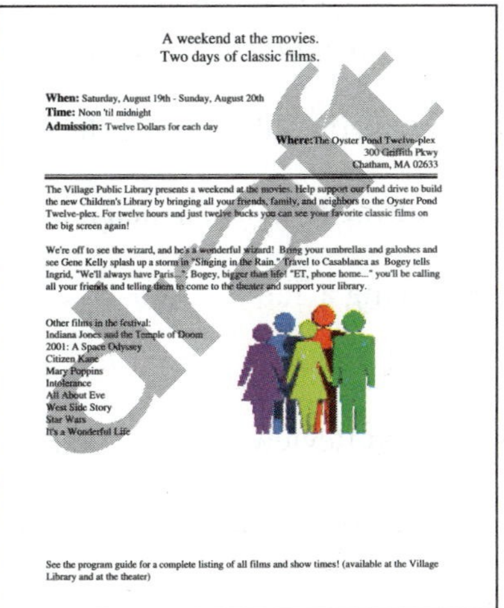

A weekend at the movies.
Two days of classic films.

When: Saturday, August 19th - Sunday, August 20th
Time: Noon 'til midnight
Admission: Twelve Dollars for each day

Where: The Oyster Pond Twelve-plex
300 Griffith Pkwy
Chatham, MA 02633

The Village Public Library presents a weekend at the movies. Help support our fund drive to build the new Children's Library by bringing all your friends, family, and neighbors to the Oyster Pond Twelve-plex. For twelve hours and just twelve bucks you can see your favorite classic films on the big screen again!

We're off to see the wizard, and he's a wonderful wizard! Bring your umbrellas and galoshes and see Gene Kelly splash up a storm in "Singing in the Rain." Travel to Casablanca as Bogey tells Ingrid, "We'll always have Paris...", Bogey, bigger than life! "ET, phone home..." you'll be calling all your friends and telling them to come to the theater and support your library.

Other films in the festival:
Indiana Jones and the Temple of Doom
2001: A Space Odyssey
Citizen Kane
Mary Poppins
Intolerance
All About Eve
West Side Story
Star Wars
It's a Wonderful Life

See the program guide for a complete listing of all films and show times! (available at the Village Library and at the theater)

Contents

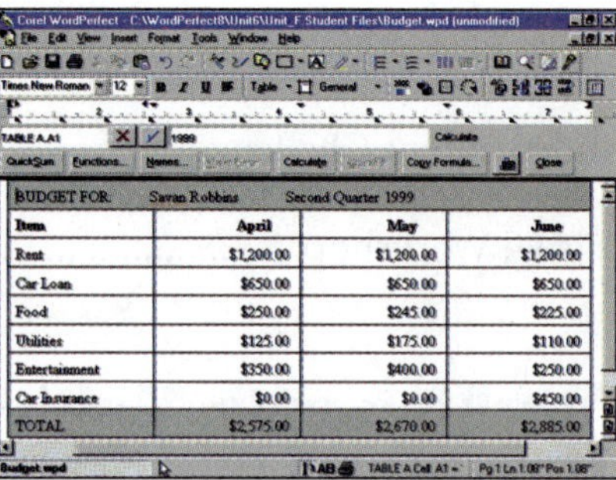

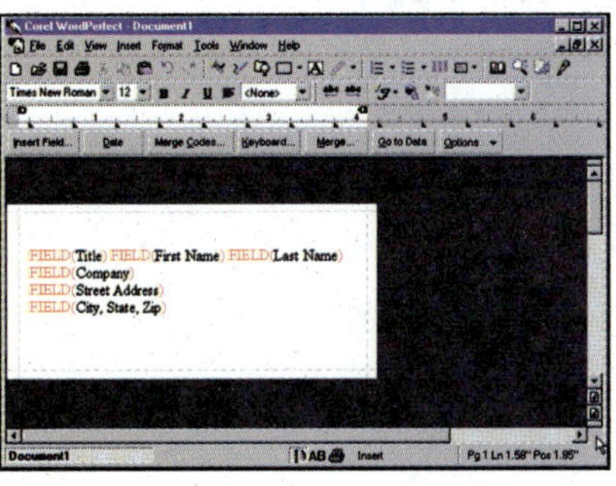

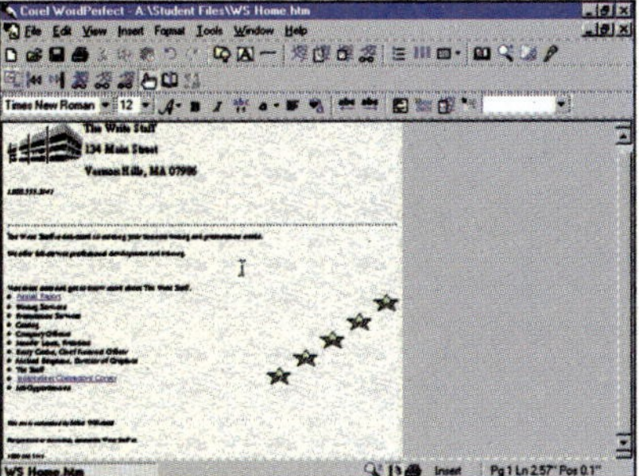

Contents

Getting Started with Corel WordPerfect 8

Objectives

- Define word processing software
- Start Corel WordPerfect 8
- View the WordPerfect window
- Open an existing document
- Move around the document
- Get Help
- Save a document
- Print a document
- Close a document

This unit introduces WordPerfect and its basic features. It also introduces the company that will be used as a case study throughout this book, The Write Staff. The Write Staff provides writing services for small businesses. It has recently upgraded its office software to Corel WordPerfect Suite 8; all documents will be written using WordPerfect 8. Jennifer Laina, the company's owner, has hired you to join her team of professional writers. As part of your responsibilities, you will write descriptions for catalogs, compose letters to clients, draft press releases, design advertising copy, send memos to other employees, and prepare written reports. You'll need to familiarize yourself with WordPerfect 8 quickly so that you can begin your assignments.

Defining Word Processing Software

You use a **word processor** to organize and present text on a page. Text entered into a word processor is defined as a **document**. In addition to words, text-based documents can include numbers and graphic images. WordPerfect is a word processor that enables you to produce a variety of documents including letters, memos, newsletters, and reports. Figure A-1 shows sample documents created with WordPerfect. WordPerfect's easy-to-use features and tools facilitate writing, revising, and printing documents.

Using a word processor provides you with the ability to:

Make editing changes, delete unwanted text, and insert new text at any location in a document.
WordPerfect lets you enhance your work by adding and deleting text anywhere in your document.

Move text from one location in a document to another without having to reenter the text.
WordPerfect lets you change text rather than retyping it, making writing more efficient and enjoyable.

Locate and correct grammatical errors and common spelling mistakes.
WordPerfect provides tools to improve your grammar and vocabulary as well as correct spelling errors.

Move quickly to any point in the document.
WordPerfect provides tools that facilitate working with large documents, so that you can access specific sections or words directly.

Make formatting changes to enhance a document's appearance.
WordPerfect has several formatting features which enable you to convey your message not only with words, but also by the look of text on the page.

Align text in rows and columns using tables.
WordPerfect provides Table tools to organize your tabular data in the proper format.

Create customized form letters, envelopes, and labels.
WordPerfect can print documents in special pre-designed formats, so that you can conduct business and personal correspondence with professionalism and flair.

Use PerfectExpert to create pre-designed documents.
WordPerfect's PerfectExpert helps you create a variety of business and personal documents based on pre-designed formats, so great-looking materials take only minutes to produce.

Add visual interest to your documents by inserting graphics and arranging text in interesting ways.
With WordPerfect graphics, a picture can convey your message or reflect the theme of your document.

Preview a document before printing to see what it will look like.
WordPerfect preview features let you see what your document will look like before printing, to save time and paper.

FIGURE A-1: Documents created using Corel WordPerfect 8

Rose Costumers
35 Bedminster Road
Orangetown, NY 10987
212-555-6334

August 22, 1999

Jourdain Dance Company
383 Holiday Avenue
River Edge, New Jersey 07628

Dear Ms. Jourdain:

Thank you for your interest in our services. Recently our company provided costumes for the National Ballet School's production of *The Nutcracker Suite*.

If you would like to preview our latest dance attire, please call for a personal appointment.

Sincerely,

Bella Boyd Rose,
Owner

...Perfection in Costuming Since 1972

Letter with graphics

Sun	Mon	Tue	Wed	Thu	Fri	Sat
May 1999						1
2	3	4	5	6	7	8 Water Lawn for Garden Walk
9 Plant Peas	10	11	12	13	14	15 Garden Walk
16 Garden Walk	17	18	19	20	21	22
23	24	25	26	27	28	29
30 State Fair Deadline	31					

Pre-designed document format

Corel WordPerfect Suite

Corel WordPerfect 8 is the word processor in Corel WordPerfect Suite 8. This suite of programs also includes Quattro Pro 8, a spreadsheet program; Presentations 8, a presentation graphics program; Corel Photo House, a graphics program; Netscape Navigator 3.0, an Internet browser; and other applications designed to increase your productivity in business, academic, and personal projects.

WordPerfect 8

Starting Corel WordPerfect 8

To use WordPerfect, you must first turn on your computer and make sure Windows is running. Next, either double-click the WordPerfect icon on the desktop, or click the Start button on the taskbar, open the Corel WordPerfect Suite program menu, then click Corel WordPerfect 8. A slightly different procedure might be required for computers on a network. Your work day has begun at The Write Staff, so you need to start WordPerfect. If you have any problems accessing Windows or starting WordPerfect, consult your instructor or technical support person for assistance.

Steps

1. **Be sure that your computer and monitor are on, and that the Windows 95 desktop is displayed on your computer screen**
2. **Locate the taskbar**
   The taskbar is usually located at the bottom of your screen. On some systems, you must move the mouse pointer down to the bottom of the screen to display the taskbar. The **Desktop Applications Director (DAD)** is a Corel WordPerfect Suite feature that gives you quick access to other programs in the WordPerfect Suite. You can click DAD icons on the right side of the taskbar to move to other programs installed on your system.
3. **Click the Start button on the taskbar to display the Start menu**
   The Start menu opens.
4. **Point to Corel WordPerfect Suite 8**
   The Corel WordPerfect Suite 8 program group opens, as shown in Figure A-2, displaying the WordPerfect Suite programs installed on your computer.
5. **Click Corel WordPerfect 8**
   WordPerfect starts and opens the WordPerfect window, as shown in Figure A-3. You use this window to create a document.

QuickTip

Depending on your installation, you may have to point to Programs to display the Programs menu, then locate Corel WordPerfect 8 on this menu.

Compatibility with other word processors or previous WordPerfect versions

If you've created documents with some other word processor or another version of WordPerfect, you can work with them in WordPerfect 8. WordPerfect 8 recognizes and converts documents to work with the current version, so there is no need to spend time recreating existing work.

FIGURE A-2: Corel WordPerfect Suite 8 program group on Start menu

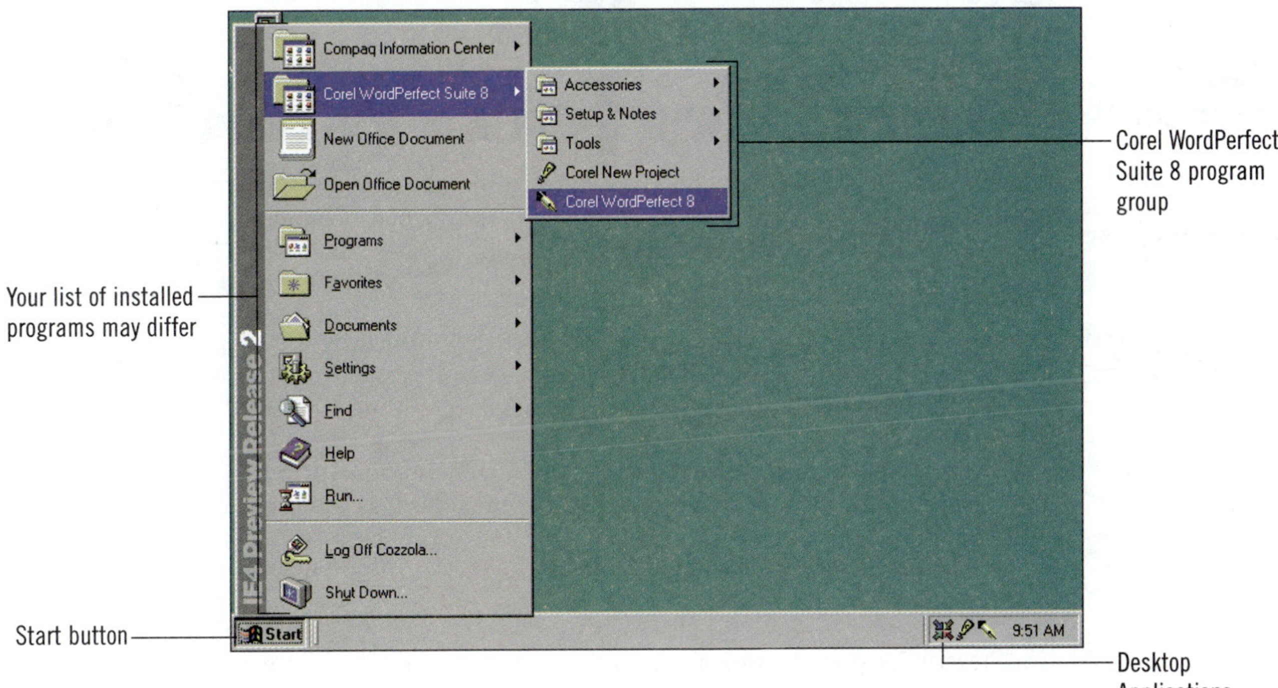

FIGURE A-3:WordPerfect window

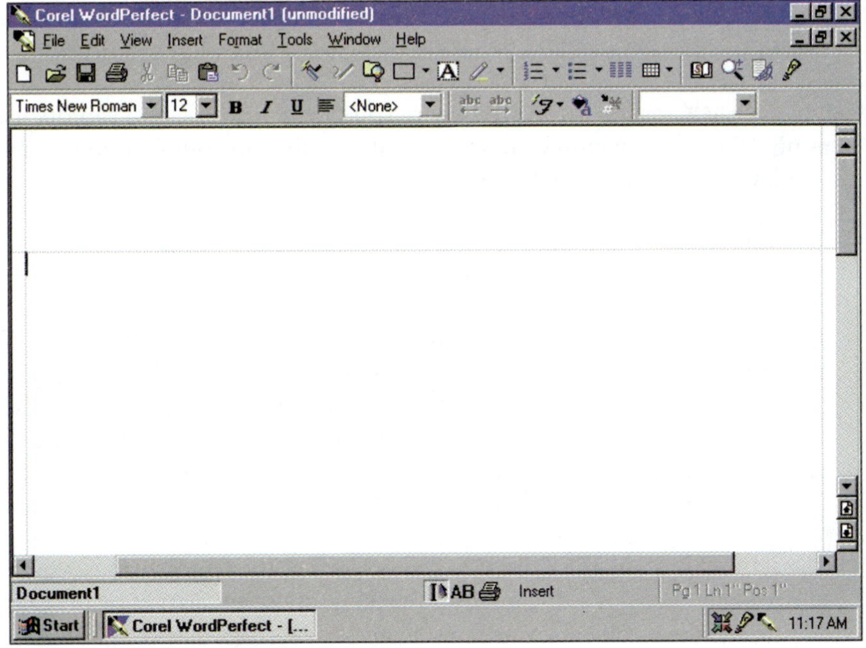

WordPerfect 8

WordPerfect 8

Viewing the WordPerfect Window

When you start WordPerfect, the WordPerfect program window appears. The items on the WordPerfect window enable you to create, edit, and format documents. Familiarize yourself with the WordPerfect window by comparing the descriptions below with Figure A-4.

Trouble?

If your WordPerfect window does not fill the entire screen, click the Maximize button on the program window.

The **title bar** contains the name "Corel WordPerfect" to identify the program, the drive and directory path, and the name given a document when it is saved and named. The title bar also indicates whether the document has been modified since it was last saved.

The **menu bar** lists the names of the menus that contain WordPerfect commands. Clicking a menu name on the menu bar displays a list of commands that you can choose.

The **WordPerfect 8 Toolbar** provides buttons for quick access to frequently used features and to additional Toolbars.

The **Property Bar** provides easy access to the most frequently used features in the current activity. For example, when you are working with text, the Property Bar displays common text editing and formatting commands such as a Font Face list box and a Bold formatting button.

The **Ruler** allows you to set and move tabs and margins, and to make paragraph adjustments quickly. Unless WordPerfect has been customized, the Ruler Bar does not appear above the document window. You will learn how to display the Ruler Bar in upcoming lessons.

The **document window** is the area where you type and work. You can open and arrange as many as nine document windows at one time, depending on your computer's available memory. Each window can be maximized, minimized, and sized.

The **insertion point** (blinking vertical bar) indicates the position on the screen where text will be inserted.

The **mouse pointer** indicates the position of the mouse on the screen. This pointer changes appearance, depending on where you point it and current Display options. The **I-beam pointer** I indicates that you are moving the mouse over existing text in the document. The **select pointer** indicates that you are pointing outside an editable area, such as in the left margin. When the **shadow cursor** is active, you can move the insertion point anywhere it appears in the document window by clicking the mouse button.

The **scroll bars** along the right side and bottom of the window allow you to move vertically and horizontally through a document by clicking the scroll arrows or dragging the scroll boxes. In addition to the scroll bars, you can use the **Previous Page button** and the **Next Page button** to move quickly through multiple-page documents.

The **Application Bar** displays and accesses information about all open WordPerfect documents, such as the active document, the current pointer, the current printer, and other general information.

The **Reveal Codes bar** allows you to drag open and size the Reveal Codes window.

The **Reveal Codes window** displays the codes behind the document that determine how the text is displayed and formatted on the page.

The **margin guidelines** define the page. The text you type appears within these dotted lines.

FIGURE A-4: The WordPerfect window

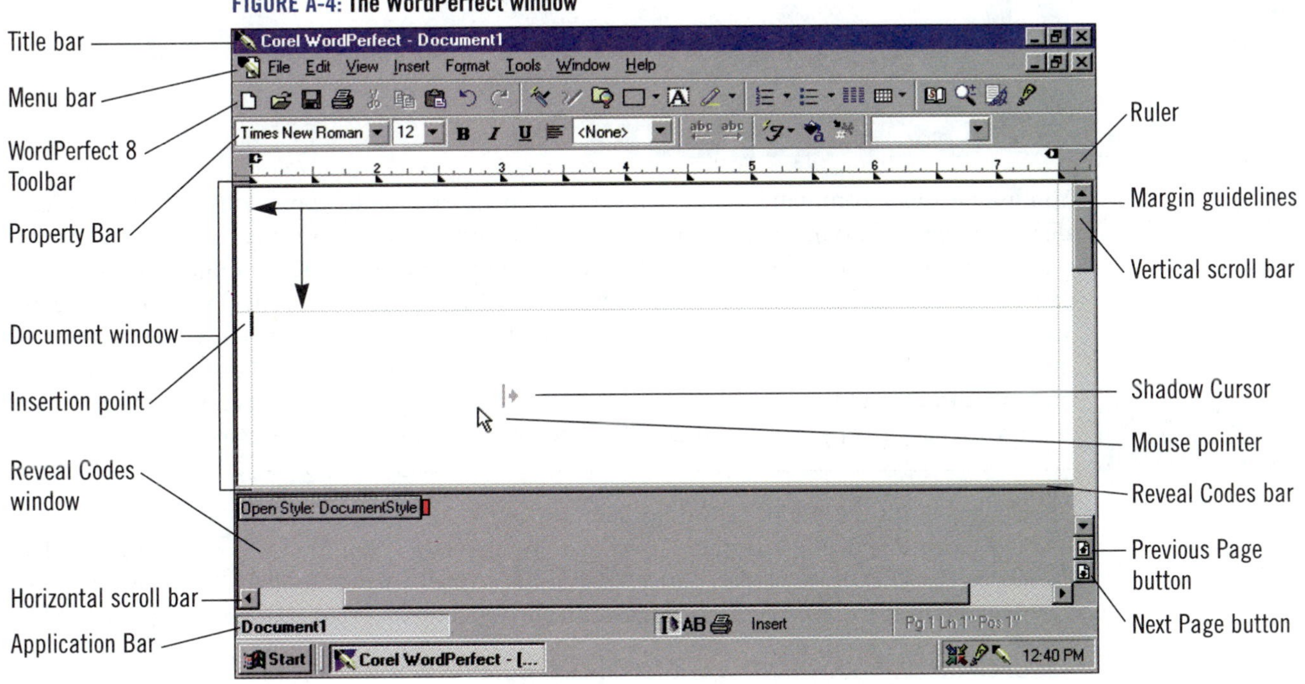

WordPerfect 8

Choosing a different Toolbar

WordPerfect provides 14 different Toolbars. You can display one or more Toolbars to give you easy access to commonly used commands. If, for example, you are a WordPerfect 6.1 user, you might want to display the WordPerfect 6.1 Toolbar until you are more familiar with WordPerfect 8. You choose a new Toolbar by right-clicking anywhere on a currently displayed Toolbar. A menu opens, listing the descriptive names of the available toolbars. Choose a new Toolbar by clicking to select it. Hide a currently displayed Toolbar by clicking to deselect it.

Opening an Existing Document

You use the Open command to open an existing document you have previously saved on a hard disk or floppy disk. When you open an existing document, a new document window opens displaying the document. You can then revise the document or modify it for another purpose. You can also open a file as a copy of itself. The Write Staff has a policy of saving all correspondence in client files. Jennifer, the president of The Write Staff, has written a contact letter to attract a new client. She asks you to review the document. This file, and all documents you open and save throughout this book, are located in the drive and folder that contain your student files. Be sure to make a copy of your Student Disk before proceeding with the lessons in this book.

1. **Click File on the menu bar, then click Open**
   The Open File dialog box opens, as shown in Figure A-5. You can also open the Open dialog box by clicking the Open button on the WordPerfect 8 Toolbar. The title bar shows the current drive. You need to change to the drive and folder that contain your Student files.
2. **Click the Look in: list arrow, then click the name of the drive and folder that contain your student files**
   A list of documents appears in the list box.
3. **Click WP A-1, then click Open**
   The file opens and is displayed in the document window, as shown in Figure A-6. Notice that the words Laina and Bashir are underlined in red; this is a feature of the WordPerfect Spell Checker, which you will learn more about in a future unit. Jennifer wants you to read the document and quickly check her writing. You can do this right in the document window.

QuickTip

To change the way your file list displays, click the View menu in the Open dialog box, and then click Large icons, Small icons, List, or Details.

Open as Copy

The Open dialog box gives you the option to open a file as a copy. When you choose the Open as Copy button instead of the Open button, the file you open is **read-only**. This means that you can view the document and you can make changes to it, but when you try to save the document, you will have to give it a new name. This protects your original document from any changes.

FIGURE A-5: Open File dialog box

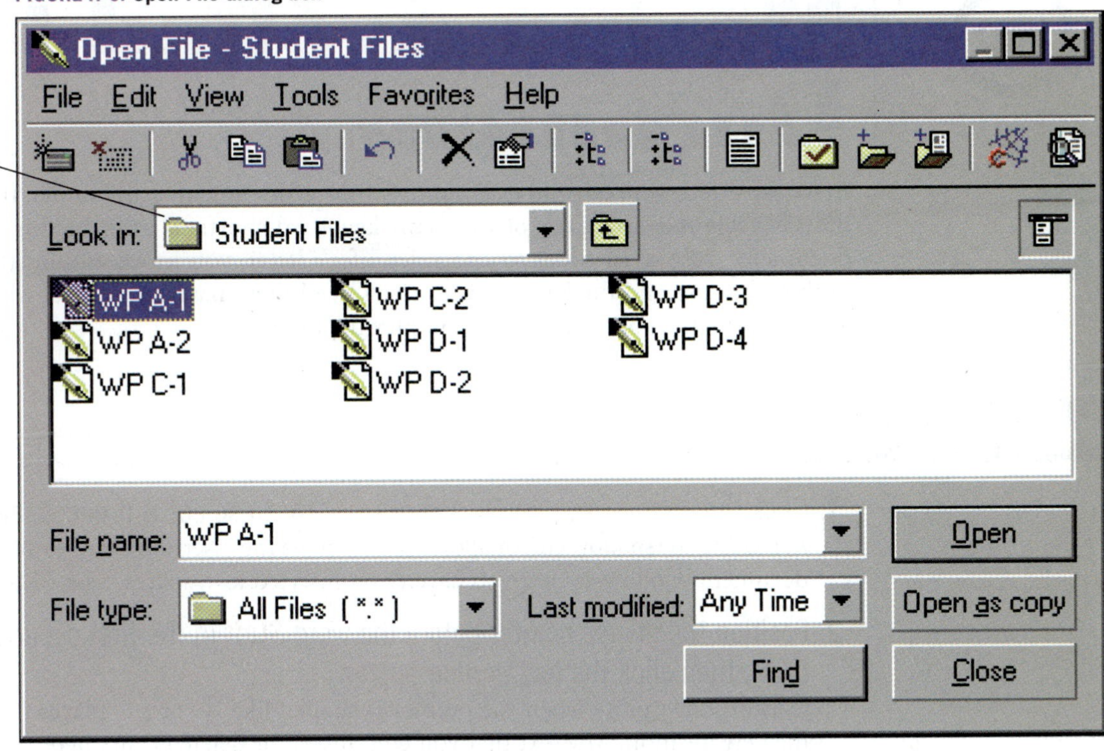

FIGURE A-6: WP A-1 document

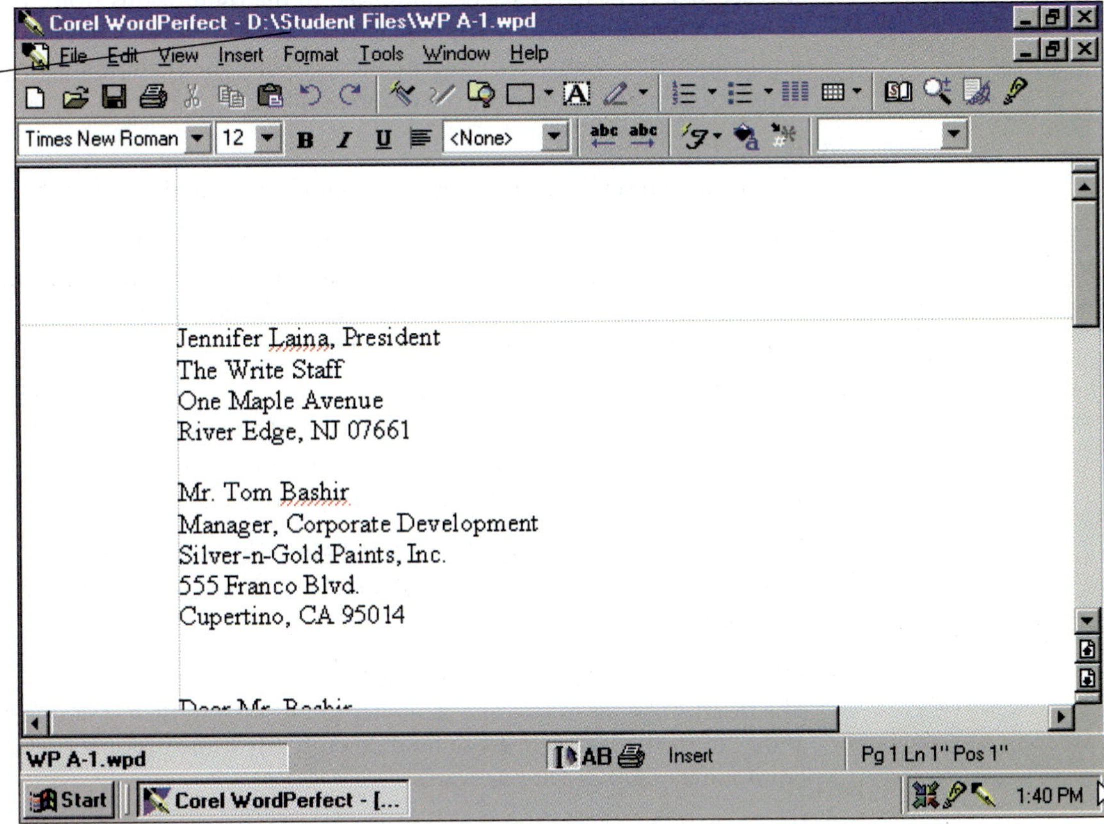

WordPerfect 8

WordPerfect 8

Moving Around the Document

In WordPerfect you can move around within a document using either the keyboard or the mouse. Table A-1 lists a few of the many keyboard shortcuts available for moving around the document. In order to check Jennifer's letter, you move around the document using both the mouse and the keyboard. You will need these navigation skills when you edit, delete, and insert text as you create more complex documents.

Steps

1. **Click the shadow cursor On/Off button to select it if necessary**
   Activating the shadow cursor allows you to move the insertion point to any editable area in the document window, even if you haven't yet inserted text, spaces, tabs, or paragraph returns.

2. **Position the mouse pointer before the word Staff in the first occurrence of The Write Staff, then click the left mouse button**
   Clicking the mouse when the pointer is shaped like I or places the insertion point at the new location. Any text that you edit, insert, or delete occurs here.

QuickTip
Throughout this book, the instruction "Point" means to position the mouse pointer where directed.

3. **Point far to the right of the word Staff, then when the pointer changes to , click with the left mouse button**
   No text, spaces, or tabs have been inserted to the right of this word, yet you can still move the insertion point here because the shadow cursor is active. If you have worked with a word processor before, you will appreciate the flexibility the shadow cursor provides. Now use a keyboard shortcut to move the insertion point.

4. **Press [Ctrl][End]**
   The document scrolls and the insertion point moves to the end of the document.

QuickTip
Depending on the screen size and resolution of your monitor, your view may differ from the screen shots shown in this book.

5. **Click the up scroll arrow on the vertical scroll bar 12 times**
   The closing line of the document scrolls out of view, as shown in Figure A-7, and you can no longer see the insertion point. However, if you entered text now, it would appear at the insertion point, and your screen would reposition the document so that you could see the text again.

6. **Drag the vertical scroll box up to the top of the vertical scroll bar**
   The top of the document is visible in the document window. You also can scroll using the keyboard. However, using the keyboard repositions the insertion point.

7. **Press [↑] to move the insertion point before the word Dear**
   You can use the arrow keys to move line by line, or character by character through your document.

8. **Press [→] then press [Ctrl][→] twice**
   The insertion point moves one character to the left and then over one word, and should be at the "B" in "Bashir." When you hold down [Ctrl] while pressing [→] or [←], the insertion point moves right or left one word.

9. **Press [Ctrl][Home]**
   The document scrolls and the insertion point moves to the beginning of the document. After reading the document you tell Jennifer that you haven't found any errors. It is a terrific letter that will generate business for the company.

FIGURE A-7: Document scrolled

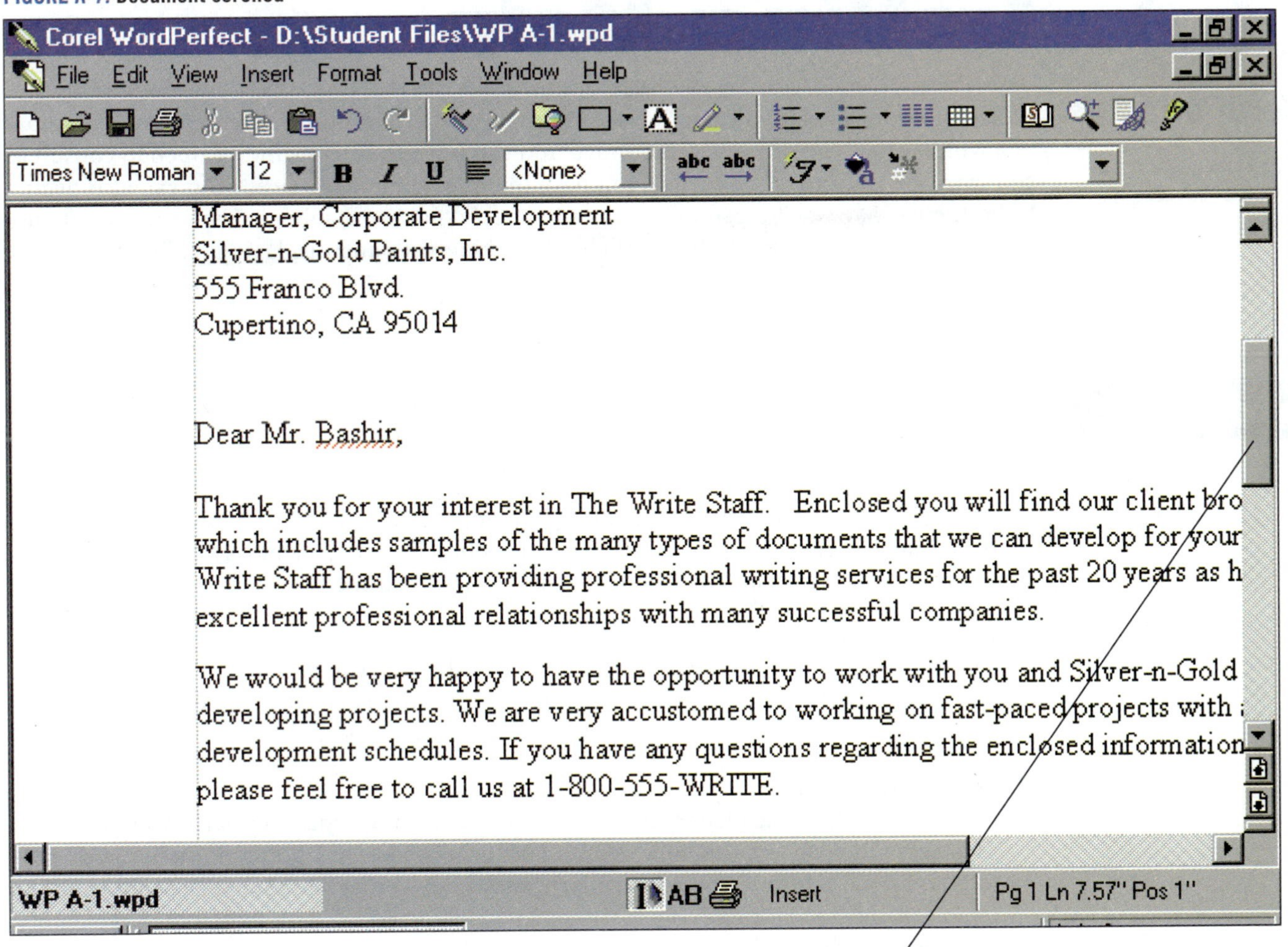

TABLE A-1: Shortcut navigation keys

button	description
[↑], [↓], [←], [→]	Moves insertion point up one line, down one line, left one character, and right one character
[Home]	Moves insertion point to beginning of line
[End]	Moves insertion point to end of line
[Pg Up]	Moves insertion point to previous page in a multiple-page document
[Pg Dn]	Moves insertion point to next page in a multiple-page document
[Ctrl][Home]	Moves insertion point to beginning of document
[Ctrl][End]	Moves insertion point to end of document

Getting Help

WordPerfect comes with an extensive online **Help system** that gives you definitions and explanations, or guides you step by step through tasks. Help information appears in a separate window that you can resize and move. You can leave the Help window open to consult as you work, or you can close it when you have the information you need. You can also print a Help topic. To get up to speed quickly for your job at The Write Staff, use WordPerfect's Help system to find out about working with and displaying different Toolbars.

Steps

1. Click **Help** on the menu bar, then click **Help Topics**
   The Help Topics: WordPerfect Help dialog box appears. You can browse through topics using the Contents tab, look up a topic from an alphabetical list using the Index tab, search the Help database for a term using the Find tab, or ask a question using the Ask the PerfectExpert tab.
2. Click the **Index tab**
   The Index tab opens, as shown in Figure A-8. In this tab, you type the first few letters of a term in the text box, and the list of help topics scrolls to match what you've typed as closely as possible.
3. Type **toolbar**
   Notice as you type each letter, the contents of the list box appear to match your selection. The term "Toolbar" appears followed by a list of related topics. You can use the scroll buttons and scroll box to read the entire list of matching words if necessary. Depending on the topic you choose, clicking Display will open a Help window describing it, or a dialog box asking you to choose the specific topic you want help with.
4. Click **about** in the list headed by "Click the index entry you want, and then click Display" list, click **Display**, in the Topics Found dialog box click **About the Toolbar**, then click **Display**
   The topic appears in a Help window, as shown in Figure A-9. Read the Help topic. You can use Help throughout your work with WordPerfect, accessing a wide variety of topics. Now familiarize yourself with PerfectExpert, a powerful tool that can answer questions you ask about using WordPerfect, and also help you to complete more complex tasks.
5. Click **Help Topics** to return to the Index tab, then click the **Ask the PerfectExpert tab**
   The Ask the PerfectExpert tab opens. In this window, you ask a question by typing it in your own words.
6. Under "What do you want to know?" if necessary, type **How do I close a toolbar?**, then click **Search**
   The PerfectExpert displays a list of topics likely to answer your question, as shown in Figure A-10.
7. Click **To display or hide toolbars**, then click **Display**
   A Help window opens and lists the steps necessary to complete this task. The PerfectExpert can also guide you step-by-step through complex projects, as you will see in later lessons.
8. Read the information in the Help window, then click the **Close button**

FIGURE A-8: Help Topics: WordPerfect Help dialog box

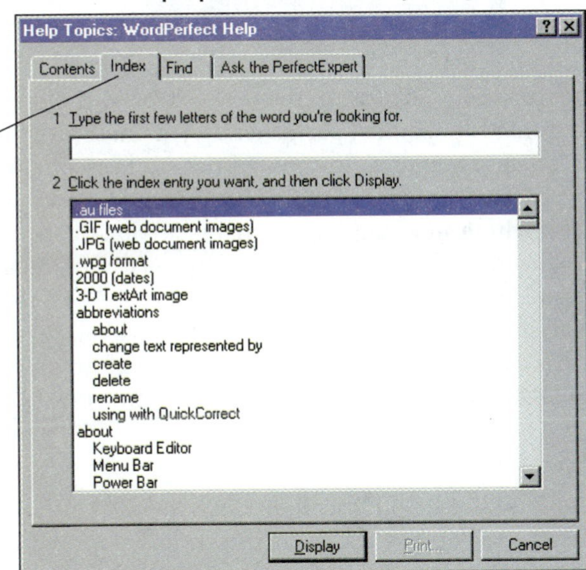

FIGURE A-9: Help topic displayed in Help window

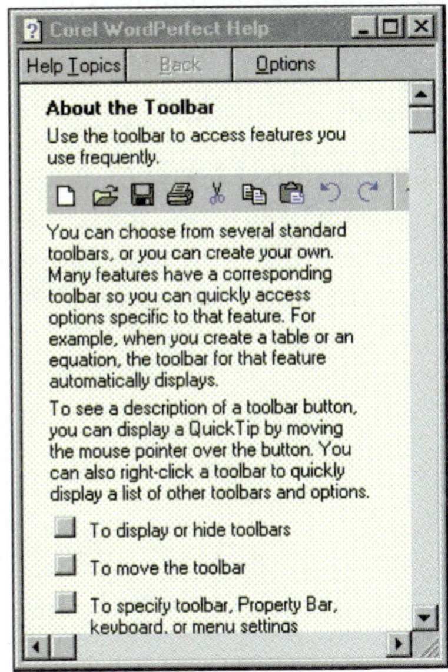

FIGURE A-10: Asking the PerfectExpert

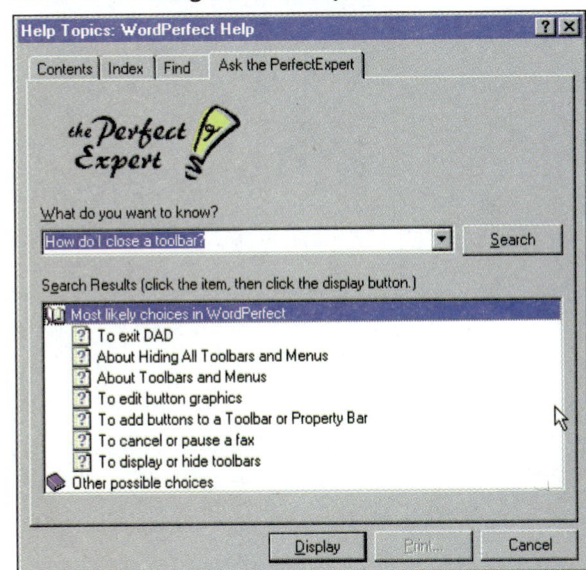

WordPerfect 8

Saving a Document

As you enter text in a document, the text is kept in the computer's **random access memory (RAM)**. To store the document permanently, you must save it to a file on a disk. It's a good practice to save often so you don't lose your work. To prevent any accidental changes to the original document, now and throughout this book, you will save each document that you open from your Student Disk with a new name. This makes a copy of the document in which you can make changes, leaving the original unaltered so that you can repeat a lesson. You should save your work frequently, and always save before printing. At The Write Staff, documents are routinely saved and given descriptive names to facilitate retrieval. Saved documents can be shared among the staff, parts can be used in new documents, and most important, you can continue to work on your document another day. You save the document you are working on for Jennifer.

Steps

1. Click **File** on the menu bar, then click **Save As**
   The Save As dialog box opens, as shown in Figure A-11. To preserve the original file, you need to save this document with a new name.

2. Be sure that the drive containing your student files is open, or open it if necessary
   This document will be saved using the company's name. The Write Staff has a policy of always including the company name in the filename of any document, along with a brief description of the type of letter.

3. Type **Silver-n-Gold contact letter** in the File name text box, then click **Save**
   The file is saved with a new name, "Silver-n-Gold contact letter". The original document is automatically closed. The default file extension .wpd is assigned automatically. Depending on the configuration of your computer system, the extension may not appear in the files and folders listing.

QuickTip

To save the file to disk with the same filename, you can click the Save button on the toolbar, or click File on the menu bar, then click Save.

FIGURE A-11: Save As dialog box

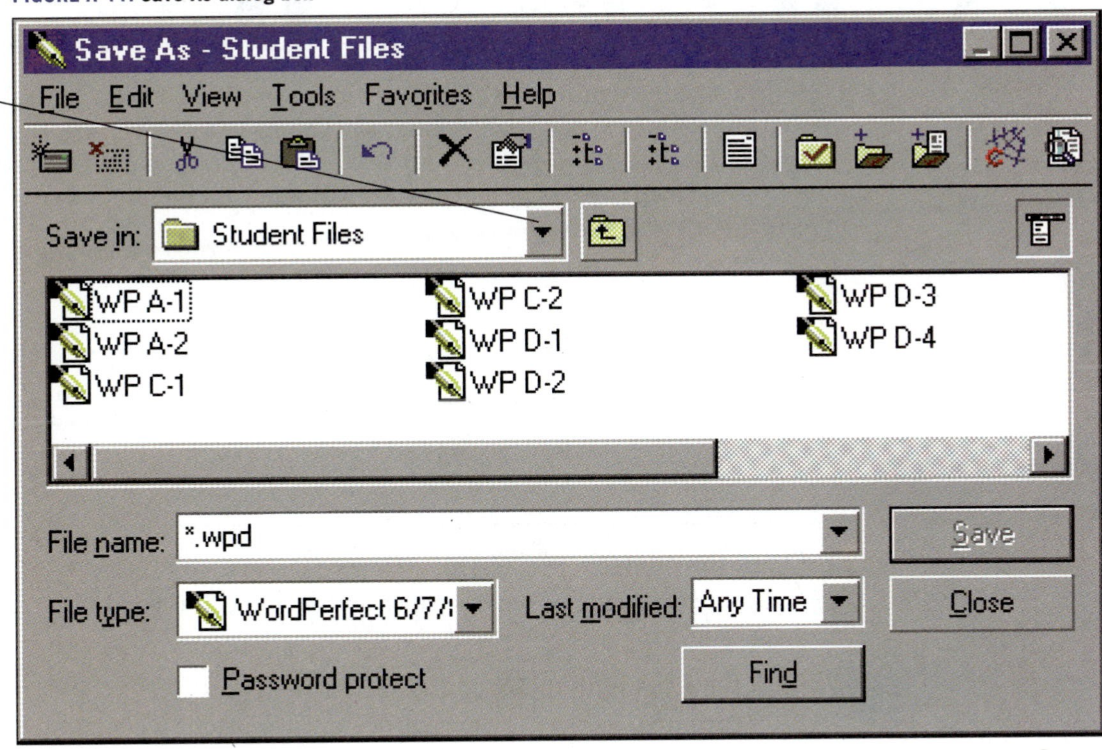

Setting a timed backup

You can set WordPerfect to automatically save your documents at timed increments. The Timed Document Backup feature automatically makes a copy of the document you are working on. The default setting is every 10 minutes. Click Tools on the menu bar, click Settings, double-click the Files icon, then click the Document tab if necessary. Click the Timed document backup every check box, then specify the backup folder and the file and set the time interval. To guard against accidentally replacing work that you did not intend to replace, select Original Document Backup. Note that this is *not* a substitute for saving your work regularly, but rather a backup you can access if your computer loses power or is turned off prematurely.

Printing a Document

Printing a document provides a paper copy to read, send to others, or file. You also might want to print an incomplete document so that you can review it or work on it when you're not at a computer. It's a good idea to save your document immediately before printing. You want to keep a hard copy of the letter to Mr. Bashir in your files for future reference, so you need to print it out.

1. **Check the printer**

   Make sure the printer is on, has paper, and is online. It is good to get in the habit of saving before you print your document.

2. **Click the Save button on the Toolbar**

   Before printing, check to see how the document will look when printed. For example, if you add several paragraphs to your document, you might want to check that it still fits on one page. WordPerfect provides a method for viewing the entire page of the document before printing it.

To specify a Zoom size not available on the Zoom button menu, click View on the menu bar and then click Zoom.

3. **Click the Zoom button on the Toolbar, then click Full Page**

   The document view changes, as shown in Figure A-12, to display the letter in Full Page view. This view is 30% of the actual size of the document. Depending on the size of your actual document, Full Page view might be larger or smaller. If you are working on a legal-sized document, for example, Full Page view is only 24% of the actual size of the page. As you can see, the letter fits nicely on one page.

4. **Click , then click Margin Width**

   The view returns to Margin Width, a convenient view for entering and editing text. Now you are ready to print the document.

To open the Print dialog box, you can also click the Print button on the toolbar.

5. **Click File on the menu bar, then click Print**

   The Print dialog box opens, as shown in Figure A-13. There are many options that you can control in this dialog box. For now, you will accept all the default values.

6. **Click Print**

   The document is sent to the printer.

FIGURE A-12: Document in Full Page view

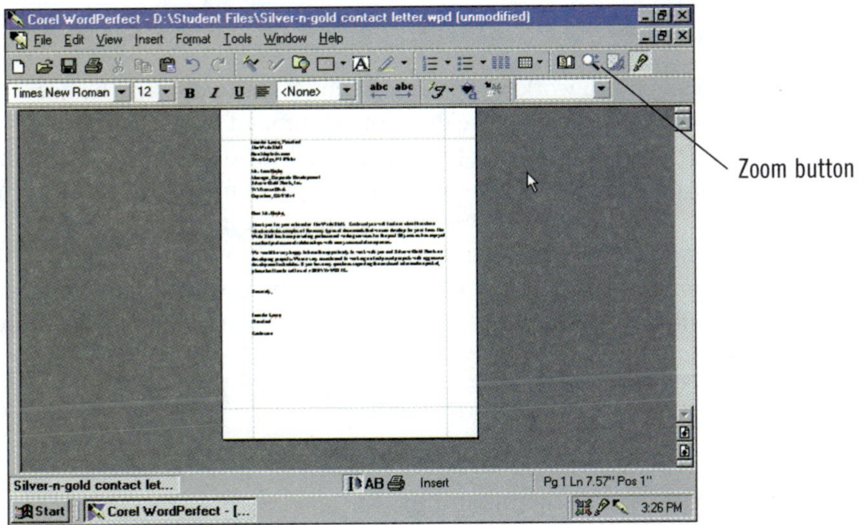

FIGURE A-13: Print to dialog box

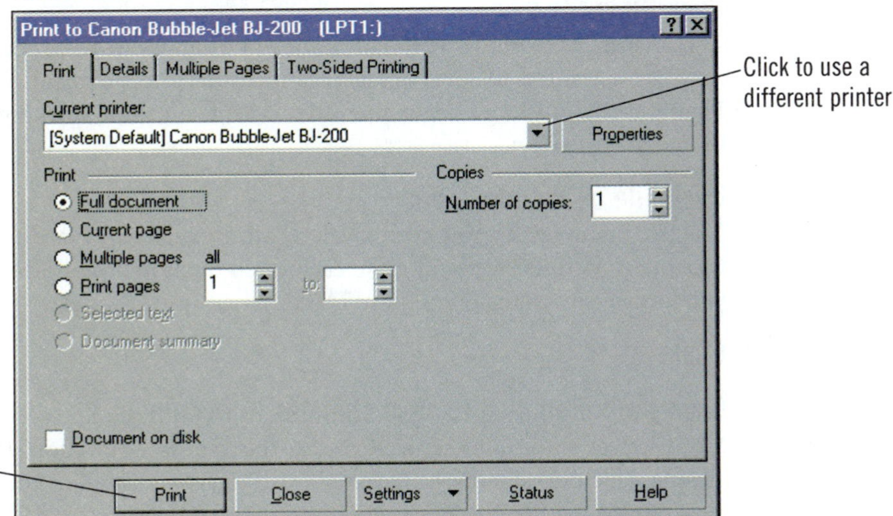

Zooming a document

You can also use the Zoom button on the Toolbar, or the Zoom command on the View menu to change the view of your document. The Zoom button lists commonly used Zoom sizes. When you click Other on the Zoom button menu or click Zoom on the Zoom menu, the Zoom dialog box shown in Figure A-14 opens. This dialog box lets you view the document at any size. After you specify or enter a view size, this size appears in the Zoom menu and is highlighted until you change it. Choose Full Page to see exactly how a document will look on the printed page. If you choose a percentage less than 100, the size of your document is reduced, making more of it visible. If you choose a percentage greater than 100, the size of your document is enlarged, showing greater detail—but making less of it visible.

FIGURE A-14: Zoom dialog box

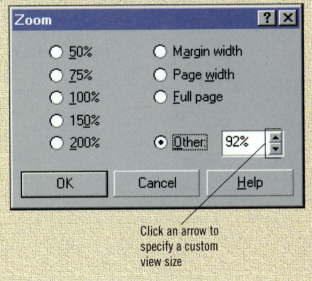

Zoom

50% | Margin width
75% | Page width
100% | Full page
150%
200% | Other: 92%

OK | Cancel | Help

Click an arrow to specify a custom view size

WordPerfect 8

Closing a Document

When you finish working on a document, you usually save the document to a disk and then close it. To close a document, use the Close command on the File menu. WordPerfect always provides a dialog box before closing the document if the document has been modified, meaning that new text or revisions have been made since the document was last saved. You have the choice of closing the document without saving, saving the changes, or canceling the Close command. When you are finished using WordPerfect, you need to exit the program. To exit WordPerfect, use the Exit command on the File menu. It's the end of the day and you have done a great job of familiarizing yourself with WordPerfect. Before going home, close the Silver-n-Gold contact letter, and then exit WordPerfect.

QuickTip

Clicking the WordPerfect document window Close button to the right of the menu bar closes the document.

1. **Click File on the menu bar**
   The File menu opens.
2. **Click Close**
   The document closes. If you had made any changes to the document, WordPerfect would ask if you wanted to save changes. Notice that the program remains open, as shown in Figure A-15. You could begin a new document, continue working on an existing document, or exit WordPerfect.
3. **Click File on the menu bar**
   The File menu opens. You need to click Exit. You can exit WordPerfect with many document files open. WordPerfect will close each open document window, one at a time, prompting you to save any changes you have made.
4. **Click Exit**
5. **Click No if prompted to save changes to Document 1**
   WordPerfect closes and returns you to the Windows desktop. It's important to note that closing a file puts it away, but leaves WordPerfect running. In contrast, exiting WordPerfect closes any open files and also closes WordPerfect.

FIGURE A-15: Document closed

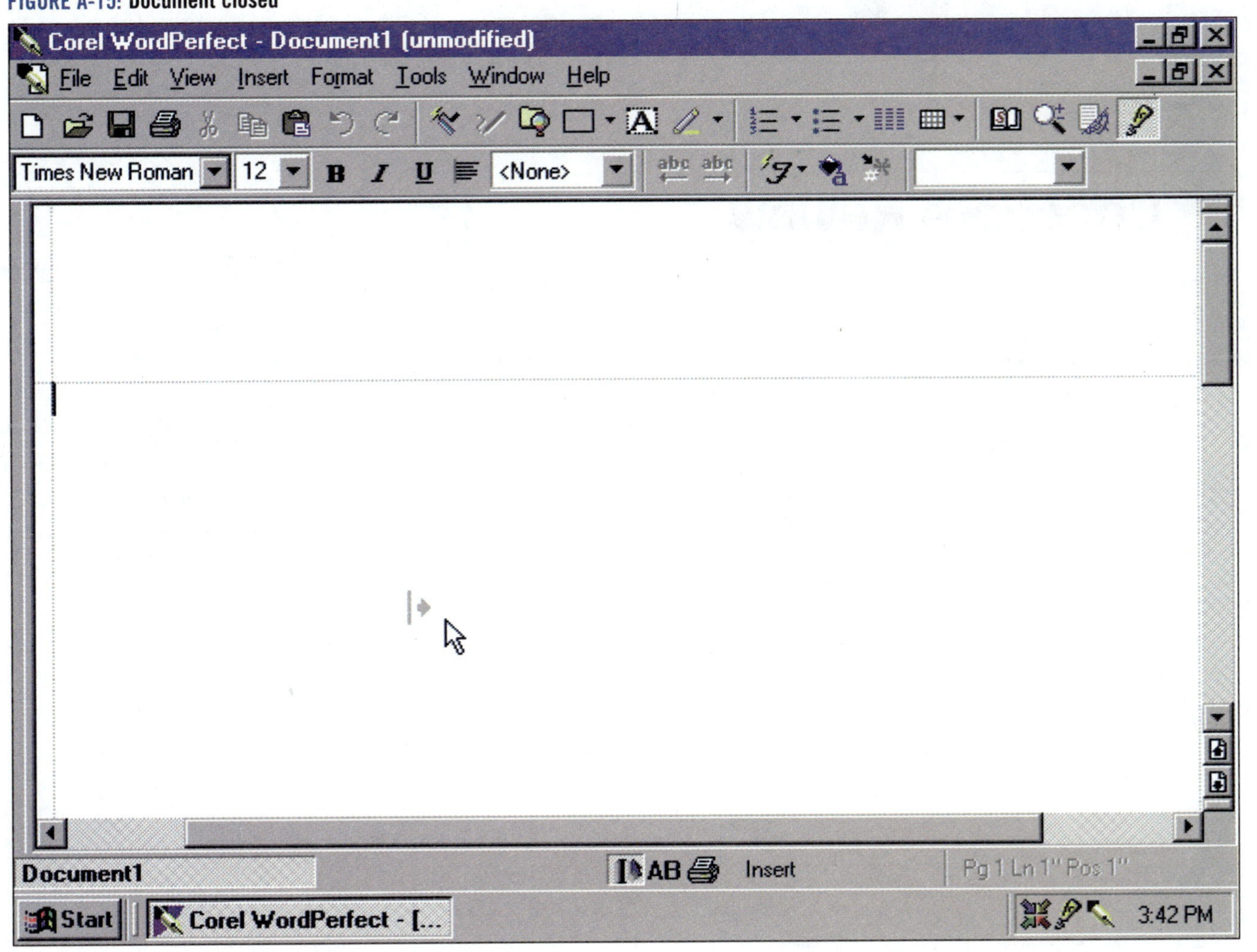

WordPerfect 8

Practice

Concepts Review

Label each element of the WordPerfect window shown in Figure A-16.

FIGURE A-16

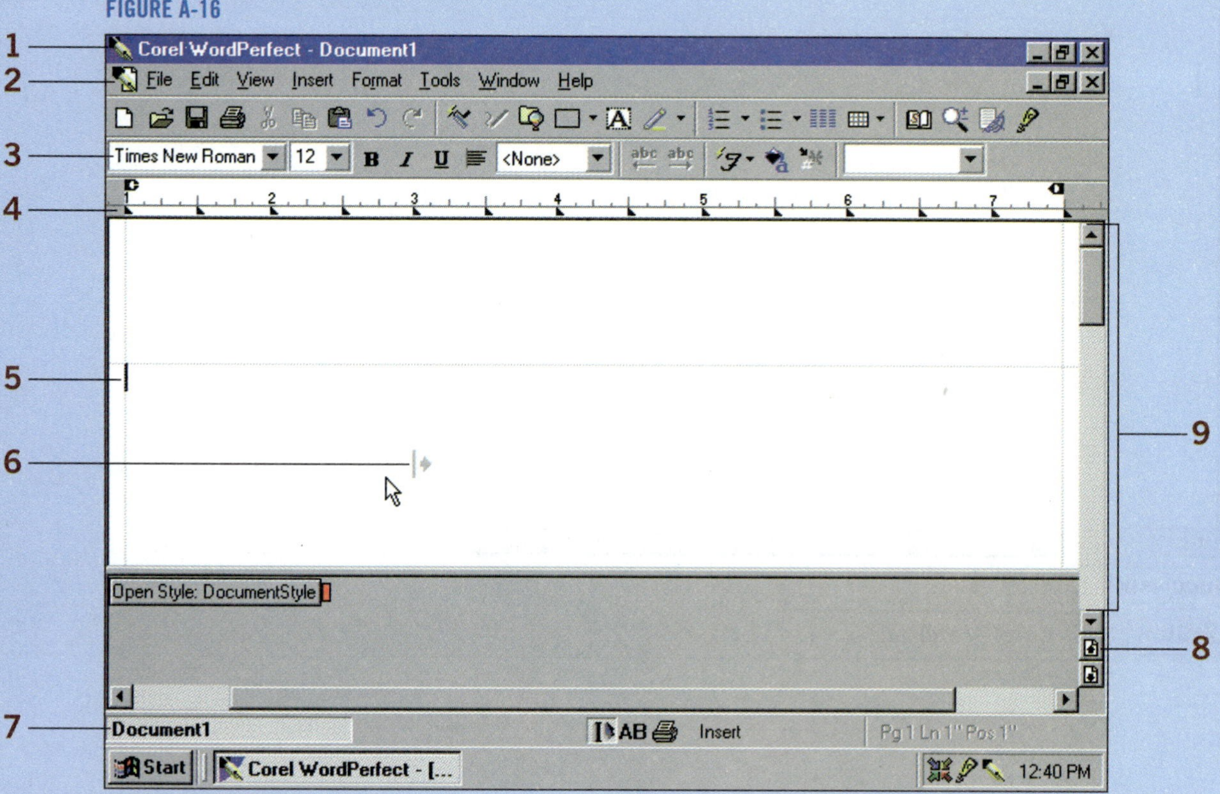

Match each statement with the term it describes.

10. Shows the name of the current document
11. Automatically creates a copy of the file
12. Shows page, line, and vertical and horizontal position of the insertion point
13. Identifies the file on the disk
14. Lists the menus that contain WordPerfect commands

a. Status bar
b. Timed Document Backup
c. Filename
d. Menu bar
e. Title bar

Select the best answer from the list of choices.

15. The WordPerfect menu command that removes all open documents from the screen is
- **a.** Close.
- **b.** Exit.
- **c.** Cancel.
- **d.** Minimize.

16. The best way to quickly learn about an unfamiliar topic in WordPerfect is to
- **a.** Refer to the documentation provided with the software.
- **b.** Click Edit on the menu bar, then click Help Topic.
- **c.** Click Help on the menu bar, then click Help Topics.
- **d.** Press [Alt][H] to open a Help window.

17. **To ask a question of the PerfectExpert, you**
   a. Click the Contents tab in the Help Topics window.
   b. Click the PerfectExpert tab in the Help Topics window.
   c. Click Help on the menu bar, then click PerfectExpert.
   d. Both b and c are correct.

18. **Word-processing software can be used to create all of the following except**
   a. Documents.
   b. Reports.
   c. Letters.
   d. Sound.

19. **Printing a document is useful when**
   a. You want a copy of the document to use again.
   b. You want a hard copy to share with others.
   c. You need to have multiple copies of the same document.
   d. You save a file.

20. **Press [Ctrl][End] to move to the**
   a. Beginning of the document.
   b. End of the line.
   c. End of the document.
   d. Beginning of the line.

21. **The insertion point**
   a. Is always at the beginning of the document.
   b. Is where text will be entered or deleted.
   c. Is always visible on the screen.
   d. Has the shape of an arrow.

Skills Review

1. **Define word processing software.**

2. **Start Corel WordPerfect 8.**
   a. Turn on the computer if necessary.
   b. Click the Start button on the taskbar.
   c. Point to the Corel WordPerfect Suite 8 Program group.
   d. Click Corel WordPerfect 8.

3. **View the WordPerfect window.**
   a. Try to identify as many items in the WordPerfect window as you can without referring to the lesson.
   b. On a notepad, write all the items you can identify, then compare your notes with Figure A-4.

4. **Open a document.**
   a. Click File on the menu bar.
   b. Click Open.
   c. Open WP A-2.

5. **Move around the document.**
   a. Scroll to view the first paragraph in the letter.
   b. Place the insertion point before the word "Sincerely".
   c. Move to the end of the document.
   d. Move to the beginning of the document.

6. **Get Help.**
   a. Click Help on the menu bar.
   b. Click Help Topics.
   c. Click the Index tab.
   d. Click the list arrow on the list box scroll bar to view possible word choices.
   e. Click a word from the list box.
   f. Choose a topic to read by clicking it.

g. Click Display.
h. Read the Help screen. Click any additional topics that appear at the bottom of the file.
i. Read the additional topics.
j. Click the Close button.
k. Click Help on the menu bar, then click Ask the PerfectExpert.
l. In the What do you want to know? text box, type "What's the shadow cursor?"
m. In the list of topics that appear, click one of interest and read the contents.
n. Click the Close button on the Help window to close Help.

7. Save a document.
a. Click File on the menu bar.
b. Click Save As.
c. Save the document with the new filename "Silver2".

8. Print a document.
a. Check to see that the printer is on.
b. Click File on the menu bar, then click Print.

9. Close a document and exit WordPerfect.
a. Click File on the menu bar, then click Close.
b. Close any other documents you have opened.
c. Click File on the menu bar, then click Exit.

Independent Challenges

1. WordPerfect provides you with powerful tools to create and edit documents. Without even realizing it, many documents you encounter in your daily life have been created using powerful word processors. These might include your daily newspaper, the college newsletter, a piece of mail advertising a new product, or any business correspondence.
To complete this independent challenge:

1. Gather four different documents that you have recently received.
2. Identify each as either a letter, newsletter, brochure, or other category.
3. Circle two elements in each document that cannot be created easily with a typewriter.
4. For each document, write a brief paragraph explaining how word processing made the creation of the document easier.

2. Explore the various tools on the Toolbar. Start WordPerfect, you do not need an open document to complete this independent challenge.

1. Right-click the Toolbar and be sure that the WordPerfect 8 Toolbar is displayed.
2. Slowly place the pointer on each button on the Toolbar. The yellow box that appears is a QuickTip. Make a list of all the QuickTips on the WordPerfect 8 Toolbar.
3. Slowly place the pointer on each button on the Power Bar. Make a list of all the QuickTips that explain the buttons.

3. WordPerfect has a very extensive online help system. You learned how to use the Index and the PerfectExpert in WordPerfect Help to get information about a topic in question. WordPerfect also contains a Find tab, so that you can search for a Help topic by typing a word or phrase. This can be helpful when you're not sure of the name of the feature you need help with. Familiarize yourself with the Find tab.
To complete this independent challenge:

1. Start WordPerfect if necessary.
2. Click Help on the menu bar, then click Help Topics.

3. Click the Find tab. If this is the first time you've used the Find tab, the Find Setup Wizard opens. The Find feature requires a database of all words contained in the WordPerfect Help feature in order to run. Depending on the speed of your computer, this process takes from a few moments to a few minutes.
4. In the Find Setup Wizard dialog box, click the Minimize database size option button if necessary, click Next, then click Finish. When the database is compiled, the Find Setup Wizard closes. Use the Find tab to learn more about faxing a document.
5. In the Find tab, type the word "faxing" in the text box. The Select some matching words to narrow your search list box lists all topics found that contain the word faxing, or the word Faxing (note the difference in capitalization).
6. Press [↓] if necessary, then click the word "Faxing". A list of Help topics containing the word Faxing appear in the Click a topic then click Display list. Obtain some general information on faxing a document.
7. In the Click a topic then click Display list, click "To fax a document", then click Display.
8. Read the Help window that opens.
9. When you are finished, return to the Find tab and search for another word or phrase of interest to you.
10. When you are finished, close the Help window and exit WordPerfect.

4. As you continue to explore the WordPerfect features that will help you create professional-looking documents, you will find that you often need help. In addition to the PerfectExpert and Find, you can also create very complicated documents by having PerfectExpert "walk" you through the steps. Use the PerfectExpert to create a basic calendar.

To complete this independent challenge:

1. Start WordPerfect if necessary.
2. Click File on the menu bar, then click New. Your screen should look similar to Figure A-17.
3. Scroll the list box and click Calendar, Monthly, then click Create.
4. Follow the instructions on the screen to create one calendar for the current month and year, and to indicate your style preferences.
5. Click Finished. The completed calendar will appear in your document window.
6. Save the document as "Calendar". Print the document, then close it and exit WordPerfect.

FIGURE A-17

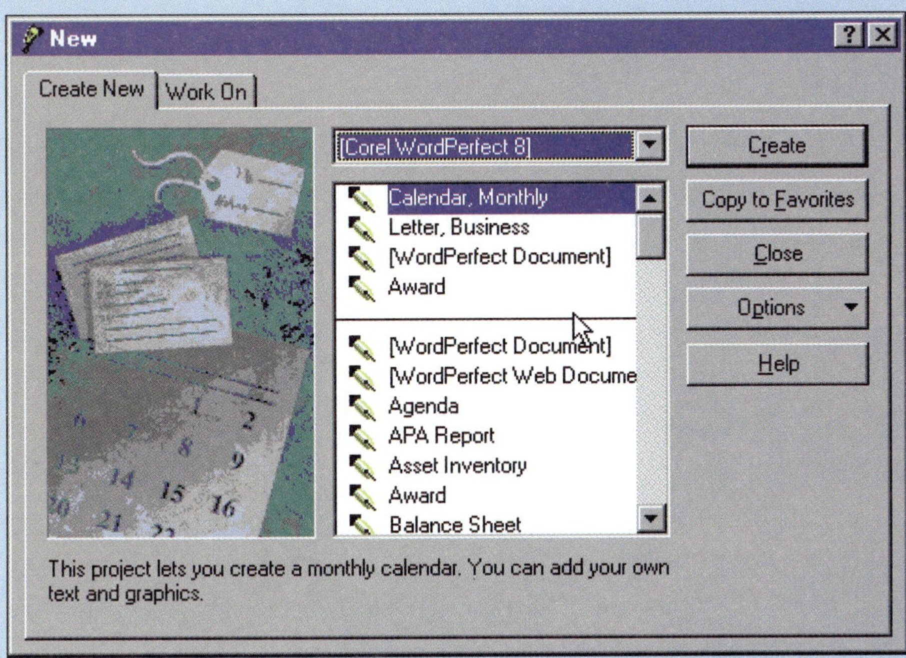

Visual Workshop

Use the skills you learned in this unit to display and hide various toolbars, so that your screen matches Figure A-18. When you are finished, display the original combination of toolbars (Property Bar, Application Bar, and WordPerfect 8) as a convenience to others. Then, exit WordPerfect without saving changes.

FIGURE A-18

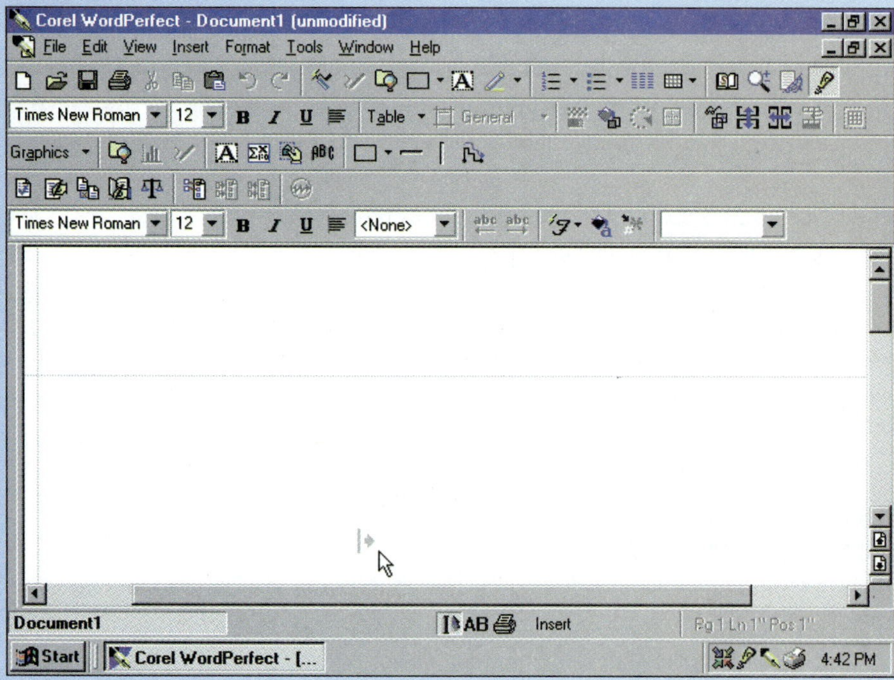

WordPerfect 8

Creating a Document

Objectives

- Plan a document
- Enter text
- Select text
- Delete and insert text
- Undo changes
- Cut, copy, and paste text
- Drag and drop text
- Create an envelope

Your first day working with WordPerfect at The Write Staff went well. Now you are ready to create your own document. To create a document, you first plan it, and then enter text in the document window. Once you create a document, you can add, delete, or copy and move text. You can also change the document view to make working in the document window easier. When you are finished, you are ready to print the document. On your second day at The Write Staff, the owner, Jennifer Laina, has asked you to write an upbeat and informative welcoming note to all new employees. You will first plan the letter, then create it using WordPerfect.

Planning a Document

Planning a document before you write it improves the quality of your writing, makes your document more attractive and readable, and saves you time and effort. You can divide your planning into four parts: content, organization, style, and format. First determine what you want to say, or, the **content**. Next, organize the information so that your ideas appear in a logical and coherent sequence. After you have decided the content and organization, you can begin writing, using a style that satisfies your purpose and meets the needs of your audience. For example, if you are writing a promotional piece for The Write Staff or a letter to the corporate office, you will use a different writing style in each. Finally, you should make your document visually appealing, using WordPerfect's formatting features. The Write Staff needs a general welcoming note introducing all new employees to the company and its policies. You begin your first job assignment by planning the document.

Steps

1. **Determine the content: Choose the information you want to include**
   Jennifer leaves a note for you that lists the staff, describes some basic procedures, and specifies general company policies, as shown in Figure B-1. This is the information you need for the document.

2. **Organize the information: Decide how you will construct the document**
   You need to mention names in order to introduce new employees and make them feel welcome and comfortable. You want the memo to be brief because you want the staff to post it on their bulletin boards to use as a reference. However, you must also include all of the information Jennifer provided.

3. **Decide on the style: Pick the tone you will use**
   You want The Write Staff to sound like a fun, exciting, and cutting-edge place to work; use a lively, positive tone to help the new people relax and feel good about their jobs.

4. **Choose the formatting: Think about how you want your document to look**
   Jennifer wants this document to be friendly and informal. It must be a single-page document. WordPerfect's default format settings are perfect for this document.

FIGURE B-1: Jennifer's note

The Write Staff
Jennifer Laina, President
Emily Caitlin, Chief Financial Officer
Michael Benjamin, Director, Graphics Department
David Choi, Writer
Arianna Quintana, Writer
Erica Brennan, Writer
[your name], Writer

Office Procedures
Backup all work regularly
Label each disk and tape cartridge by job number
Include client name in each filename
Print all documents on the laser printer
Requests for any graphics must go through the Graphics Department

Company Policies
Create all documents with Core WordPerfect 8
Be professional and polite with all clients and coworkers
Have fun and work creatively
No smoking in the office

WordPerfect 8

Entering Text

After you plan your document, you are ready to begin entering text. When you start WordPerfect, an empty document window appears. You enter text at the insertion point in the first line. You can use the Show Paragraph command to identify the basic symbols for spaces and hard returns in your document. With the information Jennifer provided and the planning you did in the previous lesson, you are ready to begin entering text for the welcoming letter.

Steps

1. Start WordPerfect 8

   WordPerfect opens and a blank document appears in the document window. Near the upper-left corner, just below the intersection of the two margin guidelines, the insertion point appears as a blinking vertical bar. You will type your text here. Table B-1 lists some of WordPerfect's basic key functions to help you enter text.

2. Carefully type the following text; when you reach the end of a line, keep typing without pressing [Enter]

   Welcome to The Write Staff! We are so happy to have you as a member of our team of professional writers. You'll find our offices at One Main Street to be sunny and bright. Frazzle's Diner down the block has a superb lunch special. If you like dining outdoors, you may bring a bag lunch and eat on our beautiful cedar deck.

   Text automatically wraps, or moves, to the next line. This is called **word wrap**. A hidden symbol called a soft return is placed at the end of a line of type. Press [Enter] only at the end of the paragraph to generate a hard return that forces a new line. Hard returns can be deleted with [Backspace]. You cannot delete soft returns. Use [Backspace] to correct any errors you make.

3. Press **[Enter]** twice to create a blank line between the paragraphs

4. Click **View** on the menu bar, then click **Show ¶**

   Notice that a • symbol appears at each space in the paragraph, and wherever you press [Enter] the ¶ symbol appears. The **Show Paragraph command** makes it easy to see if you've pressed [Spacebar] or [Enter] too many times. These symbols do not appear when a document is printed. Clicking Show Paragraph again turns the command off.

5. Type the new text as shown in Figure B-2, pressing **[Enter]** at the end of each line

   As you enter more lines, the first few lines will scroll off the screen and out of the document window.

6. Press **[Enter]**

   Notice that the insertion point is repositioned to the blank line below the paragraph. Your screen should look like Figure B-3. Now you need to name and save the document.

7. Click the **Save button** on the Toolbar

   The Save As dialog box opens.

8. Click the directory that contains your student files, click in the **File name text box**, type **The Write Staff welcome letter**, then click **Save**

   Your document "The Write Staff welcome letter" is saved.

QuickTip

If you have not yet saved the document you are creating, the Save command opens the Save As dialog box so that you can specify a name and location to save the file.

FIGURE B-2: Text to be typed in the document

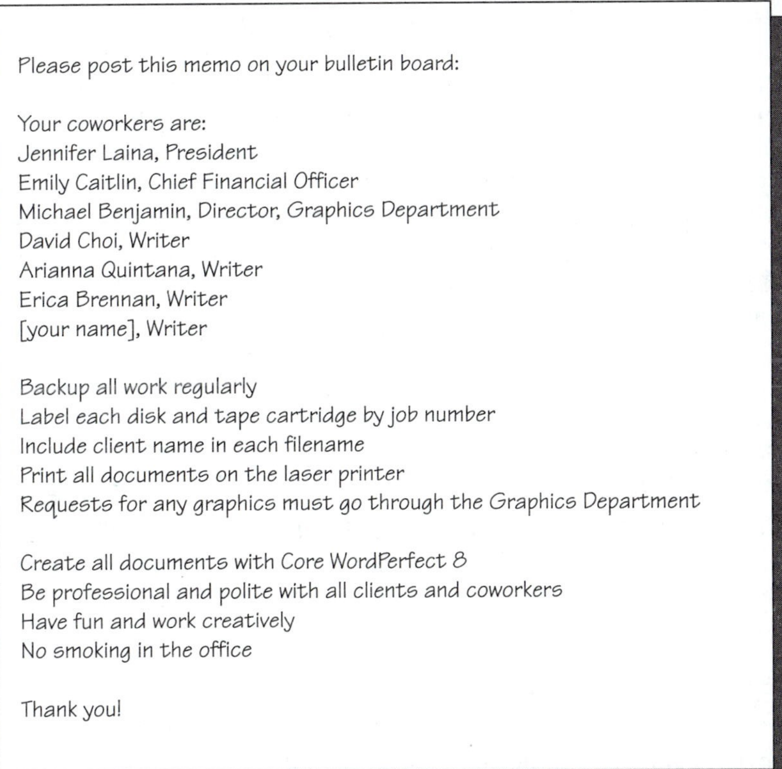
Please post this memo on your bulletin board:

Your coworkers are:
Jennifer Laina, President
Emily Caitlin, Chief Financial Officer
Michael Benjamin, Director, Graphics Department
David Choi, Writer
Arianna Quintana, Writer
Erica Brennan, Writer
[your name], Writer

Backup all work regularly
Label each disk and tape cartridge by job number
Include client name in each filename
Print all documents on the laser printer
Requests for any graphics must go through the Graphics Department

Create all documents with Core WordPerfect 8
Be professional and polite with all clients and coworkers
Have fun and work creatively
No smoking in the office

Thank you!

FIGURE B-3: Document with text and symbols

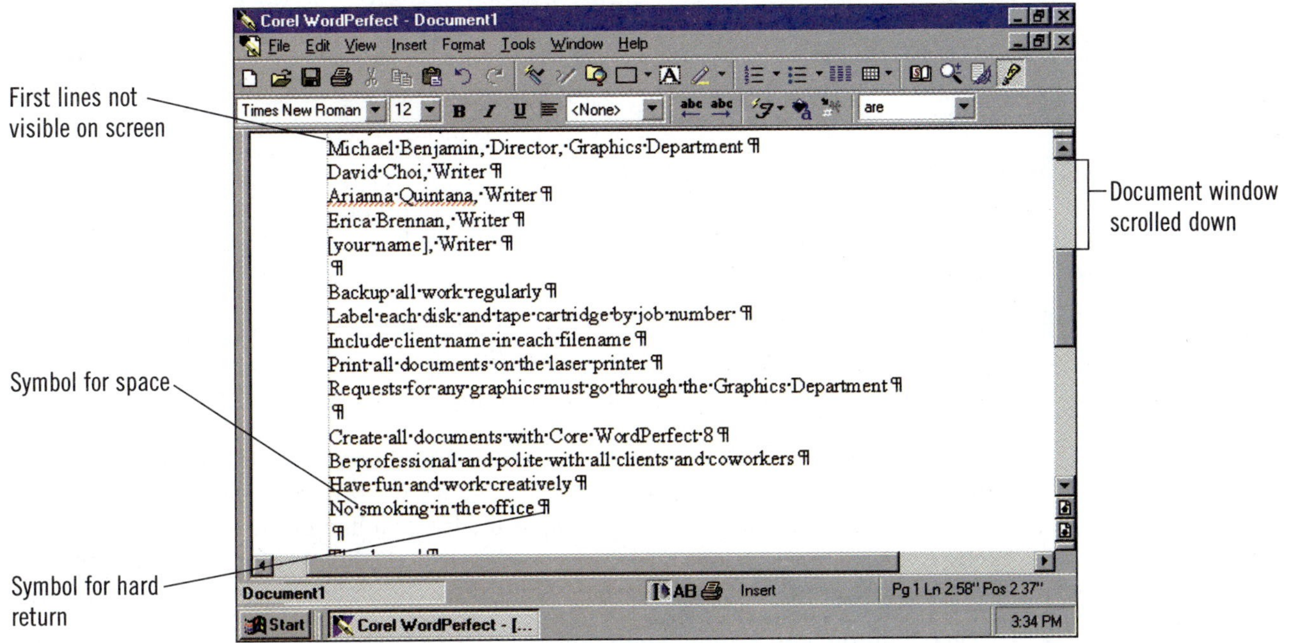

TABLE B-1: Basic key functions for entering text

key	action
[Spacebar]	Press once between words and sentences to leave a space
[Enter]	Press at the end of a paragraph or when you want text to begin a new line; pressing more than once creates blank lines
[Backspace]	Press to correct any character you mistype; deletes text to the left of the insertion point
[Delete]	Press to delete text to the right of the insertion point

Selecting Text

Selecting text is an essential word processing skill because you must **select** text, or highlight it, in order to work with it. There are many options for selecting text in WordPerfect. You can use the Select command on the Edit menu, or use **QuickSelect** to select text by clicking. You also can click and drag the mouse pointer over the text to highlight it. You can select a letter, a word or words, a sentence or several sentences, one or more paragraphs, a page, or an entire document. Once text is selected, you can format (change the appearance), cut, copy, or move it. You want to learn to select text so that you can work efficiently on the welcome letter and other documents.

Steps

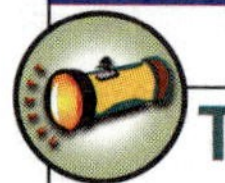

Trouble?

If the pointer changes to [pointer icon], click outside the selected text, then try again.

QuickTip

Whenever you select text, release the mouse button after you reach the end of the text you need to select.

1. **Press [Ctrl][Home] to place the insertion point at the beginning of the letter, then click and drag the mouse pointer to the end of the first paragraph**
   As you drag the mouse, the text is highlighted; the characters appear light and the area behind them appears dark. Highlighting indicates that text is selected and ready for you to work with. When you reach the end of the text you want to select, you release the mouse button.
2. **Release the mouse button**
   You can deselect text by selecting other text or clicking outside the selected area.
3. **Click anywhere outside the selected area, then click before the word happy in the middle of the first line**
4. **Click Edit on the menu bar, click Select, then click Paragraph**
   Your screen should look like Figure B-4. You can select an entire paragraph from anywhere within the paragraph using Select. You can select a sentence, a paragraph, a page, or the entire document using the Edit menu in this manner. Clicking All selects the entire document.
5. **Click anywhere outside the selected text**
   The paragraph is no longer selected. As a writer, you'll find that keeping the pointer on the document for simple tasks is easier than moving up to the menu bar to get commands. Now try using QuickSelect.
6. **Double-click the word sunny in the third sentence of the first paragraph to select the word, then triple-click sunny**
   You selected the sentence by triple-clicking just one word in the sentence.
7. **Practice using QuickSelect by double-, triple-, and quadruple-clicking to select text**
   Refer to Table B-2 for a summary of QuickSelect and the many ways to select text. You can also use the left margin to select items. Clicking to the left of a line in the left margin when the pointer is shaped like [pointer icon] selects the left-most sentence in the line, even if it starts or ends on a different line. You want to select the names of the three coworkers, Emily, Michael, and David.
8. **Position [pointer icon] in the left margin beginning at Jennifer Laina, then drag down the margin to select text from Emily Caitlin, Chief Financial Officer through David Choi, Writer**
   Your screen should look like Figure B-5.
9. **Position the insertion point before the word Frazzle, click and drag the mouse pointer across four characters to select Fraz**
   Selecting characters and words takes practice. Continue selecting and deselecting characters and words until you are comfortable selecting small amounts of text.

FIGURE B-4: First paragraph selected

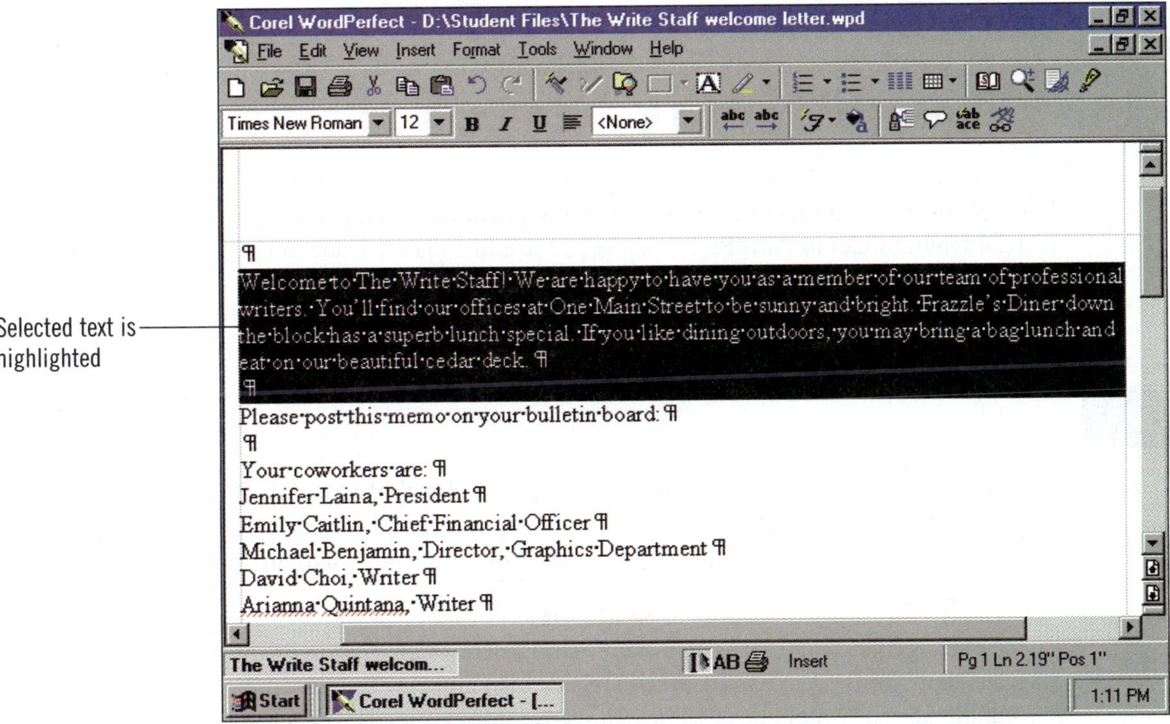
Corel WordPerfect - D:\Student Files\The Write Staff welcome letter.wpd
File Edit View Insert Format Tools Window Help
Times New Roman 12 <None>
Welcome to The Write Staff! We are happy to have you as a member of our team of professional writers. You'll find our offices at One Main Street to be sunny and bright. Frazzle's Diner down the block has a superb lunch special. If you like dining outdoors, you may bring a bag lunch and eat on our beautiful cedar deck.
Please post this memo on your bulletin board:
Your coworkers are:
Jennifer Laina, President
Emily Caitlin, Chief Financial Officer
Michael Benjamin, Director, Graphics Department
David Choi, Writer
Arianna Quintana, Writer
The Write Staff welcom...
Insert
Pg 1 Ln 2.19" Pos 1"
Start
Corel WordPerfect - [...
1:11 PM
Selected text is highlighted

FIGURE B-5: Four lines selected

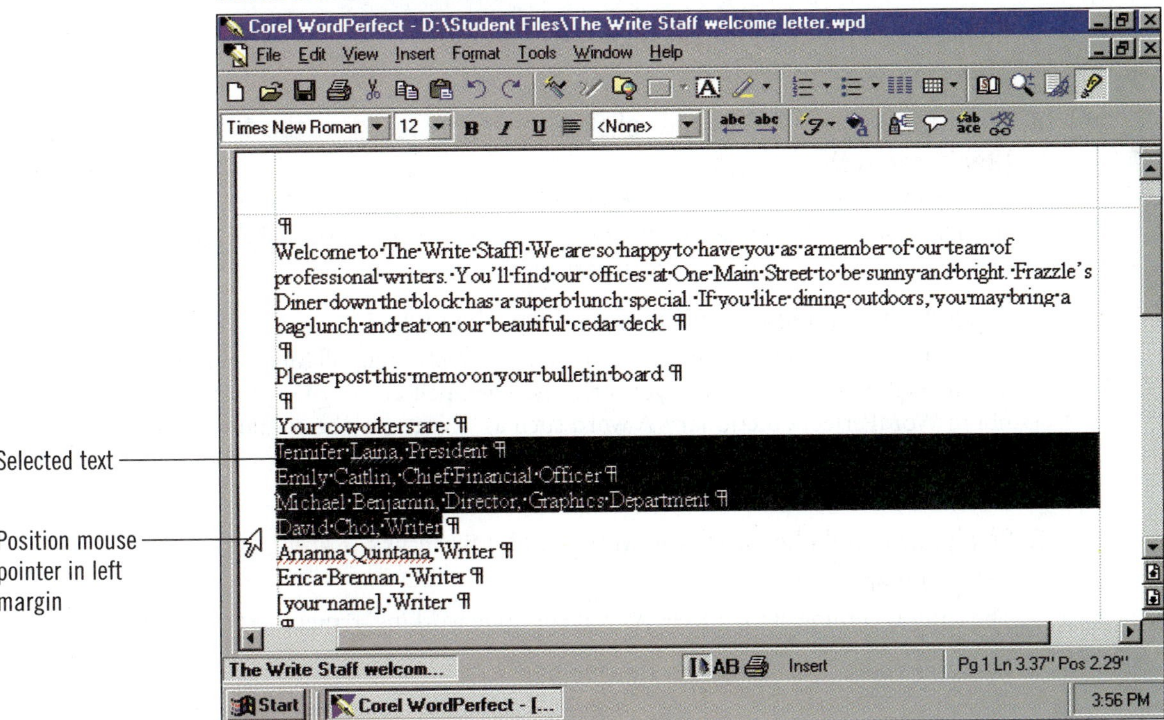
Corel WordPerfect - D:\Student Files\The Write Staff welcome letter.wpd
File Edit View Insert Format Tools Window Help
Times New Roman 12 <None>
Welcome to The Write Staff! We are so happy to have you as a member of our team of professional writers. You'll find our offices at One Main Street to be sunny and bright. Frazzle's Diner down the block has a superb lunch special. If you like dining outdoors, you may bring a bag lunch and eat on our beautiful cedar deck.
Please post this memo on your bulletin board:
Your coworkers are:
Jennifer Laina, President
Emily Caitlin, Chief Financial Officer
Michael Benjamin, Director, Graphics Department
David Choi, Writer
Arianna Quintana, Writer
Erica Brennan, Writer
[your name], Writer
The Write Staff welcom...
Insert
Pg 1 Ln 3.37" Pos 2.29"
Start
Corel WordPerfect - [...
3:56 PM
Selected text
Position mouse pointer in left margin

TABLE B-2: Selecting text

select	with a mouse	using QuickSelect
Character	Click and drag across the letter	
Word	Click and drag across the word	Double-click the word
Sentence	Click and drag across the sentence	Triple-click anywhere in, or next to, the sentence
Paragraph	Click and drag across the paragraph	Click four times anywhere in, or next to, the paragraph

Deleting and Inserting Text

You often need to edit a document by deleting text or inserting new text. WordPerfect's correcting tools save you time and energy by deleting portions of text, adding new text, or correcting text. Different modes in WordPerfect allow you to add and delete text as well. Table B-3 lists methods of changing or correcting text. Emily Caitlin reviewed your first draft and marked a few words that you need to change. Figure B-6 shows the changes she wants you to make.

Steps

1. **Click before the D in Diner in the first paragraph of text, then press [Delete] six times**
   The Delete key is a **destructive movement key**; it deletes characters to the right of the insertion point. The word "Diner" is deleted. The correct name is actually "Frazzle's Restaurant."
2. **Type Restaurant, then press [Spacebar]**
   The text is entered at the insertion point. The General Status button on the Application Bar indicates that WordPerfect is in **Insert** mode, as shown in Figure B-7. Insert mode allows you to type additional text without deleting or writing over the existing text. The existing text moves to the right as you type and automatically wraps to the next line. Next, you'll use the Delete key again.
3. **Double-click the word block, then press [Delete]**
   The word "block" is deleted.
4. **Press [Spacebar], type road, click after the word so in the first line, then press [Backspace] three times**
   The [Backspace] key is also a destructive movement key; it deletes characters to the left of the insertion point. You deleted the two letters and the extra space between the words "are" and "happy." Now you need to correct the Corel product name.
5. **Scroll down and click after the word Core, then type l**
   The word Corel is now spelled correctly. This correction highlights the importance of reading through your work before you print it. The Spell-As-You-Go feature only flags words not in WordPerfect's dictionary. A word such as "Core" may be contained in the dictionary, yet still be a misspelling in the context of a particular sentence. Next, Emily wants you to include a note about recycling paper.
6. **Scroll down and click after the word creatively, press [Enter], then type Recycle all scrap paper**
   The letter is coming along nicely. As you continue working, remember to save your changes.
7. **Click the Save button on the Toolbar**

Typeover and Insert Modes

Double-click Insert on the Status bar or press the Insert key to display "Typeover" in place of "Insert" on the Application bar. Double-click Typeover on the Status bar or press the Insert key to display "Insert." This Status bar item is called a **toggle button** because it switches WordPerfect back and forth between two modes: Insert and Typeover. In Insert mode, as each character is added, the text shifts to the right to make room for the inserted text. In Typeover mode, you "type over" or replace existing text when making a correction.

FIGURE B-6: Emily's notes for editing the document

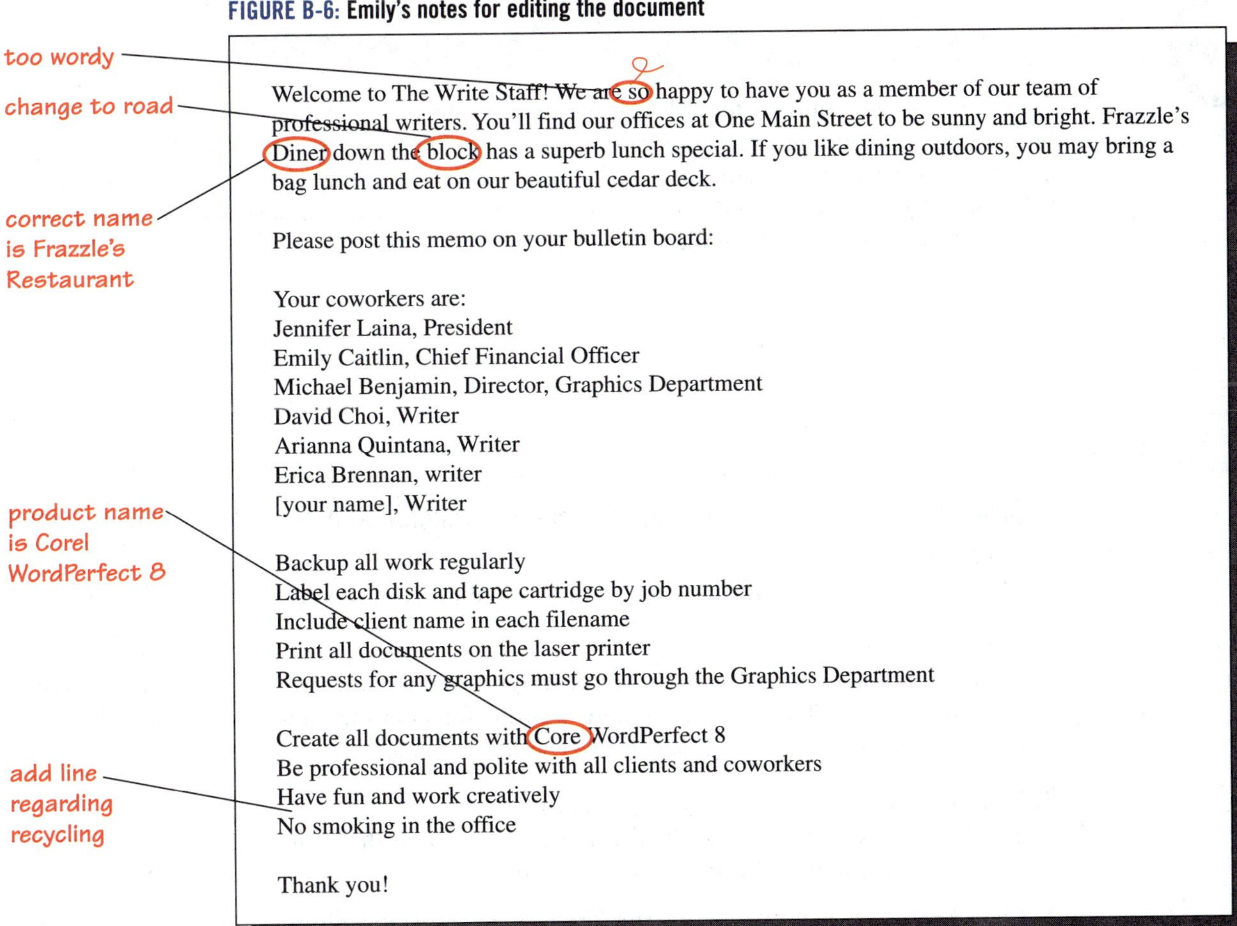

Welcome to The Write Staff! We are so happy to have you as a member of our team of professional writers. You'll find our offices at One Main Street to be sunny and bright. Frazzle's Diner down the block has a superb lunch special. If you like dining outdoors, you may bring a bag lunch and eat on our beautiful cedar deck.

Please post this memo on your bulletin board:

Your coworkers are:
Jennifer Laina, President
Emily Caitlin, Chief Financial Officer
Michael Benjamin, Director, Graphics Department
David Choi, Writer
Arianna Quintana, Writer
Erica Brennan, writer
[your name], Writer

Backup all work regularly
Label each disk and tape cartridge by job number
Include client name in each filename
Print all documents on the laser printer
Requests for any graphics must go through the Graphics Department

Create all documents with Core WordPerfect 8
Be professional and polite with all clients and coworkers
Have fun and work creatively
No smoking in the office

Thank you!

FIGURE B-7: Working in Insert Mode

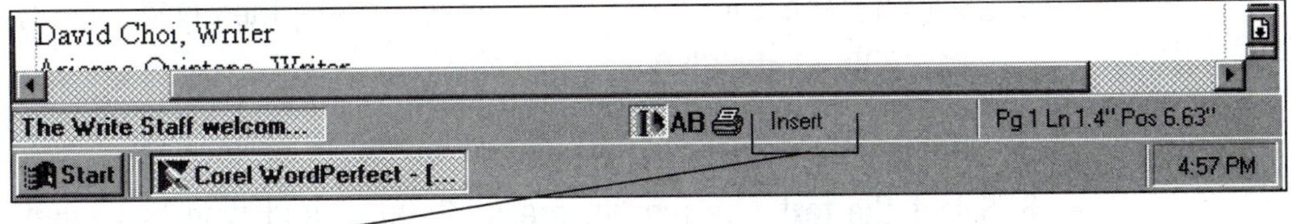

TABLE B-3: Changing or correcting text

method	action
[Delete]	Deletes a character to the right of the insertion point
[Backspace]	Deletes a character to the left of the insertion point
Typeover mode	Replaces existing text with new text
Insert mode	Inserts new text into existing text at the insertion point
Undo button	Reverses your last action
Redo button	Reverses the last undo

WordPerfect 8

Undoing Changes

If you change your mind after deleting or inserting text, or making other edits or changes, WordPerfect lets you undo your actions. You can undo the last action by using the Undo button on the toolbar or the Edit menu, and you can undo previous changes in the Undo/Redo History dialog box. After making the changes Emily requested, you have some ideas for additional edits that might improve the letter.

Steps

1. Select the text **and polite** in the line "Be professional and polite with all clients and coworkers"
   This directive seems condescending to the new employees, so you decide to delete it.
2. Press **[Delete]**
   On second thought, you decide that Emily might want the line to appear as is. You decide to undo this change. The Toolbar contains buttons for undoing and redoing edits. The Redo button is grayed because you have not yet "undone" an edit.
3. Click the **Undo button** on the Toolbar
   The deleted text is restored to the document. Notice that the Redo button is no longer dimmed. Try using this button to repeat the edit.
4. Click the **Redo button** on the Toolbar, observe the change on the screen, then click again
   Now you decide to add information about requesting vacation time.
5. Click after the word **coworkers**, press **[Enter]**, then type **Submit vacation requests one month in advance**
   You check this policy in the employee manual and find that employees should actually submit requests for extended time off two months in advance.
6. Select the text **one month**, press **[Delete]**, and type **two months**, then select the entire line and click the **Underline button** on the Property Bar
   You mention to Emily that you've added this line, and she informs you that The Write Staff is considering changing this policy so that employees have more flexibility in planning their vacations. You can undo more than one edit by using the Undo/Redo dialog box. Use the Undo/Redo menu to undo the series of edits you just made.
7. Click **Edit** on the menu bar, then click **Undo/Redo History**
   The Undo/Redo History dialog box opens, as shown in Figure B-8. The Undo list lists the recent edits you have made, beginning with the last edit, ("AttributeAppearanceToggle" refers to the underline attribute you applied to the new line) and allows you to select as many as you wish to undo. Undoing any item automatically undoes all the previous items.
8. Click the lines **AttributeAppearanceToggle**, **SelectDelete**, **HardReturn**, and **SelectDelete**, and **SelectDelete**, click **Undo**, then click **Close**
   You have made all the edits Emily requested as shown in Figure B-9.
9. Click the **Save button** on the Toolbar.

QuickTip

The Undo and Redo commands on the Edit menu are the menu equivalents of the Undo and Redo buttons on the Toolbar.

FIGURE B-8: Undo/Redo History dialog box

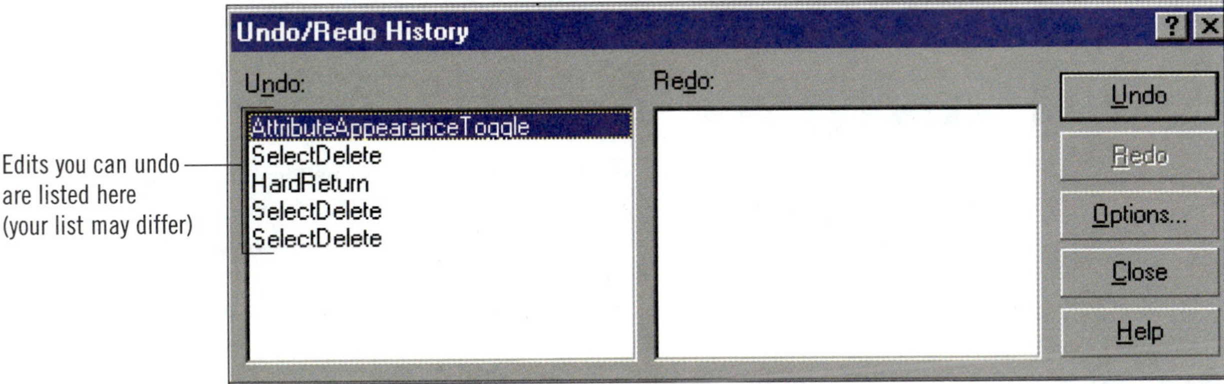

Edits you can undo are listed here (your list may differ)

FIGURE B-9: All corrections made in the document

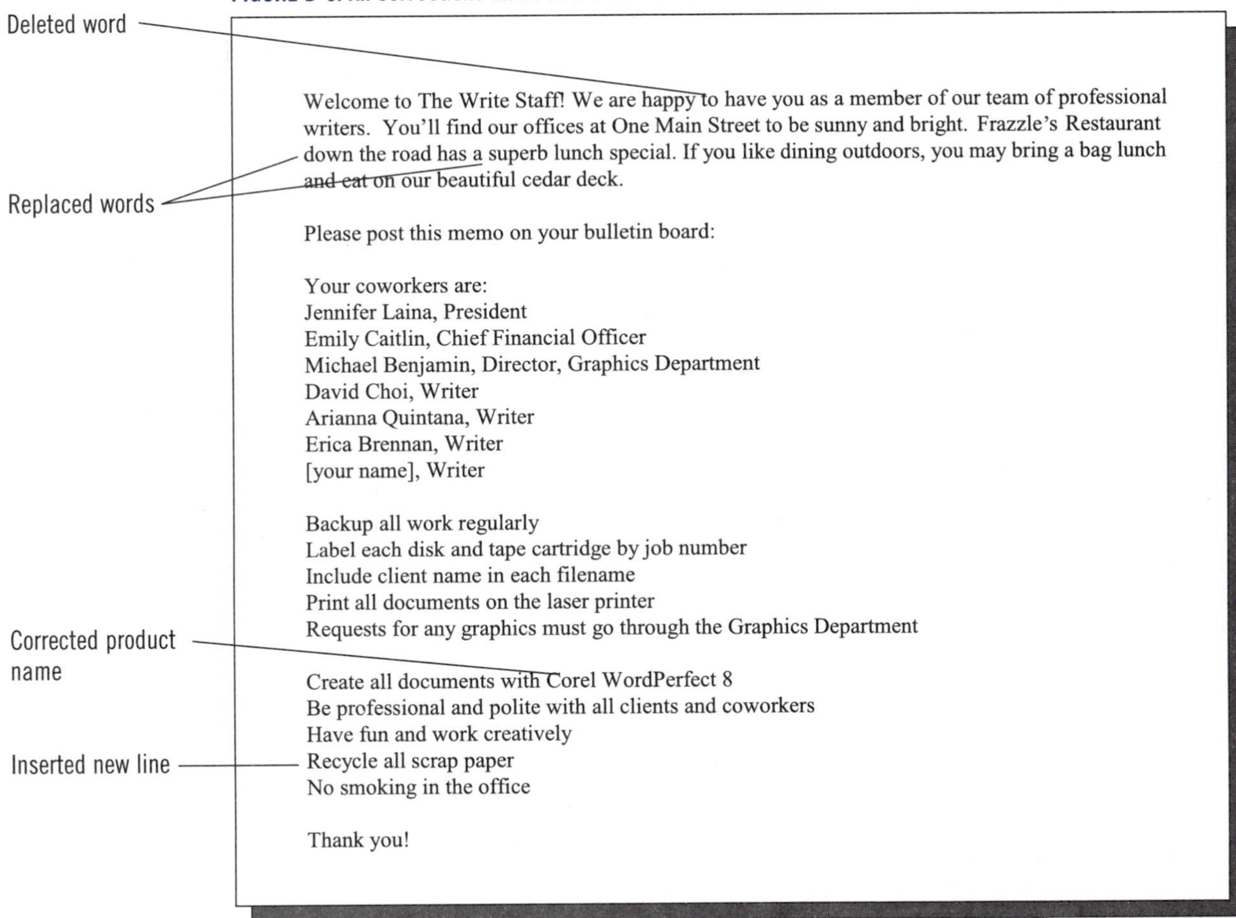

Deleted word
Replaced words
Corrected product name
Inserted new line
Welcome to The Write Staff! We are happy to have you as a member of our team of professional writers. You'll find our offices at One Main Street to be sunny and bright. Frazzle's Restaurant down the road has a superb lunch special. If you like dining outdoors, you may bring a bag lunch and eat on our beautiful cedar deck.
Please post this memo on your bulletin board:
Your coworkers are:
Jennifer Laina, President
Emily Caitlin, Chief Financial Officer
Michael Benjamin, Director, Graphics Department
David Choi, Writer
Arianna Quintana, Writer
Erica Brennan, Writer
[your name], Writer
Backup all work regularly
Label each disk and tape cartridge by job number
Include client name in each filename
Print all documents on the laser printer
Requests for any graphics must go through the Graphics Department
Create all documents with Corel WordPerfect 8
Be professional and polite with all clients and coworkers
Have fun and work creatively
Recycle all scrap paper
No smoking in the office
Thank you!

Setting the Undo/Redo level

The number of edits you can undo or redo is determined by the Undo/Redo Options dialog box. By default, this number is set at 10, but you can change it to suit your preferences. To open the Undo/Redo dialog box, click Options in the Undo/Redo History dialog box. When the Options dialog box opens, change the number of edits by clicking the up arrow or the down arrow in the Number of Undo/Redo items box, or entering a different number. You can also control when the edit history is saved with the document after you close it, by selecting or deselecting the Save Undo/Redo items with document check box.

WordPerfect 8

Cutting, Copying, and Pasting Text

In WordPerfect, there are two ways to move or copy text from one location in your document to another. You can use the **Clipboard**, a temporary storage place in the computer's memory, or you can drag text using the mouse. In this lesson, you will use the Clipboard. By placing text on the Clipboard using either the Cut or Copy commands, you can paste the text as many times as you want anywhere in the document. Jennifer wants you to add a short phone list at the bottom of the document. Instead of retyping the names in the list, use Copy and Paste to make the additions.

QuickTip

Before you can cut or copy text, you must first select it.

1. Scroll up, point in the left margin to **Jennifer** in the name list, and drag the mouse to the end of the name list as shown in Figure B-10
   Now that you've selected the text, you can copy it to the Clipboard, so that you can paste it to the bottom of the document.
2. Click the **Copy button** on the Toolbar
   This copies the selected text to the Clipboard, leaving the selected text in place. You can now paste this text anywhere in your document.
3. Click anywhere to deselect the text, press **[Ctrl][End]** to position the insertion point at the end of the document, then press **[Enter]** twice
   This is where you want to paste the copied text.

Trouble?

If you paste something in the wrong place by mistake, click the Undo button, or press [Delete] or [Backspace] to erase it; then paste it again at the correct location.

4. Click the **Paste button** on the Toolbar
   The copied list of names appears in the document. You want to call this list the phone list.
5. Click before **Jennifer** in the newly copied list, type **Phone List:**, then press **[Enter]**
6. Double-click **President**, type **x2402**, then continue to delete the position titles (Writer, for example) following each last name in the copied list, and replace the position titles with these phone extensions:

Jennifer	Emily	Michael	David	Arianna	Erica	[your name]
x2402	x2401	x2305	x2409	x2306	x2408	x2500

   Now you realize that the words "Thank you!" should be at the end of the document. Move the text using the Cut and Paste buttons.

QuickTip

When new text is copied to the Clipboard, the selection that was in the Clipboard previously is erased.

7. Select the **paragraph mark** ¶ above **Thank you!** and the text **Thank you!**, then click the **Cut button** on the Toolbar
   The selected text and hard return code is cut from the document and placed on the Clipboard. Because you want to move it, not delete it, you now need to paste it from the Clipboard to a new location in your document.
8. Press **[Ctrl][End]** to position the insertion point at the end of the document, press **[Enter]** twice, then click
   Your screen should now look like Figure B-11. Remember to save your changes.
9. Click the **Save button** on the Toolbar

FIGURE B-10: Text to be copied

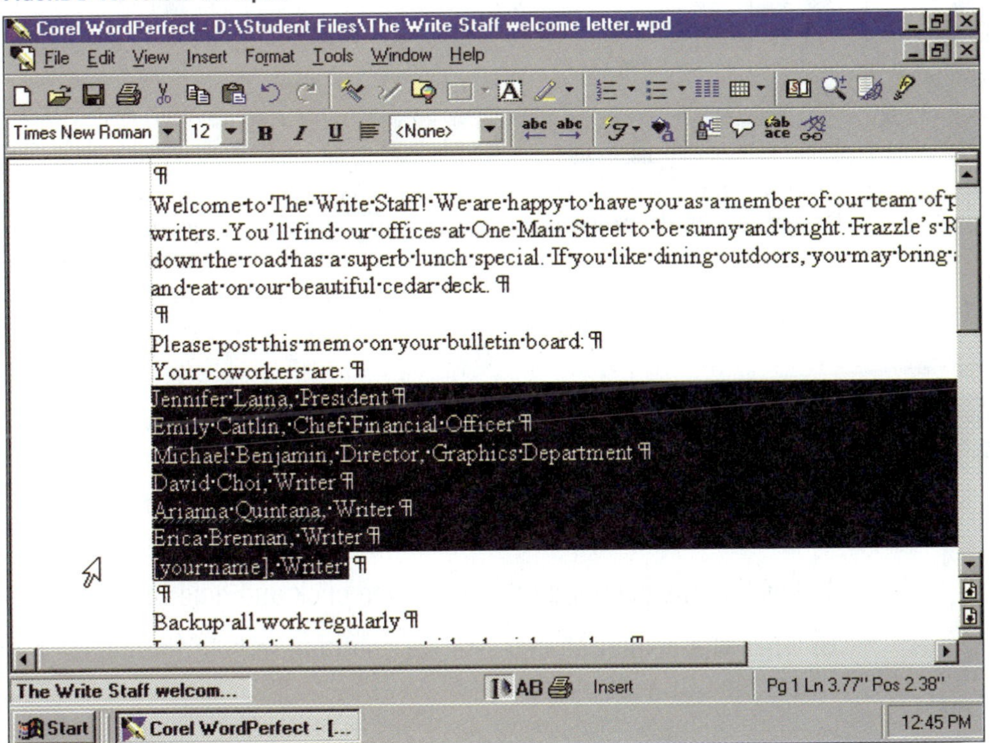

Corel WordPerfect - D:\Student Files\The Write Staff welcome letter.wpd
File Edit View Insert Format Tools Window Help
Times New Roman 12 <None>
Welcome to The Write Staff! We are happy to have you as a member of our team of
writers. You'll find our offices at One Main Street to be sunny and bright. Frazzle's R
down the road has a superb lunch special. If you like dining outdoors, you may bring
and eat on our beautiful cedar deck.
Please post this memo on your bulletin board:
Your coworkers are:
Jennifer Laina, President
Emily Caitlin, Chief Financial Officer
Michael Benjamin, Director, Graphics Department
David Choi, Writer
Arianna Quintana, Writer
Erica Brennan, Writer
[your name], Writer
Backup all work regularly
The Write Staff welcom...
AB Insert
Pg 1 Ln 3.77" Pos 2.38"
Start
Corel WordPerfect - [...
12:45 PM

FIGURE B-11: Document with text cut, copied, and pasted

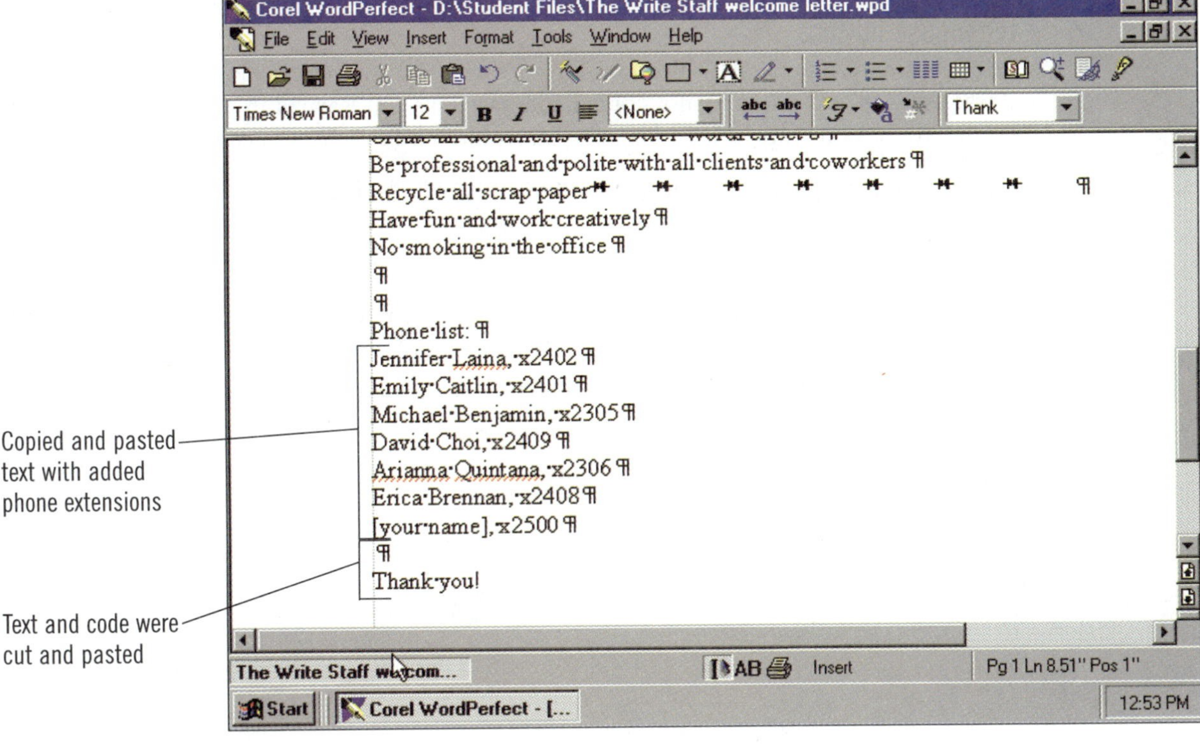

Corel WordPerfect - D:\Student Files\The Write Staff welcome letter.wpd
File Edit View Insert Format Tools Window Help
Times New Roman 12 <None> Thank
Be professional and polite with all clients and coworkers
Recycle all scrap paper
Have fun and work creatively
No smoking in the office
Phone list:
Jennifer Laina, x2402
Emily Caitlin, x2401
Michael Benjamin, x2305
David Choi, x2409
Arianna Quintana, x2306
Erica Brennan, x2408
[your name], x2500
Thank you!
The Write Staff welcom...
AB Insert
Pg 1 Ln 8.51" Pos 1"
Start
Corel WordPerfect - [...
12:53 PM
Copied and pasted text with added phone extensions
Text and code were cut and pasted

WordPerfect 8

CLUES TO USE

Delete vs. Cut

Pressing [Delete] is not the same as using the Cut command. The Cut command places the selected text temporarily on the Clipboard after removing it from the document. Pressing [Delete] removes the text permanently and the text is not available for pasting.

Dragging and Dropping Text

There are times when you want to move selected text without first copying it to the Clipboard. **Dragging and dropping** text is a very easy way to move text using the mouse. Jennifer reviewed the welcome letter and asks you to place the note about posting the message on the bulletin board at the top of the document. You will drag the sentence from its current location and drop it at the new location.

Steps

1. Press **[Ctrl][Home]**, then select **Please post this memo on your bulletin board**:
   Your screen should look like Figure B-12.
2. Position the pointer on the **text**, then click and hold the **mouse button**
3. When the pointer changes to , continue to hold the mouse button and drag it to the top of the document
   The blinking vertical bar up and to the left of the move pointer indicates where the text will be inserted.
4. Position the pointer so that the vertical bar is before the word **Welcome**, then release the mouse button
   The text is moved to the new location. This dragged text was never copied to the Clipboard. It was dragged and dropped, not copied and pasted as you learned in the last lesson. If you wanted to move or copy this text again, you would have to select it again.
5. Click in front of the word **Welcome**, then press **[Enter]** to insert a new line
   Your screen should look like Figure B-13. Jennifer is pleased with the way the letter looks. Save the document, then print copies to send to all members of the staff.
6. Click the **Save button** on the Toolbar, click the **Print button** on the Toolbar, then click **Print**
   The letter prints to your printer. Now you can close the document, but since you have more work to do, keep WordPerfect open.
7. Click the **document window Close button**

FIGURE B-12: Selected text to be dragged

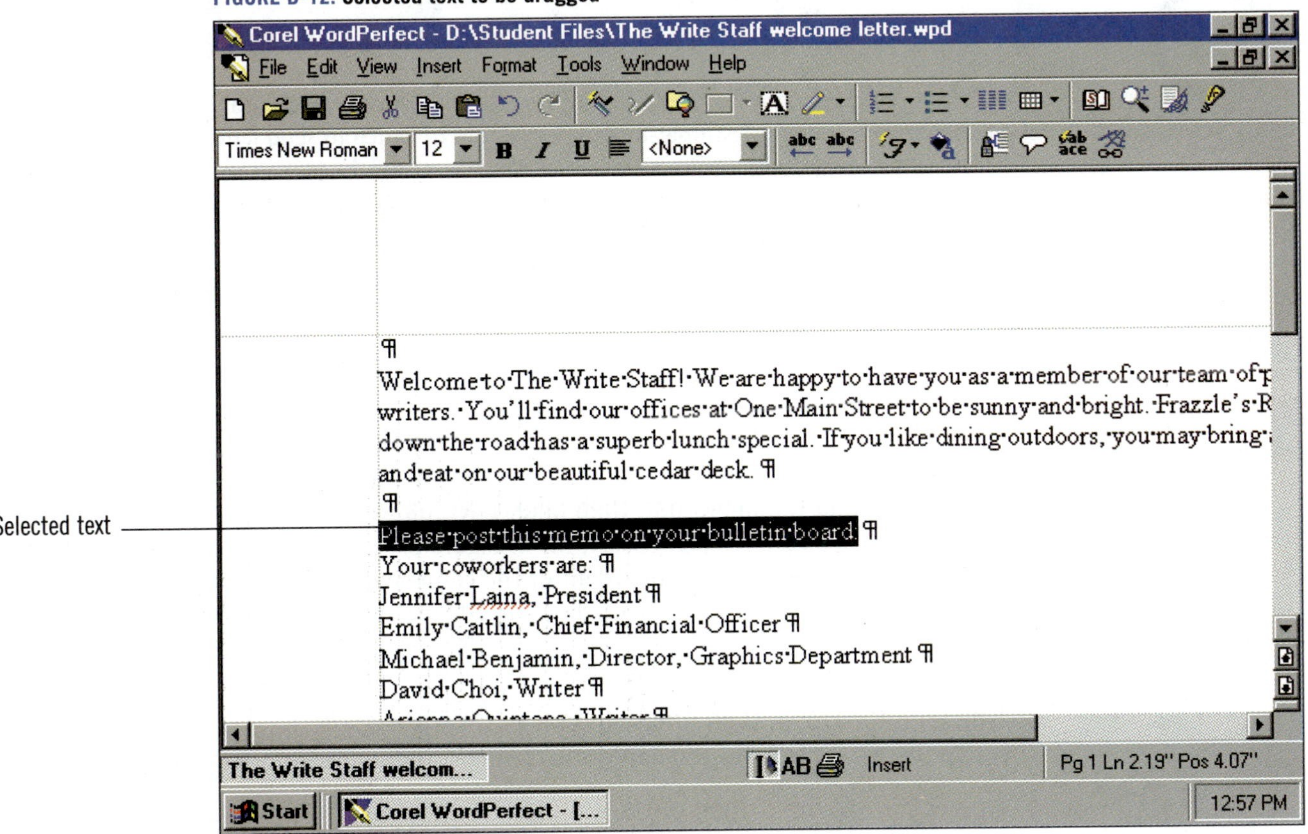
Corel WordPerfect - D:\Student Files\The Write Staff welcome letter.wpd
File Edit View Insert Format Tools Window Help
Times New Roman 12 <None>
Welcome to The Write Staff! We are happy to have you as a member of our team of p
writers. You'll find our offices at One Main Street to be sunny and bright. Frazzle's R
down the road has a superb lunch special. If you like dining outdoors, you may bring
and eat on our beautiful cedar deck.
Please post this memo on your bulletin board.
Your coworkers are:
Jennifer Laina, President
Emily Caitlin, Chief Financial Officer
Michael Benjamin, Director, Graphics Department
David Choi, Writer
The Write Staff welcom...
Insert
Pg 1 Ln 2.19" Pos 4.07"
Start
Corel WordPerfect - [...
12:57 PM
Selected text

FIGURE B-13: Text dropped in new location

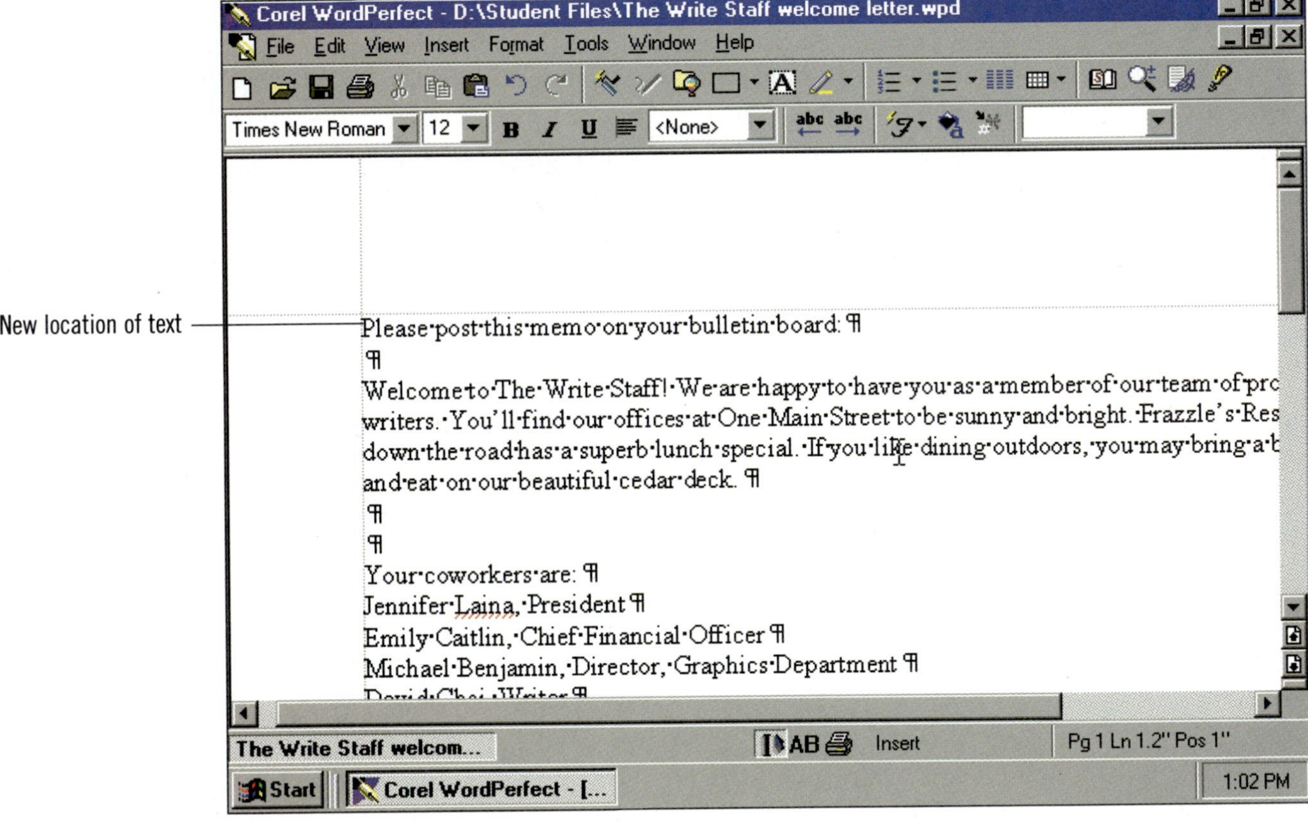
Corel WordPerfect - D:\Student Files\The Write Staff welcome letter.wpd
File Edit View Insert Format Tools Window Help
Times New Roman 12 <None>
Please post this memo on your bulletin board.
Welcome to The Write Staff! We are happy to have you as a member of our team of pro
writers. You'll find our offices at One Main Street to be sunny and bright. Frazzle's Res
down the road has a superb lunch special. If you like dining outdoors, you may bring a b
and eat on our beautiful cedar deck.
Your coworkers are:
Jennifer Laina, President
Emily Caitlin, Chief Financial Officer
Michael Benjamin, Director, Graphics Department
The Write Staff welcom...
Insert
Pg 1 Ln 1.2" Pos 1"
Start
Corel WordPerfect - [...
1:02 PM
New location of text

Creating an Envelope

WordPerfect provides many features to complete tasks that may appear complicated. The Envelope feature helps you create professional-looking envelopes in which to send letters. An envelope has a **return address** which typically gives the name and address of the person mailing the letter, and a **mailing address**, the person and address who will receive the letter. Now that you have completed the letters for all new staff members, you want to send each one through the interoffice mail in an envelope.

1. Click **Format** on the menu bar, then click **Envelope**
   The Envelope dialog box opens, as shown in Figure B-14. You want the recipients to know that this letter came from the president of the company, Jennifer Laina. You will type her name in the From text box, however, there already may be information in the From box.
2. If necessary, select the text in the From text box, then press **[Delete]**
3. Type **Jennifer Laina**, then press **[Enter]**
   Notice that as you type, the text appears in the image of the envelope in the appropriate place.
4. Type **The Write Staff**, then press **[Enter]**
   Since this letter is just going within this office you do not need to give the complete street addresses. At The Write Staff, mail boxes are the same as the phone extensions.
5. Click in the **To text box**, then type **Emily Caitlin**, press **[Enter]**, type **Chief Financial Officer**, press **[Enter]**, then type **Mail Box 2401**
   Emily's office address is clearly visible in the sample envelope in the dialog box, as shown in Figure B-15. The Write Staff uses #10 business envelopes, so you need to specify this before printing.
6. Click the **Envelope definitions** list arrow, then click **Envelope #10** or **Envelope Landscape**
7. If you have a #10 envelope available at this time, place it in the envelope feed of your printer; if not, click **Close** and skip to Step 9
8. Click **Print**
   You continue to create envelopes for all new staff members in this manner. When all the envelopes are printed, you place the copies of the welcome letter in the envelopes and distribute them through the mailroom. You are very pleased with your work on your second day. Now it is time to go home.
9. Click **File** on the menu bar, then click **Exit**
   All open documents are closed, and you exit WordPerfect.

QuickTip

You can change the Font style or size of the return address or the mailing address by clicking the Font button in the Envelope dialog box. You do not need to select the text first. Note that the new font will not appear in the dialog box.

FIGURE B-14: Envelope dialog box

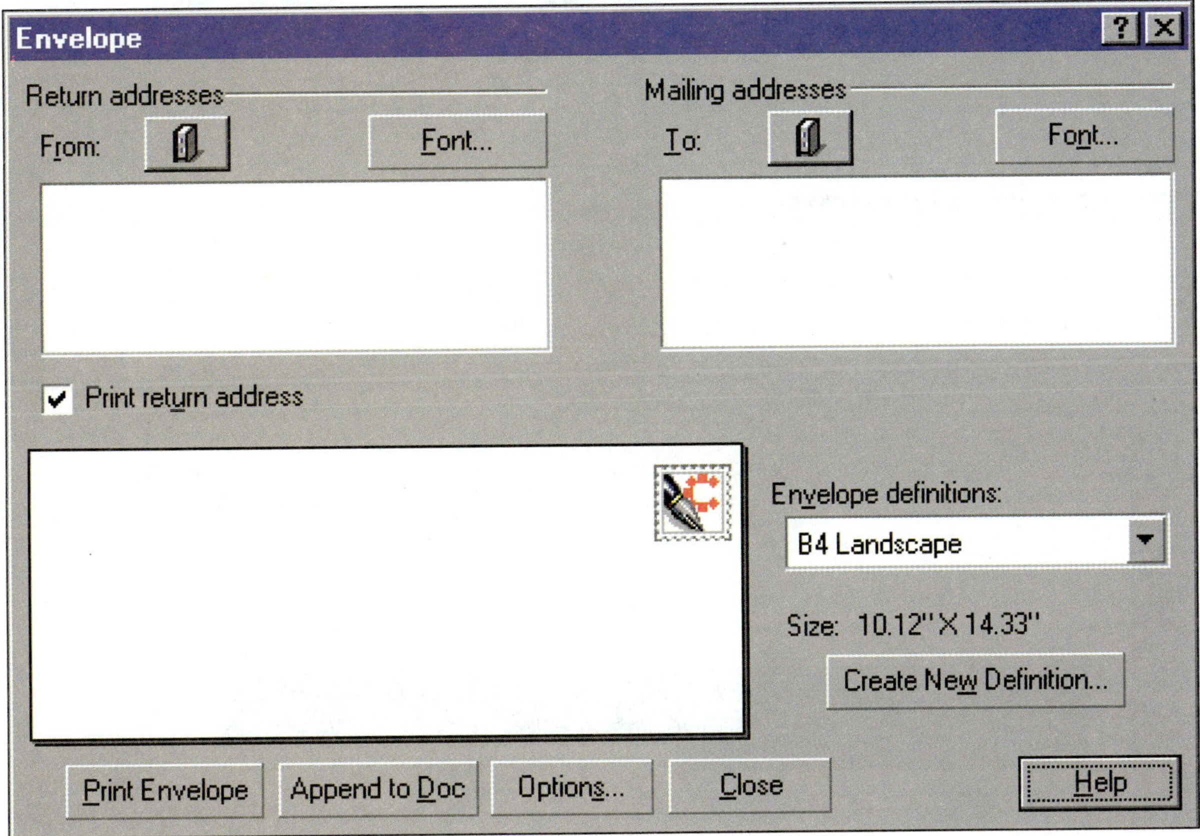

FIGURE B-15: Completed Envelope dialog box

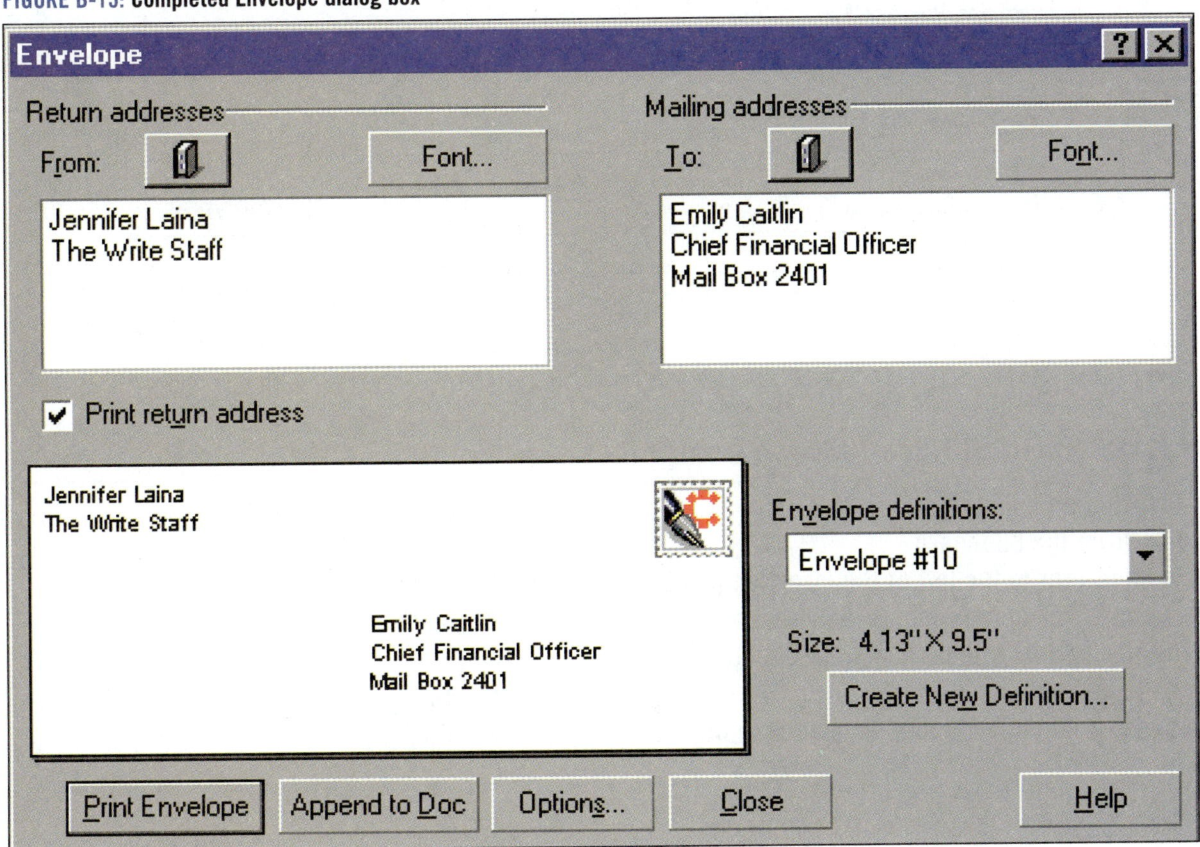

Practice

Concepts Review

Label each element of the WordPerfect window shown in Figure B-16.

FIGURE B-16

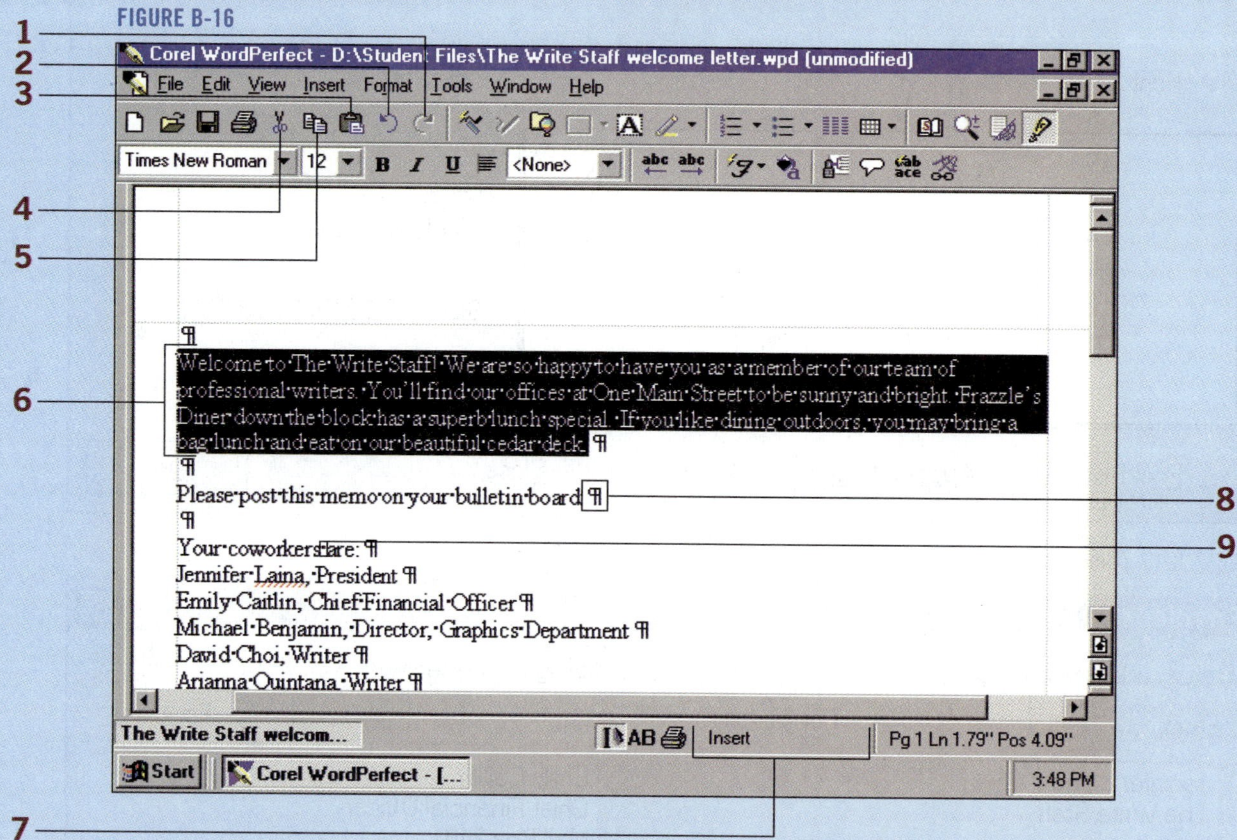
1
2
3
4
5
6
7
8
9
Corel WordPerfect - D:\Student Files\The Write Staff welcome letter.wpd (unmodified)
File Edit View Insert Format Tools Window Help
Times New Roman
12
<None>
Welcome to The Write Staff! We are so happy to have you as a member of our team of professional writers. You'll find our offices at One Main Street to be sunny and bright. Frazzle's Diner down the block has a superb lunch special. If you like dining outdoors, you may bring a bag lunch and eat on our beautiful cedar deck.
Please post this memo on your bulletin board.
Your coworkers are:
Jennifer Laina, President
Emily Caitlin, Chief Financial Officer
Michael Benjamin, Director, Graphics Department
David Choi, Writer
Arianna Quintana, Writer
The Write Staff welcom...
Insert
Pg 1 Ln 1.79" Pos 4.09"
Start
Corel WordPerfect - [...
3:48 PM

Match each statement with the function it describes.

10. Copies text to the Clipboard
11. Pastes text from the Clipboard
12. Deletes a character to the left of the insertion point
13. Deletes a character to the right of the insertion point
14. Useful for moving text without using the Clipboard
15. Restores the last action
16. Removes text from current location, places in Clipboard

a. [Backspace]
b. (Undo button)
c. Drag and drop
d. [Delete]
e. (Cut button)
f. (Copy button)
g. (Paste button)

Select the best answer from the list of choices.

17. You can select several lines of text

a. By triple-clicking a word in a sentence.
b. By clicking and dragging in the left margin.
c. By double-clicking the paragraph.
d. You cannot select by line, only by sentences or paragraphs.

18. To quickly create an envelope

a. Click Insert on the menu bar, then click Envelope.
b. Click Format on the menu bar, then click Envelope.
c. Click Format on the menu bar, click Envelope, then click Create.
d. Click Edit on the menu bar, then click Envelope.

19. Which commands would you use to copy a sentence to another paragraph in your document?

a. Cut, Copy, Paste
b. Copy, Paste
c. Paste, Copy
d. Move, Copy

20. Which commands would you use to move a paragraph to another page in your document?

a. Move, Paste
b. Cut, Paste
c. Paste, Move
d. Copy, Move

21. If you position the mouse pointer on a word and triple-click the mouse, you

a. Select the word.
b. Select the page.
c. Select the paragraph.
d. Select the sentence.

► Skills Review

1. **Plan a document.**
   - **a.** Think about and write notes on how a greeting card company might plan its advertising copy.
   - **b.** Determine the tone of the text and write notes.
   - **c.** Decide what important facts should be included in the text.
   - **d.** Sketch out how you might want it to look.

2. **Enter text.**
   - **a.** Type the following text exactly as shown below, including errors:
     Holiday Gliter. You'll find lots of fun uses for this totally outrageous holiday glitter. Sprinkle on greeting cards or use it to decorate a table top. Packed in a handy 3" plastic tube. Pre-inflated "Happy Valentine's Day" Balloon Assortment. Includes 48 4" clear, round red and white confetti. Each assortment rests on a 7" cup and stick decorated with an "I Love You." Stand included.
   - **b.** Save the document as "Glitter".

3. **Select text.**
   - **a.** Select the paragraph using the Select menu.
   - **b.** Drag to select the words "I Love You."
   - **c.** Use the Select pointer in the left margin to select the first three lines.

4. **Insert and delete text.**
   - **a.** Change the word "Gliter" to "Glitter."
   - **b.** The word "Pre-inflated" should begin a new paragraph. Insert a blank line between the paragraphs.
   - **c.** Position the insertion point at the end of the word "round" and insert the words "balloons with".
   - **d.** Click View on the menu bar, then click Show Paragraph to check for extra spaces in the document.
   - **e.** If you don't like working with the Show Paragraph feature, click Show Paragraph again to turn this feature off.
   - **f.** Save the corrected document with the same filename.

5. **Undo changes.**
   a. Delete the sentence "Stand Included."
   b. Undo this deletion.
   c. Click after the sentence, "Stand Included.", and type "Also includes gift insertion card."
   d. Press [Enter].
   e. Select the sentence you just typed, then click the Bold button **B** on the Property Bar.
   f. Use the Undo/Redo History dialog box to remove the new sentence and the hard paragraph return you just inserted.

6. **Cut, copy, and paste text.**
   a. Use the Cut command to make the last sentence the first sentence.
   b. Insert a date at the end of the document.
   c. Copy the date to the top of the document.
   d. Type your name at the top of the document.
   e. Print the document.

7. **Drag and drop text.**
   a. Drag your name to the bottom of the document.
   b. Save and print the file.

8. **Create an envelope.**
   a. Click Format, click Envelope.
   b. Type your name and home address in the Return Address text box.
   c. Type your friend's address in the Address text box.
   d. Print the envelope.
   e. If the document has been changed since the last save, make sure to save it before exiting.
   f. Click File on the menu bar, then click Exit.

Independent Challenges

1. You are a product manager for Lawn Tools, Inc, a company that designs and manufactures lawn mowers and trimmers. For the past 24 months, you have been developing a new, low-cost, environmentally safe push mower called the SwiftBlade. You are confident that the new product has significant market potential, but you must get final approval from the Corporate Products Group before beginning production.

Write a memo to the Corporate Products Group in which you explain that the SwiftBlade is ready for production, but needs final corporate approval. Point out that you conducted a market study that showed consumers were very interested in the SwiftBlade because it is quiet and light. Explain that the suggested retail price of $198 makes it attractive to new home buyers.

To complete this independent challenge:

1. Make a list of the ideas you want to present to the Corporate Products Group in your memo.
2. Make a rough sketch of how you would like the memo to look on paper.
3. Remember to include a standard memo heading, like the one shown here:
   Memo To: Corporate Products Group
   From: {your name}
   Date: {current date}
   Subject: SwiftBlade Product Proposal
4. Use WordPerfect to create the document.
5. Carefully review the document and use the WordPerfect editing features to correct any errors.
6. Save the document as "Swiftblade Memo".
7. Print the completed document.
8. Submit any preliminary notes or sketches and the completed memo.

2. Practice your WordPerfect skills by taking a break to write a letter to a friend.
To complete this independent challenge:

1. Write a letter to your friend telling him or her about your new job at Great Expectations, a party–planning service. Be sure to date the letter.
2. After you write the letter, save it with the filename of your choice to your Student Disk, print it, and read it over. Then use the skills you've learned in this unit to move text around, insert, delete, and correct errors to make it the best letter possible.

3. The Morning StarLight Cereal Company has asked you to write a short description of their new Colorful StarLight cereal which will be placed on the side panel of the cereal box. The description should be exciting and interesting, and it should promote this new low-fat kid's cereal. The cereal clusters are in the shape of stars, and they glow when milk is poured on them.
To complete this independent challenge:

1. Make a list of the ideas you want to include in the copy.
2. Make a rough sketch of how you would like the text to look on the cereal box.
3. Use WordPerfect to create the document.
4. Include your name and the current date at the top of the document.
5. Carefully review the document and use the WordPerfect editing features to correct any errors.
6. Save the document as "Starlight1".
7. Print the completed document.
8. Submit any preliminary notes or sketches and the completed memo.

4. You are going to send a series of letters to your neighbors asking them to join you in planning a New Year's Eve party. You completed the letters, but need to create envelopes for them.
To complete this independent challenge:

1. Start WordPerfect and open a new document.
2. Use the Envelope feature to create and print five envelopes addressed to your friends.
3. Close the document without saving changes.

Visual Workshop

Use the skills you learned in this unit to create the document shown in Figure B-17. Use as many of the selecting, copying, pasting, inserting, and deleting skills that you can. Use copying and pasting for repeating words such as Western Wear, Hotel California, shareholders, and ballroom. Save the document as "Western Wear letter." When you are finished with the letter, create the envelope as shown in Figure B-18.

FIGURE B-17

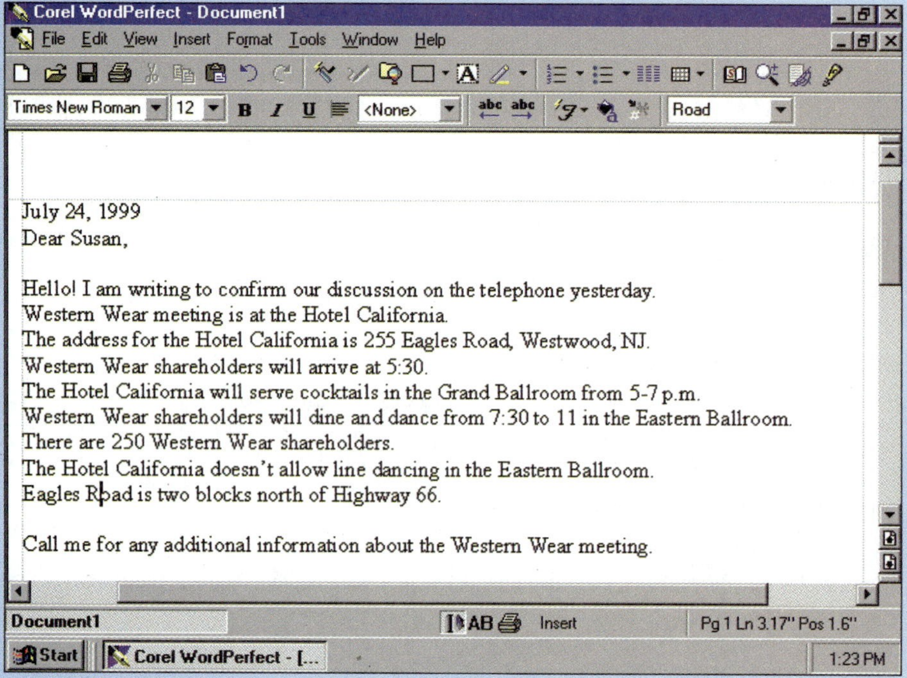

FIGURE B-18

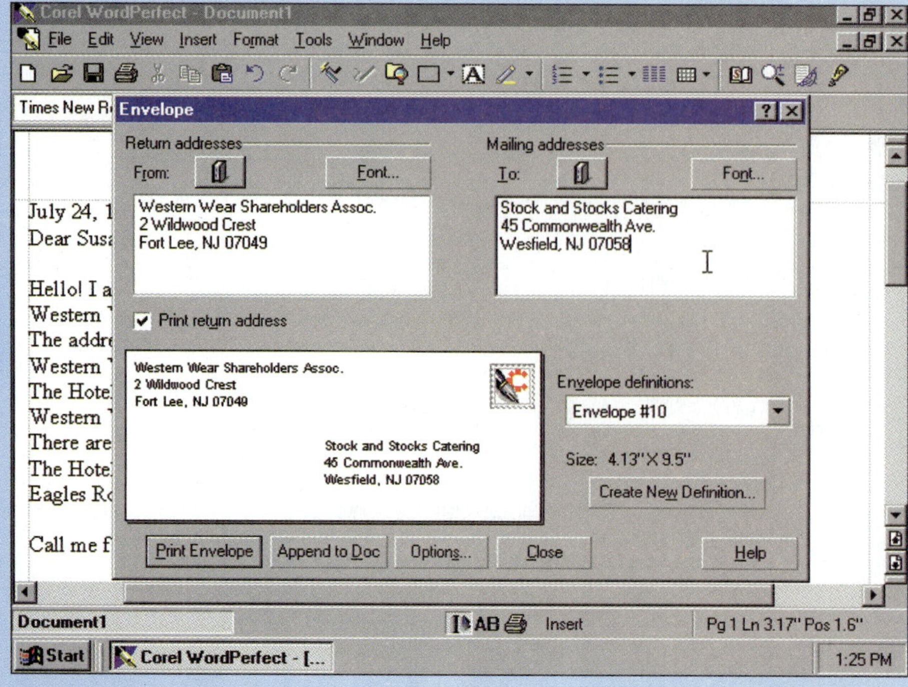

WordPerfect 8

Editing

a Document

Objectives

- Correct spelling in a document
- Customize QuickCorrect
- Use the Thesaurus
- Use Grammatik
- Find and replace text
- View Reveal Codes
- Delete codes
- Use Make It Fit

When you edit a document, you try to improve it by copying, cutting, and moving sections of text. You also check to make sure it is well organized and error free. In this unit, you will learn to further refine a document by using WordPerfect's proofreading tools. For example, you can check for spelling and typographical errors using the Spell Checker, find and replace text, find a synonym or antonym for a particular word using the Thesaurus, or check for grammatical mistakes using Grammatik. You can use these tools while you are typing a document or after you have created it. There also are various display options in WordPerfect that help you edit your document. In this unit, you'll make corrections to a letter written by Jennifer to promote The Write Staff 's catalog writing department. You'll correct errors in grammar and style, and then use the Make It Fit feature to make the letter a single-page document.

Correcting Spelling in a Document

As a writer, you ultimately decide whether words in a document are correct or should be changed. However, the WordPerfect **Spell Checker** assists you in creating professional documents by checking for misspelled words, duplicate words, words containing numbers, or irregular capitalization. Jennifer Laina has asked you to check her letter to a mail-order clothing company for possible spelling errors, then make any final edits needed.

Steps

1. **Start WordPerfect, click the Open button on the Toolbar, click the drive that contains your Student Disk, click WP C-1, then click Open**
   WP C-1 opens in the document window, as shown in Figure C-1. This is the letter you will work on in this unit.

QuickTip

To enable or disable Spell-As-You-Go, click Tools on the menu bar, then click Spell-As-You-Go.

2. **Click File on the menu bar, click Save As, type Clothing Adventures contact letter in the File name text box, then click Save**
   The WP C-1 file is saved with a new name, "Clothing Adventures contact letter". As you scroll through the document, notice that many words are underlined with hatched red lines. This is the **Spell-As-You-Go** feature. WordPerfect checks the spelling of each word as you enter it and marks those words that aren't in the dictionary. You can choose to correct spelling "as you go" by right-clicking a misspelled word, then choosing from a list of alternative spellings that opens in the shortcut menu. Or, you can wait until you've completed your document and check the entire document at one time, which you will now do.

QuickTip

To make additional changes to text while the Spell Check dialog box is open, click in the document window. When you are ready to continue the Spell Check, click Resume.

3. **Click Tools on the menu bar, then click Spell Check**
   The Writing Tools dialog box opens with the Spell Checker tab selected, as shown in Figure C-2. The document appears in a scrollable window so that you can make additional changes to text without closing the dialog box. The Spell Checker looks at each word but stops only on words it does not recognize. It does not stop on correctly spelled words that are used incorrectly in a sentence. The first misspelled word it found is "competative". You can choose the suggested spelling of the word in the Replace with text box, choose a suggested word from the Replacements list, or manually make corrections in the Replace with text box.
4. **Click Replace to choose the word in the Replace with text box**
   "Competative" is replaced with "competitive", and the Spell Checker continues looking for the next spelling error or repeated word. The next misspelled word found is "infrormation."
5. **Click Replace to correctly spell "information"**
   The next word the Spell Checker stops on is a duplicate word. You need to delete "to".
6. **Click Replace to replace "to to" with "to", click "essentials" in the Replacements text box, then click Replace**
   Continue spell checking the document until the Spell Checker finds the word "Laina." Since this word is not in the dictionary, Spell Checker suggests correctly spelled words that are similar. Laina is a proper noun and is spelled correctly.
7. **Click Skip All**
   After the last correction, a dialog box informs you that the spell check is completed.
8. **Click Yes**
   This closes the Spell Checker and the corrected document appears.
9. **Click the Save button on the Toolbar to save your changes**

FIGURE C-1: Clothing Adventures contact letter

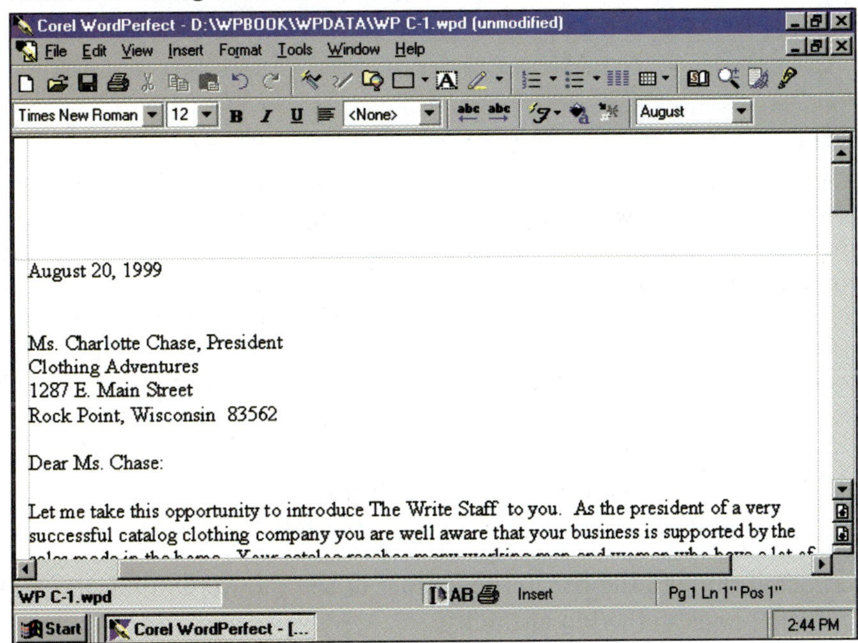

FIGURE C-2: Spell Checker tab of Writing Tools dialog box

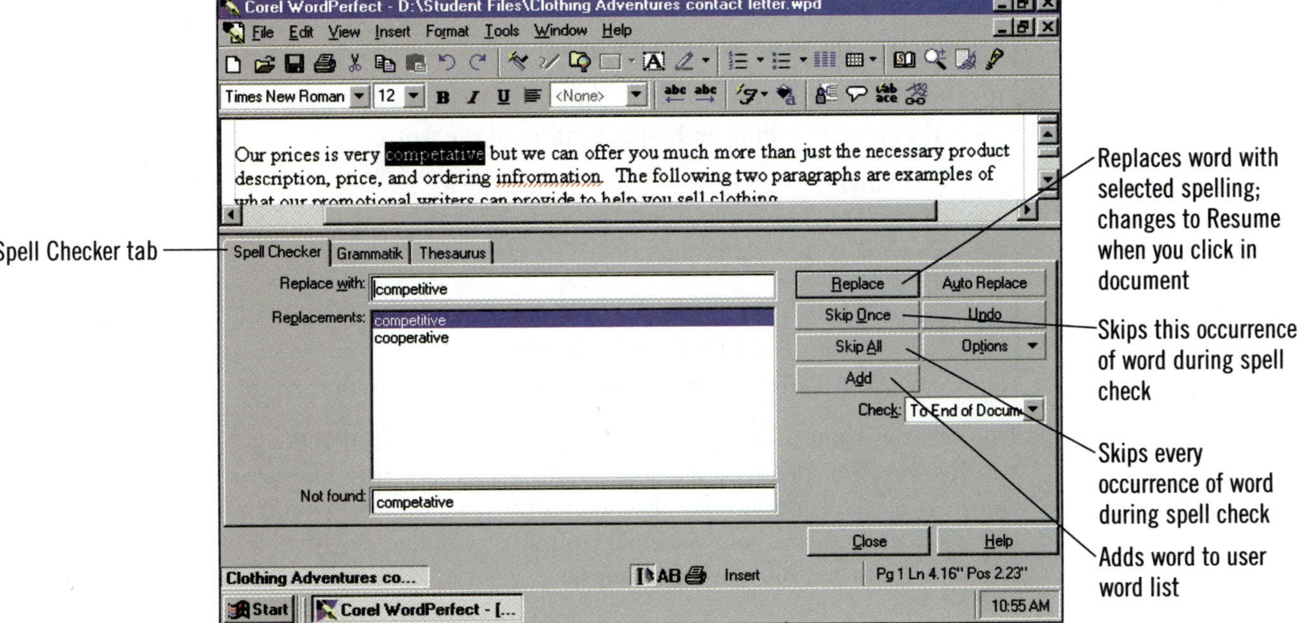

CLUES TO USE

Adding to your word list

You can customize the Spell Checker to skip words that are not in the main dictionary (your name, for example) by adding them to a **user word list**, a supplemental dictionary for words and phrases. WordPerfect maintains an active word list for each document you create and for the registered user of the program. You can also create additional word lists for specific purposes, such as for your company, for specific types of writing you do (such as legal or medical writing), or for others who use your computer. When checking for spelling errors, the Spell Checker searches the current document word list and your user word list and skips any words you have added. To add a word to a word list, click the Add to list in the Spell Check dialog box, click the name of the word list, and then click Add. If you are working in a lab setting, check with your instructor or technical support person before adding words to the dictionary.

WordPerfect 8

Customizing QuickCorrect

Keyboarding is not an exact science, and often you will find that you repeatedly make the same errors for common words. QuickCorrect in WordPerfect has predefined words and characters that automatically change as specified so that "teh" changes to "the" for example. The related feature, Format-As-You-Go, automatically corrects irregular capitalizations such as "THe" to "The". See Table C-1 for a list of the Format-As-You-Go options. You can customize QuickCorrect to meet your specific needs. As a writer at The Write Staff, you are having trouble typing Jennifer's name correctly. You continually type "Jenifer" rather than "Jennifer". You decide to customize QuickCorrect to always spell her name correctly.

Steps 1 2 3 4

1. Click **Tools** on the menu bar, then click **QuickCorrect**
   The QuickCorrect dialog box opens, as shown in Figure C-3.
2. Scroll through the list to the bottom to see the words that are predefined, and then scroll back to the top of the list
   You can see that WordPerfect corrects many common typing and spelling errors. However, Jenifer is not on the list, so you will add it.
3. Type **Jenifer** in the **Replace text box**
   Now, you type the word as it should appear.
4. Press **[Tab]**, then type **Jennifer** in the **With text box**
   This is the correct spelling and capitalization of the word.
5. Click **Add Entry**
   The entry is added to the list and is now part of the QuickCorrect settings as shown in Figure C-4.
6. Click **OK**, press **[Ctrl][End]** to move to the end of the document, type **Jenifer**, then press **[Spacebar]** to signal the end of the word
   Notice how WordPerfect automatically corrected your error.
7. Type **jenifer**, then press **[Spacebar]** to signal the end of the word
   WordPerfect also corrects the case if you forget to capitalize her name. Making changes to QuickCorrect will affect everyone who uses the machine after you. This feature is document independent. If this is your personal computer, you can decide to leave the change in the program. However, you can delete entries.
8. Click **Tools**, click **QuickCorrect**, scroll down, click **Jenifer**, click **Delete Entry**, confirm the entry you are deleting, then click **Yes** in the **Delete Selected QuickCorrect entry-message box**, then click **OK**
   Now you need to delete the extra text "Jennifer Jennifer" at the end of the document.
9. Select the extra text **Jennifer Jennifer**, then press **[Delete]**

Overriding QuickCorrect settings

There may be times when you don't want QuickCorrect to take over and change characters. To temporarily disable the QuickCorrect feature, click Tools on the menu bar, then click QuickCorrect, and click to remove the checkmark in the Replace words as you type checkbox.

FIGURE C-3: QuickCorrect dialog box

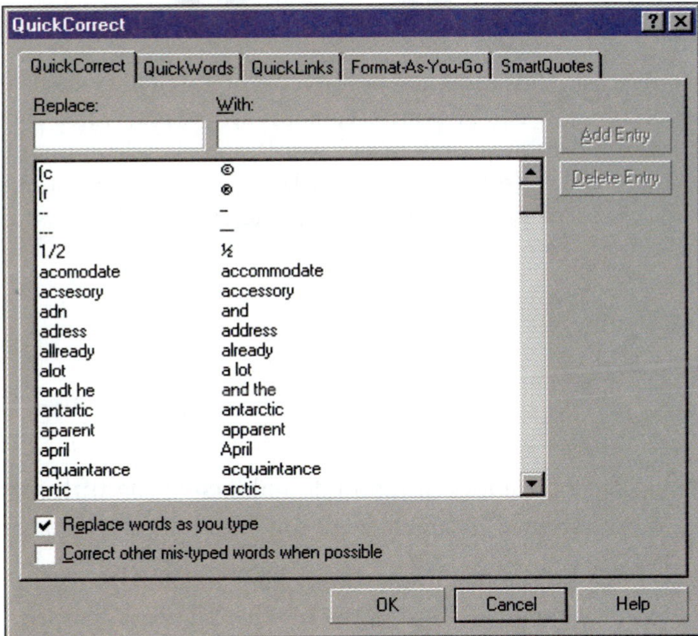

FIGURE C-4: Jennifer entry added to QuickCorrect dialog box

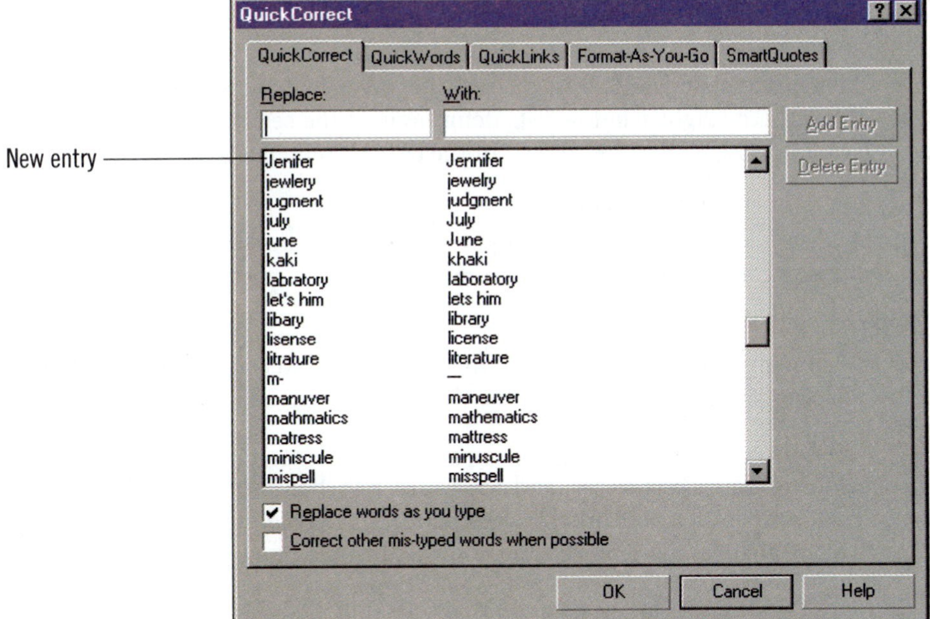

TABLE C-1: Format-As-You-Go options

feature	description
CapsFix	Corrects irregular capitalization
QuickBullets	Converts certain characters to a bulleted list, or numbers to a numbered list at the beginning of the line
QuickIndent	Tabs over at the beginning of any line to begin a paragraph
QuickLines	Converts dashes or hyphens to graphic lines
QuickOrdinals	Converts to ordinal numbers using superscript, such as 1st, 2nd, 3rd
QuickSymbols	Converts hyphens to en-dashes and em-dashes

Using the Thesaurus

The WordPerfect **Thesaurus** offers you a list of alternative words that enhance the vocabulary in your documents. The Thesaurus contains **synonyms**, words with like meanings; **antonyms**, words with opposite meanings; related words, and even definitions to ensure that you choose an appropriate word. After reading Jennifer's letter several times, you don't like the use of the word "products" in the second to last paragraph. Use the Thesaurus to find a synonym to use as a substitute.

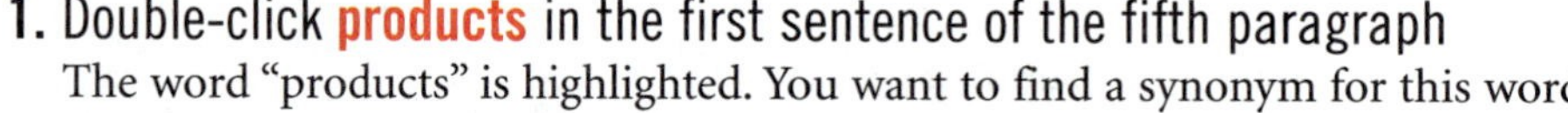

1. Double-click **products** in the first sentence of the fifth paragraph
   The word "products" is highlighted. You want to find a synonym for this word.

2. Click **Tools** on the menu bar, then click **Thesaurus**
   The Writing Tools dialog box opens with the Thesaurus tab selected, as shown in Figure C-5. The word "products" appears in the Replace with text box, and a list of synonyms for "products" appears, followed by a list of antonyms. The word "merchandise", the first word in the list of synonyms, is highlighted.

3. Scroll down through the choices in the list box
   Suggested replacement words and phrases are organized by Synonyms, Antonyms, and Related Words. The right window lists definitions of the selected word and highlights the most likely meaning within the context of the current sentence.

4. Scroll back up through the choices
   "Merchandise" seems like a good synonym to use. Just to be sure that "merchandise" is the best word, you can display alternatives to this word.

5. Double-click **merchandise**
   A list of synonyms appears for the noun "merchandise" as well as for the verb "merchandise" in the adjacent list boxes. The noun is the word you choose to use.

6. Click **Replace**
   The Thesaurus dialog box closes, and the word "merchandise" replaces "products" in the document. Compare your document with Figure C-6. Reread the sentence to ensure that the word change enhances the sentence and conveys the meaning you wanted.

7. Click the **Save button** to save changes to your document

Trouble?

Depending on your installation, the thesaurus dialog box may differ from the one pictured here. To complete the lesson, scroll to find the word "merchandise" and skip to Step 5.

Trouble?

If the Select Word Form dialog box opens, make sure the word "merchandise" is selected, then click OK.

FIGURE C-5: Thesaurus tab of Writing Tools dialog box

Selected word

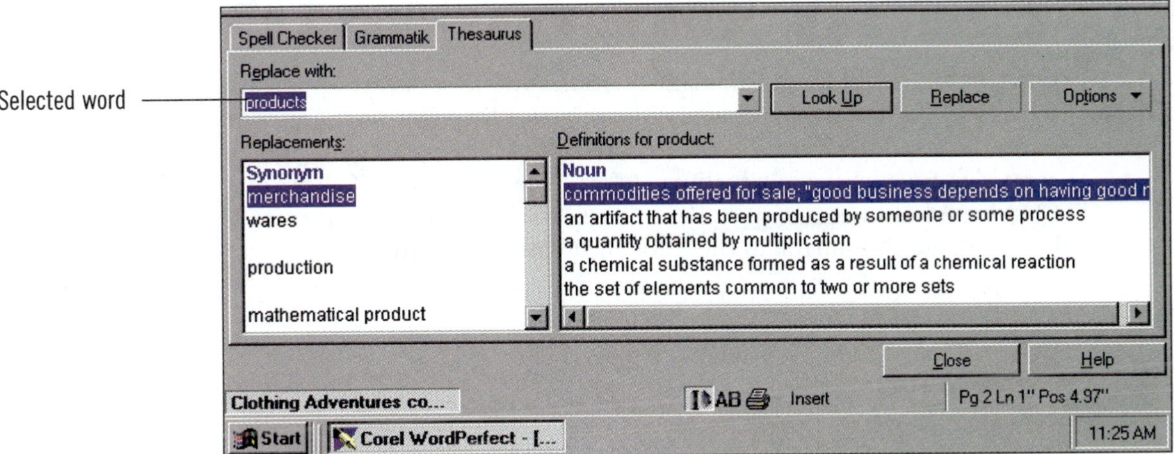

Prompt-As-You-Go list box

FIGURE C-6: Document with word change

Synonym in document

Corel WordPerfect - D:\Student Files\Clothing Adventures contact letter.wpd

File Edit View Insert Format Tools Window Help

Times New Roman | 11. | <None> | merchandise

The Write Staff can provide you with descriptions for your merchandise that will help you sell high quality clothing essentials. Quality garments deserve quality descriptions. You have already demonstrated your knowledge that words sell, by your company name, Adventure Clothing. This title piques the interest of readers who then want to open the catalog and view the merchandise your company makes available.

The Write Staff can provide you with the promotional text that will sell your clothing. I will contact you early next week to share additional examples of other clients' catalogs for which we have written successful descriptions that have boosted their sales dramatically. Quality garments deserve quality descriptions.

Sincerely,

Jennifer Laina

Clothing Adventures co... Insert Pg 2 Ln 1" Pos 5.73"

Start | Corel WordPerfect - [... | 11:34 AM

WordPerfect 8

Prompt-As-You-Go

Prompt-As-You-Go is a context-sensitive feature that makes it easy to correct spellings and grammatical errors, or make word changes, without ever opening a dialog box. As you type, the Prompt-As-You-Go list box on the Property bar displays an alternative spelling in red for the word you are typing if it appears to be misspelled; click the list box to see other alternate spellings. It displays the word in blue to indicate a possible grammatical error. It displays the word in black to indicate alternate word choices; click the list box to choose a different word.

Using Grammatik

Grammatik (rhymes with "dramatic") enables you to review your documents for grammatical errors such as mistakes in punctuation, sentence fragments, or agreement. When Grammatik locates an error, you can review an explanation of the corresponding grammar rule and select a correction from a list of alternatives.  You are not sure if all the grammar in the letter to Clothing Adventures is correct. Because you want the letter to represent The Write Staff in the best light, use Grammatik to check for any grammatical errors.

Steps

QuickTip

Grammatik always begins at the top of a document. This ensures that Grammatik checks the entire document for grammatical errors.

1. **Click Tools on the menu bar, then click Grammatik**
   The Writing Tools dialog box opens with the Grammatik tab selected, as shown in Figure C-7. The first phrase Grammatik stops on is "prices is". Grammatik has detected an error in the number agreement. Read the suggested change in the New sentence text box and the description of the error in the Subject-Verb Agreement text box. You want additional information about why Grammatik flagged this error.
2. **Position the mouse pointer on the green underlined word subject so the pointer changes to** ?
3. **Click subject in the Subject-Verb Agreement text box**
   The Grammatik Help on Grammar window opens, as shown in Figure C-8. After reading the Help text, you agree that "are" is the correct verb and the sentence needs to be corrected.

QuickTip

While using Grammatik, you can edit text manually by placing the insertion point in the document window, clicking, typing in the new text, then clicking Resume.

4. **Click the Help window Close button to close Help, click prices are in the Replacements text box, then click Replace**
   Grammatik makes the replacement in the document and continues checking for errors. The next item it stops on is the sentence "Looks good with slacks and skirts," because the verb "Looks" may be lacking a subject. You decide that this grammatical construction is appropriate to the informal style of promotional text, so you do not want to change it.
5. **Click Skip Once**
   Grammatik continues checking the document.
6. **Click Skip Once for any remaining words or phrases Grammatik stops on**
   When Grammatik is finished, it displays a dialog box asking if you want to close.
7. **Click Yes, then click the Save button on the Toolbar**

FIGURE C-7: Grammatik tab of Writing Tools dialog box

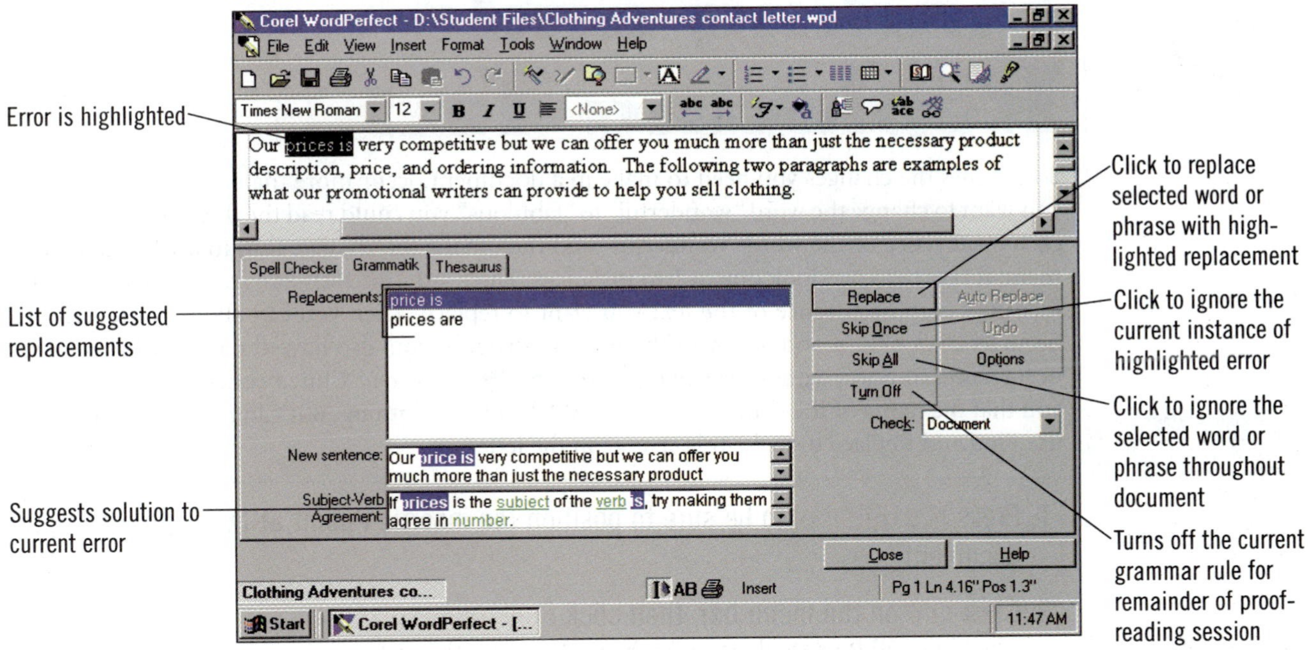

Error is highlighted

List of suggested replacements

Suggests solution to current error

Click to replace selected word or phrase with highlighted replacement

Click to ignore the current instance of highlighted error

Click to ignore the selected word or phrase throughout document

Turns off the current grammar rule for remainder of proofreading session

Corel WordPerfect - D:\Student Files\Clothing Adventures contact letter.wpd

Our prices is very competitive but we can offer you much more than just the necessary product description, price, and ordering information. The following two paragraphs are examples of what our promotional writers can provide to help you sell clothing.

Spell Checker | Grammatik | Thesaurus

Replacements: price is / prices are

Replace | Auto Replace | Skip Once | Undo | Skip All | Options | Turn Off

Check: Document

New sentence: Our price is very competitive but we can offer you much more than just the necessary product

Subject-Verb Agreement: If prices is the subject of the verb is, try making them agree in number.

Close | Help

FIGURE C-8: Explanation of grammar rule

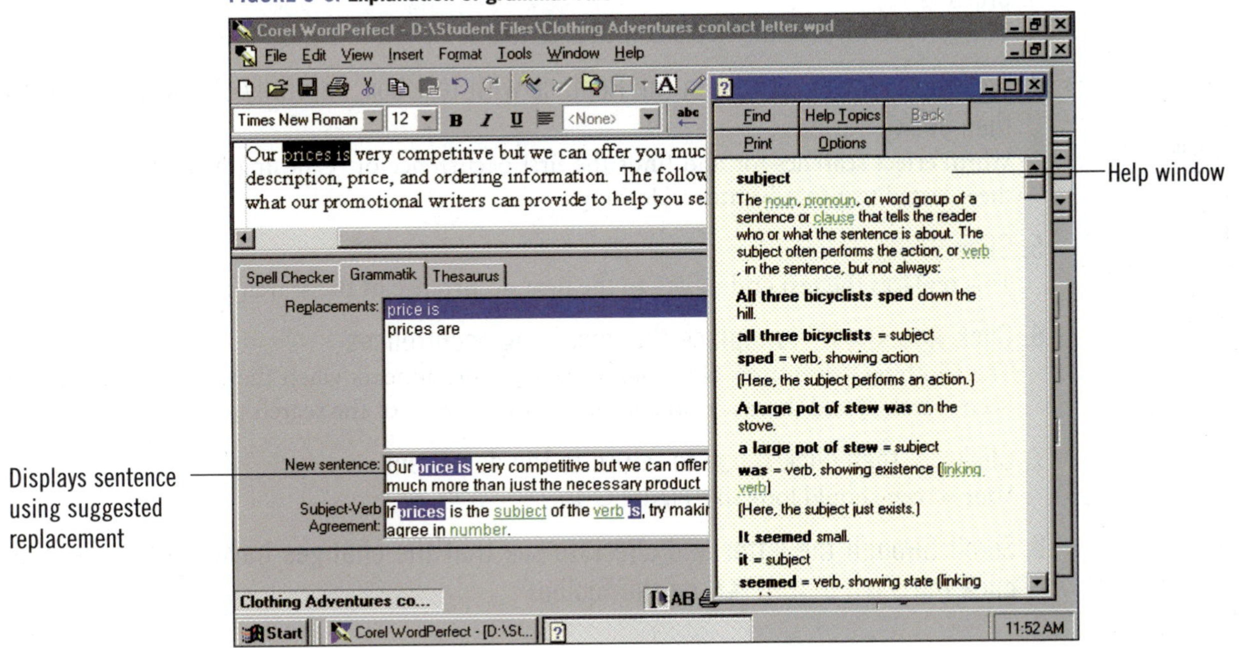

WordPerfect 8

Finding and Replacing Text

Sometimes the changes you need to make in a document occur more than once. For example, if you want to change the word "wonderful" to "fabulous", you could read the document looking for each occurrence of the word "wonderful" and then make the change. But, in a very large document, it is easy to overlook one or two instances. The **Find and Replace** feature in WordPerfect identifies each occurrence of the text you want to replace. Then you can choose to replace that occurrence or skip it and go on to the next occurrence. You also have the option to replace all occurrences at once, without verifying each one. David Chu, a colleague, just informed you that the name of the company is actually Adventure Clothing, not Clothing Adventures. You use Find and Replace to make this change in the letter.

Steps

1. Press **[Ctrl][Home]** to be sure to position the insertion point at the beginning of the document

2. Click **Edit** on the menu bar, then click **Find and Replace**
   The Find and Replace dialog box opens. You type the text you want to find in the Find text box. You can choose to search the document in either direction. The Find Next button searches forward and Find Prev searches backward in your document. Now enter the text you want to search for.

3. Type **Clothing Adventures** in the Find text box, carefully check your spelling, then press **[Tab]**
   The cursor moves to the Replace with text box, as shown in Figure C-9.

4. Type **Adventure Clothing** in the Replace with text box, carefully check your spelling, then click **Find Next**
   WordPerfect searches for and finds the first occurrence of "Clothing Adventures." Change the selected text to Adventure Clothing.

5. Click **Replace**
   This replaces the text and moves to the next occurrence of the search text.

6. Click **Replace All** to replace the remaining occurrences
   The Clothing Adventures Not Found message box appears when the entire document has been searched and there are no additional occurrences of the search text.

7. Click **OK**, then click **Close** to return to the document
   Your screen should look like Figure C-10.

8. Scroll through the letter and check to see that the changes have been made, then click the **Save button** on the Toolbar

QuickTip

To select a word or phrase you searched for previously, you can click the arrow to the right of the Find text box in the Find and Replace dialog box, then click to select the word from the list that you want to find.

Trouble?

If you're accidentally replacing parts of words in a Find and Replace, click Match on the menu bar in the Find and Replace Text dialog box, then click Whole Words to find whole words only.

FIGURE C-9: Find and Replace dialog box

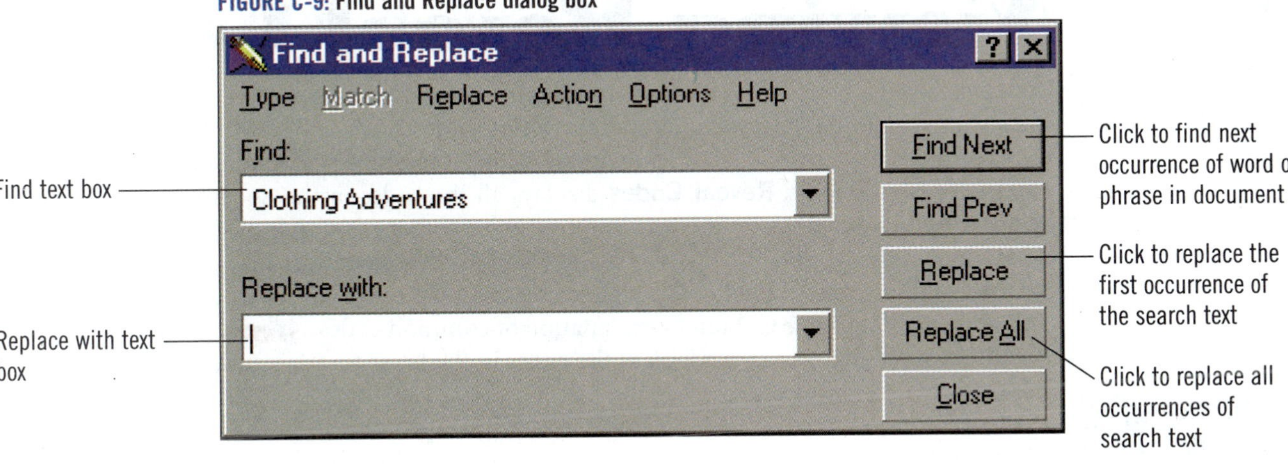

WordPerfect 8

FIGURE C-10: Document with replaced text

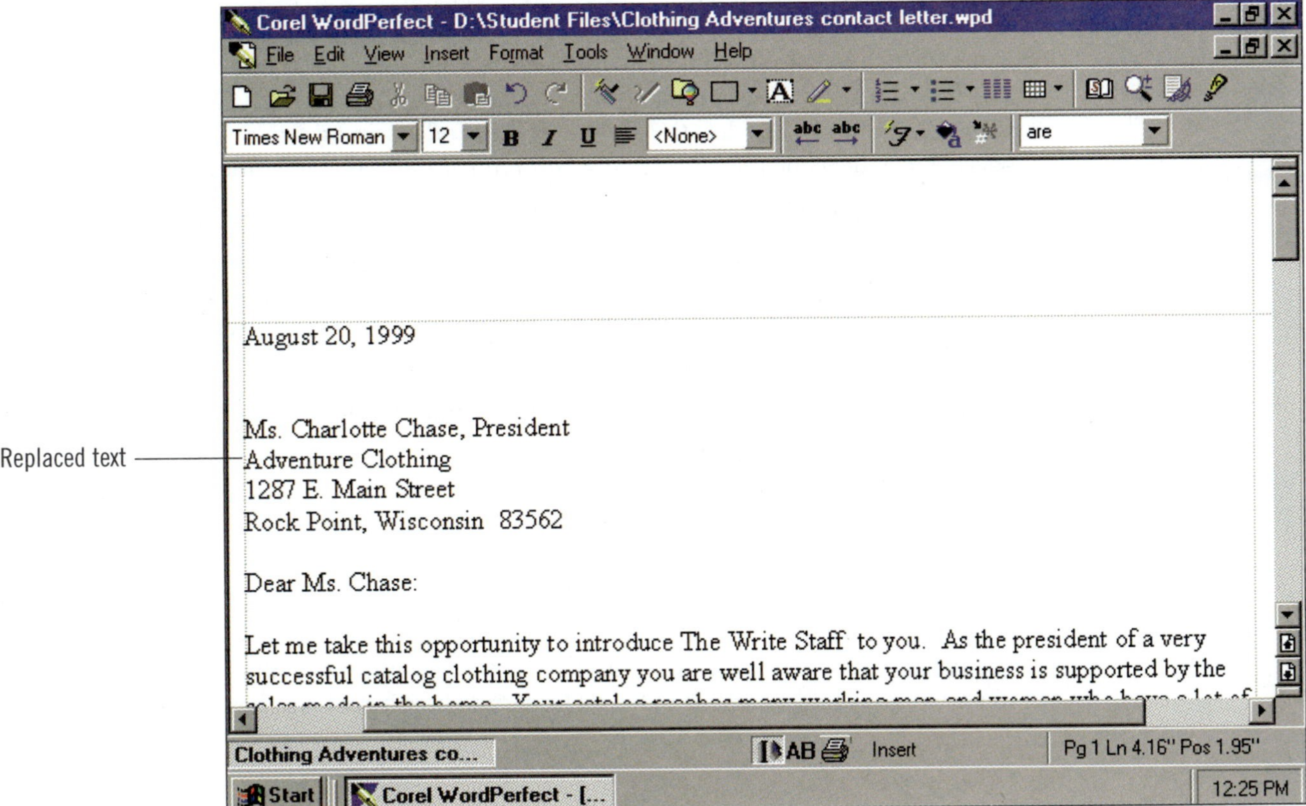

WordPerfect 8

Viewing Reveal Codes

Codes determine how your document looks on the screen and how it will appear on paper. A code is inserted in the document almost every time you use a WordPerfect feature. You cannot see these codes in a normal document window. While the **Show** ¶ command displays a limited number of key symbols, **Reveal Codes** displays all the codes in the document and helps you determine why your document is treating text in ways that you might not understand. Reveal Codes divides the document window into two parts split by a divider line. The top part is your normal editing window. The lower part displays the same text as in the upper part, with all the codes showing. See Table C-2 for an explanation of common codes. To familiarize yourself with this feature, you take a look at the codes in the letter to Adventure Clothing.

QuickTip

You can also open the Reveal Codes window by dragging the small bars on the vertical scroll bar below the Next Page button to where you want the Reveal Codes window to begin.

1. Press **[Ctrl][Home]** to position the insertion point at the top of the document
2. Click **View** on the menu bar, then click **Reveal Codes**
   Your screen splits into two windows to display the Reveal Codes window, revealing the codes in your document. Refer to Figure C-11; notice the location of the insertion point.
3. Scroll the document until the second paragraph appears, then double-click **competitive**
   The Reveal Codes screen scrolls to display the corresponding text, and the red insertion point moves to the new location in the Reveal Codes window. The Select code identifies selected text, the code [SRt] identifies a soft return, and [HRt] identifies a hard return.
4. Position the mouse pointer on the **divider line**; when the cursor shape changes to ↕ drag the line up until it is directly under the first paragraph
   You can adjust the ratio of the text window to Reveal Codes window by dragging the dividing line to any desired position. While working at The Write Staff, you may need to adjust this window as you create documents.
5. Position the mouse pointer in the **Reveal Codes window**, then click and drag to select the phrase **prices are very**
   The Select code identifies the selected text (see Figure C-12). You can select text as well as codes within the Reveal Codes window.
6. Right-click in the **Reveal Codes window**
7. Click **Hide Reveal Codes** in the pop-up menu
   The Reveal Codes window closes, and the text window returns to a full screen display. Now you have a good understanding of Reveal Codes and how it can help you edit your documents.

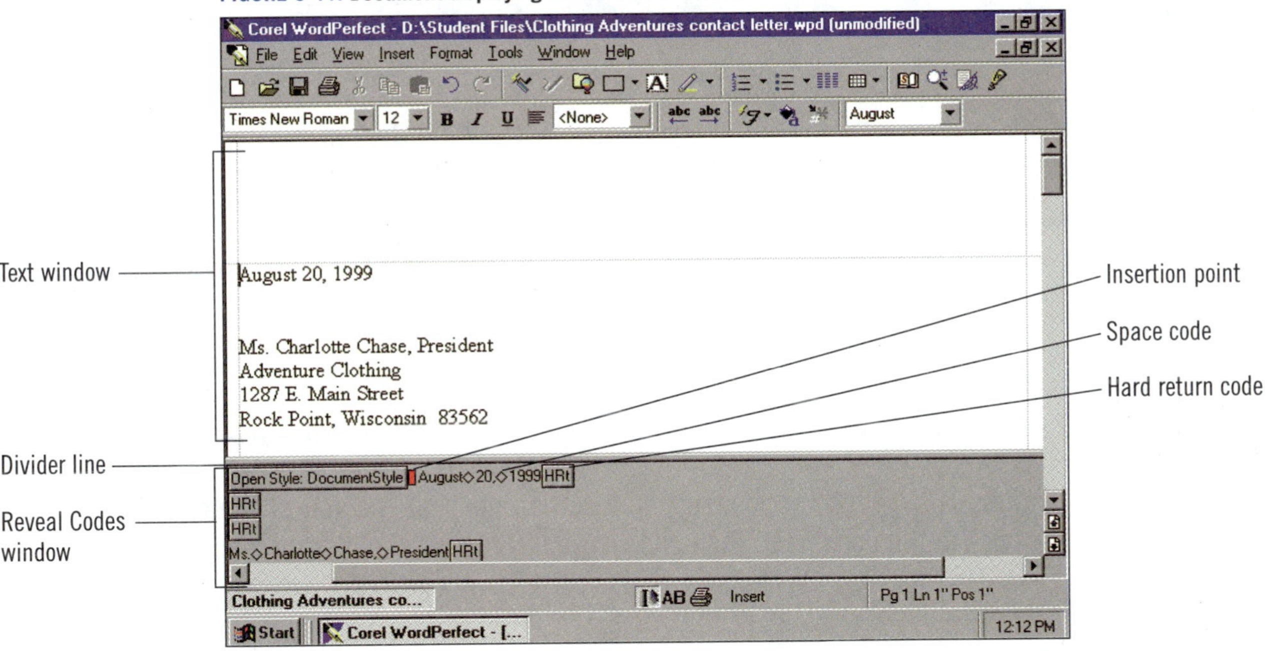

FIGURE C-11: Document displaying Reveal Codes window

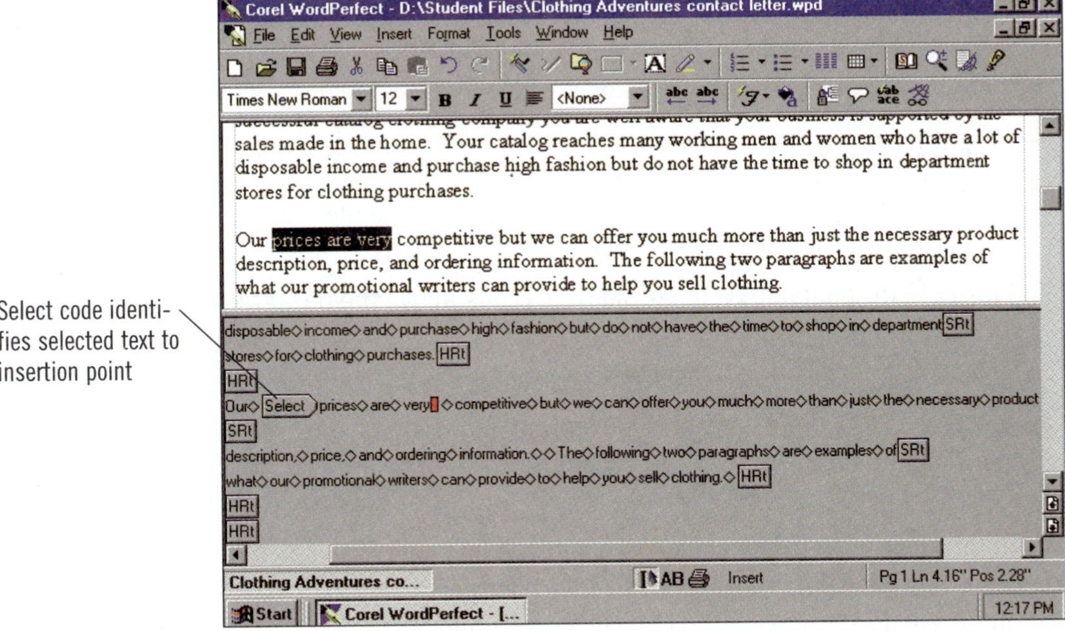

FIGURE C-12: Selected text in Reveal Codes window

TABLE C-2: Some common codes in Reveal Codes

code	meaning
[SRt]	Soft return
[HRt]	Hard return
[HPg]	Hard page break
[SPg]	Soft page break
[<>]	Space

Deleting Codes

As you edit your document and insert and delete spaces, returns, and text, the corresponding codes are inserted or deleted. However, sometimes it is not clear why your document appears a certain way, and you may want to delete the codes directly from the Reveal Codes window. After completing a trial printout run of Jennifer's letter, you discover an extra blank page in the middle of the letter. Scrolling through the document does not reveal why WordPerfect added the extra page. Use Reveal Codes to identify any extra codes in the letter.

Steps 1 2 3 4

1. Press **[Ctrl][End]** to position the insertion point at the end of the document, right-click in the document, then click **Reveal Codes** in the pop-up menu
   A [Hrt] appears in the Reveal Codes window, but the last line of text in the document is not visible. It looks like this extra code may be the cause of your extra page.
2. Press **[↑]** until the last line of text appears
   There are seven extra [HRt] codes at the bottom of the document. You can see how those extra codes might create blank pages in the document. You will learn about multiple-page documents in later lessons. For now, you want to get rid of those extra codes.
3. Position the mouse pointer on the last **[HRt] code**, then click and drag the code up into the normal text area, as shown in Figure C-13
   Dragging the codes off the Reveal Codes window deletes them.
4. Drag the next six **[HRt] code**, into the normal text area to delete them
   The final codes at the bottom of the document should look like Figure C-14. You are not convinced that those codes are the only problem with Jennifer's letter. You scroll the document to look for more problem codes.
5. Press **[↑]** to scroll until you see the [HPg] code above the paragraph that begins "The Write Staff can provide you with descriptions for your merchandise"
   This code generates an extra page. You want to delete it from the document.
6. Drag the **[HPg] code** out of the Reveal Codes window
   You scroll up through the document and see that, for now, there are no more extraneous codes. You can print the document.
7. Right-click in the Reveal Codes window, click **Hide Reveal Codes**, then click the **Save button** on the Toolbar to save your document
   You check the document once more before printing.
8. Scroll to the bottom of the document
   As you can see, the letter still takes up two pages. There is more text than can fit on a page (notice the [SRt] code near the bottom of the first page). Even though Jennifer is very pleased with the final letter and is confident The Write Staff will receive a positive response and get the account, she wants to fit this on one page. You will do this in the next lesson.

QuickTip

You can find and replace codes in your document just as you find and replace text; click Match in the Find and Replace dialog box, then click Codes.

QuickTip

You cannot delete the [SRt] soft return code in WordPerfect. Only [HRt] hard return codes at the end of lines can be deleted. Hyphenate a word or delete text to change the position of a soft return.

FIGURE C-13: **Dragging a code to delete it**

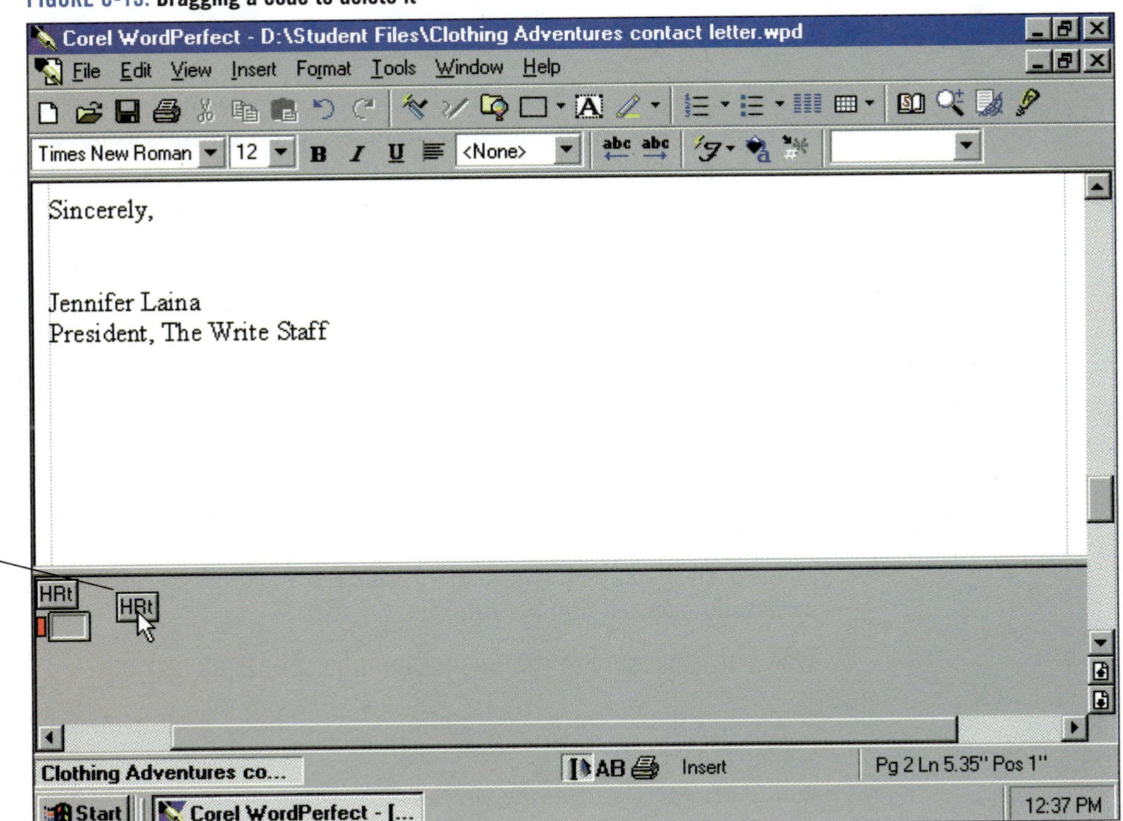

FIGURE C-14: **Codes at the end of the document**

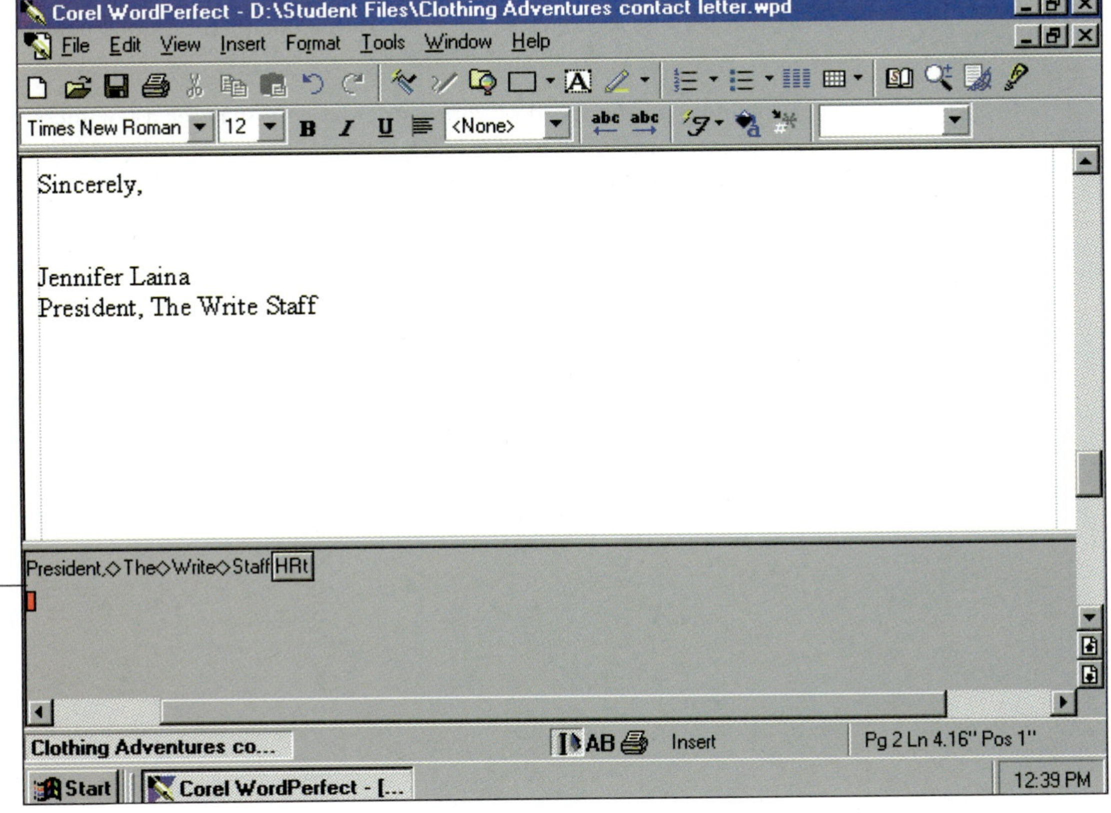

Using Make It Fit

When a document doesn't fit on one page, there are a few options you can use to reduce its size. You can edit the text and delete words to make the document shorter, you can delete any extra lines between paragraphs, you can change the margins, or you can reduce the size of the characters. This can be a tedious trial and error process. An easier alternative is to use the WordPerfect **Make It Fit** feature, which finds the best way to adjust your document to fit the page. Make It Fit can also expand your document. An effective contact letter or cover letter should fit on a single page. You decide to use WordPerfect's Make It Fit feature to fit the letter to Adventure Clothing on a single page.

Steps 1 2 3 4

1. **Click Format on the Toolbar, then click Make It Fit**
   The Make It Fit dialog box opens, as shown in Figure C-15. You can determine which elements of the document you want WordPerfect to adjust, to either expand or shrink a document to the desired number of pages.
2. **Type 1 if necessary in the Desired number of pages text box**
3. **Verify that the Line spacing and Font size check boxes are checked in the Items to adjust area**
   WordPerfect lets you choose which combination of elements to change to make the document the size you specify. You do not want to adjust the margins, because this letter will be printed on The Write Staff stationery which has text and designs preprinted in the margins.
4. **If any of the margin options are checked in the Items to adjust area, click to remove the checkmark**
   Now you are ready to let WordPerfect fit the document on one page.
5. **Click Make It Fit**
   Depending on the speed of your computer, you may see a few message boxes flash on the screen, as WordPerfect works through several passes adjusting the line spacing and font size to make the document one page.
6. **Click the Zoom button on the Toolbar, then click Full Page**
   The letter fits on a single page. Your screen should look like Figure C-16. Now you can save the document with the new font size and line spacing, and print the document to mail to Ms. Chase.
7. **Click the Save button on the Toolbar, then click the Print button**
   The printed document will be mailed out in the office mail. You can close the document and exit WordPerfect.
8. **Click File on the menu bar, then click Exit**

FIGURE C-15: Make It Fit dialog box

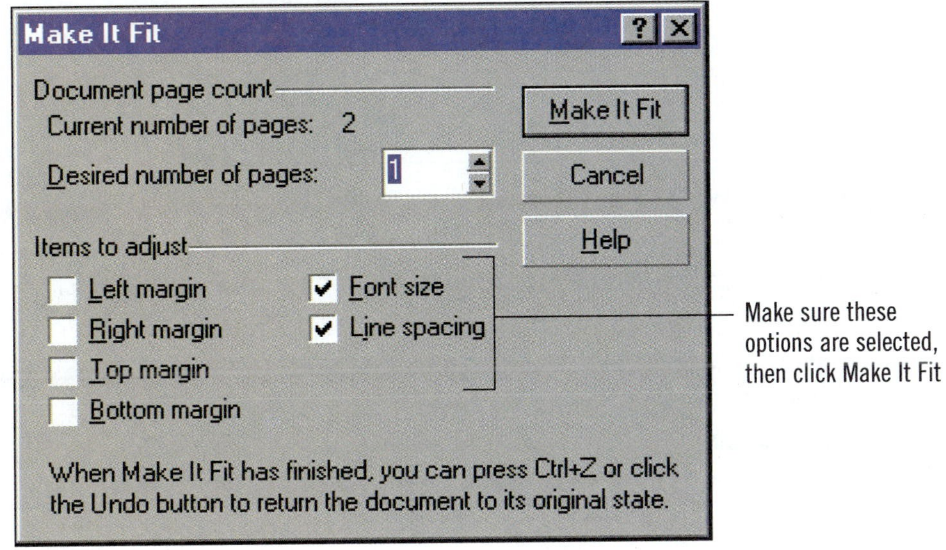

Make sure these options are selected, then click Make It Fit

WordPerfect 8

FIGURE C-16: Letter reduced to fit on one page

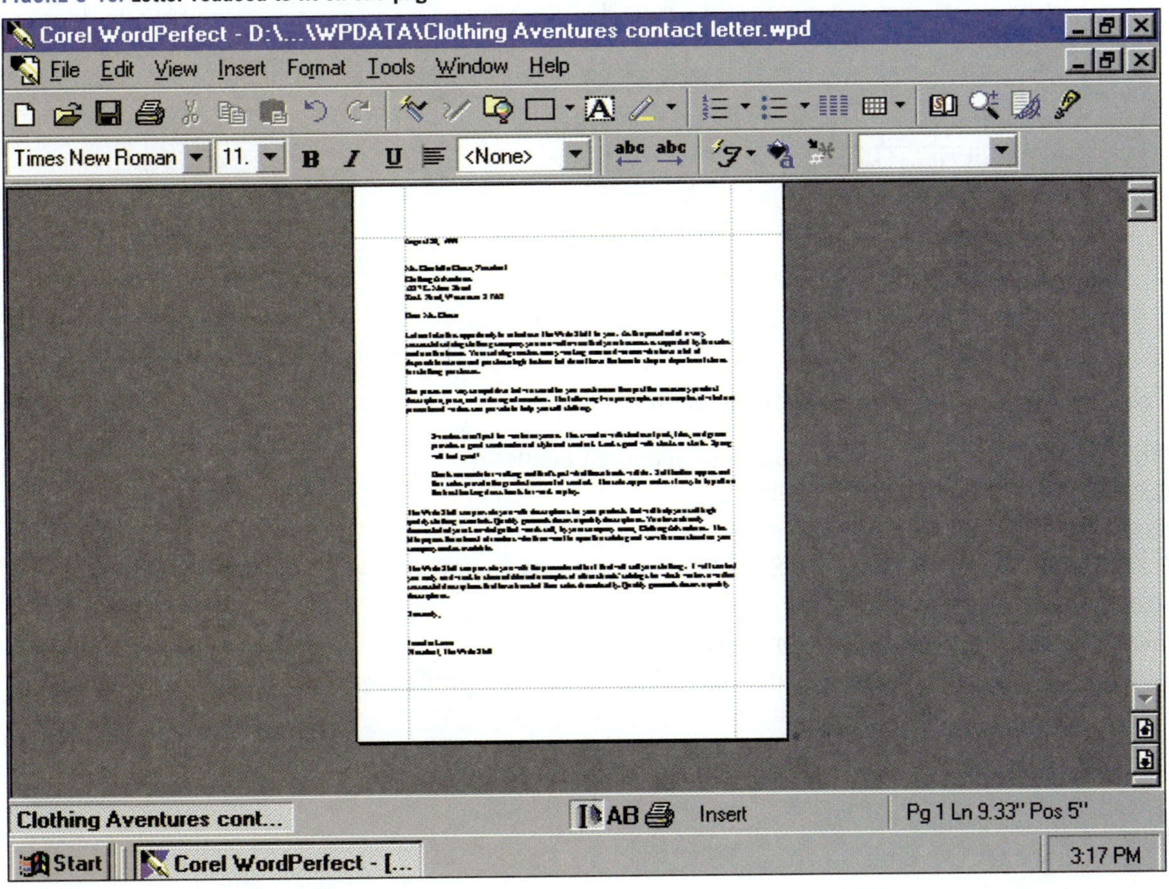

Practice

► Concepts Review

Label each element of the WordPerfect window shown in Figure C-17.

FIGURE C-17

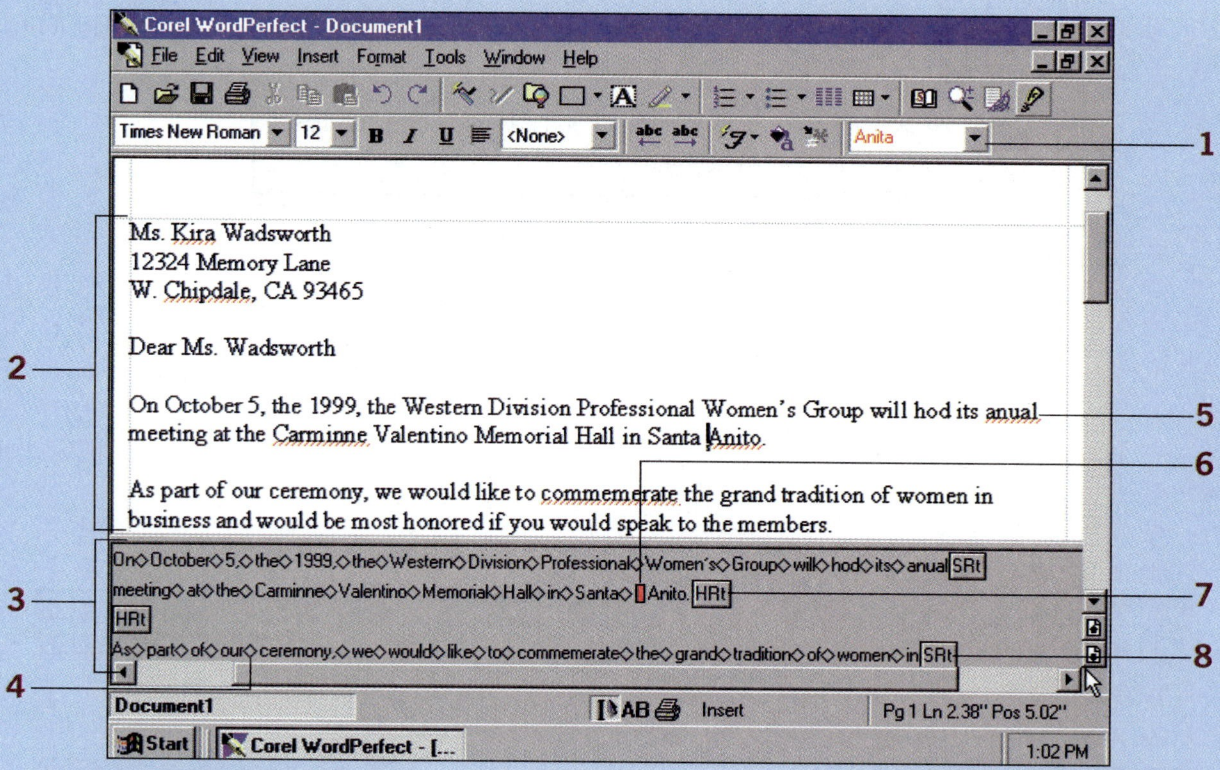

Match each statement with the term it describes.

9. Shrinks or expands a document by adjusting specified elements
10. Checks documents for errors in spelling
11. Replaces a word in the text with a synonym
12. A personalized list of words that the Spell Checker will skip even if they are not contained in the main dictionary
13. Checks documents for errors in writing style
14. Corrects common spelling errors as they are typed based on a predefined list

a. Thesaurus
b. QuickCorrect
c. Word list
d. Spell Checker
e. Grammatik
f. Make It Fit

Select the best answer from the list of choices.

15. Spell-As-You-Go identifies words not found in its dictionary by
- **a.** Highlighting the word in yellow.
- **b.** Placing a code in the Reveal Codes window.
- **c.** Placing red hatched lines under the word.
- **d.** Correcting the word automatically.

16. Which of these is *not* displayed as a code in the Reveal Codes window?
- **a.** Tab
- **b.** Capitalization
- **c.** Hard return
- **d.** Hard page

17. Which tool identifies the word "two" as misspelled when the correct word should be "too"?
- **a.** Spell Checker
- **b.** Grammatik
- **c.** Thesaurus
- **d.** All of the above

18. The code [HPg] in a document
- **a.** Opens a new document.
- **b.** Hyphenates a word.
- **c.** Generates a new page.
- **d.** Wraps the text to a new line.

19. You can hide Reveal Codes by
- **a.** Clicking Reveal Codes on the View menu.
- **b.** Right-clicking in Reveal Codes and then clicking Hide Reveal Codes.
- **c.** Dragging the divider to the bottom of the window.
- **d.** All of the above.

20. Make It Fit can adjust all of the following except
- **a.** Font size.
- **b.** Font style.
- **c.** Line spacing.
- **d.** Margins.

Skills Review

1. **Correct spelling in a document.**
   a. Start WordPerfect and open WP C-2.
   b. Enter the current date and your name in the first line. Save the file to your Student Disk as "Robinson Greenhouse letter".
   c. Spell check the document from the beginning of the document.
   d. In the address at the beginning of the document, skip words that WordPerfect doesn't recognize.
   e. Remove duplicate words.
   f. Replace misspelled words with the appropriate suggested words.

2. **Customize QuickCorrect.**
   a. Customize the QuickCorrect list to change any spelling of Robison to Robinson.
   b. Test your change to the QuickCorrect list by typing Robison in the document.
   c. Delete the item Robison Robinson from the QuickCorrect list.

3. **Use the Thesaurus.**
   a. Move the insertion point to the word "jealousy" in the first paragraph.
   b. Open the Thesaurus dialog box.
   c. Replace "jealousy" with a synonym such as "envy".

4. **Use Grammatik.**
   a. Open the Grammatik dialog box.
   b. Decide whether to skip or replace the words or phrases Grammatik identifies as errors.

5. **Find and replace text.**
   a. Open the Find and Replace Text dialog box.
   b. Replace each occurrence of "flowers" with "flowering plants".
   c. Replace each occurrence of "clients" with "customers".

6. **View Reveal Codes.**
   a. Display Reveal Codes.
   b. Drag the window up to display Reveal Codes in more than half the screen.
   c. Identify four different codes and write them on a note pad.
   d. Hide Reveal Codes using any method other than dragging the window.

7. **Delete codes.**
   a. Open the Reveal Codes window.
   b. Locate any extra [HRt] codes in the document.
   c. Delete the codes.
   d. Close the Reveal Codes window.

8. **Use Make It Fit.**
   a. Save your work.
   b. Print a copy of the letter to Robinson Greenhouse.
   c. Make the document fit on one page.
   d. Save your work.
   e. Print the document and exit WordPerfect.

Independent Challenges

1. You are the assistant manager of Ocean Breeze Book Store. One of your responsibilities is to respond to customer complaints, comments, and questions. A customer, Teresa Alvarez, of 888 Manzana Street, La Jolla, CA 92122, has recently written to compliment the store on its excellent service. Write a letter to Ms. Alvarez, thanking her for her kind letter and telling her about the Ocean Breeze Book Store philosophy.

To complete this independent challenge:

1. Start WordPerfect and type the letter using the standard letter format, beginning with the current date, an inside address, and salutation.
2. In the first paragraph of the letter, thank Ms. Alvarez for her kind remarks about Ocean Breeze Book Store.
3. In the second paragraph, tell her that the bookstore's philosophy is summarized in the two words "quality service".
4. In the third paragraph, list the company goals: (1) a clean, attractive, well-organized sales floor; (2) a large inventory of quality books and magazines; and (3) knowledgeable, enthusiastic employees.
5. In the final paragraph, explain that through quality service, Ocean Breeze Book Store maintains loyal customers, benefits from volume sales, and gives customers the best prices in the industry.
6. At the end of the letter, include a cordial closing (such as "Sincerely yours") and your signature block.
7. Save the letter as "Ocean Breeze letter" to your Student Disk. Print the document.
8. Review the document and change all occurrences of "Ocean Breeze Book Store" to "Ocean Breeze Bookstore".
9. Use the Spell Checker to check the spelling of your document.
10. Use the Thesaurus to replace the first occurrence of "customers" with "clients".
11. Use Grammatik to check the grammar in your document.
12. Use Make It Fit to make sure the document fits on one page.
13. Save your final letter, print the document, and exit WordPerfect.

2. The local library is sponsoring a writing contest for community-related fiction and poetry. The winners will read their fiction at a city festival, and their work will be published in the local newspaper. You have decided to enter the children's fiction category. Conservation and the benefits of recycling are very important to your town, so you decide to write a story that encourages children to recycle.
Your story is about a huge monster who is created out of trash and rises out of the landfill. Although citizens are initially frightened by the monster, he is a good monster who wants to tell people to recycle more. The monster's name is Gargantutrash and he lives in Trashville.
To complete this independent challenge:

1. Start WordPerfect and type a title for the story at the top of a new document.
2. In the first paragraph, describe how the monster looks and the effect he has on townspeople who don't know he is a good monster. Use his name and the town name several times in this paragraph.
3. In the second paragraph, mention the monster's mission to get people to recycle glass, paper, and plastics. Describe how he accomplishes this mission by visiting townspeople at home and work.
4. Include a paragraph that describes how the monster spreads his good message to children and how they teach adults not to be afraid of him.
5. Conclude the story with a message about how all towns can be cleaned up, even without a monster.
6. Make sure to include your name and current date in the document.
7. Save the story as "Trashman contest" and print one copy.
8. Use Find and Replace to change the monster's name from Gargantutrash to Trashman.
9. Use the Spell Checker to check the spelling of your document. Be careful not to change the name of the monster.
10. Use the Thesaurus to replace the first occurrence of "trash" with "garbage".
11. Use Grammatik to check the grammar in your document.
12. Use Reveal Codes to be sure the document doesn't have any extra codes that would generate unwanted pages.
13. Save the document as "Trashman contest revision" to retain your previous copy on file.
14. The story should fit on one page. Use Make It Fit to either shrink or expand the document.
15. Save the document, print the document, then exit WordPerfect.

3. You are the Marketing Manager at Greenview Film & Video, a Milwaukee-based company that produces training films and videos. You recently received a request to propose a series of six employee training videos for Wagner-Hill College Bookstores. Wagner-Hill is a leading retailer with stores on most college campuses throughout the country. One of the producers at Greenview Film & Video, Mitch Green, has created an initial proposal to send to the client. You want the final proposal to look professional and engage the client's interest, so that they hire Greenview Film & Video to produce their series. You know that proposals of this nature are usually limited to one page. Review Mitch's proposal now and make some improvements before sending it to the client.
To complete this independent challenge:

1. Start WordPerfect, open the file WP C-3 and save it as "Wagner-Hill proposal".
2. Check the document for spelling and grammatical errors, and make the necessary corrections.
3. Make any other changes you feel will improve the document.
4. Print a copy of the document.
5. Use Make It Fit to shrink the proposal to one page. Select and deselect checkboxes as necessary in the Make It Fit dialog box to fit the document on one page.
6. Print one copy of the one-page proposal, then close the file, saving changes when prompted.
7. Write a brief memo to Mitch telling him which version of the proposal you think should be sent to the client. Be sure to explain why you think that version looks better.
8. Save the memo as "Wagner-Hill memo".
9. Print one copy of the memo, then close it and exit WordPerfect.

4. The QuickCorrect feature in WordPerfect is very useful for correcting common typing errors. QuickCorrect also has other benefits. If you use QuickCorrect you can fix common case errors, such as changing the word STanley to Stanley, as well as common spelling errors such as acommodate to accommodate. QuickCorrect also has other handy features to help you with your typing. Use the WordPerfect Help feature to learn more about these, and then create a document using QuickBullets, one of the helpful features.

To complete this independent challenge:

1. Start WordPerfect.
2. Press [F1] to open the Help Topics, WordPerfect Help dialog box.
3. Click the Index tab if necessary.
4. Type QuickBullets.
5. Click Display. The Topics Found dialog box displays the topic: To create a bulleted list using QuickBullets.
6. Click Display if necessary.
7. The WordPerfect Help window shown in Figure C-18 opens.
8. Read this Help topic carefully. If necessary, click Options, and click Keep Help on Top if you want to keep the Help topic available while you create your document.
9. Create a document that includes a bulleted list. The document can be a list of your classes and teachers, or upcoming and ongoing work projects. Be sure to use at least two of the bullet styles.
10. Save and print the document and exit WordPerfect.

FIGURE C-18

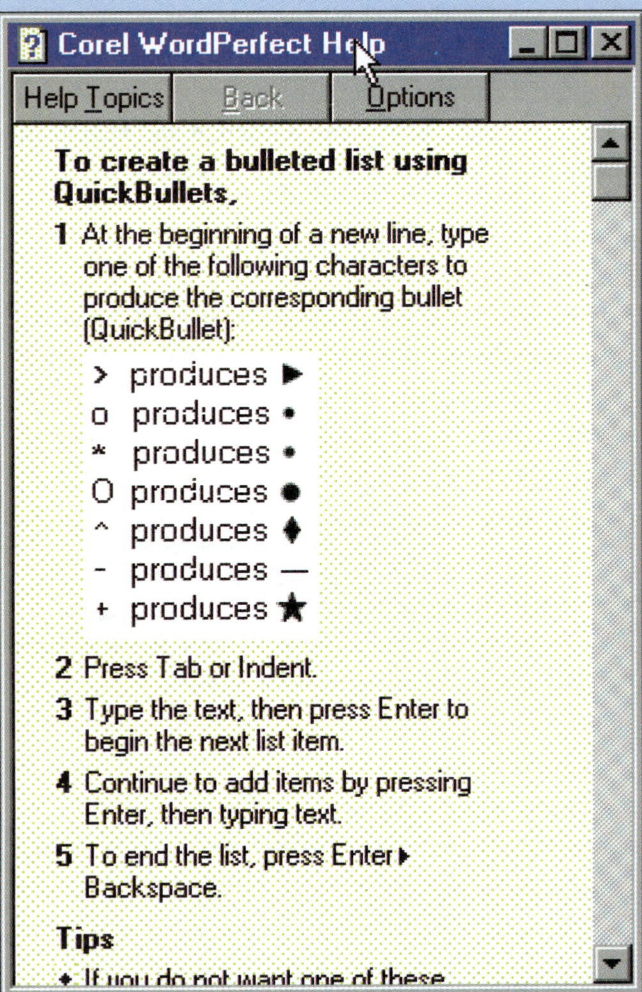

WordPerfect 8

Visual Workshop

Create and format the document shown in Figure C-19. This is the beginning of a short story about what might happen if companies and government agencies fail to make proper adjustments to their computer systems for the year 2000. Complete the story using the skills you have learned in this book. Be sure to use the Spell Checker to correct any spelling errors, use the Thesaurus to find synonyms for the repeating words, use Grammatik for improving the document's language, and use Reveal Codes to find any unwanted codes. Continue the short story so that the document goes beyond a single page, then use Make It Fit so the final document fits on one page. Save your document as "Year 2000 Story" to your Student Disk, and then print it.

FIGURE C-19

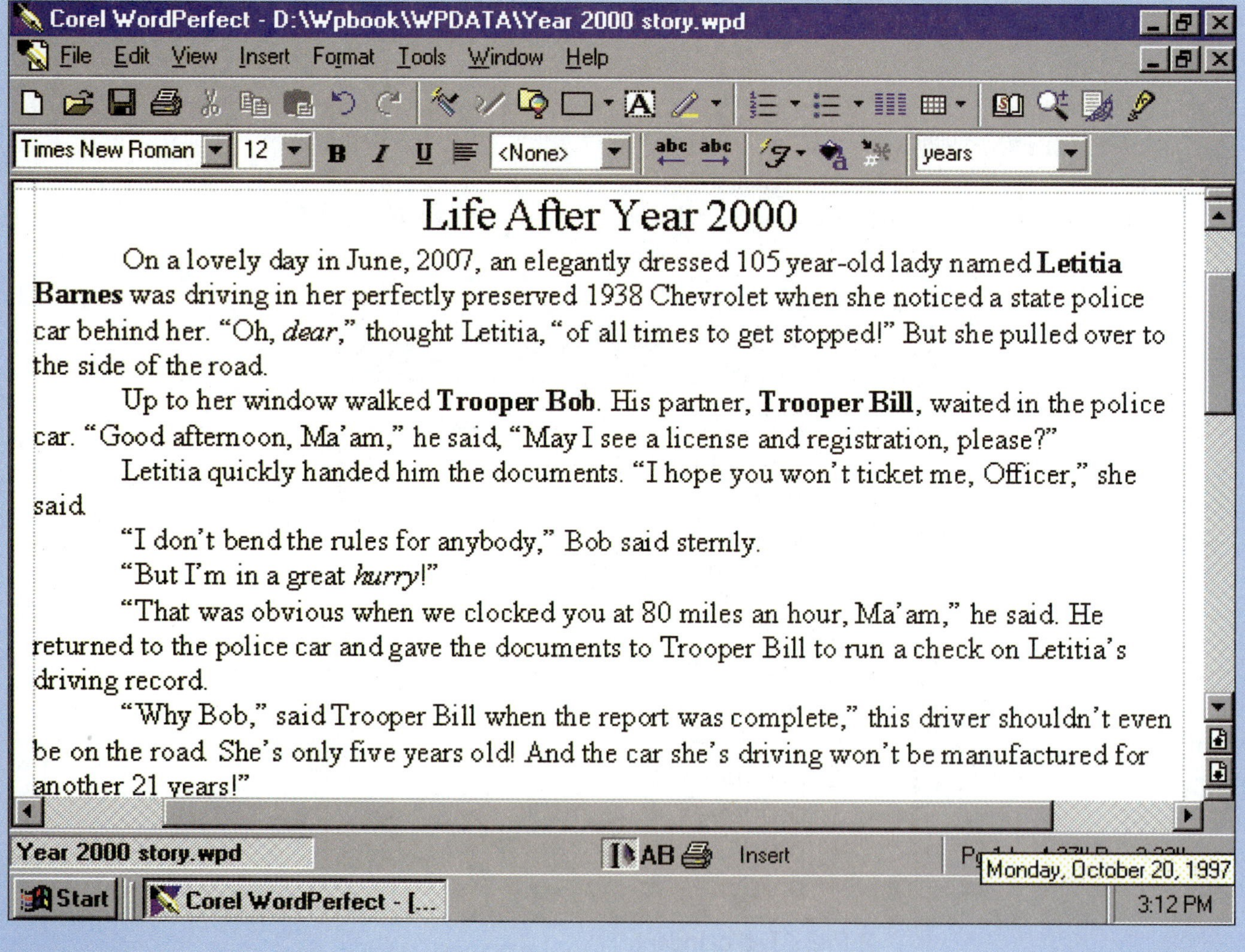

WordPerfect 8

Formatting a Document

Objectives

- Choose fonts and sizes
- Change the appearance of text
- Set margins and line spacing
- Align text and use justification
- Set tabs
- Use tabs
- Indent paragraphs
- Use QuickFormat

Once you create a document, you can use a variety of formatting tools to improve its appearance. You can change the way the characters look: text can be bold, italic, or underlined, and characters can be in different fonts and point sizes. You can format the way the text is placed on the page by changing the margins, setting tabs, indenting paragraphs, and changing the spacing between lines and paragraphs. Audiosyncracies is an upscale electronics boutique with locations in fashionable shopping malls. The chain is opening a new branch location. The Write Staff has been hired to write a press release announcing the new store. In this unit, you'll format the press release.

WordPerfect 8

Choosing Fonts and Sizes

Fonts refer to the **typeface**, or style, and size of computer-generated letters and numbers. The size of a font is measured in **points**, and each font is available in a range of sizes: from 4 points, which is a very small size and not considered readable—to 10 or 12 points, which is commonly used in documents—to 72 points, which is a very large size. Using different fonts and point sizes can improve a document's appearance and readability. Your coworker Erica Brennan wrote, edited, and proofread the press release for Audiosyncracies but did not have time to format the document. She asks you to use fonts to highlight the important words.

Steps 1 2 3 4

1. **Start WordPerfect, open the file WP D-1 and save it to your Student Disk as Audiosyncracies press release**
   The first thing you notice when you look at Erica's document is that she used the same font, Times New Roman 12 point, throughout the entire document (see Figure D-1). You want to change the format of the entire document to a sharper-looking font. When you select text and choose a formatting option, the formatting affects only the selected text; otherwise the formatting affects either the word, paragraph, or page after the insertion point.
2. **Click the Font Face list arrow on the Property Bar**
   An alphabetical list of available fonts appears. A preceding a font name indicates that it is **True Type** font, a type of font that remains embedded in a document even when you open it on a computer that may not have the font installed. You should use a True Type font whenever possible.
3. **Click the Arial True Type font**
   The current font and the text after the insertion point changes to Arial. Next, you decide that the first line should catch the reader's attention. You choose another font, but this time you use the Font dialog box.
4. **Click in the left margin to select the line Press Release: October 1, 1999, click Format on the menu bar, then click Font**
   The Font dialog box opens, as shown in Figure D-2. This dialog box contains all the font formatting tools available on the Formatting Toolbar, such as font style, size, and appearance, plus additional attributes such as double underline, small caps and positioning text.
5. **Scroll the Font face list, then click BinnerD**
   The font for the selected text is now BinnerD. Check the preview window to see how this font change will look with the currently selected text. You decide it would look better in a larger point size.
6. **Click 18 in the Font size list**
   This increases the point size of the characters.
7. **Click OK**
   Erica wants the name of the store, Audiosyncracies, to appear in a special font and size. To make this change, use the Property Bar.
8. **Double-click the first occurrence of the word Audiosyncracies, click the font face list arrow, scroll the Font face list if necessary, click PT Barnum BT, click the Font size list arrow, then click 14**
   The most recently used fonts are added to the QuickFonts list on the Property Bar, which also shows what the resulting font looks like right on the list. Use the same font, PT Barnum 14, for the words "Washington Mall!"
9. **Select Washington Mall! in the first line, click the QuickFonts button on the Property Bar, then click PT Barnum 14**
   Your screen with font changes should now look like Figure D-3.

Trouble?
If the fonts used in the lessons are not available on your system, choose some that are similar.

QuickTip
To open the Font dialog box quickly, press [F9].

QuickTip
To change the case of letters, you click Edit on the menu bar, point to Convert Case, then click the type of conversion you want.

FIGURE D-1: Audiosyncracies press release

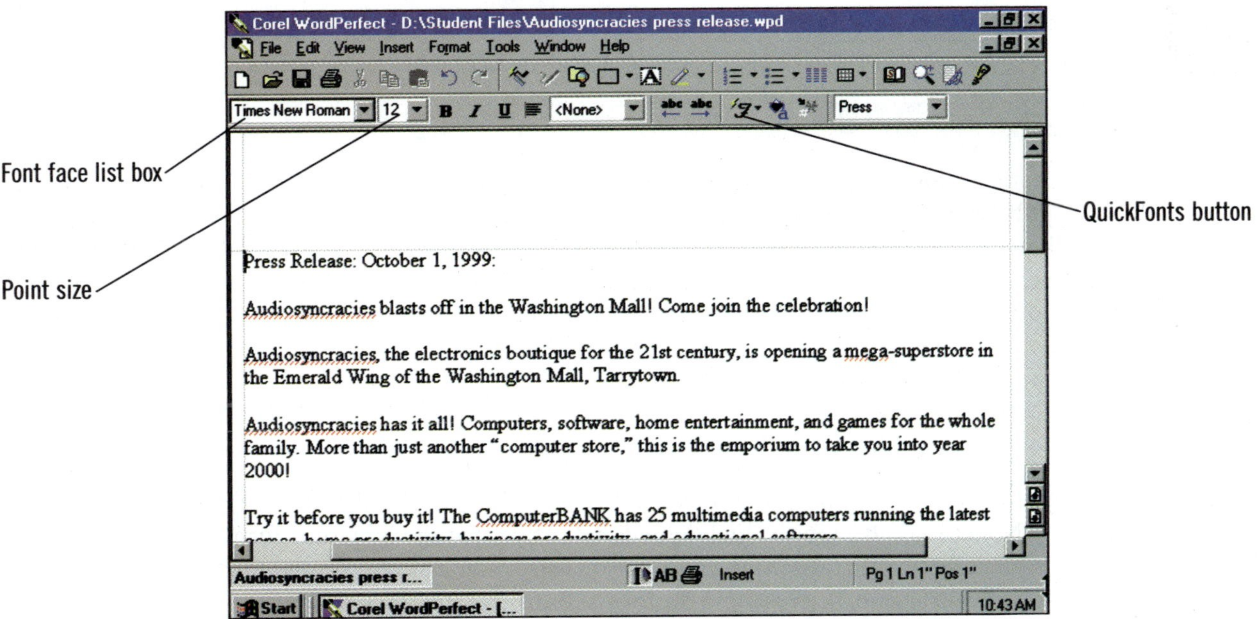

FIGURE D-2: Font dialog box

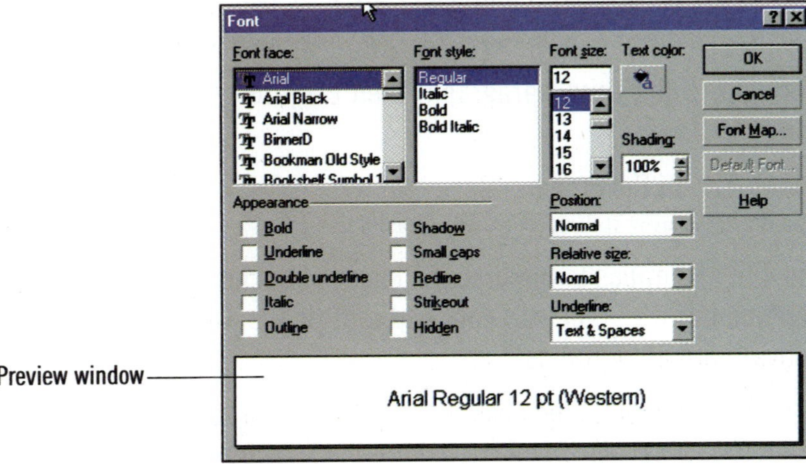

FIGURE D-3: Press release after font and size changes

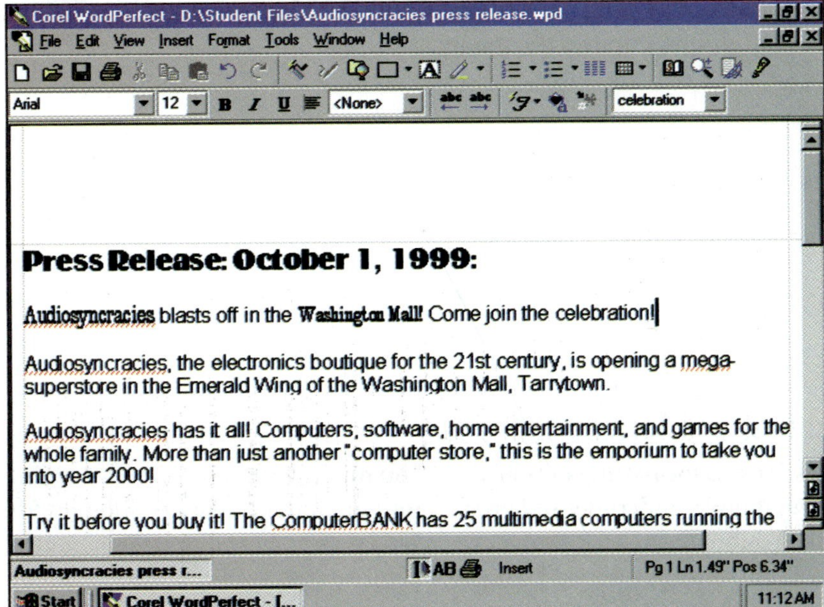

WordPerfect 8

Changing the Appearance of Text

Character formats such as bold, italics, and underline add emphasis to a document. You can apply character formats to single characters, words, lines, and whole documents. Table D-1 shows some common WordPerfect character formats. The writers at The Write Staff use character formats to draw the reader's attention to product names, pricing strategies, and important facts. Michael Benjamin, the graphics director, advises you to try using character formats to enhance the document for Audiosyncracies.

Steps

QuickTip

Remember that you can apply formatting changes to selected text you have already typed, or turn on the attributes so that they are applied to text you type.

1. **Press [Ctrl][Home], then click the Underline button on the Property Bar**
   Notice that the button appears highlighted, indicating that the underline format is on. If you accidentally format the wrong character or word, you can remove the format by selecting the same text again, then clicking the format button again. Click the button once to turn the formatting on and click it again to turn it off.

2. **Type For General Release, click the Underline button, then press [Enter]**
   "For General Release" is underlined. Compare your screen with Figure D-4.

3. **Point in the left margin to the third paragraph, then click to select the sentence Audiosyncracies has it all!**

4. **Click the Italic button on the Property Bar**
   "Audiosyncracies has it all!" is now italicized for emphasis.

5. **Repeat Steps 3 and 4 to add italics to the first sentences of the next four paragraphs so that "Try it before you buy it!," "Let your ears and eyes do the walkin'!," "Play and Play!," and "Take five!" are all in italics**

6. **Select the last line in the document, then click the Bold button on the Property Bar**
   The phone and fax numbers for Audiosyncracies are now bold. Figure D-5 shows the document with formatting changes.

Trouble?

If you forget to click outside the selected text before clicking the Save button, a dialog box opens asking whether you want to save the entire file or only the selected text. Click the Entire file option button, then click OK.

7. **Click outside the selected text, then click the Save button on the Toolbar to save your changes to the document**

Additional font and format changes

The Font dialog box has various formatting options, such as strikeout, shadow, double-underline, and even colored text. Because the Font dialog box shows an example of each selected font and appearance change, you might wish to use it when trying an unfamiliar font or combinations of different formatting options. This way, you can decide on a font, size, and/or format before entering new text or changing existing text.

FIGURE D-4: Underlining text

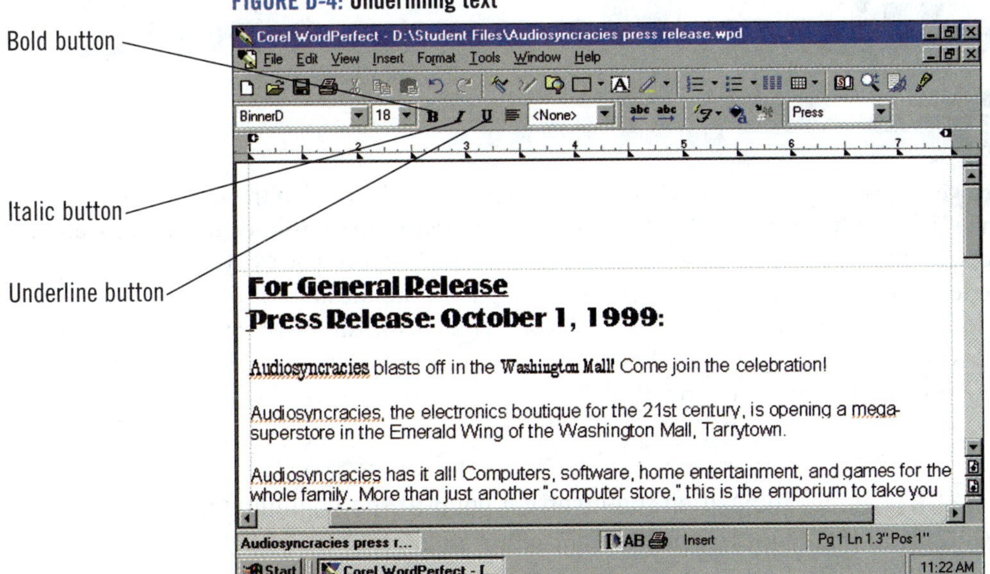

FIGURE D-5: Document with formatting changes

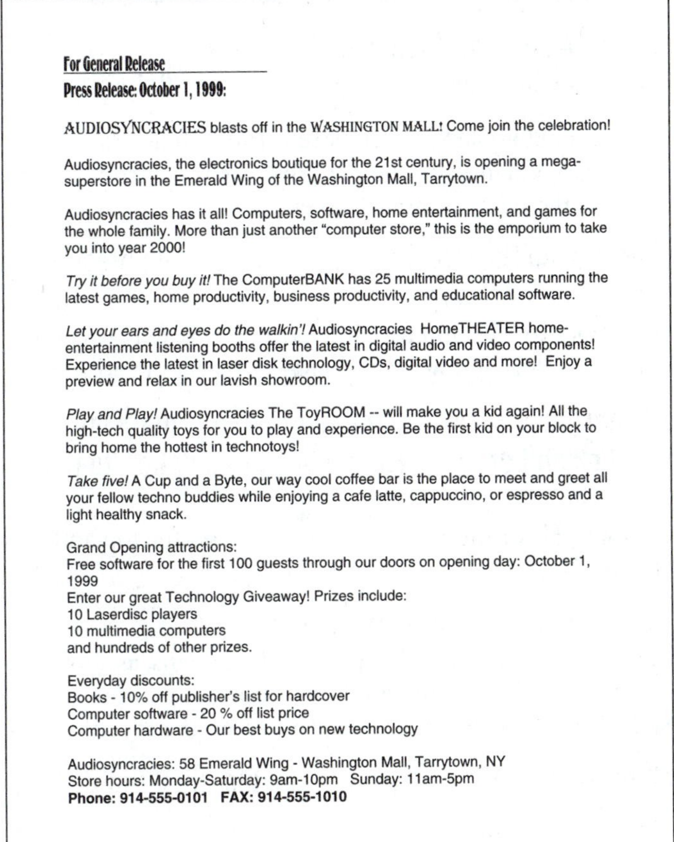

For General Release
Press Release: October 1, 1999:

AUDIOSYNCRACIES blasts off in the WASHINGTON MALL! Come join the celebration!

Audiosyncracies, the electronics boutique for the 21st century, is opening a mega-superstore in the Emerald Wing of the Washington Mall, Tarrytown.

Audiosyncracies has it all! Computers, software, home entertainment, and games for the whole family. More than just another "computer store," this is the emporium to take you into year 2000!

Try it before you buy it! The ComputerBANK has 25 multimedia computers running the latest games, home productivity, business productivity, and educational software.

Let your ears and eyes do the walkin'! Audiosyncracies HomeTHEATER home-entertainment listening booths offer the latest in digital audio and video components! Experience the latest in laser disk technology, CDs, digital video and more! Enjoy a preview and relax in our lavish showroom.

Play and Play! Audiosyncracies The ToyROOM -- will make you a kid again! All the high-tech quality toys for you to play and experience. Be the first kid on your block to bring home the hottest in technotoys!

Take five! A Cup and a Byte, our way cool coffee bar is the place to meet and greet all your fellow techno buddies while enjoying a cafe latte, cappuccino, or espresso and a light healthy snack.

Grand Opening attractions:
Free software for the first 100 guests through our doors on opening day: October 1, 1999
Enter our great Technology Giveaway! Prizes include:
10 Laserdisc players
10 multimedia computers
and hundreds of other prizes.

Everyday discounts:
Books - 10% off publisher's list for hardcover
Computer software - 20 % off list price
Computer hardware - Our best buys on new technology

Audiosyncracies: 58 Emerald Wing - Washington Mall, Tarrytown, NY
Store hours: Monday-Saturday: 9am-10pm Sunday: 11am-5pm
Phone: 914-555-0101 FAX: 914-555-1010

TABLE D-1: Common character formats

character formats	sample text
Bold	**Audiosyncracies**
Italics	*Audiosyncracies*
Underline	Audiosyncracies
Double-underline	Audiosyncracies

WordPerfect 8

Setting Margins and Line Spacing

You use two formatting options to change the placement of the text on the pages of your document: margins and line spacing. **Margins** are the boundaries that produce white space around the edges of the document. **Line spacing** is the amount of space between lines of text. WordPerfect's default setting for margins is one inch around all sides of the page. The default setting for line spacing is single-spaced. The client, Audiosyncracies, requested that their press releases be double-spaced and have ½" left margins and 1½" right top and bottom margins. You will change these formats.

Steps

1. **Press [Ctrl][Home] to position the insertion point at the beginning of the document, click View on the menu bar if the Ruler is not displayed, then click Ruler**
   The Ruler, which shows the margin markers, appears just below the Property Bar. See Figure D-6. The guidelines, the dashed vertical lines, also show the boundaries for your text. Be sure the guidelines are on; you will use them to change the margins.
2. **Click View on the menu bar, then click Guidelines**
   The Guidelines dialog box opens. You want to display all the guidelines listed.
3. **Verify that all the checkboxes are selected, then click OK**
   The dialog box closes. Changes to the margins take place from the insertion point forward in the document to the next margin changes.
4. **Position the pointer on the left-margin guideline, then press and hold the left mouse button**
   Your pointer changes to ↔ and a yellow pop-up box tells you it is set at the 1" mark, as shown in Figure D-7. This number will change to reflect the position of your margin setting.
5. **Drag the left-margin guideline to the left to the ½" mark on the Ruler, 0.5" in the yellow box, then click and drag the right-margin guideline to the left to the 7" mark for a 1½" right margin**
   This resets the margins for the entire document. To set the top and bottom margins, use the Margins dialog box.
6. **Click Format on the menu bar, then click Margins**
   The Page Margins tab of the Page Setup dialog box opens, as shown in Figure D-8. You can specify the exact number for right, left, top, or bottom margins in this dialog box. It shows you a representation of the document page based on the specified margins.
7. **Double-click the Top text box, type 1.5, double-click the Bottom text box, type 1.5, then click OK**
   The top and bottom margins are now set to 1½". The guidelines have been adjusted to reflect the change. Next, before printing, you will change the line spacing from single- to double-spaced to make the document easy to read. The insertion point should still be at the top of the document.
8. **Click Format on the menu bar, point to Line, then click Spacing**
9. **In the Line Spacing dialog box, type 2.0 in the Spacing box, click OK, then save your changes to the document**
   The press release is coming along nicely.

QuickTip

When you print a document on three-hole paper, or if you need to put the document in a binder, set the left margin to 2" or 2.5" to provide an adequate left margin.

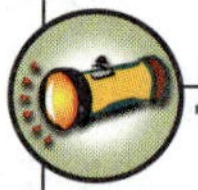

Trouble?

If the ½" margin isn't visible on your screen, the document window will scroll as necessary to display it as you drag the margin guideline.

FIGURE D-6: Ruler with margin markers

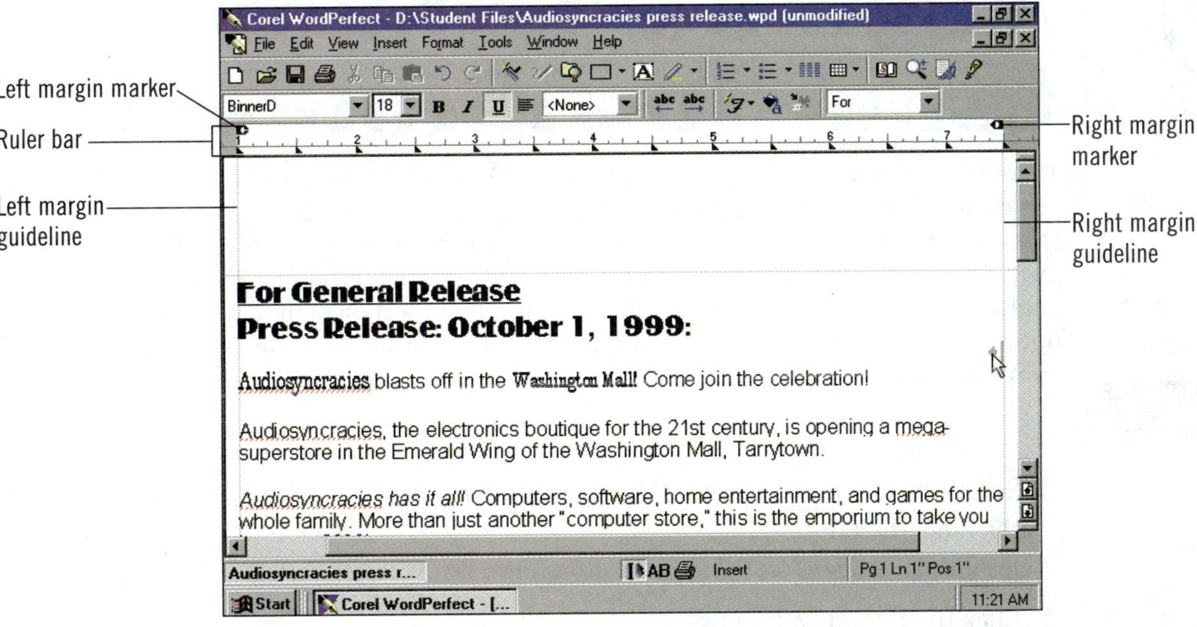

FIGURE D-7: Guideline selected

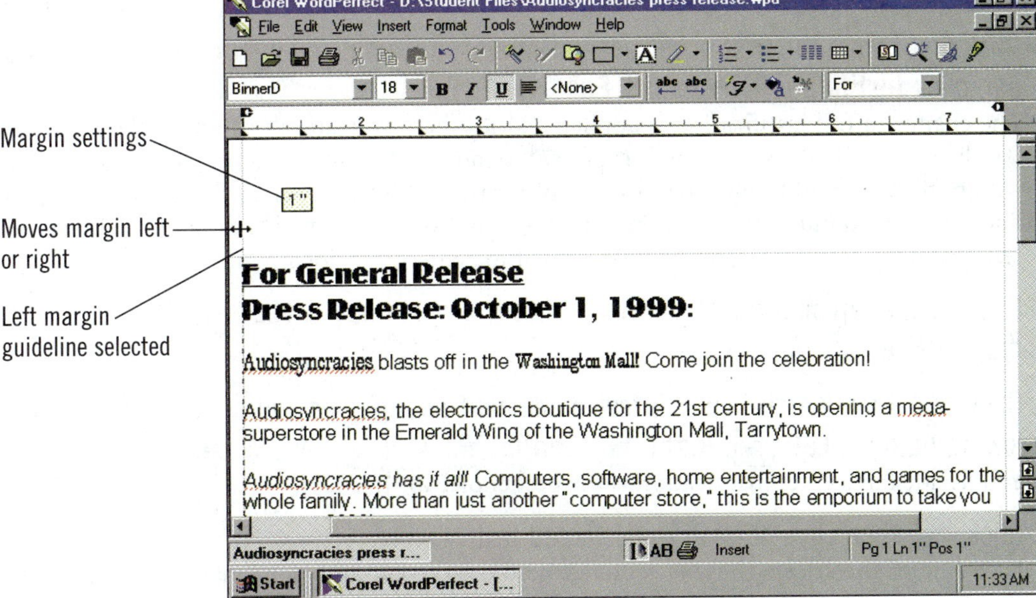

FIGURE D-8: Page Margins tab of Page Setup dialog box

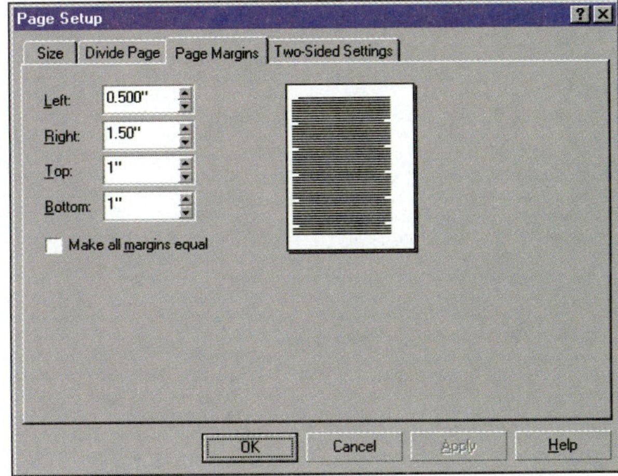

WordPerfect 8

WordPerfect 8

Aligning Text and Using Justification

There are several ways to **align**, or adjust, text in WordPerfect documents. **Justification** aligns text on the right or left margins, along both margins, or centered between the margins. Table D–2 shows the different justification buttons and their functions. You can also change the alignment of part of a line, leaving the other part at its original position. For the press release, Michael asks you to center the heading, justify the text on both margins, change the justification of the section on prizes, and align the telephone and fax numbers along the left and right margins.

Steps

1. Select the heading **For General Release**, then click the **Justification button** on the Property Bar
   Justification options are listed in the drop-down list, as shown in Figure D-9.
2. Click the **Center button**
   The heading is aligned evenly between the left and right margins. Next, you want to justify all the text on both margins, from the insertion point forward.
3. Click just before the first occurrence of **Audiosyncracies**, click **Format** on the menu bar, click **Justification**, then click **Full**
   The change to full justification is applied. Notice the Justification button on the Property Bar displays the Full Justification button to indicate full justification. The text is aligned with both the left and right margins, except for the last line. The change is most evident in lines that extend fully to the right margin. You want to see the effect of different justification settings in the section describing the prizes at the end of the document.
4. Click in the left margin at **Enter our great Technology Giveaway**, then click and drag to select the four lines
5. Click , then watch how the text placement changes as you slowly click the following buttons: **Left** , **Right** , **Center** , **Full** , and **All**
   You decide that center justification is the best choice for this text.
6. Click , then click outside the selected text
   Each line of the selected text is centered between the left and right margins. Your screen should match Figure D-10.
7. Save your changes to the document

FIGURE D-9: Justification button drop-down list

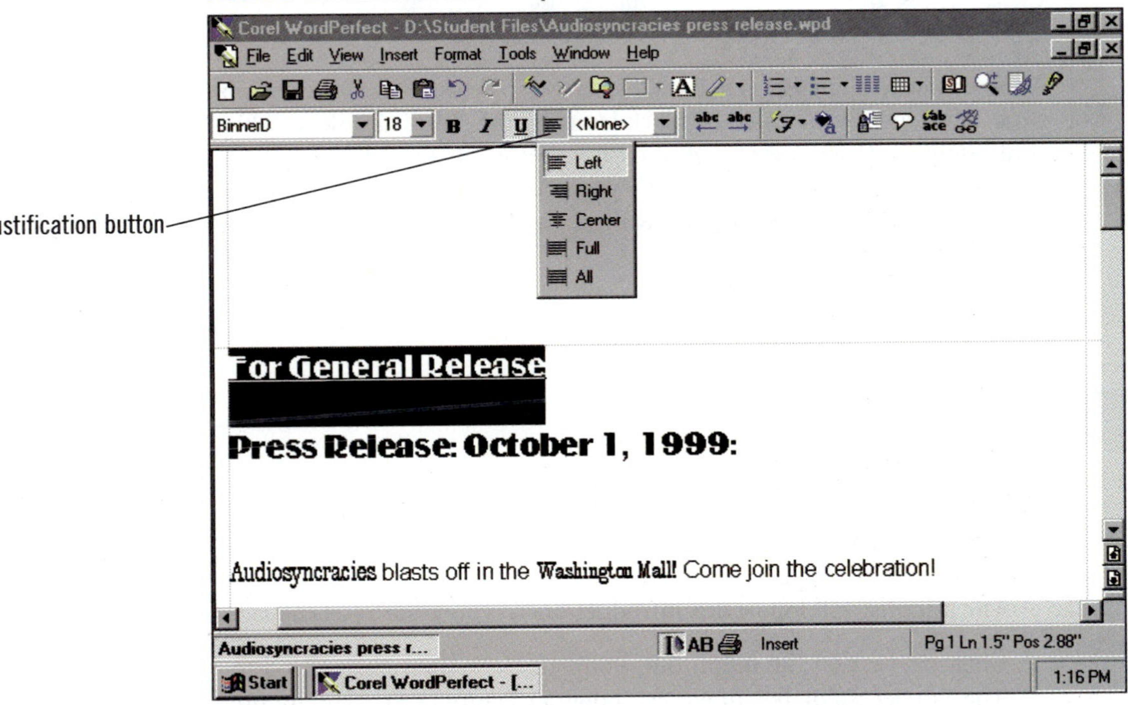

FIGURE D-10: Text with justification changes

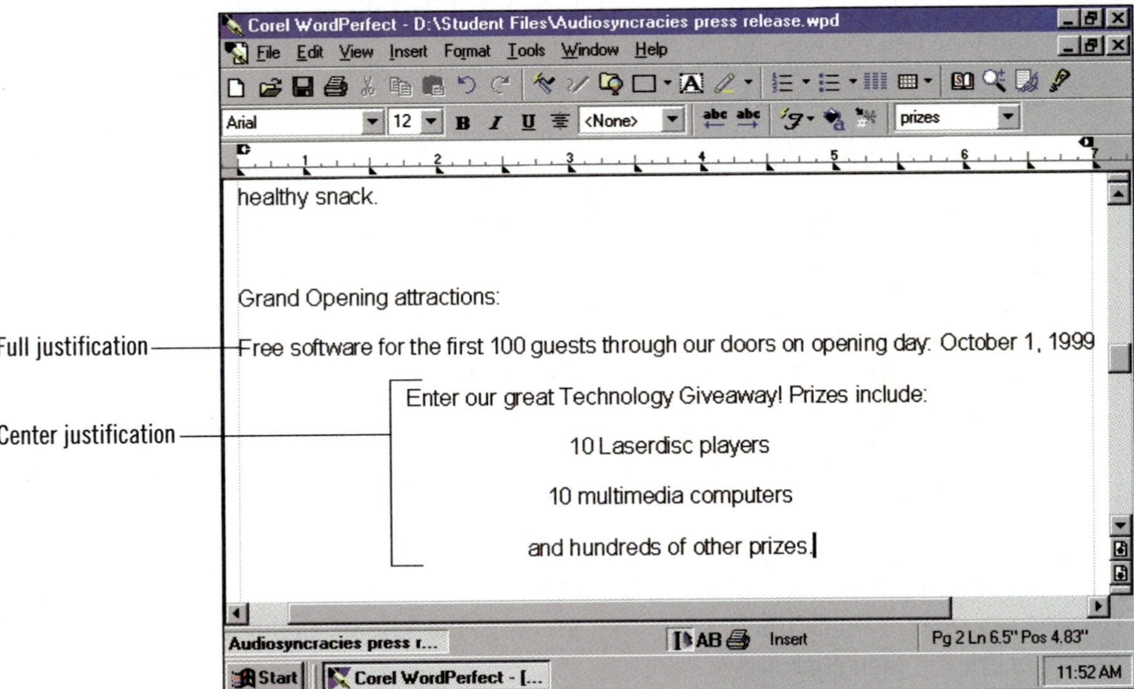

TABLE D-2: Types of justification

justification	button	description
Left		Aligns text along the left margin, producing ragged-right margins
Right		Aligns text along the right margin, producing ragged-left margins
Center		Centers each line of text between the right and left margins
Full		Aligns text along the left and right margins, except for the last line of the paragraph
All		Aligns text along the left and right margins, including the last line of the paragraph

Setting Tabs

Another way to align text is to use tabs. Tabs move text after the insertion point to the next tab stop. Tab stops are indicated by black icons on the Tab and Rulers. Table D-3 lists and defines commonly used tabs. Audiosyncracies wants to include a sample pricing list for their discount televisions at the end of the press release. Use the following steps to set tabs for this pricing list. In the next lesson, you will create the list. The Ruler should still be open at the top of the document window.

Steps

1. **Press [Ctrl][End], press [Enter], type To our valued customers! Here is just one small sampling of the competitive pricing we offer at Audiosyncracies!, then press [Enter] twice**
   The price list will follow this introduction, so you want to set the tabs here.
2. **Click Format on the menu bar, point to Line, then click Tab Set**
   The Tab Set dialog box opens, as shown in Figure D-11. Tabs are preset at every half inch, but you can reset these as needed. When you change the tab settings in a document, the changes take effect from that paragraph on. You'll clear the preset tabs so that you can set just the tabs you want for the pricing table.
3. **Click Clear All, then click OK**
   This clears all the tabs on the Ruler. When you change a tab setting in your document, the Tab Set icon appears in the left margin. You may need to scroll to view the Tab Set icon.
4. **If necessary, scroll to the left until appears in the left margin**
5. **Click**
   The Tab bar opens. A yellow pop-up box tells you the position of the tab when you move the mouse pointer. The Tab bar works like the Ruler. To set tabs you click on the Tab bar; to remove tabs you drag the tab marker off the Tab bar.
6. **Drag the Tab Marker on the Tab bar until the box indicates a Relative left tab: 3.5"**
   A left tab marker appears at 3.5" on the Tab bar. See Figure D-12. Use the Ruler as your guide. You want this to be a decimal tab because you plan to list prices at this tab, and you want the decimal points of each price to line up.
7. **Click on the Tab bar and drag to create a Relative left tab: 5", double-click the 5" tab marker, click the Tab type list arrow in the Tab Set dialog box, click Decimal, click OK, then click**
   A decimal tab appears at 5" mark on the Tab bar to align the prices. In the next lesson, you will use these tabs to create the price list.
8. **Click the Save button on the Toolbar**
   Your changes are saved to the document.

Trouble?

To return to the default tab settings, click Default in the Tab Set dialog box.

Absolute and relative tabs

You can position tabs from the left edge of the paper (**absolute** tabs), or you can position the tabs from the left edge of the margin (**relative** tabs). The default tabs in WordPerfect are relative tabs.

FIGURE D-11: Tab Set dialog box

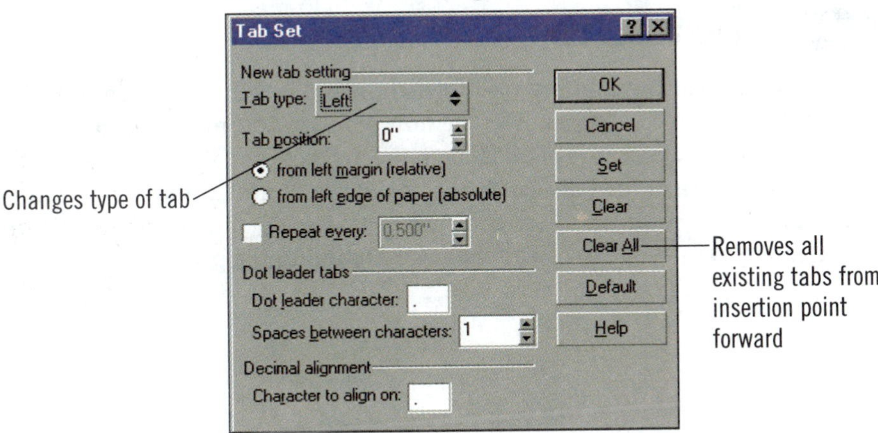

FIGURE D-12: Tab bar

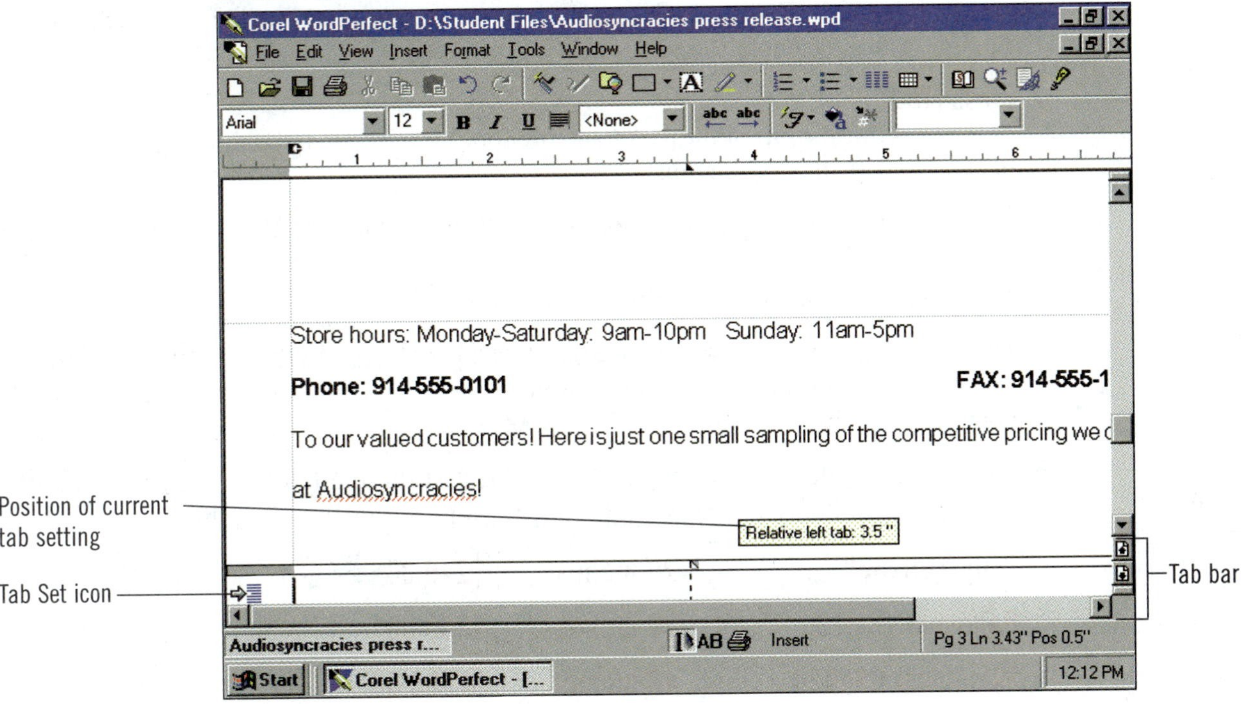

TABLE D-3: Tab types

tab icon	description	effect
	Left	WordPerfect default tab; text moves to right of tab
	Center	Text centers around the tab
	Right	Text moves backward to the left of the tab
	Decimal	Text you type before you insert the decimal point moves to the left of the tab, text entered after the decimal moves to the right of the tab, decimals are aligned
	Dot Left	Left tab with dot leader (a row of dots between the insertion point and the next tab setting)
	Dot Center	Center tab with dot leader
	Dot Right	Right tab with dot leader
	Dot Decimal	Decimal tab with dot leader

WordPerfect 8

Using Tabs

Tabs are useful when you want to create columns of information and indent paragraphs for certain styles of business correspondence. You are now ready to add pricing information for a list of televisions to the press release. You want to align the first column of information with the left margin, the second column at the 3.5" mark, and the third column at the 5" mark. You will use the tabs you set in the previous lesson to create the list quickly and efficiently. Before entering the table, you decide to insert a tab before the introduction to the price list.

1. **Click before the word To in the introduction of the price list**
   Note that the Ruler changes to display the tabs set for this line. You did not clear the tabs in this line, so the default tab stops appear at every ½-inch.
2. **Press [Tab]**
   This moves the first line of the paragraph over one tab, or .5" to the right. Now you are ready to enter the pricing information.
3. **Click at the beginning of the second blank line following the introduction of the price list**
   Notice that the tab stops you set here appear on the Ruler.
4. **Type Mfr/Model, press [Tab], type Size, press [Tab], type Price, then press [Enter]**
   The three headings are aligned respectively at the left margin, the 3.5" point, and the 5" point, creating three columns.
5. **Type the following information, using the left margin to align the first column, press [Tab] between items you type, and press [Enter] at the end of each line**

Sony XBR2650	26 inches	$249.00
Panasonic KM29	29 inches	$309.00
Mitsubishi CS402R	40 inches	$1999.00
Sony XBR4255	42 inches	$2215.00

6. **Click the Save button on the Toolbar**
   Your screen should look like Figure D-13.

QuickTip

To move text back to the previous tab setting, press [Shift][Tab].

FIGURE D-13: Press release with tabular information

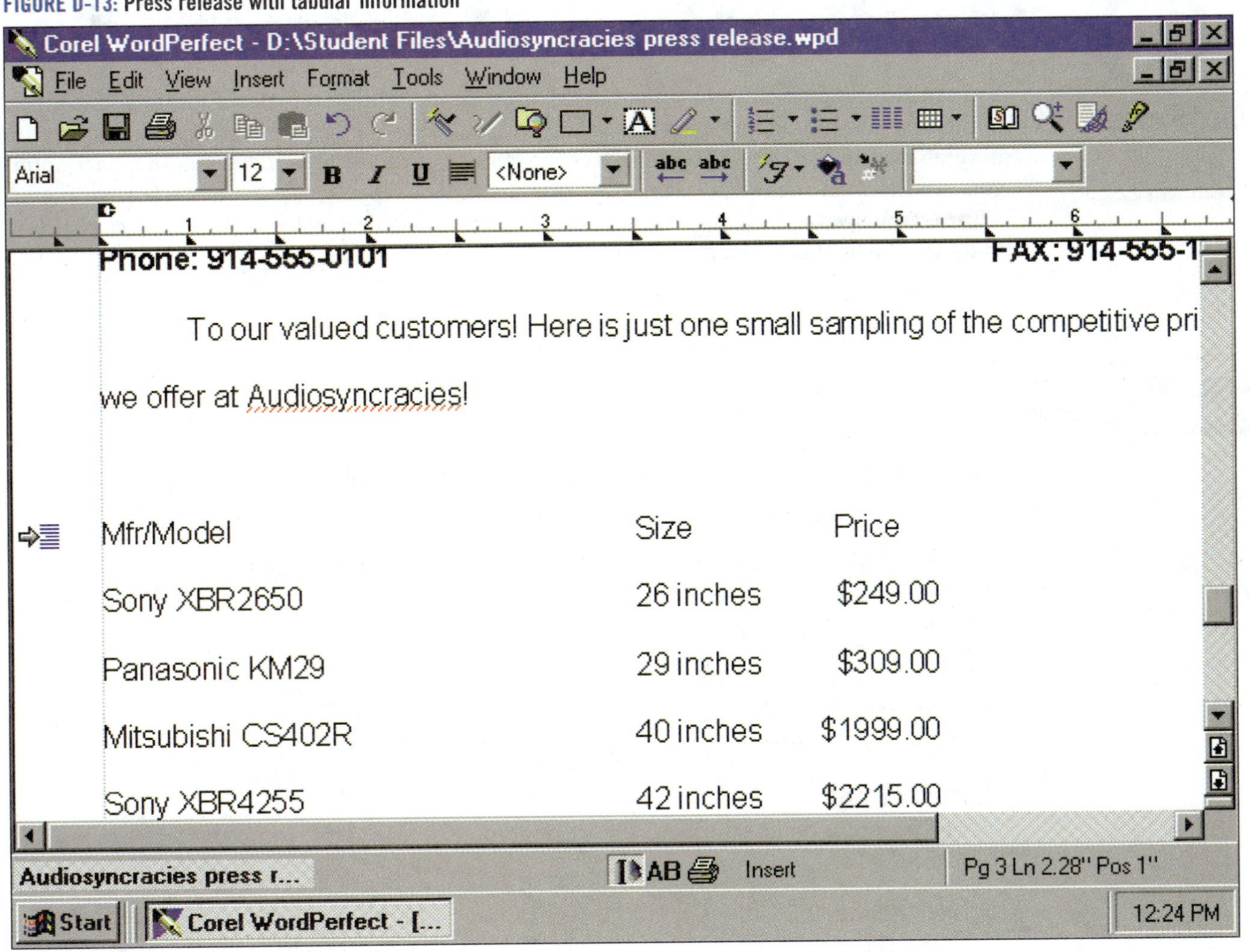

Indenting Paragraphs

You can also align text in a document by setting indents. While a tab moves just one line of text to the next tab stop, an indent moves all subsequent lines of text in the current paragraph to the next tab stop. Indents are canceled by pressing [Enter]. If you want to indent another paragraph, you need to reset the indent. Table D-4 lists the indent types available on the Format menu. You need to add promotional text to the end of the press release. Follow the steps below to indent the final paragraph.

Steps

1. **Position the insertion point at the end of the document, then press [Enter]**
   This inserts a blank line and positions the insertion point for the new paragraph.
2. **Click Format on the menu bar, point to Paragraph, then click Indent**
   The insertion point is repositioned to the temporary indent. Because you did not reset the tabs after adding the price list, it moves the tab stop to the current 3.5" mark.
3. **Type Watch out for our next Audiosyncracies grand opening in Paramus on November 1, 1999 and in Manhattan on January 2, 2000!**
   The text automatically wraps to the new temporary left margin.
4. **Press [Enter]**
   The insertion point returns to the left margin. Compare your completed paragraph with Figure D-14.
5. **Click the Save button on the Toolbar**

FIGURE D-14: Press release with tabs and indented paragraph

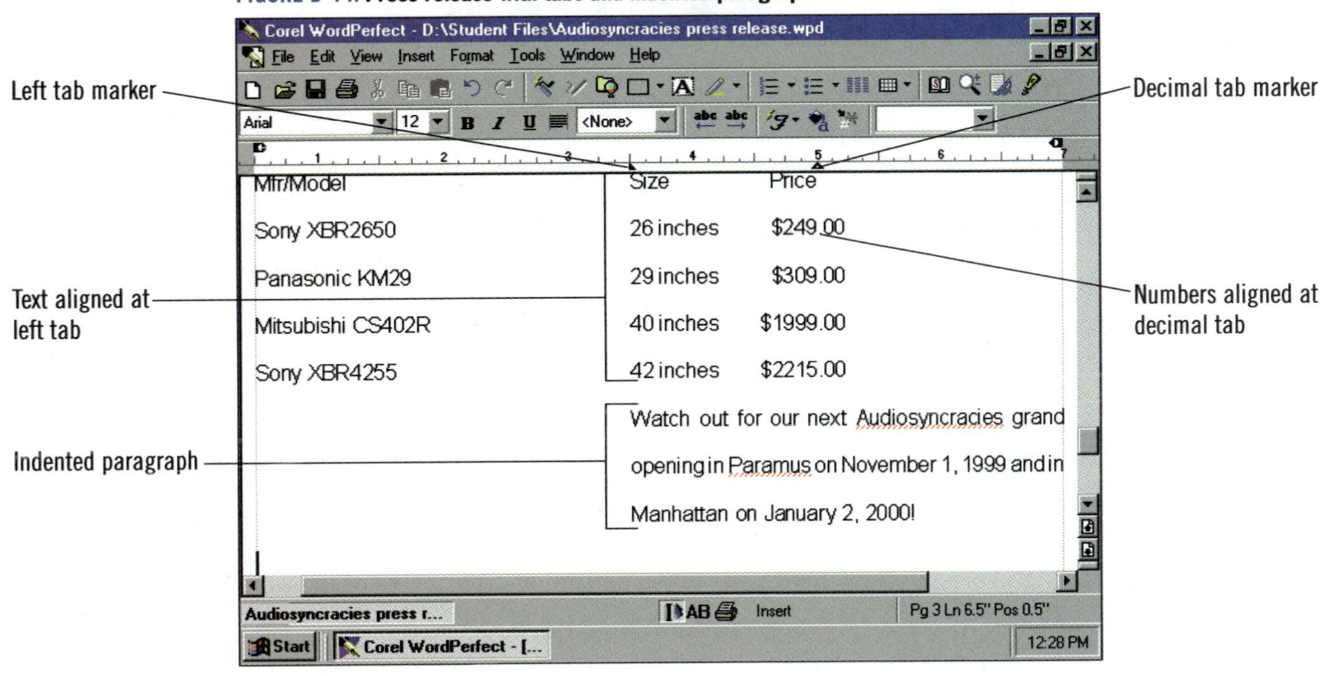

TABLE D-4: Indent types

indent type	action
Indent	Indents entire paragraph to the right one tab stop
Double indent	Indents entire paragraph inward one tab stop from each margin
Hanging indent	Indents all but the first line of a paragraph one tab stop to the right

Using QuickFormat

QuickFormat lets you easily copy fonts and alignment styles from one area of text to another. By placing the insertion point in the paragraph containing the format you want to copy and clicking the QuickFormat button on the Toolbar, you can specify where to place the formatting styles you want to copy by simply dragging over the text you want to reformat. To turn off QuickFormat, click the QuickFormat button again. After reviewing your document, you realize that you want to format the name of the store, Audiosyncracies, using PT Barnum BT 14 pt everywhere in the press release. Use QuickFormat to make this change throughout the document.

Steps 1 2 3 4

1. **Press [Ctrl][Home], then double-click the first occurrence of the word Audiosyncracies to select it**
   You need to copy this format to the remaining occurrences of the word in the document.
2. **Click the QuickFormat button on the Property Bar**
   The QuickFormat dialog box opens as shown in Figure D-15. The Characters option copies only the fonts and attributes of the current text.
3. **Click the Selected characters option button if necessary, then click OK**
   The mouse pointer changes to the QuickFormat pointer. Drag this special mouse pointer over any text to apply the new format.
4. **Double-click the next occurrence of Audiosyncracies**
   QuickFormat changes the word from the document's default font to the QuickFormat font.
5. **Scroll through the document, then double-click to select and QuickFormat all the Audiosyncracies in the document**
   As long as the QuickFormat pointer is active, text changes to match the format. See Figure D-16. To turn off QuickFormat, simply click the button again.
6. **Click**
   The press release looks terrific. You want to spell check it.
7. **Click Tools on the menu bar, click Spell Check, then spell check the entire document, skipping and correcting words as necessary**
   Now you are ready to print the press release to show it to your colleagues at The Write Staff.
8. **Click the Save button on the Toolbar, click the Print button, then press [Enter]**
   One copy of the document prints out. Now you're ready to close the document and exit WordPerfect.
9. **Click File on the menu bar, then click Exit**

FIGURE D-15: QuickFormat dialog box

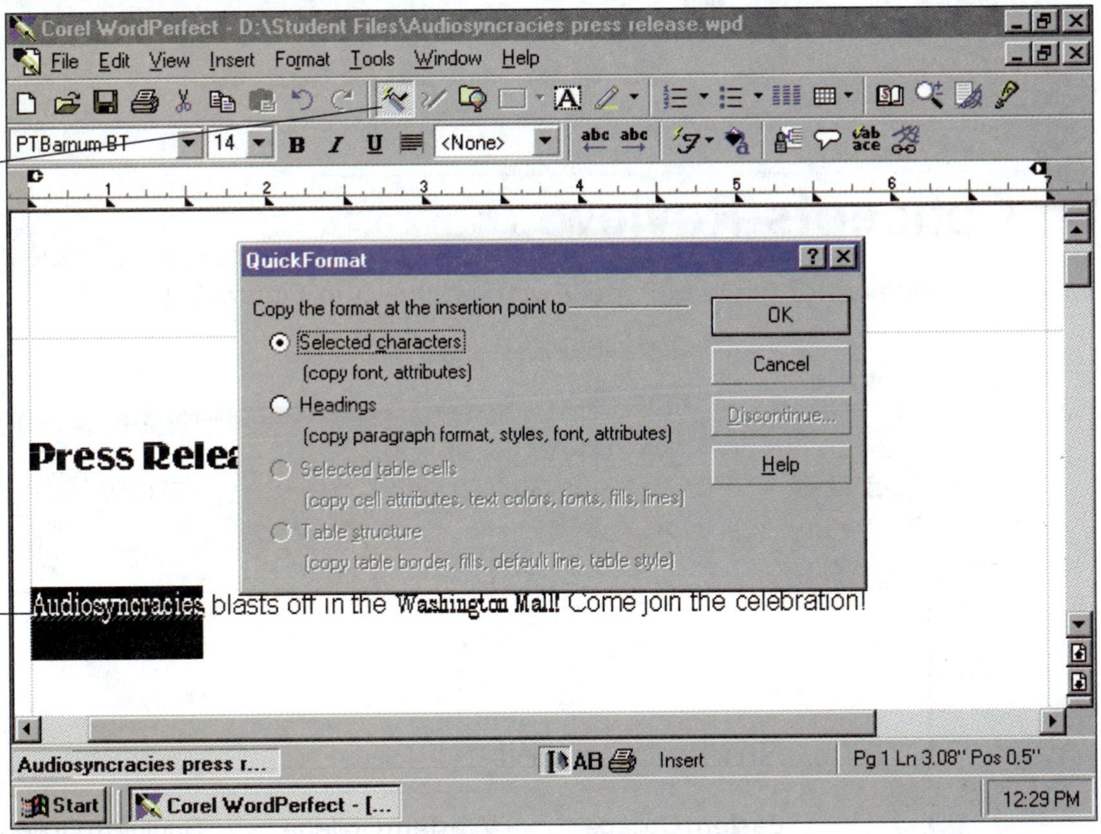

QuickFormat button

Format of selected text will be copied

FIGURE D-16: Using the QuickFormat pointer

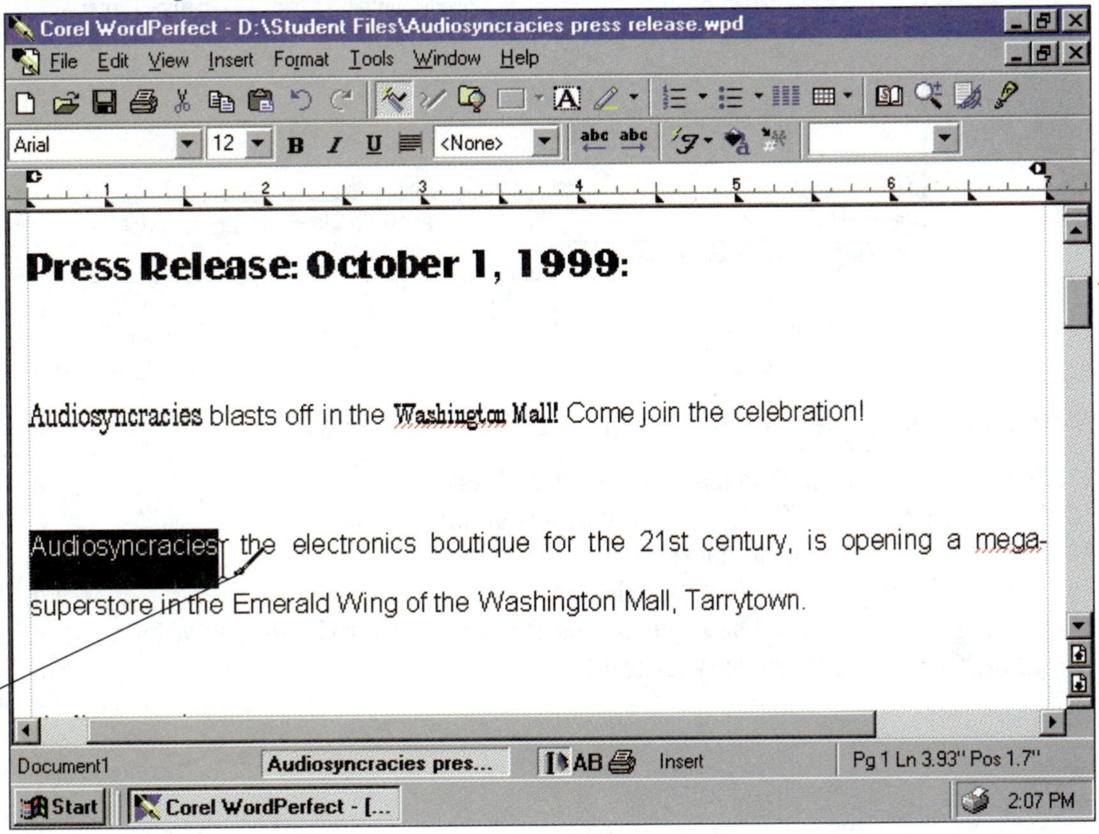

QuickFormat pointer

Practice

Concepts Review

Label each element of the WordPerfect window shown in Figure D-17.

FIGURE D-17

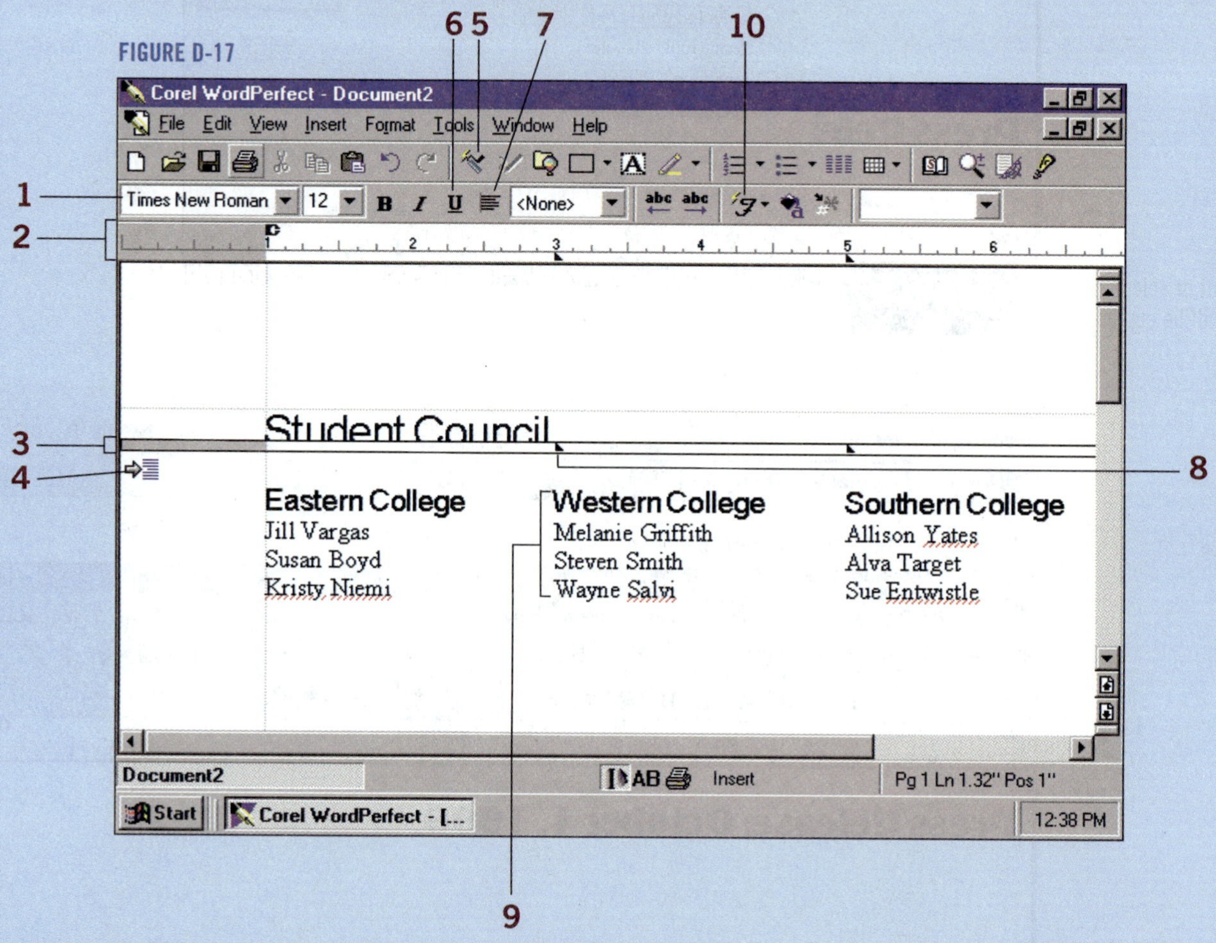

Match each statement with the format command it describes.

11. Specifies the amount of space between lines of text
12. Indents a single line of text or aligns columns of information
13. Makes text look thicker or darker
14. Aligns the entire paragraph at the tab stop
15. Specifies that text should be aligned along the left margin, right margin, or both
16. Creates a temporary boundary for text

a. Tab
b. Margin
c. Indent
d. Justification
e. Line spacing
f. Bold

Select the best answer from the list of choices.

17. Text aligned on both the left and right margins is what type of justification?
- **a.** Right
- **b.** Full
- **c.** Left
- **d.** Center

18. The easiest way to change line spacing is to
- **a.** Click the Tab Set button on the Property Bar.
- **b.** Press [Enter] after each line.
- **c.** Click Format on the menu bar, point to Line, then click Spacing.
- **d.** Increase the top and bottom margins.

19. Which Property Bar element would you click to change the height of the font in your document?
- **a.** Font Size list box
- **b.** Font Face list box
- **c.** Underline Button
- **d.** Justification Button

20. The easiest way to copy character formats is to use
- **a.** QuickSelect.
- **b.** QuickFormat.
- **c.** QuickCharacter.
- **d.** QuickCopy.

Skills Review

1. **Choose fonts and sizes.**
   a. Start WordPerfect, open the document WP D-2 and save it as "Creative Kitchens" to your Student Disk.
   b. Select the words "Creative Kitchens" in the first sentence of the letter.
   c. Click the Font Face button on the Property Bar, then click any font of your choice. The phrase appears in the new font.
   d. Use the Font Face button to select a few fonts until you find one to your liking.
   e. Click the Font Size button on the Property Bar, then click 14. The words appear in a larger font size.
   f. Click anywhere in the document to deselect the highlighted words.
   g. Select the text "Creative Kitchens" in the second paragraph of the body of the letter.
   h. Click the QuickFonts button on the Property bar, then click the font you chose for the previous instance of "Creative Kitchens."
   i. Save your changes to the document.

2. **Change the appearance of text.**
   a. Select the first occurrence of "Creative Kitchens" in the document.
   b. Click the Bold button on the Property bar.
   c. Select the word "variety" in the second paragraph in the document.
   d. Click the Italic button on the Property bar.
   e. Save your changes to the document.

3. **Change margins and line spacing.**
   a. Move the insertion point to the beginning of the document, and save the document to your Student Disk as "Creative kitchens letter".
   b. If the Ruler isn't already visible, click Ruler on the View menu.
   c. Click and drag the left guideline to change the margin to the 1½" mark. Click and drag the right margin to the 6½" mark.
   d. Click Format on the menu bar, then click Margins.
   e. Double-click the Top text box, type 2, double-click the Bottom text box, type 2, then click OK.
   f. Press [Ctrl][Home] to move the insertion point to the beginning of the document.
   g. Click Format on the menu bar, point to Line, then click Spacing.
   h. In the Line Spacing dialog box, type 1.5 in the Spacing box, then click OK.
   i. Save your changes to the document.

4. **Align text and use justification.**
   a. Select the text that displays the date at the top of the document.
   b. Click the Justification button on the Property bar, then change the justification of the selection so that it is aligned along the right margin.
   c. Click at the beginning of the first paragraph in the document.
   d. Change the justification to Full.
   e. Save the document, then close it.

5. Set tabs.

a. Open the document WP D-3 and save it to your Student Disk as "Memo".
b. If the Ruler is not already visible, click Ruler on the View menu.
c. Click Format on the menu bar, point to Line, then click Tab Set.
d. Click Clear All, then click OK.
e. Move the insertion point to the beginning of the document.
f. If necessary, scroll to the left until the Tab Set icon appears in the left margin.
g. Click the Tab Set icon in the left margin to open the Tab bar.
h. Set a left tab by clicking and dragging on the Tab bar until the yellow pop-up box reads "Relative left tab: 1.25"."
i. Use the tab bar to set another relative left tab at 2.00".
j. Save your changes to the document.

6. Use tabs.

a. Move the insertion point immediately to the right of the colon (:) after "Date", then press [Tab].
b. Click after the colons (:) in "To", "From", and "RE", and press [Tab] to align the information after each colon at 2".
c. Save your changes to the document.

7. Indent paragraphs.

a. Click at the beginning of the first paragraph, which begins "Accompanying this memo".
b. Click Format on the menu bar, point to the paragraph, then click Indent.
c. Repeat the steps above to indent the other two paragraphs of the memo at the 1.25" tab.
d. Save your changes to the document.
e. Print one copy of the document.

8. Use QuickFormat.

a. Click at the beginning of the document.
b. Type "INTER-OFFICE MEMO" and then press [Enter].
c. Select the line of text you just typed, then change the font to Arial and the font size to 14 points.
d. Click the QuickFormat button on the Toolbar.
e. Click the Selected Characters option button, then click OK.
f. Apply the QuickFormat to the text "Date:" in the second line of the document.
g. Apply the QuickFormat to the text "To:", "From:", and "RE:" in the next three lines. (Be careful not to move the margin guidelines when selecting text.)
h. Save your changes to the document.
i. Print one copy of the memo.
j. Close the document and exit WordPerfect.

Independent Challenges

1. You are a sales representative for Clearwater Valve Company. You have a list of prospective clients, one of whom is Mr. Ken Kikuchi of CryoTech Pharmaceuticals, 891 Avocado Avenue, Escondido, CA 92925. As part of your job, you write letters to prospective clients, introducing yourself as a sales representative for Clearwater Valve Company and explaining that Clearwater designs and manufactures the highest quality valves in the industry. You explain that Clearwater can design valves to meet extreme conditions of temperature, pressure, and acidity.

To complete this independent challenge:

1. Write a short letter using WordPerfect introducing yourself to Mr. Kikuchi, briefly explaining what your company does, and asking to visit him and others at CryoTech Pharmaceuticals.
2. Save the letter as "CryoTech", then print it.
3. Now make the following changes in the format of the letter:
   a. Move the left margin to 1.5", and move the right margin to 7.25".
   b. Make the line spacing 2.0.
   c. Change the font for every occurrence of "Clearwater Valve Company" to Bodoni Black or a similar font. If that font isn't available, choose one of your liking.
   d. Make every occurrence of "Cryo" bold, and italicize every occurrence of "Tech" so that the company name is formatted as "**Cryo***Tech* Pharmaceuticals."
   e. Set a left tab stop 0.4" from the left margin. Indent the first line of every paragraph to this tab stop.
4. Save the letter as "CryoTech2", then print it and exit WordPerfect.
5. Submit the first and final drafts of the letter.

2. Find the lyrics to one of your favorite songs. You can locate these on the jackets of cassette tapes or often inside the booklet that comes with compact discs. If you don't have access to CDs or cassette tapes, go to your local library and get a song book. Find a book that has the lyrics for all the verses of the song you choose. Try to find a song that has a repeating chorus.

To complete this independent challenge:

1. Create a document using WordPerfect, typing all the lyrics. Be sure to end each line with [Enter] as required.
   a. Proofread the document and correct any spelling errors.
   b. Be sure to enter the song title and the lyricist (the person who wrote the song) at the top of the document.
   c. Use the song title as the filename to save the document to your Student Disk.
2. Now make the following changes to the format of the lyrics:
   a. Move the left margin to 1.25". Move the right margin to 6.75".
   b. Make the line spacing 1.5.
   c. Change the font face and font size for every occurrence of the chorus so that it is different from the other verses. Choose a font and size of your liking. Use QuickFormat to complete this step.
   d. Make every occurrence of the song title bold, both in the heading and throughout the lyrics.
   e. Set a left tab stop 0.5" from the left margin. Use a hanging indent on this tab stop at the first line of every verse.
   f. Italicize the lyricist's name.
   g. Type your name and date at the bottom.
3. Save the song as the song title but add "revised" to the filename.
4. Print the song and exit WordPerfect.
5. Submit the first and final drafts of the song.

3. Formatting enhances a document by making the text look interesting. You will take a letter you wrote to Ms. Charlotte Chase at Adventure Clothing and format the text to make it look more interesting.

To complete this independent challenge:

1. Start WordPerfect, open the file WP D-4 and save it as "Formatted letter to Adventure Clothing."
2. Change the font in the letter from Times New Roman to a font of your choice.
3. Format the name of the store in a different font from the rest of the letter.
4. Change the margins and the line spacing.
5. Change the tab settings to .75" and tab each paragraph.
6. Save your changes.
7. Print the revised letter, close your document, and exit WordPerfect.

4. Review several documents from commercial establishments that you either received in the mail or found inserted in a newspaper or magazine. The documents can be serious or junk mail, advertisements, flyers, catalogs, or brochures. Be sure they are professionally printed. From these documents, select four that have at least four font styles in them. See how the font sets the tone for the documents.

To complete this independent challenge:

1. Select your favorite document with the most interesting font styles.
2. Try to select one that is no more than 1 page.
3. Highlight the font changes.
4. Mark any text formatting or use of tabs in the document.
5. Type the document in WordPerfect and save it as "Font challenge."
6. Try to match the fonts, line spacing, and margins of the selected document as you create your own document.
7. When you are done, save and print your document.
8. Now save the document as "Font fun" to preserve the original file before moving on to the next step.
9. Identify key words in the document and change the fonts. Try using fonts that you have never heard of, those with interesting names on the font list.
10. Print and save the file, then exit WordPerfect.
11. Compare all three documents: the original, your first draft, and then your revised copy. Which fonts work best? Which distract from the text? Write your notes on the printouts.

Visual Workshop

Create the document shown in Figure D-18. Be sure to format the text as shown using fonts, different point sizes, and character formatting such as bold, italics, and underline. Use the QuickFormat button to set the repeating character formats. Set the line spacing as shown on the Property Bar, and adjust the margins to match the figure. You can continue to add your own favorites to this list. Be sure to save it as the name of your choice to your Student Disk, and then print it.

FIGURE D-18

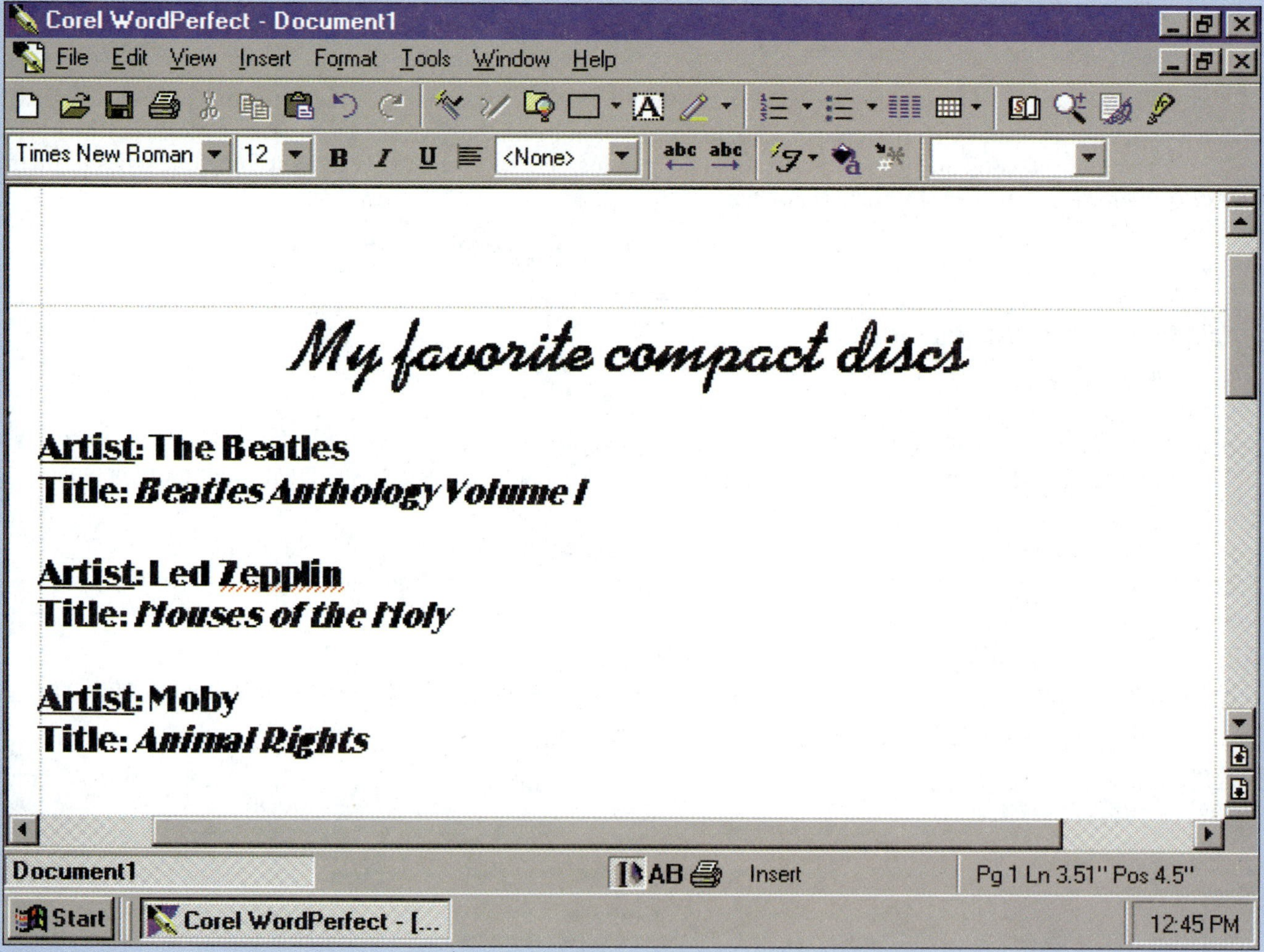

Corel WordPerfect - Document1

File Edit View Insert Format Tools Window Help

Times New Roman 12 B I U <None>

My favorite compact discs

Artist: **The Beatles**
Title: ***Beatles Anthology Volume I***

Artist: **Led Zepplin**
Title: ***Houses of the Holy***

Artist: **Moby**
Title: ***Animal Rights***

Document1 AB Insert Pg 1 Ln 3.51" Pos 4.5"

Start Corel WordPerfect - [... 12:45 PM

Working with Multiple-Page Documents and Graphic Images

Objectives

- Add and customize page numbers
- Insert headers and footers
- Keep text together
- Plan a graphic image
- Insert a graphic image
- Move and size a graphic image
- Add a graphical line to your document
- Create a watermark

Although some of the documents you create are simple single-page letters or papers, many will consist of multiple pages, presenting new word processing challenges. For example, you may want to keep track of the pages by using page numbers or by including headers or footers. You may also want to enhance the appearance of your documents by adding graphic images. WordPerfect helps you with these tasks by providing many features to facilitate working with longer documents and with graphics. Jennifer Laina just finished writing a company style guide entitled "Promotional Text Writing Guidelines," which will be distributed to the staff. It is a multiple-page document that includes the condensed version of the "General Writing Style Guide." Before distributing the guidelines to other writers, Jennifer asks you to add page numbers and a header to the document.

Adding and Customizing Page Numbers

If a document includes more than one page, you may want to add page numbers. You can choose the type of page numbers you want, any text to be included with the page numbers, and where the page numbers should appear on the printed page. Table E-1 shows different page number types and suggested uses for each. One issue that Jennifer addresses in her guidelines is the company policy for putting page numbers in documents longer than one page. Jennifer also provides guidelines for how to include the document title and the total number of pages in the document. Jennifer has asked you to add page numbers to the style guide document.

Steps

1. **Start WordPerfect, open the file WP E-1 from your Student Disk, then save it to your Student Disk as Style Guide**
   There are intentional errors in the document that you will correct in a later lesson.

2. **Scroll down the page until a thick horizontal bar appears across your document window**
   This line identifies the page break. The second page of your document begins below this line; the first page ends above this line. You want the page numbers to start on page 2.

3. **Position the insertion point on the second page before the word Identify**
   The location of the insertion point determines where page numbering will begin.

4. **Click Format on the menu bar, click Page, then click Numbering**
   The Select Page Numbering Format dialog box opens, as shown in Figure E-1.

5. **Click Page 2 of 4 in the Page numbering format list box, then click Custom Format**
   The Custom Page Numbering dialog box opens as shown in Figure E-2.

6. **If necessary, click the Custom page numbering format text box, then press [Home]**
   The insertion point is positioned before the word "Page". You want to insert the text "Style Guide" before the page numbering to identify the document.

7. **Type Style Guide, press [Spacebar], click OK, click OK to return to the document, scroll to the bottom of page 2, then save your document**
   Your page numbering at the bottom of the page should read "Style Guide Page 2 of 4".

QuickTip

To change page numbers font, click Font in the Select Page Numbering Format dialog box. Choose a new font in the Font dialog box.

Trouble?

You must be in Page or Draft view to see page numbers in your document.

TABLE E-1: Types of page numbers and how they are used

type	example	suggested uses
Arabic numerals	1, 2, 3,	WordPerfect's default setting; body of a document
Lower-case roman numerals or letters	i, ii, iii, a, b, c	Table of contents, acknowledgments
Upper-case roman numerals or letters	I, II, III, A, B, C	Table of contents, acknowledgments, appendices

FIGURE E-1: **Select Page Numbering Format dialog box**

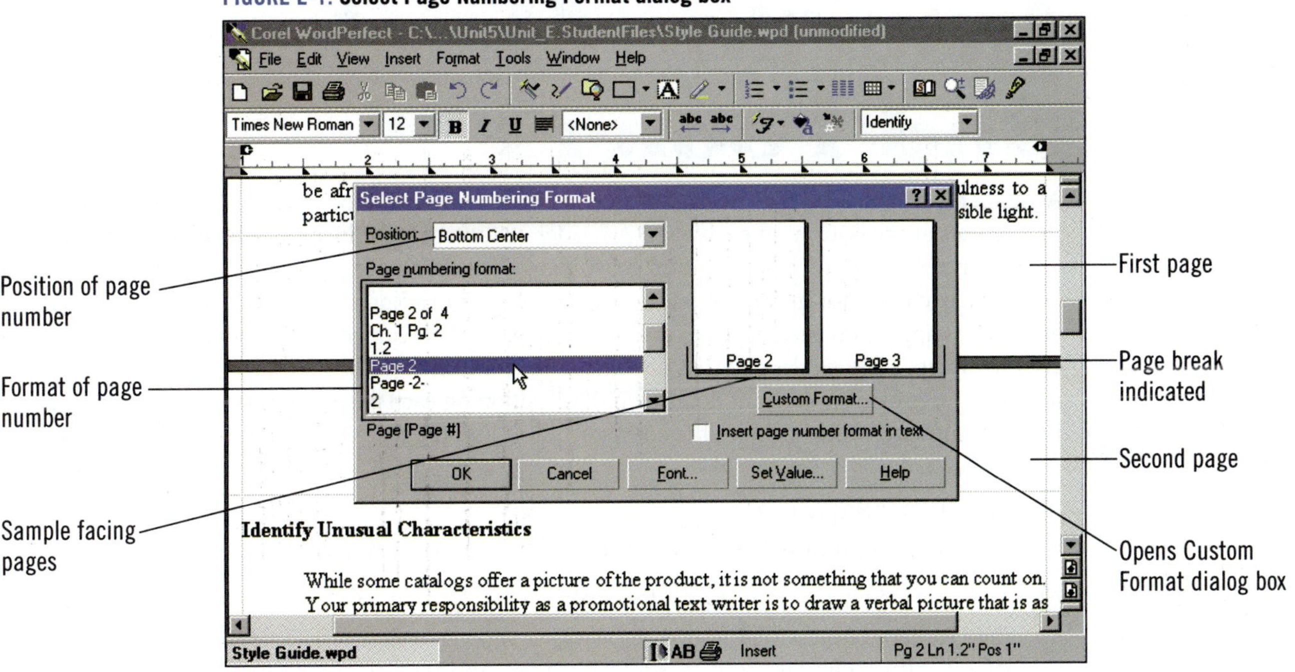

FIGURE E-2: **Custom Page Numbering dialog box**

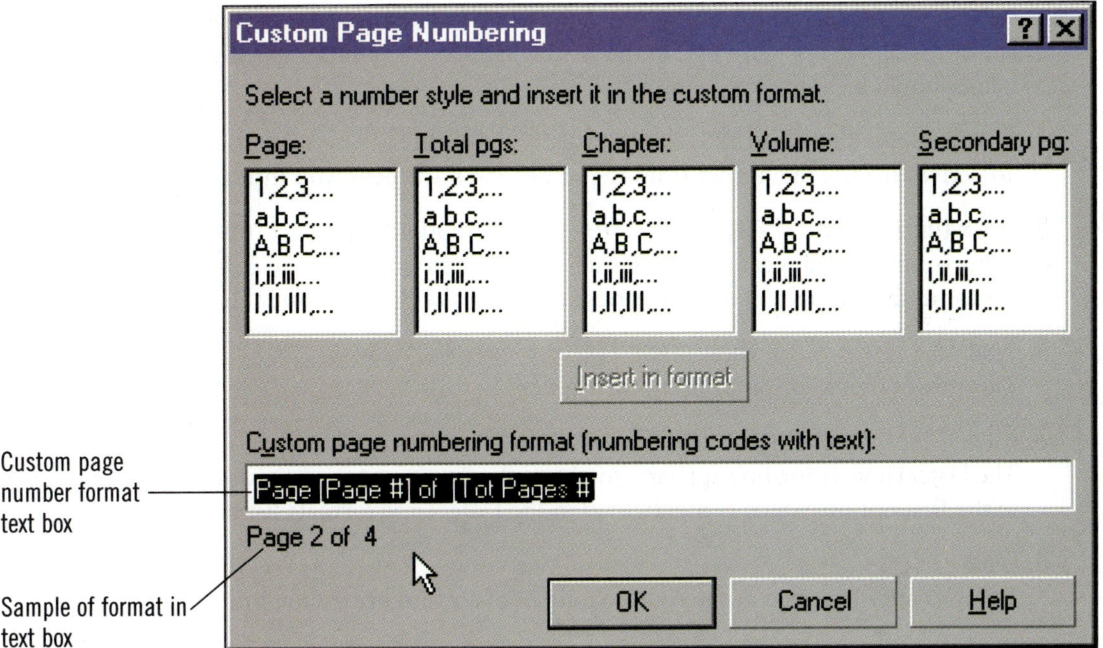

Page Numbering options

The Select Page Numbering Format dialog box has several options. If you want to include a page number directly into the document, click the box next to Insert page number format in text. This option creates a **relative reference** in your document. A relative reference always adjusts to represent the desired page as your document length changes. If you want to change the value of the page number, click the Set Value button. This option is useful if you want to combine or append one document with another. To find out how many pages there are in your document, click File on the menu bar, select Properties, then click Information.

WordPerfect 8

WordPerfect 8

Inserting Headers and Footers

A **header** is information that repeats at the top of each page of a document; a **footer** is information that repeats at the bottom of each page. A header or footer might include your name and the company name. Some header information may change for each page, such as a section heading, or a header may change for groups of pages, such as chapter headings. You can choose to have headers and footers appear on each page or on alternating pages. You can also edit, suppress, or delete headers and footers. Jennifer has discussed the importance of using headers and footers, explaining that they provide important document information on each page. She asks you to insert a header in the document, which includes the company name and the date that the guide was last revised.

Steps

QuickTip

The header will start on the current page and will appear on every subsequent page.

QuickTip

To create a footer, click either Footer A or Footer B, then continue with the following steps.

1. **Press [Ctrl][Home]**
   The insertion point is positioned at the beginning of the document.
2. **Click Insert on the menu bar, then click Header/Footer**
   The Headers/Footers dialog box appears, as shown in Figure E-3. Header A is selected by default. Although you can have several headers and footers in a document, only two can be active on any page.
3. **Click Create in the Headers/Footers dialog box**
   Header guidelines, which define the header area, and the Headers/Footers Property Bar appear, as shown in Figure E-4. In the writing guidelines, Jennifer specifies that the company name should be at the left margin.
4. **If necessary, clear all tabs, then set a right tab at 7½"**
   To better separate the header from the rest of the document, you insert a horizontal line.
5. **Click the Horizontal Line button on the Headers/Footers Property Bar**
   A horizontal line appears in the header area. When you type the company name, it will appear at the left margin of the header and above the thin horizontal line.
6. **Type The Write Staff, then press [Tab]**
   This moves the insertion point to the right.
7. **Click Insert on the menu bar, then click Date/Time**
   The Date/Time dialog box appears. You want the date to appear in your document as it does in the first option, which is highlighted in the Date/Time formats list box.
8. **Click Insert**
   Today's date is inserted at the right margin above a thin horizontal line.
9. **Click the Close Headers/Footers button on the Headers/Footers Property Bar, then save your document**
   The header appears as shown in Figure E-5. This header appears on all pages of the document.

Suppressing a header or footer

In many cases, you will find that you don't want to include a header or footer on the first page of a document. To suppress the header or footer on the first page, press [Ctrl][Home]. Place the insertion point outside of the header/footer area, click Format, click Page, click Suppress, click Header A check box, then click OK. When your document prints, it will be without a header or footer on the first page.

FIGURE E-3: Headers/Footers dialog box

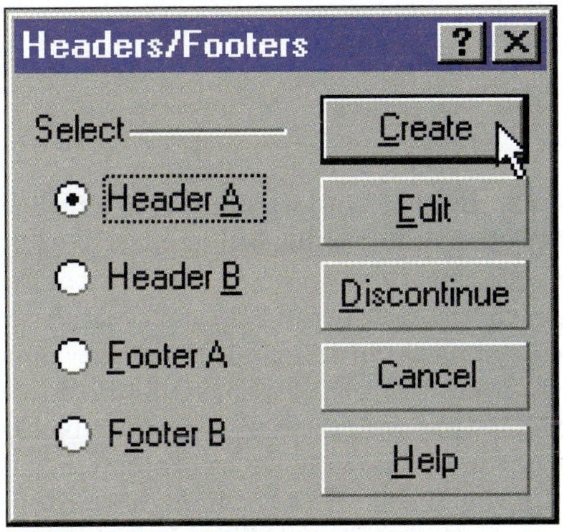

Headers/Footers

Select

- Header A
- Header B
- Footer A
- Footer B

Create | Edit | Discontinue | Cancel | Help

FIGURE E-4: Headers/Footers Property Bar

Corel WordPerfect - C:\...\Unit5\Unit_E.StudentFiles\Style Guide.wpd (Header A)

File Edit View Insert Format Tools Window Help

Times New Roman 12 <None>

Inserts page, chapter, or volume number

Inserts a line

Specifies pages on which header or footer should appear

Specifies amount of space between text and header or footer

Closes Headers/ Footers Property Bar

Area for header

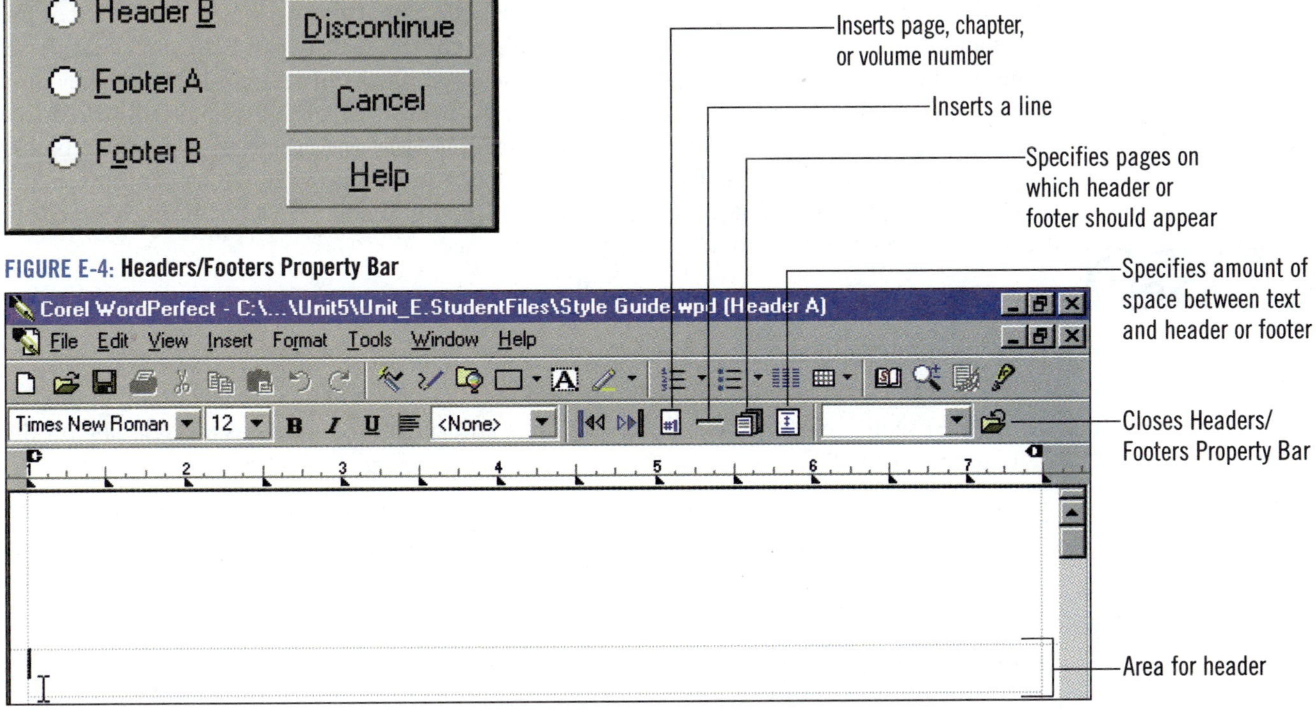

FIGURE E-5: Document header

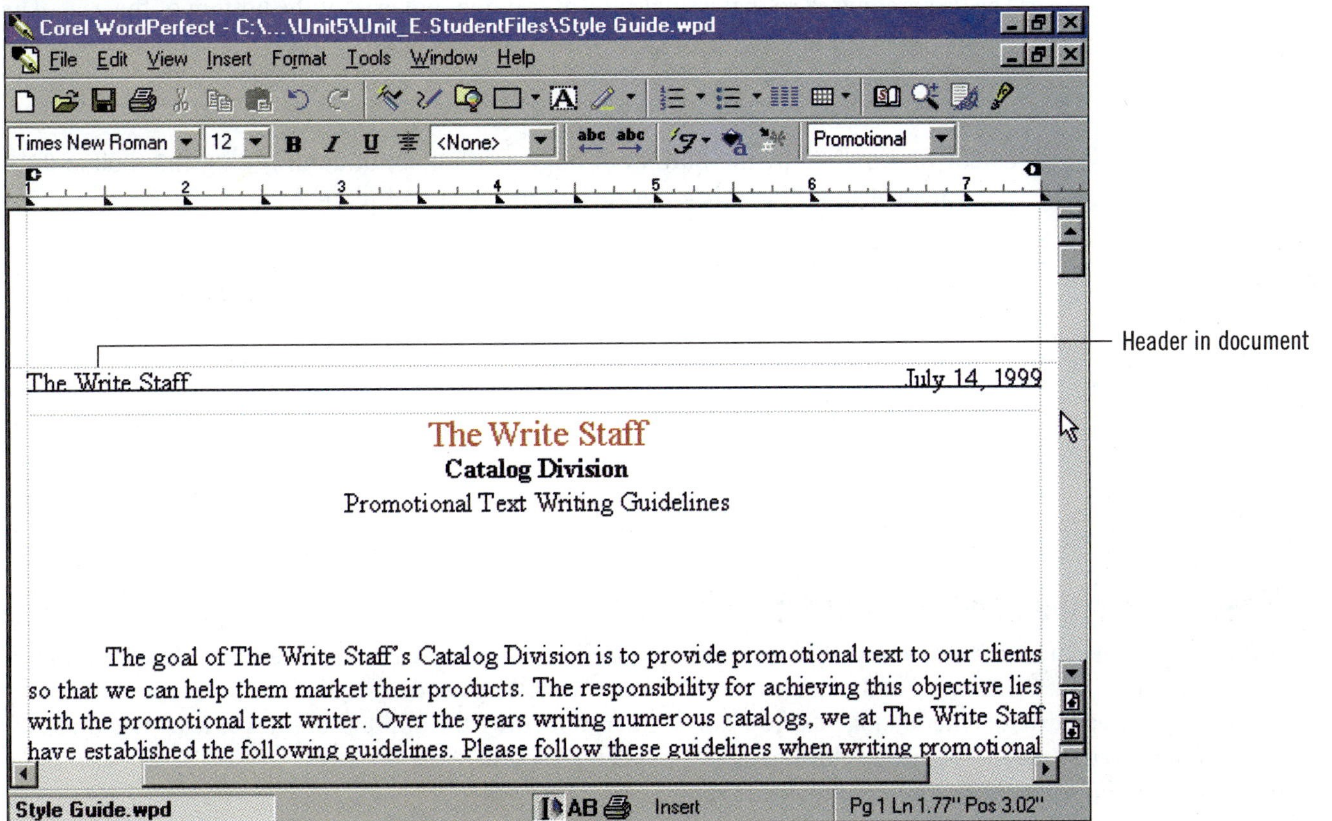

WordPerfect 8

WordPerfect 8

Keeping Text Together

Sometimes in multiple-page documents paragraphs begin or end awkwardly, leaving one line of text alone at the bottom or top of a page. A single line of text at the beginning of a paragraph that appears alone at the bottom of a page is called an **orphan**; a single line of text at the top of a page is called a **widow**. The Widow/Orphan control feature can help you avoid these. Similarly, the Block Protect option ensures that selected blocks of text are kept together on a page. Jennifer wants you to be sure that no widows or orphans appear in the document. She also asks you to be sure that section headings stay with their respective text blocks and don't split between pages. To keep text together, you use the Widow/Orphan option and the Block Protect option. But first, Jennifer has asked you to add a new beginning sentence to the section, "Be Positive." You add this sentence for her.

Steps

1. Scroll to the bottom of Page 1, click before **Get**, type **A positive attitude comes from the writer and is conveyed through the written word.**, then scroll to the beginning of page 2
   The first sentence in the Be Positive section is an orphan. It appears as a single line on the bottom of page 1.

QuickTip

The Widow/Orphan control feature is in effect from the insertion point to the end of the document.

2. Press **[Ctrl][Home]**, click **Format** on the menu bar, then click **Keep Text Together**
   The Keep Text Together dialog box opens, as shown in Figure E-6. Regardless of the edits you make to this document, the software controls the flow of text so you never have a widow or an orphan in the document.
3. Click the **Widow/Orphan check box**, then click **OK**
4. Click the **Next Page button**
   The text is adjusted so that a single line of text does not exist at the bottom of the page. The last line of text from the first page has been moved to the second page so that an orphan does not exist. However, now the section "Be Positive" is split between the first and second pages. You want this section all on one page. You use Block Protect to correct this problem.
5. Select **Be Positive** at the bottom of page 1, then continue dragging the mouse until you have selected the entire paragraph at the top of page 2

Time To

- Spell check
- Save
- Print
- Close

6. Right-click the selected text, then click **Block Protect**
   The text "Be Positive" is now together on page 2 with the paragraph. See Figure E-7. You are pleased with the finished product.

Using the Conditional end of page command

Another way to keep blocks of text together on a single page is to use the Conditional end of page command in the Keep Text Together dialog box. You can use this to prevent a paragraph from splitting between pages by setting the number of lines to keep together. Click Format, click Keep Text Together, click the Conditional end of page check box, type the number to identify the number of lines to keep together, then click OK.

FIGURE E-6: Keep Text Together dialog box

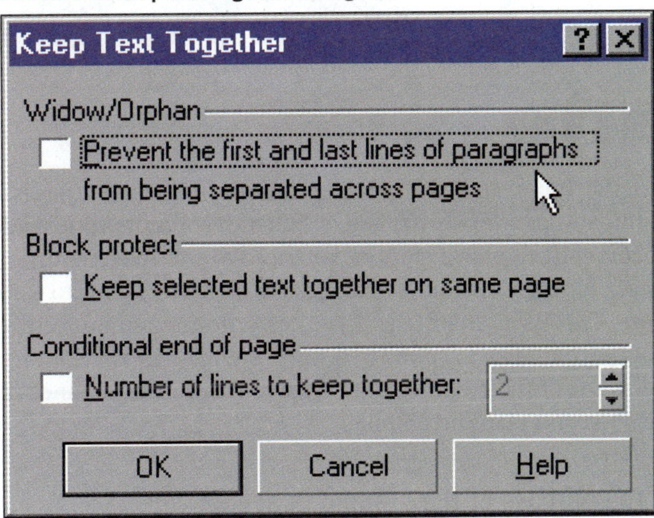

FIGURE E-7: Text together on one page

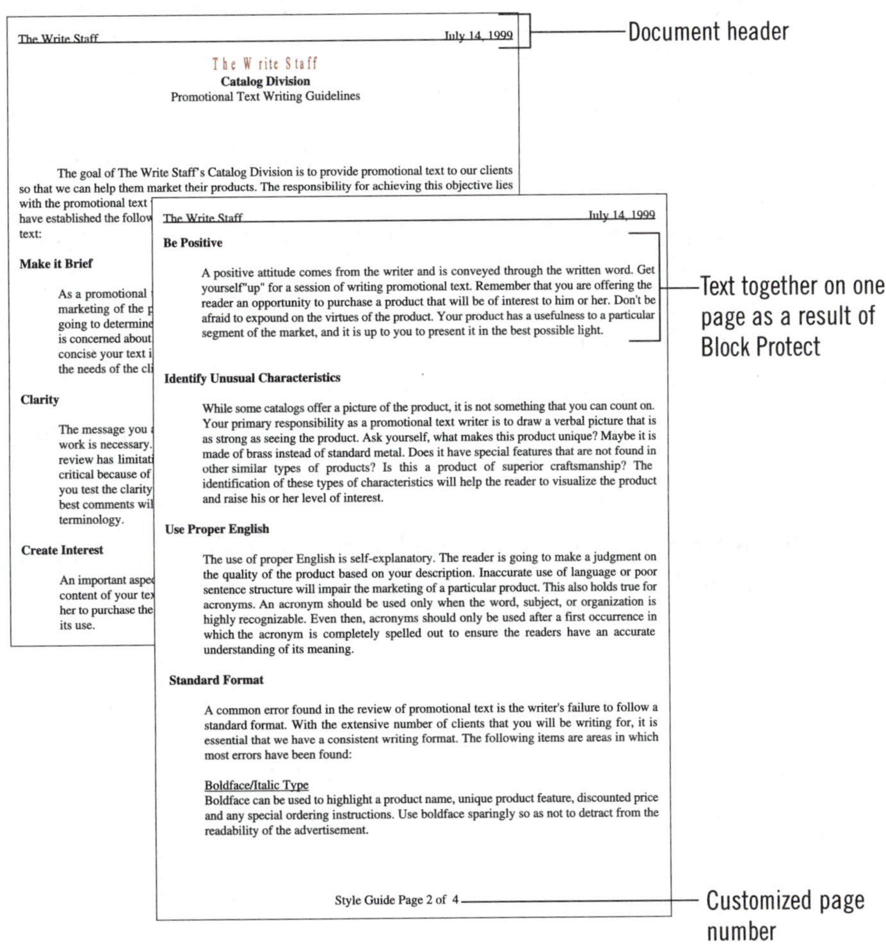

The Write Staff July 14, 1999

The Write Staff
Catalog Division
Promotional Text Writing Guidelines

The goal of The Write Staff's Catalog Division is to provide promotional text to our clients so that we can help them market their products. The responsibility for achieving this objective lies with the promotional text [...] have established the follow[...] text:

Make it Brief

As a promotional [...] marketing of the p[...] going to determine[...] is concerned about[...] concise your text i[...] the needs of the cl[...]

Clarity

The message you [...] work is necessary. [...] review has limitati[...] critical because of [...] you test the clarity [...] best comments wi[...] terminology.

Create Interest

An important aspe[...] content of your te[...] her to purchase the [...] its use.

The Write Staff July 14, 1999

Be Positive

A positive attitude comes from the writer and is conveyed through the written word. Get yourself"up" for a session of writing promotional text. Remember that you are offering the reader an opportunity to purchase a product that will be of interest to him or her. Don't be afraid to expound on the virtues of the product. Your product has a usefulness to a particular segment of the market, and it is up to you to present it in the best possible light.

Identify Unusual Characteristics

While some catalogs offer a picture of the product, it is not something that you can count on. Your primary responsibility as a promotional text writer is to draw a verbal picture that is as strong as seeing the product. Ask yourself, what makes this product unique? Maybe it is made of brass instead of standard metal. Does it have special features that are not found in other similar types of products? Is this a product of superior craftsmanship? The identification of these types of characteristics will help the reader to visualize the product and raise his or her level of interest.

Use Proper English

The use of proper English is self-explanatory. The reader is going to make a judgment on the quality of the product based on your description. Inaccurate use of language or poor sentence structure will impair the marketing of a particular product. This also holds true for acronyms. An acronym should be used only when the word, subject, or organization is highly recognizable. Even then, acronyms should only be used after a first occurrence in which the acronym is completely spelled out to ensure the readers have an accurate understanding of its meaning.

Standard Format

A common error found in the review of promotional text is the writer's failure to follow a standard format. With the extensive number of clients that you will be writing for, it is essential that we have a consistent writing format. The following items are areas in which most errors have been found:

Boldface/Italic Type
Boldface can be used to highlight a product name, unique product feature, discounted price and any special ordering instructions. Use boldface sparingly so as not to detract from the readability of the advertisement.

Style Guide Page 2 of 4

Inserting a page break

In multiple-page documents, page breaks are automatically set for you and are determined by your page margins. However, you can insert a **hard page break** anywhere in the document. A hard page break generates a new page at a specified point no matter how much text is on the page. To insert a hard page break, position the insertion point where you want the page to end. Click Format on the menu bar, click Page, click Force Page, select the Start New Page option button, then click OK. A bold, horizontal line appears in the document to show that a hard page break has been inserted.

Planning a Graphic Image

You can enhance the appearance of your document with graphic images. Graphic images can be used to create company letterheads, explain or enhance concepts, or just add decorative touches to your printed documents. To plan a graphic, you need to consider its purpose, type, size, and placement on the page. Table E-2 includes many terms that are useful to know when working with graphics. The Write Staff was asked to write the announcement for the fund-raising event, *A Weekend at the Movies,* sponsored by the Village Public Library in Chatham. Michael Benjamin, the director of the graphics department, asks you to enhance the document by adding a graphic image. First you plan the graphic.

Steps 1 2 3 4

1. **Determine the purpose of the graphic image**
   You'd like to use a graphic that promotes the message of the text and catches the reader's attention.

2. **Choose the type of graphic image to use**
   There are many types of graphics, such as pictures, logos, charts, or borders. **Clipart** is a collection of images or symbols stored on disk or available on your hard drive as part of word processing programs. To announce the fund-raising event, you select an image of a group of people to symbolize that everyone is welcome to attend the event.

3. **Decide where to insert the graphic image into the document**
   Where you place a graphic affects the way text appears in the document. You might need to move and resize the graphic after inserting it in the document. To start, you plan to place it near the top of the announcement.

4. **Determine the size of the graphic image**
   You can enlarge or shrink graphics to suit the paper size or the amount of surrounding text. You don't want the image to overwhelm the text, yet you want it to be visible and significant in the document.

5. **Create a rough sketch of how the graphic should look in the document**
   Figure E-8 shows a rough sketch of the graphic in the document.

FIGURE E-8: Sketch of the document with graphic

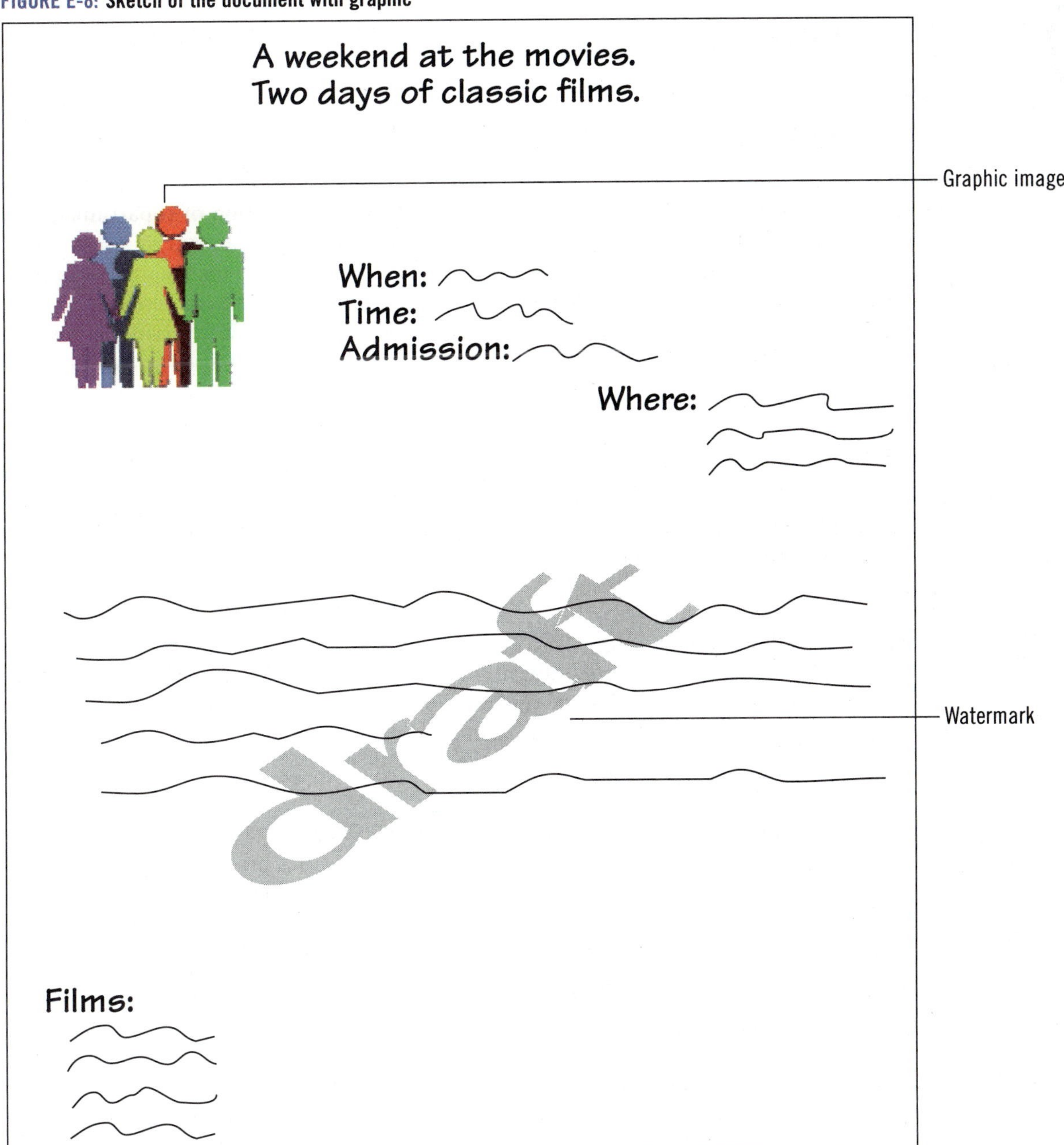

TABLE E-2: Graphics terms

term	description
Graphics figure	Clipart or an image that can be brought into a document; WordPerfect graphics figures are designated by the extension .wpg
Graphics box	A box that can contain a figure, an equation, or text
Sizing handles	Small black squares on the graphics box that indicate that the graphics box is selected and ready to be edited, sized, or moved
Image	Charts, logos, drawings created in the WordPerfect graphic format or another graphic format
Text	Quotations or other text that is set off from the main document
Equations	Mathematical, scientific, or business formulas and expressions
Tables	Spreadsheets, statistical data, or text
Charts	Graphs, including bar charts, line charts, or pie charts, to represent numerical data

Inserting a Graphic Image

Once you determine the purpose of a graphic image, you can choose one that will enhance your document. You can use the WordPerfect scrapbook, which is a collection of clipart images, to find images to include in your document, or you can use the Graphics menu to insert clipart images, logos, or drawings into your document. After planning the graphic, you have a clear image of how you want the announcement to look. While the text is interesting and the character formatting helps, the page doesn't really attract attention. You decide to insert a graphic to bring the announcement to life.

Steps

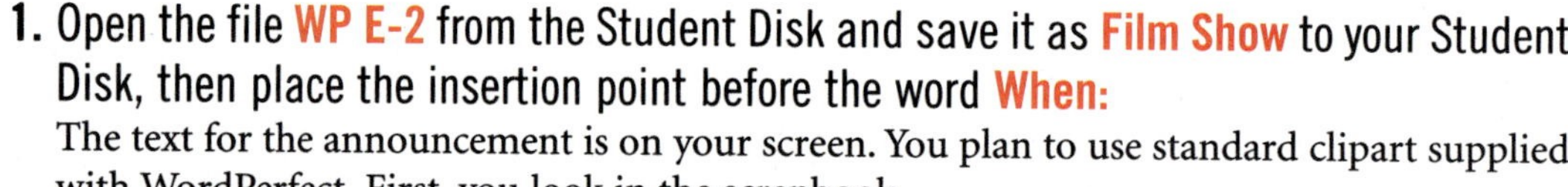

1. **Open the file WP E-2 from the Student Disk and save it as Film Show to your Student Disk, then place the insertion point before the word When:**
   The text for the announcement is on your screen. You plan to use standard clipart supplied with WordPerfect. First, you look in the scrapbook.

Trouble?
If you don't see pictures of the clipart, right-click the scrapbook background, click View, then click Large icons.

2. **Click the Clipart/Scrapbook button on the WordPerfect Toolbar, then scroll to the bottom of the scrapbook file**
   The scrapbook appears. You could drag and drop images from the scrapbook to your document. However, after reviewing the images you realize the clipart you need is not in the scrapbook. You will get the clipart image from a folder.

3. **Close the Scrapbook window**

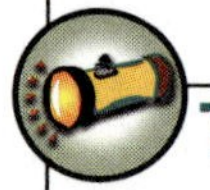

Trouble?
If you can't find the list of WordPerfect graphic images, make sure you are looking in the Graphics folder. If you find yourself in the Insert Image - Clipart window, click the folder button. The .wpg files should be on the same drive as your WordPerfect program files.

4. **Click Insert on the menu bar, click Graphics, then click From File**
   The Insert Image - Graphics window appears. WordPerfect has provided clipart related to each of the topics indicated by the file folder name. Graphic images within each folder are listed in alphabetical order. Each image has been saved with a descriptive name to help you make your selection. You want to preview the images before you select them.

5. **Click the Preview button on the Insert Image - Graphic window property bar**
   The Viewer Manager Preview window appears.

6. **Double-click Pictures, double-click Business, then click Group of People**
   The Group of People graphic image appears in the Preview window as shown in Figure E-9. This is the image you were looking for. You insert it in your document.

7. **Click the Insert button**
   Compare your screen with Figure E-10. A colorful picture of a group of people has been inserted in the document. When a graphic is imported, it is automatically placed inside a graphics box. Notice how the lines of text wrap around the image. The way the text wraps around an image is called **word wrap**. Often, when you insert an image, you need to adjust the word wrap.

8. **Click outside the graphics box to deselect the image, then save your work**
   The sizing handles on the graphics box are no longer visible. If you wish, you can add captions to any image you insert in your document.

FIGURE E-9: Insert Image dialog box

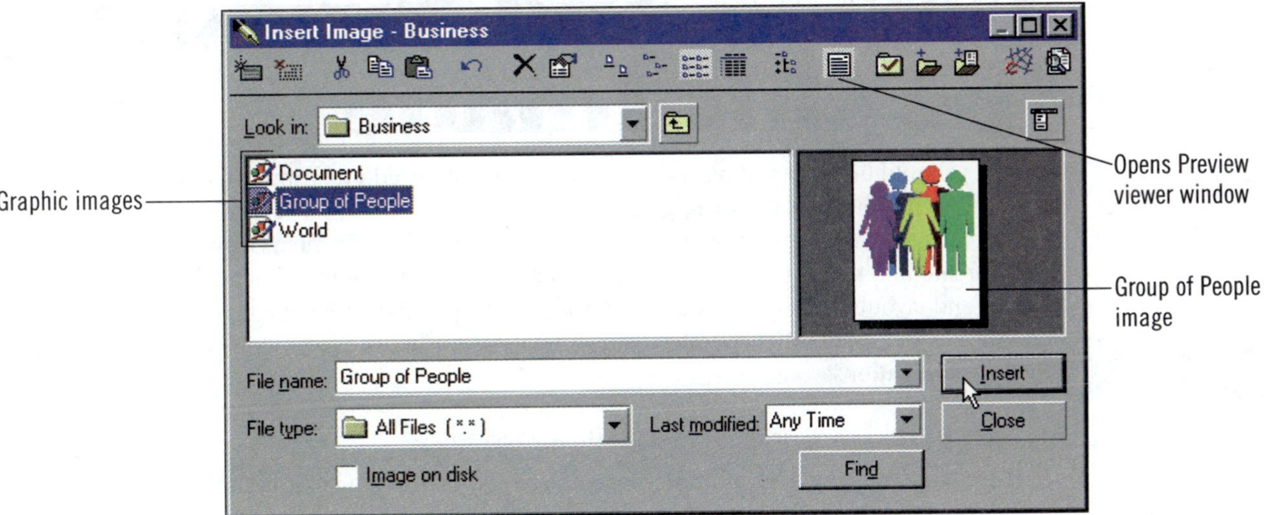

FIGURE E-10: Group of People image inserted in document

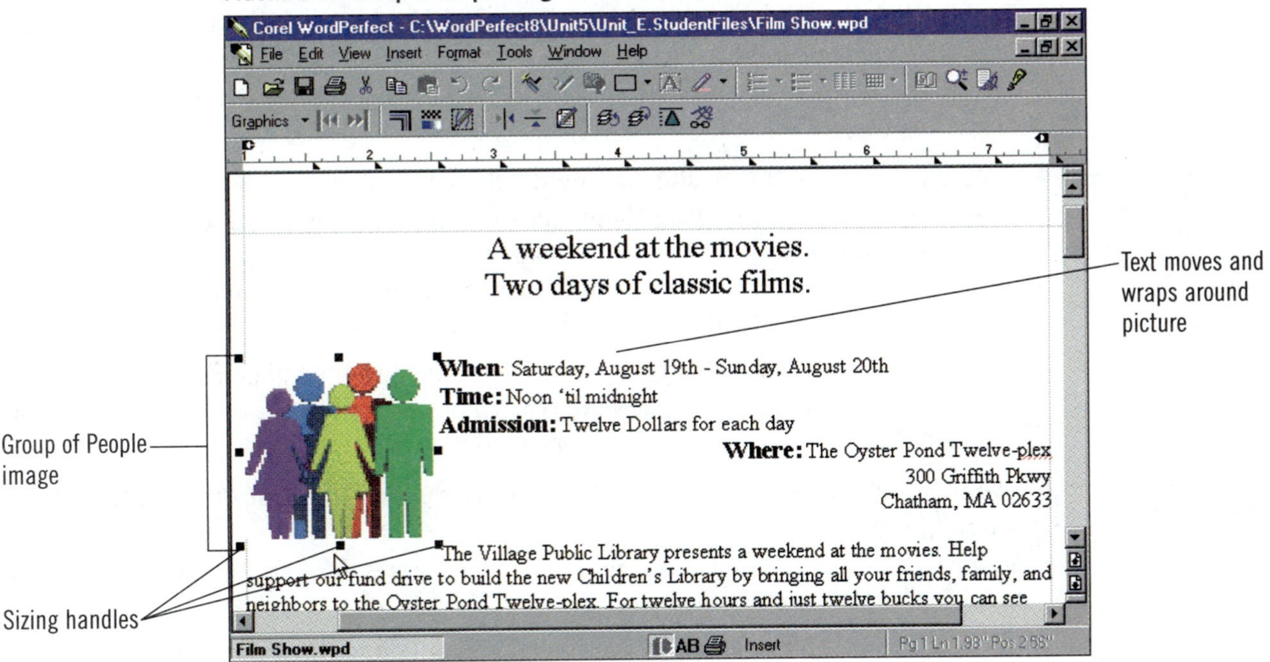

Corel WordPerfect - C:\WordPerfect8\Unit5\Unit_E.StudentFiles\Film Show.wpd
File Edit View Insert Format Tools Window Help
Graphics
A weekend at the movies.
Two days of classic films.
When: Saturday, August 19th - Sunday, August 20th
Time: Noon 'til midnight
Admission: Twelve Dollars for each day
Where: The Oyster Pond Twelve-plex
300 Griffith Pkwy
Chatham, MA 02633
The Village Public Library presents a weekend at the movies. Help
support our fund drive to build the new Children's Library by bringing all your friends, family, and
neighbors to the Oyster Pond Twelve-plex. For twelve hours and just twelve bucks you can see
Film Show.wpd
Insert
Text moves and wraps around picture
Group of People image
Sizing handles

Adding captions

You might want to add a **caption** to the graphic image. A caption is text that describes a graphic image in a document. Click the image, then right-click. Click Caption on the QuickMenu to add a caption to a graphic. The Box Caption dialog box that opens has options for positioning, styling, and editing captions. One option also automatically numbers each caption according to the location of the graphic within the document.

WordPerfect 8

Moving and Sizing a Graphic Image

Graphics should be sized and placed in a document so they add to, rather than detract from, the message. A graphic that is too large overpowers the text; one that is badly placed draws the reader's attention away from the text. You can type precise measurements or you can use the drag and drop method to position graphic images.  Jennifer and Michael review the document for text and layout. They decide that the Group of People image sets the text off-center and that the image is too small. Michael offers you some ideas for better placement. You move the image per his specifications.

Steps

QuickTip

To duplicate the graphic elsewhere in the document, select it, click Edit, then click Copy. Click the location in the document where you want the image, click Edit, then click Paste.

1. **Click the Group of People image, then right-click**
   The Group of People graphic is selected. The QuickMenu, which is shown in Figure E-11, opens with the tools you need to edit, place, and style the image.
2. **Click Position**
   The Box Position dialog box opens. Michael wants you to place the image in the upper-right corner. He suggests that you place the image .323" from the right margin and .247" from the top margin. You enter these values to see how the new placement looks.
3. **Double-click the Horizontal text box, type .323, double-click the Vertical text box, type .247, then click OK**
   The graphic moves to the specified position. However, the text is not well placed around the image. You need to adjust the word wrap.

Trouble?

If you can't select a graphic box by clicking on it, click Edit on the menu bar, then click Edit Graphic Box.

4. **If necessary, click the Group of People image, right-click the Group of People image, click Wrap in the QuickMenu, click Behind text, then click OK**
   This repositions the way the text wraps around the graphic box. After reviewing the document, you decide that the top of the document is too crowded. The image will look better to the right of the list of films. Use Full Page view to see where to place the graphic.
5. **Click the Zoom button on the WordPerfect Toolbar, then click Full Page**
   The document appears in Full Page view. When moving a graphic, be careful not to click on one of the handles, or you will resize the box rather than reposition it.

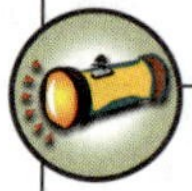

Trouble?

Be sure the Group of People image is selected.

6. **Use the drag pointer to drag the Group of People image down the page and to the right of the list of films**
   Your page should look similar to Figure E-12. The image is too small for the space. You use the sizing handles to resize the image.
7. **Click , click 100%, scroll to see the complete image, then position the insertion point on the upper-right corner sizing handle**
   The insertion point changes to as shown in Figure E-13. Resize the image so that it uses up more of the white space. Exact measurements are not critical at this time.
8. **Drag the sizing handle up and to the right to resize the image**
   You can use the sizing handles around the image to make it wider and longer. Since changing the size of the graphic box may result in poor text wrapping, you decide to change the word wrap setting back to Square.

Time To

✔ Save

9. **Right-click the Group of People image, click Wrap, click Square, click OK, then click outside the graphics box to deselect the image**

FIGURE E-11: Graphics QuickMenu

FIGURE E-12: Moving the image

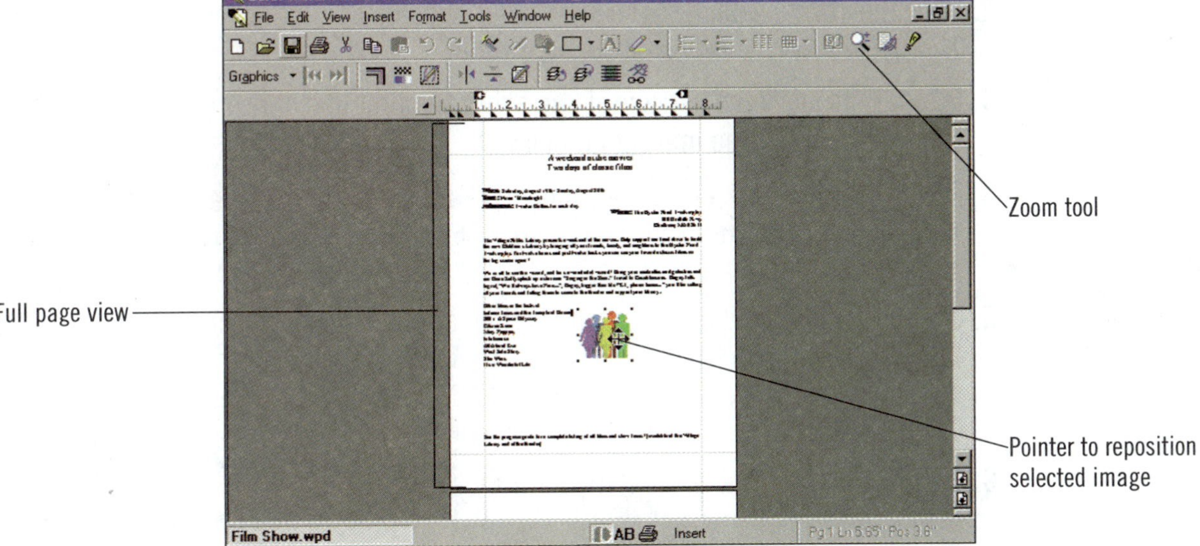

FIGURE E-13: Resizing the image

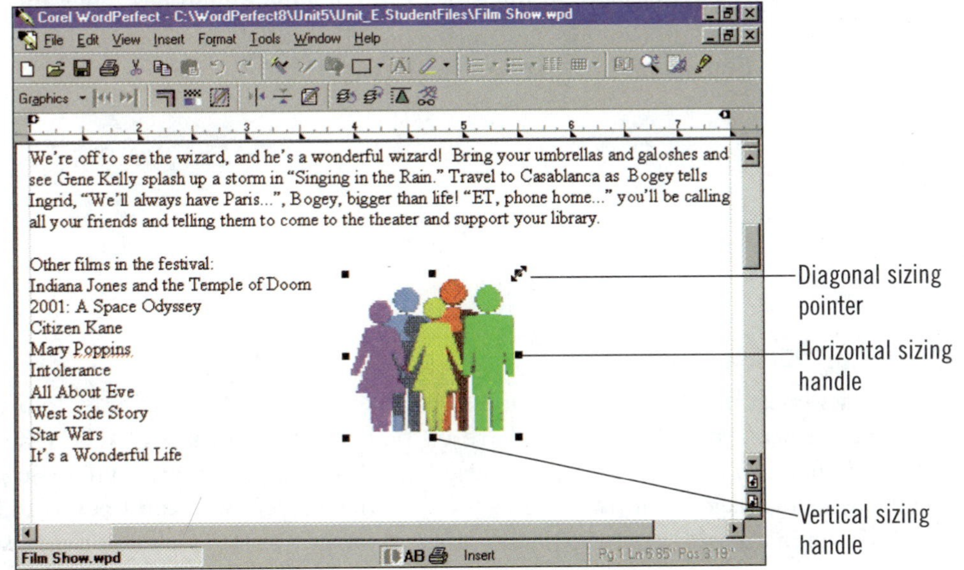

WordPerfect 8

WordPerfect 8

Adding a Graphical Line to Your Document

Horizontal and vertical lines are graphic elements that can be used to separate text on a page. Lines can be inserted anywhere in a document. You can adjust the thickness, length, width, appearance, color, or endpoints of the line. After reviewing the document, you decide that the blocks of text will read better if separated by a horizontal line, so you add a line.

Steps

1. Click before the text **The Village Public Library presents** in the first paragraph, click **Insert** on the menu bar, click **Shape**, then click **Horizontal Line**
   A horizontal line is inserted in the document, but it cuts through the text. You select the line to move it to a better position.
2. Move the insertion point to the line until it appears as ↖, then click the **horizontal line**
   The line is selected as shown in Figure E-14.
3. Drag ✥ to move the horizontal line above the first line of text in the paragraph, then center it between the margin guidelines
4. Right-click the **horizontal line**, then click **Edit Horizontal Line** from the QuickMenu
   The Edit Graphics Line dialog box opens as shown in Figure E-15. You decide to change the line style.
5. Click the **Line Styles button** at the bottom of the dialog box, scroll down the list, click **Thick/Thin 2**, then click **Select**
   The line style you selected is shown in the Edit Graphics Line dialog box. Before confirming this selection, you decide you want to see other possible line styles.
6. Click the **Line attribute Line style button** [Line Styles...]
   Graphical representations of available line styles are shown. You decide you are happy with your original selection.
7. Click anywhere in the Edit Graphics Line dialog box, click **OK**, then save your work
   The Edit Graphics Line dialog box closes. There is a thin horizontal line over a thicker horizontal line, as shown in Figure E-16.

Trouble?

Be sure the line is selected.

CLUES TO USE

Using Border/Fill

Borders frame an image on a page. When you insert an image in a document, you may want it to have a border to clearly define it on the page. You can also add fill patterns to an image. A **fill pattern** fills the empty spaces in an image with a pattern that is either colored or a shade of gray. To use Border/Fill, click an image to select it, right-click, then click Border/Fill. When the Box Border/Fill dialog box appears, click the Border tab if you want to add a border to an image. Click the Fill tab if you want to add a fill.

FIGURE E-14: Horizontal line

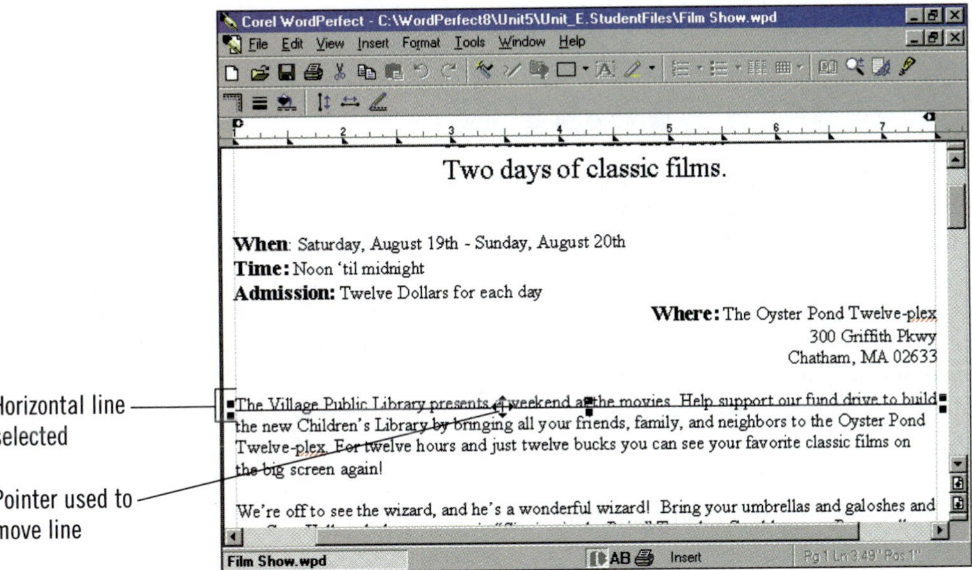

FIGURE E-15: Edit Graphics Line dialog box

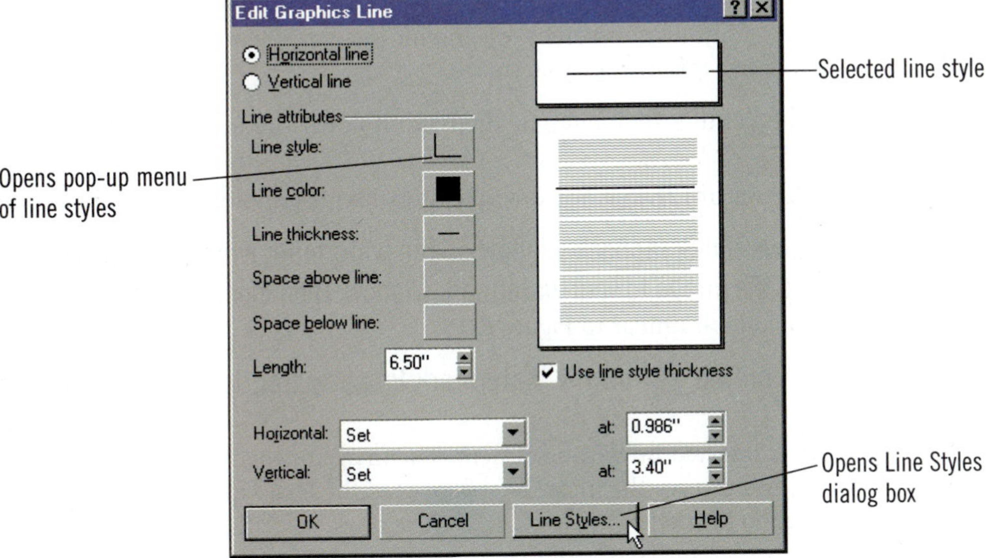

FIGURE E-16: Edited line in text

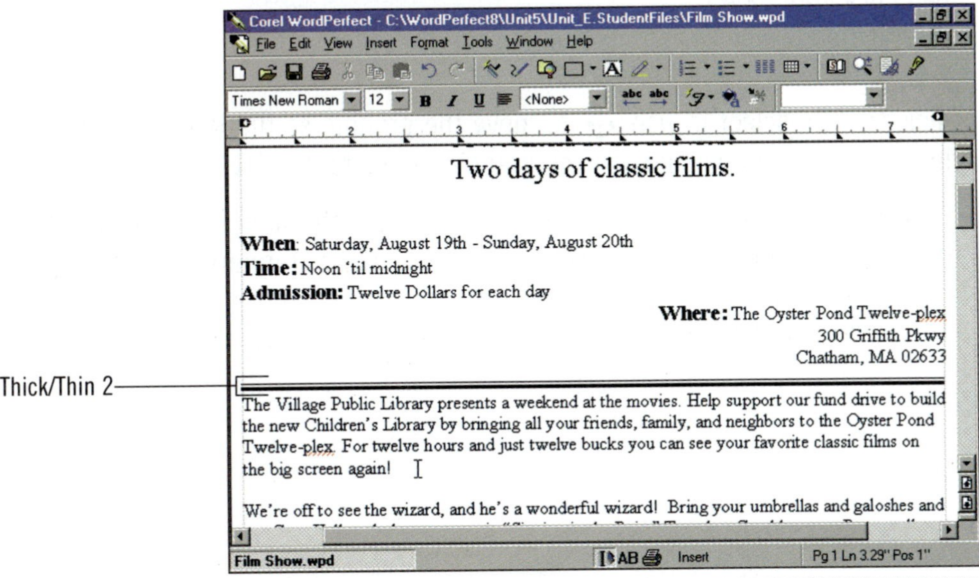

Creating a Watermark

A **watermark** is a drawing, logo, clipart image, or headline-sized text located behind the text in your document. For example, if you need to create a memo for the company picnic, you might want to include the company logo in the background of the memo. Watermarks function much the same as headers and footers. You can have one or two of them per section, and edit them individually. Michael reminds you that the dates, times, and admission fees listed on the flyer are tentative and that they could change. Michael wants to be sure that this flyer is not copied and distributed by mistake. He asks you to make it clear that this copy of the flyer is a draft copy. You decide to add a watermark to the document that clearly identifies it as a draft copy.

1. **Click Insert on the menu bar, then click Watermark**
   The Watermark dialog box opens.
2. **If necessary, click the Watermark A option button, then click Create**
   The Watermark Property Bar appears, and the watermark window is in Full Page view, as shown in Figure E-17. You know you have a graphic image of the word "draft" in your scrapbook. You want to use this as your watermark.
3. **Click on the WordPerfect Toolbar, then scroll down the screen to find the image of the word draft**
   The image is titled watrm121.wpg. You drag and drop this image onto your watermark window.
4. **If necessary, move the Scrapbook window so the watermark window is partially visible, click draft, drag the image to your watermark window, then close the Scrapbook window**
   Your screen should look similar to Figure E-18.
5. **Click the Close button on the Watermark Property Bar, then scroll down to view the document**
   The watermark is inserted in your document. The image of the word "draft" fills the page behind the text. You can see the image as well as read the text. However, you see that some adjustments need to be made.
6. **Click Insert, click Watermark, if necessary click the Watermark A option button, then click Edit**
   The watermark window appears. You can edit the watermark like any other graphic image by using the Watermark Property Bar.
7. **Click draft to select it, use ✥ to move the graphic so the letter t is in the upper-right corner, then click outside the graphic image to deselect it**
8. **Click the Watermark Shading button on the Watermark Property Bar, type 15 in the Image shading text box, click OK, then close the watermark window**
   Your document should look similar to Figure E-19. You are pleased with the results and print a copy to give to Michael.

Trouble?

If the Insert Image dialog box opens, close the dialog box, then click on the WordPerfect Toolbar.

Time To

- Spell check
- Save
- Print
- Exit

FIGURE E-17: **Watermark window**

FIGURE E-18: **Watermark**

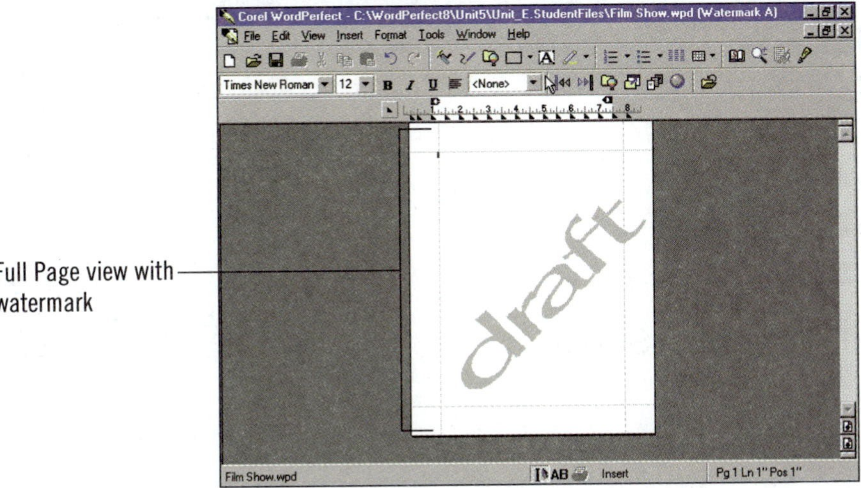

FIGURE E-19: **Printed document with watermark**

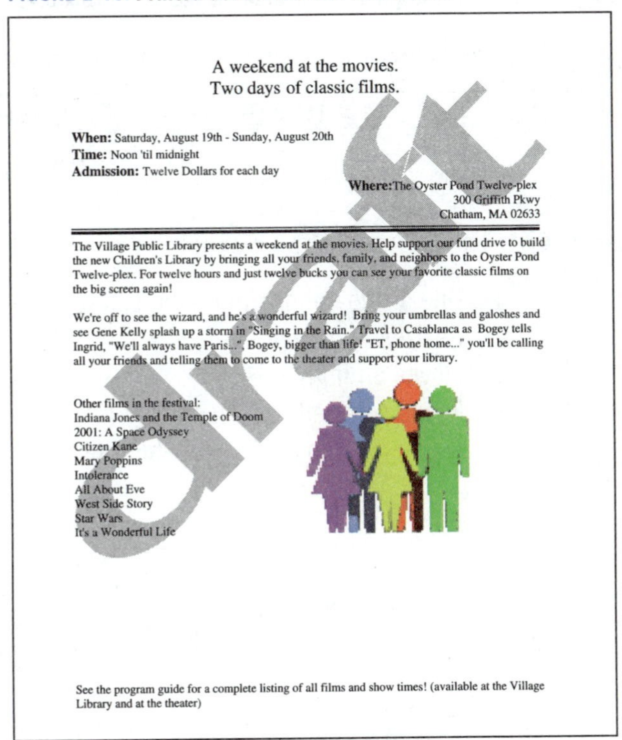

A weekend at the movies.
Two days of classic films.

When: Saturday, August 19th - Sunday, August 20th
Time: Noon 'til midnight
Admission: Twelve Dollars for each day

Where: The Oyster Pond Twelve-plex
300 Griffith Pkwy
Chatham, MA 02633

The Village Public Library presents a weekend at the movies. Help support our fund drive to build the new Children's Library by bringing all your friends, family, and neighbors to the Oyster Pond Twelve-plex. For twelve hours and just twelve bucks you can see your favorite classic films on the big screen again!

We're off to see the wizard, and he's a wonderful wizard! Bring your umbrellas and galoshes and see Gene Kelly splash up a storm in "Singing in the Rain." Travel to Casablanca as Bogey tells Ingrid, "We'll always have Paris...". Bogey, bigger than life! "ET, phone home..." you'll be calling all your friends and telling them to come to the theater and support your library.

Other films in the festival:
Indiana Jones and the Temple of Doom
2001: A Space Odyssey
Citizen Kane
Mary Poppins
Intolerance
All About Eve
West Side Story
Star Wars
It's a Wonderful Life

See the program guide for a complete listing of all films and show times! (available at the Village Library and at the theater)

Practice

► Concepts Review

Label each element in the WordPerfect window shown in Figure E-20.

FIGURE E-20

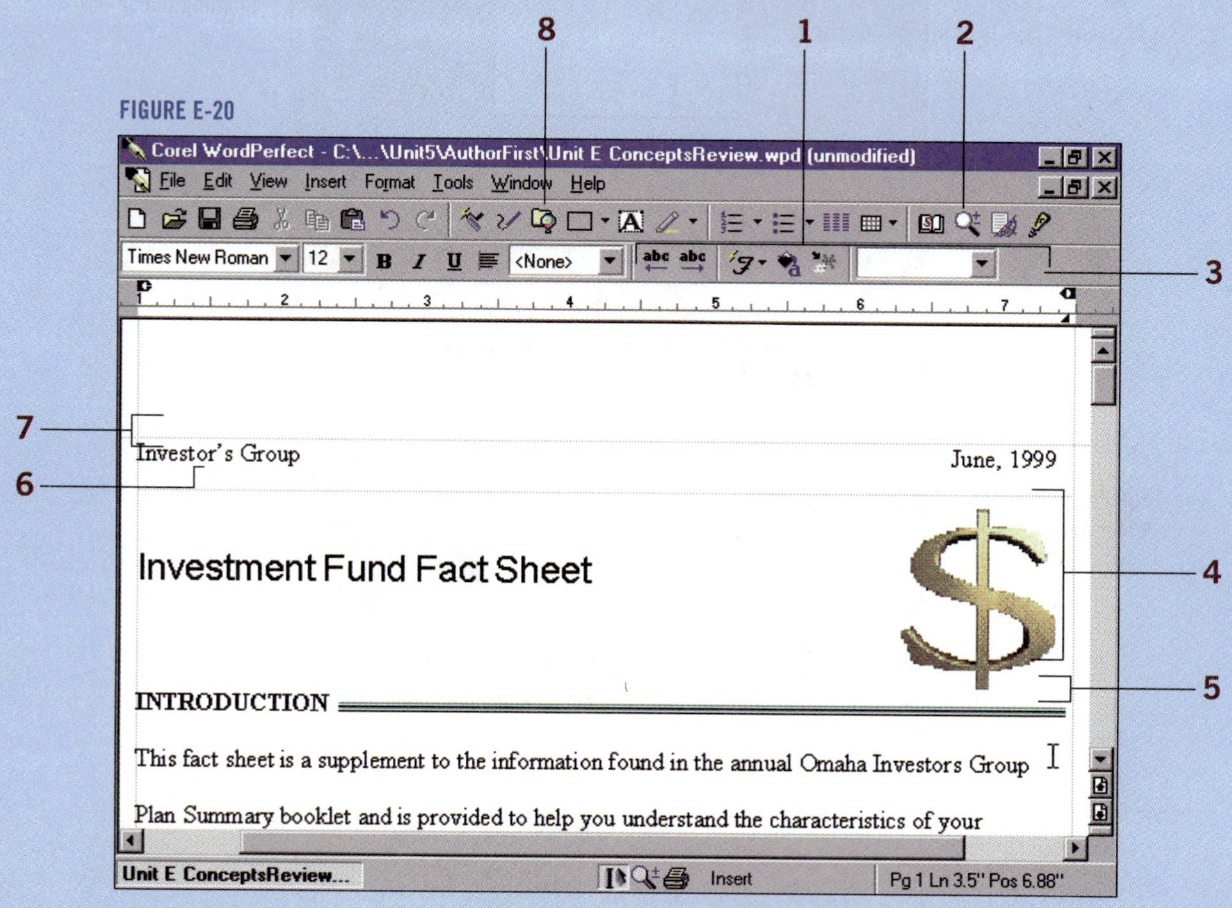

Match each WordPerfect term with the phrase that describes it.

9. ✥
10. **Watermark**
11. **Line Styles**
12. **Block Protect**
13. ⤢

a. One of the options in the Edit Graphics Line dialog box
b. Resizes an image
c. Moves an image
d. Keeps selected text together
e. A graphic image placed behind text

Select the best answer from the list of choices.

14. Which is not a Headers/Footers Property Bar button?
- a. Distance
- b. Next
- c. Position
- d. Page number

15. What is a widow?
- a. A sentence that is split between two pages.
- b. The line of text in the middle of a paragraph appearing at the bottom of a page.
- c. The first line of a paragraph appearing alone at the bottom of a page.
- d. The last line of a paragraph appearing alone at the top of a page.

16. To skip a header on a particular page without deleting it from all pages
- a. Click Format, click Page, then click Hide.
- b. Click Format, click Page, then click Suppress.
- c. Click Edit, click Header, then click Close.
- d. Click Edit, click Page, click Delete.

17. To ensure that you don't have a word sitting by itself at the bottom of your page, you should
- a. Create a footer.
- b. Write long paragraphs.
- c. Paginate the document.
- d. Activate the Widow/Orphan option.

18. When you paginate a document, the page numbers
- a. Begin on the page where the insertion point is located.
- b. Print on every other page.
- c. Print as a footer at the bottom of the page.
- d. Must be in the same font that is used throughout the document.

19. A graphic image
- a. Must be inserted at the top of a document.
- b. Must be inserted at the bottom of a document.
- c. Cannot be moved once it is in a document.
- d. Can be inserted anywhere in a document.

20. To locate clipart stored on the hard disk
- a. Click Insert, click Graphic, then click From File.
- b. Click Format, click Image, then click Get Picture.
- c. Click Tools, then click Find Graphic.
- d. Click View, then click Graphic.

21. When you right-click a graphic
- a. The graphic is deleted.
- b. A QuickMenu appears.
- c. The graphic moves to a new location.
- d. A border appears around the graphic.

22. A watermark is created
- a. When you create a header or footer.
- b. In the document window.
- c. In the watermark window.
- d. Whenever you insert a graphic.

Skills Review

1. **Add and customize page numbers.**
   a. Start WordPerfect, open file WP E-3 then save it as "Investment Fund Fact Sheet" on your Student Disk.
   b. Move the insertion point to the beginning of the document.
   c. Click Format, click Page, click Numbering, click Position list box arrow, then click bottom right.
   d. Select a page numbering format in the Select Page Numbering Format dialog box.
   e. Scroll through the document. Notice that the page number appears at the bottom right of each page.
2. **Insert headers and footers.**
   a. Move the insertion point to the beginning of the document.
   b. Click Insert, then click Header/Footer.
   c. Create Header A as "Investment Fund Fact Sheet".
   d. Scroll through the document. Notice that the header appears at the top of every page.
   e. Move the insertion point to the beginning of the document.
   f. Click Format, click Page, then click Suppress.
   g. Click Header A, then click OK.
3. **Keep text together.**
   a. Move the insertion point to the beginning of the document.
   b. Open the Keep Text Together dialog box.
   c. Set the Widow/Orphan control feature so that no widows and orphans appear in the document.
   d. Scroll through the document. Notice that no single, isolated lines of text appear at the top or bottom of the pages. Also notice that the section Fund Performance is split between two pages.
   e. Select "Fund Performance" through "(and risk) for each fund" and use the QuickMenu to activate the Block Protect control.
   f. Preview your document, then save it.
4. **Plan and insert a graphic.**
   a. Look through the document and see where you might want to insert a graphic. Place the insertion point in this area.
   b. Click Insert on the menu bar, click Graphics, then click From File.
   c. Find the Graphics Folder, double-click Pictures, then click Finance to open the Insert Image - Finance window.
   d. Select the image "Dollar Sign", then click the Insert button.
   e. Preview the document with the graphic inserted.
   f. Deselect the image.
5. **Move and size a graphic.**
   a. Select the graphic.
   b. Drag the image to the upper-right corner.
   c. Use the sizing handles to make the image small enough to fit in the upper-right corner of the first page.
   d. Right-click the graphic image, click Wrap, then place the image behind the text.
   e. Copy and paste the graphic to the upper-left corner.
   f. View the page using the Zoom feature, then return the document to 100% view.
   g. Deselect the image, then save your changes.
6. **Add a graphical line to your document.**
   a. Use the Insert menu to insert a horizontal line between the graphic and the introduction.
   b. Right-click on the line to access the Edit Horizontal line dialog box.
   c. Select a line style in the Line Styles dialog box.
   d. Verify that you have chosen a line style that you like in the Edit Graphics Line dialog box, then click OK.

e. Preview the document at 50%, then return to 100%.
f. Save your document.

7. **Create a watermark.**
   a. You want to add a watermark using an image of the world. Click Insert on the menu bar, click Watermark, click Watermark A, then click Create.
   b. Click Insert from the menu bar, click Graphics, then navigate your way to the Insert Image - Business window, where you will find the image of the world.
   c. Select the world image, then click the Insert button.
   d. Close the watermark window to see the watermark with the text.
   e. Preview the full page, then move the watermark, if necessary.
   f. If the watermark is too dark, adjust the shading using the Watermark Shading button.
   g. Spell check and save the document.
   h. Print the document, then close your document and exit WordPerfect.

Independent Challenges

1. The United Investor's Group has hired you to write a prospectus detailing their most profitable investment products. The document, which will be presented to potential investors, must be well-organized and clearly written. To complete this independent challenge:

1. Start WordPerfect, open the file WP E-4 and save it as "United Investor's Group" to your Student Disk.
2. Paginate the document beginning with the first page.
3. Format the pagination with a fancy font and include the words "Fact Sheet" before the page number.
4. Create a header for the document that includes the company name and date.
5. Suppress the header on the first page.
6. Turn on the Widow/Orphan control.
7. Insert a graphic that is relevant to the content.
8. Move and resize the graphic.
9. Insert lines and format them using features of your choice.
10. Create a watermark that shows the words "File Copy".
11. Spell check, save, and print the document, then exit WordPerfect.

2. Multiple-page documents are common when you create reports for school. You have probably written many of them throughout your school career. Examples are term papers, book reports, or research projects. When you create a report for school, it is important to proofread a draft copy before printing a final copy to submit. Find a recent report to edit or use file WP E-5 on your Student Disk.
To complete this independent challenge:

1. Start WordPerfect, open your report as a WordPerfect document or open WP E-5 and save it as My Report.
2. Paginate the report. (*Hint*: You can include pagination in either the header or footer.)
3. Create a header. Include the title of the report and the class the report is for in the report header.
4. Suppress the header on the first page of the report.
5. Create a footer that includes your name and the current date.
6. Include graphics such as charts or informative art to enhance the report.
7. Include lines to help draw attention to the sections or important information.
8. Create a watermark that identifies this paper as a draft copy.
9. Use Spell Check, print the report, proofread it, then make appropriate adjustments.
10. Save the file, then print the report and exit WordPerfect.

3. Sell It! is a Seattle-based company that specializes in training sales representatives. As an employee of the company, you write training materials for the clients who attend the company seminars. You are currently preparing a pamphlet titled "How to Sell Anything" for an upcoming seminar. The pamphlet provides tips on how to make a product more marketable, as well as advice on knowing your customer. Your instructor will let you know if you should complete this as a group or individual assignment.
To complete this independent challenge:

1. Plan the pamphlet. Decide what tips you will include on how to be a good salesperson. Include sections on topics such as selling with confidence, knowing your product, and understanding the competitors and their products. You should also detail the importance of being aware of your customers' needs. You will want to include graphics, lines, and a watermark to enhance the appearance of the pamphlet.
2. Start WordPerfect, open a new document, then type a first draft of the pamphlet, with a title page at the beginning of the document.
3. Insert the following quote at an appropriate location within the document: "Knowing something about your customer is just as important as knowing everything about your product."
4. Set the page numbering to print at the bottom center of each page.
5. Create a header with the title of the pamphlet, "How to Sell Anything."
6. Suppress the header and page numbering so that they appear only on the second and subsequent pages.
7. Use the Widow/Orphan control feature at the beginning of the document.
8. Use the Block Protect option to keep blocks of text together.
9. Use the Preview mode in the Insert Image window to find and insert three graphics that enhance the text.
10. Add lines and enhance the lines using the features of your choice.
11. Save, print, and close the document, then exit WordPerfect.

4. Several of your friends and neighbors have asked you to write a newsletter for the community. The newsletter is a new project that is intended to keep everyone informed about newsworthy items, social events, political changes, and news updates. Your instructor will let you know if you should complete this as a group or individual assignment.

Design the newsletter so that it has a few sections. These sections should have heads that are set apart using different character formats. For example: "New and Noteworthy" could discuss any new projects or activities in your neighborhood. "Our Neighbors" could include any news about the people in the neighborhood such as births, weddings, engagements, and graduations. "The Social Scene" could discuss any parties, picnics, dance recitals, movie reviews, garage or tag sales. "Our Community" could cover the political scene. You could also include a "Classified" section.

To complete this independent challenge:

1. Plan the newsletter. Do some scouting, interviewing, and reporting. Take notes about what you want to include. Decide what items you are going to cover in the first edition. Decide what graphics you will include to enhance the document.
2. Start WordPerfect, open a new document, then type a first draft of the newsletter.
3. Prepare a heading for the document. Some ideas include "The Neighborhood News," "Caryn's Chronicles," or "People's Press". Be sure to include a date in the heading.
4. Create footers or headers as appropriate.
5. Use the Widow/Orphan control feature and the Block Protect option as appropriate.
6. Insert at least one graphic per page. Include captions for each graphic.
7. Use word wrap as needed. Include borders when appropriate.
8. Insert horizontal lines. Use at least two different styles.
9. Add a watermark that prints on odd pages only.
10. Save the document, then print it and exit WordPerfect.

Visual Workshop

Create the header shown in Figure E-21. Be sure to include the page number and set the Widow/Orphan control feature at the beginning of the document. Once you create the header, write a brief essay that covers the following heads: An Overview of My Early Years, My School Years, My Likes and Dislikes, My Family, and My Friends. Center each topic on the page at the beginning of a new section as shown in the figure. Use the Keep Text Together feature to keep each section from splitting between two pages. Insert a graphic for each topic. Include lines. Save the document to your Student Disk with a name of your choice, then print it.

FIGURE E-21

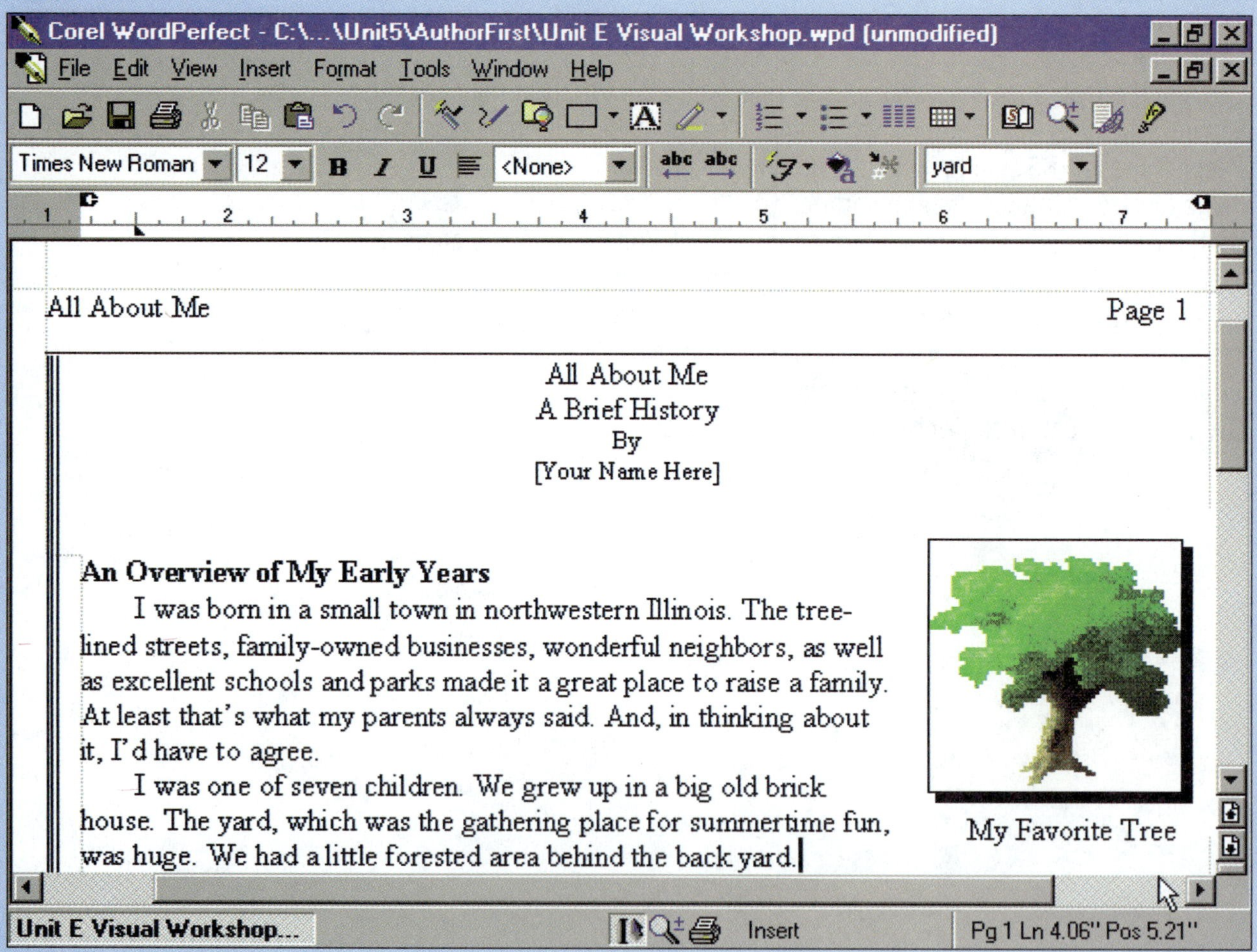

Creating Tables

Objectives

- Plan a table
- Create a table
- Enter data in a table
- Insert rows and columns
- Join and split cells
- Enter formulas in a table
- Format a table
- Enhance a table

Tables organize information into vertical columns and horizontal rows; they also enhance the appearance of your document. You can use a table to quickly arrange columns of numbers, text, or even graphics. If you include numbers in your table, you can use formulas to perform calculations. Just as you format words and paragraphs in your document, you can format tables to make them attractive and easier to read. You can also change fonts, use fills, and select borders to emphasize important information and to distinguish between different parts of the table. Each writer at The Write Staff files expense reports in order to be reimbursed for any expenses incurred as part of the job. The Chief Financial Officer, Emily Caitlin, has asked you to turn in an updated report of your monthly expenses. You will use the WordPerfect table tools to organize the information as a table of expenses to submit to Emily.

Planning a Table

To make creating your table easier, you should plan it ahead of time. Table F-1 lists some terms that you need to know when working with tables. When you plan a table, you determine the number of rows and columns you will need, the information you want to include, the cell format, and whether you will use numerical information or calculations. If you find you don't have enough information for a table, you can create a bulleted list. Your last assignment for The Write Staff was to write a promotional brochure for the new Dinosaur Wing at the American Museum of Natural History in New York City. To complete the assignment, you traveled to the museum and incurred travel expenses as well as an admission charge for entering the museum. You use the following steps as guidelines for planning your expense table.

Steps

1. **Determine the purpose of the table**
   You need to show the expenses you incurred while working for the client on this project.
2. **Make a list of the information for the table**
   Your expenses include transportation, admission to the museum, and lunch. You also bought books, a video on dinosaurs, and a software package of dinosaur clipart images that you used in the brochure.
3. **Decide how many rows and columns the table will have**
   You want to organize the expenses in rows, so you'll need nine rows: six rows for the expenses, a row for the total, a row for the column headings, and a row for the title. You need two columns: one for the expense labels and one for the expense amounts.
4. **Determine how the table should look**
   You want both the column headings and total expenses amount to appear in boldface; you want the description of the expenses left-justified in the cells, and all the numbers right-justified in the cells.
5. **Determine any calculations you may need**
   You need to add all the expenses to arrive at the total.
6. **On paper, make a rough sketch of how you want the table to look**
   You can use Figure F-1 as a guide for creating the expense report using WordPerfect.

FIGURE F-1: Rough sketch of expense table

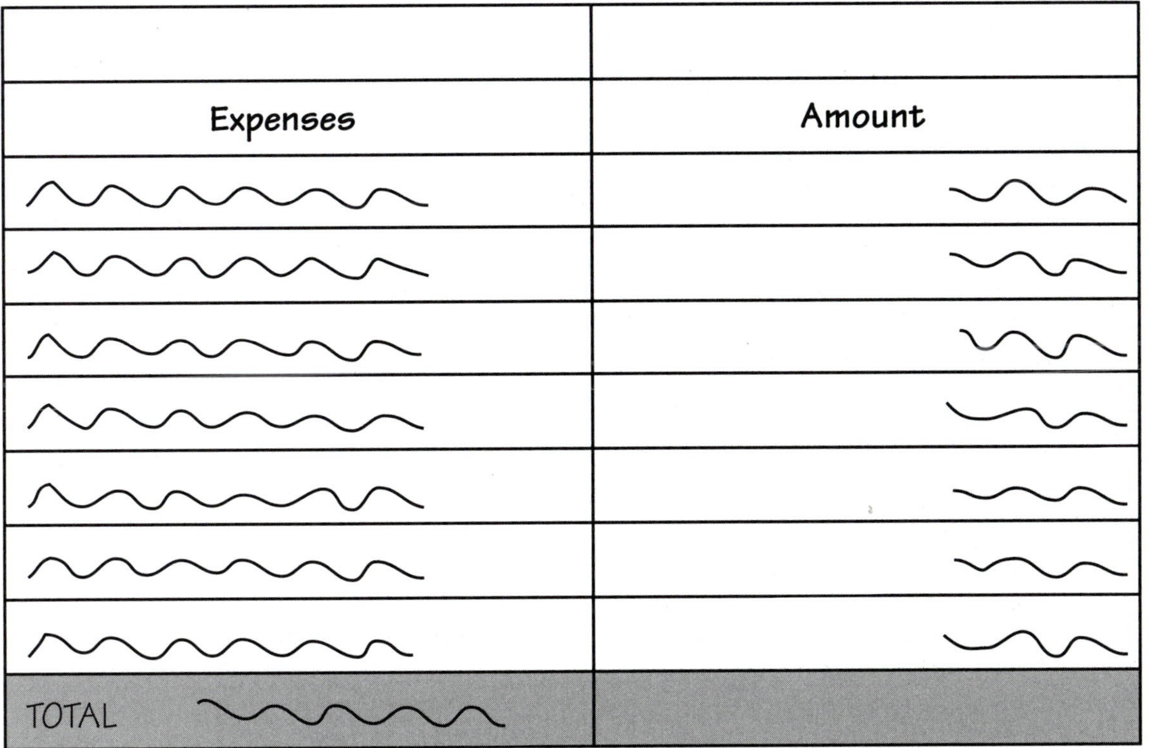

TABLE F-1: Table terms

term	description
Columns	Run vertically; assigned letters, which appear in the status bar
Rows	Run horizontally; assigned numbers, which appear in the status bar
Cell	Intersection of a row and column; for example A1, C3, etc.
Formula	Calculates totals and averages of numbers in a table
Table Formula Toolbar	Creates formulas and functions in a table

Creating a bulleted list

You need at least two columns of data to create a table. If you don't have enough information to fill a table but still want to organize the data in an itemized format, you can create a bulleted list. Use the Bullet button list arrow on the Toolbar to turn existing text into a bulleted list. First, select the text, click , click more, then select a bullet or number style in the Bullets & Numbers dialog box. You also can insert bullets before you enter text. To use QuickBullet, begin at the left margin, type an asterisk (*), press [Tab], then type your text. When you press [Enter], the bulleted list continues to the next line. For a numbered list, start with number 1 in the left margin.

WordPerfect 8

Creating a Table

A **table** consists of rows and columns. **Rows** are identified numerically from the top row down, and **columns** are identified alphabetically from left to right. Rows and columns intersect to form cells. A **cell** might contain information such as text, numbers, or formulas. A **cell name**, or **cell address**, consists of a column letter and row number that identifies the cell's position in the table. For example, cell A1 refers to the first column, first row in the upper-left corner of the table; cell B3 is in the second column, third row. Within each cell, text wraps within margins, just as it does in a document window. The height of the entire row increases to accommodate added text. Now that you have planned your expense table, you are ready to create it. Emily has requested that the table be part of an expense report memo.

Steps 1 2 3 4

1. **Start WordPerfect, open WP F-1 from your Student Disk, then save it to your Student Disk as Expense Report**
   The memo appears on the screen. When you submit the report, you want the following information to be included: your name (so Emily knows who to pay), which project and client the expenses refer to, the date or span of dates that the expenses were incurred, and what the expenses are for.
2. **Read the memo, select type your name here, then type your name**
3. **Press [Ctrl][End], then press [Enter] twice**
   A blank line appears at the end of the paragraph between the text and the beginning of the table you will create. You could use the Create Table dialog box to set up your table, but you decide to create the table quickly using the Table QuickCreate button.
4. **Click the Table QuickCreate button on the WordPerfect Toolbar**
   A pop-up grid appears. You need a table with two columns and nine rows, so you drag down and across the grid to select the number of rows and columns you want to include in the table.
5. **With still depressed, drag so that 2 x 9 appears in the horizontal bar at the top of the grid and two columns of boxes and nine rows of boxes are highlighted, as shown in Figure F-2, then release the mouse button**
   This creates a table with two columns and nine rows and a single line around each cell in the document. The width of the two columns is set automatically based on your page margins. To view the entire table you may need to scroll through the document.
6. **Scroll through the document, then save your document**
   Compare your table to the one shown in Figure F-3. Notice that the status bar indicates the position, or cell address, of the insertion point. The Tables Property Bar replaces the WordPerfect default Property Bar. Table F-2 lists ways to move around in a table.

Trouble?

If you create a table that is not 2 x 9, click Edit on the menu bar, then click Undo.

QuickTip

To avoid dividing a table by a page break, select the table, right-click, then click Block Protect.

TABLE F-2: Ways to move around a table

to move	press	to move to the	press
One cell right	[Tab] or [→]	First cell in row	[Home] [Home]
One cell left	[Shift][Tab] or [←]	Last cell in row	[End] [End]
One cell down	[↓]	Top line of multiline cell	[Alt] [Home]
One cell up	[↑]	Bottom line of multiline cell	[Alt] [End]

FIGURE F-2: Table QuickCreate button grid

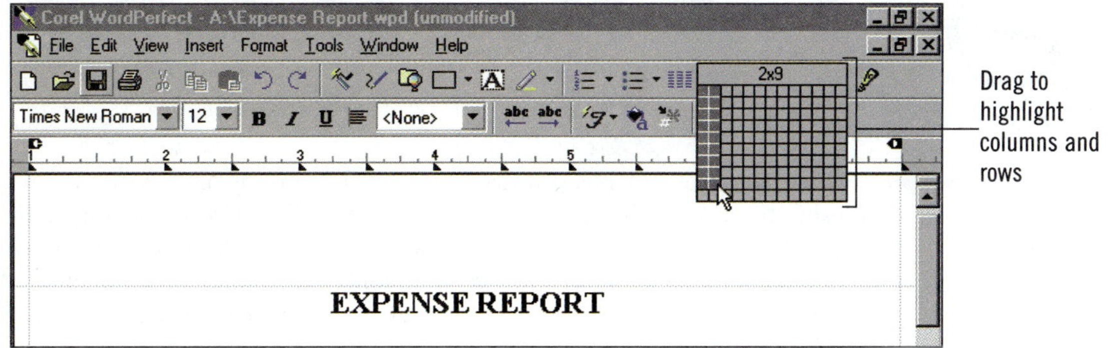

FIGURE F-3: The 2x9 table

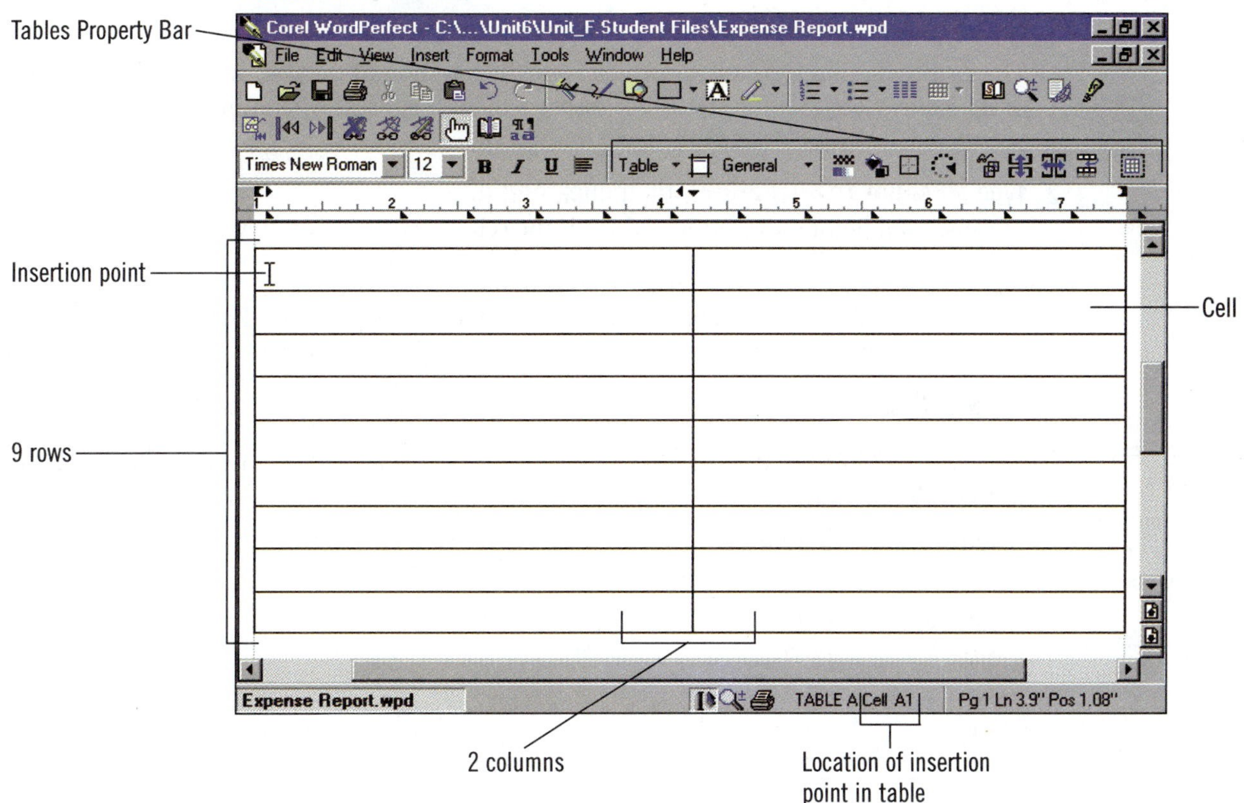

Using the Create Table dialog box

If you want to create a table with more rows or columns than are available with Table QuickCreate on the WordPerfect Toolbar, you can use the Create Table dialog box. Click Insert on the menu bar, then click Table to open the Create Table dialog box. Type the desired number in the Columns text box, press [Tab], type the desired number in the Rows text box, then click Create.

WordPerfect 8

Entering Data in a Table

Once you create a table, you need to enter data into it. You enter data into the cells of a table using the same techniques that you use to enter text into a document. The boundaries of the cells become the left and right margins. Table F-3 lists the various ways to select rows, columns, or cells. You can use all the editing commands that you use in any document. Now that you have created your table, you are ready to enter your expenses into the table.

Steps

1. Click the **top-most left cell**
   The insertion point is in cell A1, which is the intersection of the first column and first row of the table. Note that the status bar displays the cell address where the insertion point is positioned. Enter the title for the table in this cell.
2. Type **Museum Trip 10/28/99**, then click **cell A2**
   The insertion point moves to A2, which is the cell directly below cell A1.
3. Type **Expenses**, press **[Tab]**, then type **Amount**
   "Expenses" and "Amount" appear in cells A2 and B2, respectively. They are the column headings for the table.
4. Click **cell A3**
5. Type **Transportation**, press **[Tab]**, type **30**, press **[Tab]**, then enter the following data in the table using the method described in Step 3

Column A	Column B
Lunch	**15**
Admission	**6.5**
Books	**62.75**
Video	**19**
Software	**29**
TOTAL	

   Compare your table with Figure F-4. You will learn how to format numbers as currency in a later lesson. Each cell of the table contains an entry, except cells B1 and B9. Cell B9 will contain a formula for calculating the total of the expense amounts. You will enter this formula in a later lesson.

QuickTip

If you make a typing error, you can edit data in a table the same way you edit text in a document.

TABLE F-3: How to select various parts of a table

to select	move insertion point in cell	to display	action
Cell	Close to top or left cell border	⇧ or ⇦ in the cell	Click
Column	Close to top cell border	⇧ in the column	Double-click
Row	Close to left cell border	⇦ in the row	Double-click
Table	Close to top or left cell border	⇧ or ⇦ in any cell	Triple-click

FIGURE F-4: Data entered in table

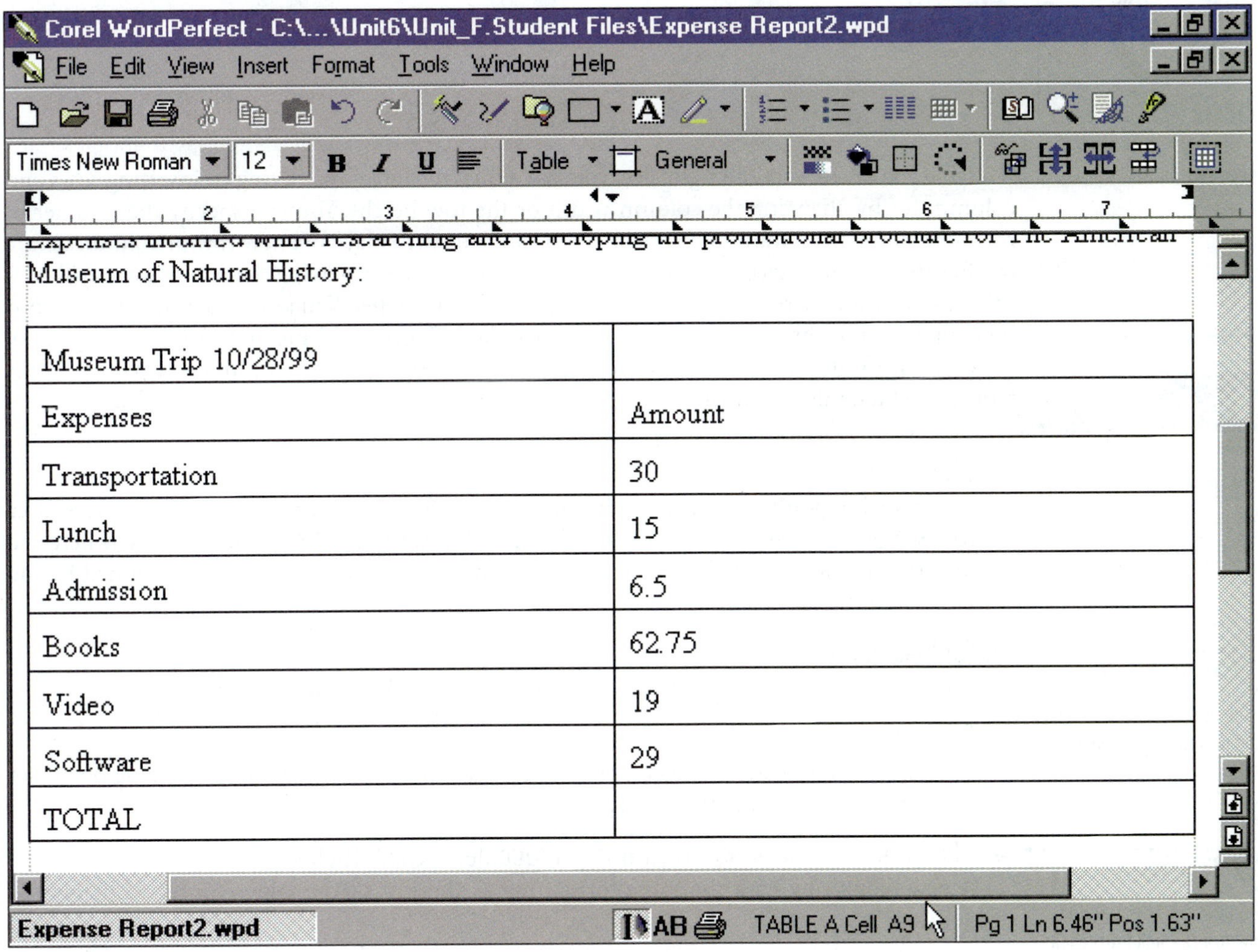

Corel WordPerfect - C:\...\Unit6\Unit_F.Student Files\Expense Report2.wpd

File Edit View Insert Format Tools Window Help

Times New Roman 12 Table General

Expenses incurred while researching and developing the promotional brochure for The American Museum of Natural History:

Museum Trip 10/28/99	
Expenses	Amount
Transportation	30
Lunch	15
Admission	6.5
Books	62.75
Video	19
Software	29
TOTAL	

Expense Report2.wpd TABLE A Cell A9 Pg 1 Ln 6.46" Pos 1.63"

Editing tables

The contents of cells can be cut, copied, and pasted using the document editing commands. You can also cut, copy, and paste parts of the table as you enter data. Select the cells, rows, or columns in the table using the directions explained in Table F-3 (note that the pointer changes appearance, depending on where it is placed within the table), right-click in the table to display a QuickMenu. Make the appropriate selection. For example, if you click Copy from the QuickMenu, the Cut or Copy Table dialog box opens. Make the appropriate selection, then click OK. The dialog box closes. Move the insertion point to the place where you want to paste what you copied, right-click, then click Paste.

Inserting Rows and Columns

If a table you create isn't the right size, you can adjust the table by deleting or inserting rows and columns, or by changing the column width or the row height. You can specify the number of rows or columns you want to insert, and you can choose to place the new row or column before or after the current insertion point position. While reviewing the receipts you will submit with the expense report, you find a receipt for special paper. You remember that during your meeting with the client, the museum director asked if you could pick up samples of a special paper to use for the brochure. Since you purchased these samples, you need to add a row to your table to include this cost with your expenses.

1. Click **cell A8**

   The insertion point is in the cell with the word "Software." You need to add a new row after row 8. New columns or rows contain the same formatting as the column or row where the insertion point is located. The placement of the new row or column is determined by the position of the insertion point.

Trouble?

Be sure to right-click in cell A8 so the new row is placed after row 8.

2. Right-click in **cell A8**

   The Table QuickMenu appears. Your screen should look similar to Figure F-5.

3. Click **Insert**

   The Insert Columns/Rows dialog box appears, as shown in figure F-6. The dialog box is set to insert one row before the selected row.

Trouble?

If the new row is not added below row 8, click Edit, click Undo, then repeat steps 1–4.

4. Click the **After option button** under Placement, then click **OK**

   A new blank row with the same formatting as the rest of the table is inserted below the Software row.

5. If necessary, click **cell A9**, type **Sample paper**, press **[Tab]**, type **10**, then save your document.

   The new data is entered in the new row. See Figure F-7.

Changing table column widths

Once you begin entering data in a cell, you might find that the column is too narrow or too wide for the entry. You can change the column width using the mouse. Position the insertion point on the **rule**, which is the line separating the columns. When the pointer changes to ↔, drag the rule to the left or right to increase or decrease the column width. A message box tells you the exact width and height of the cell.

FIGURE F-5: Table QuickMenu

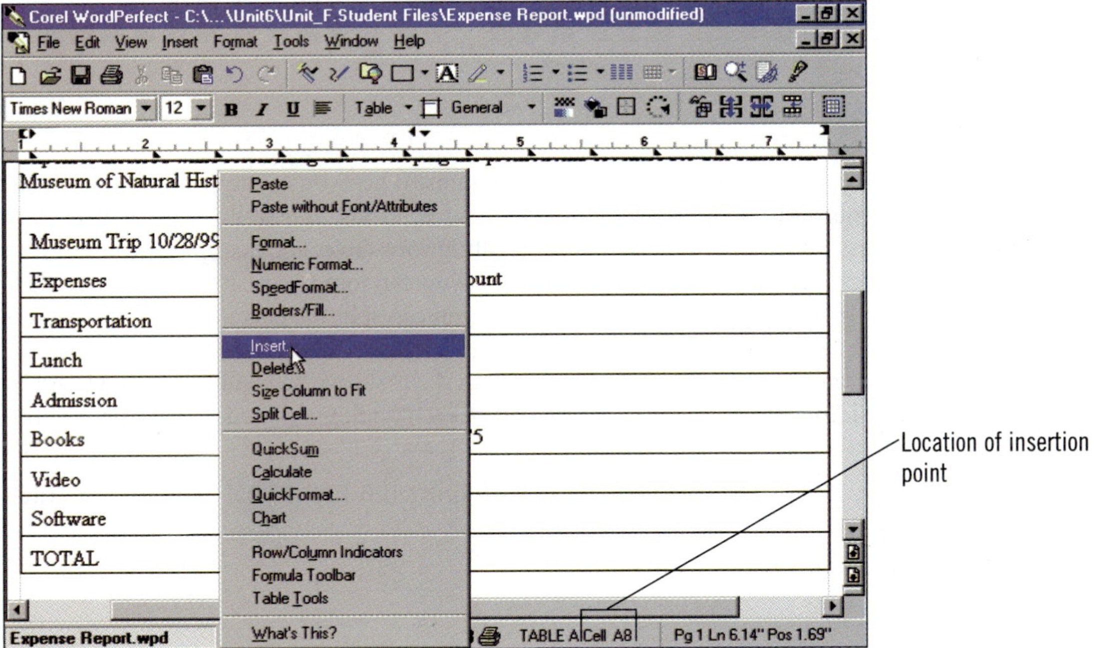

FIGURE F-6: Insert Columns/Rows dialog box

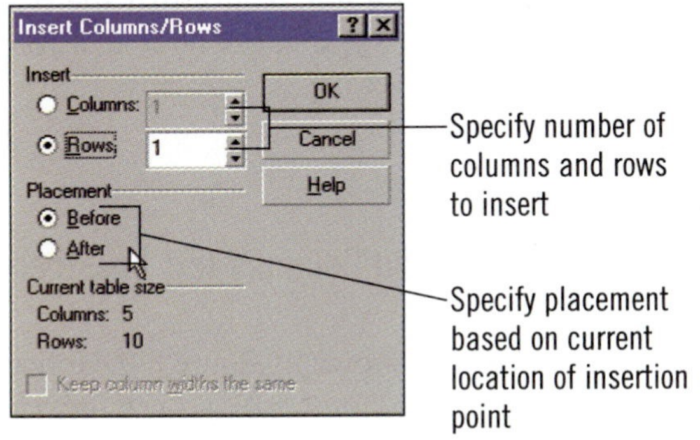

FIGURE F-7: New row in a table

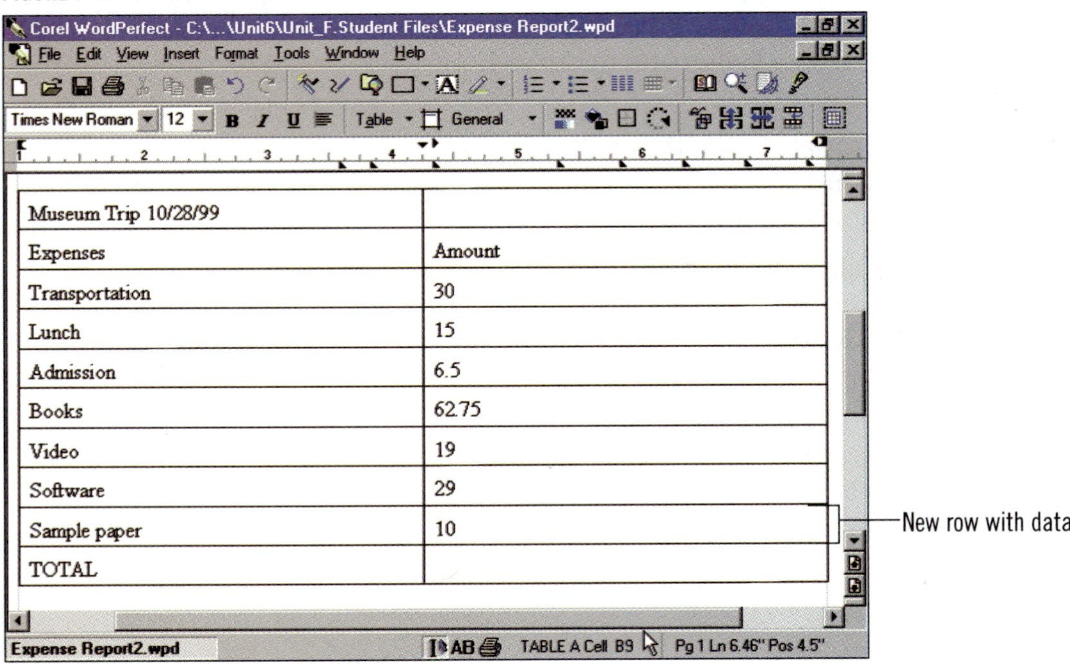

WordPerfect 8

Joining and Splitting Cells

Tables can have many configurations of rows and columns. When you create your table, you can't always predict the number and arrangement of cells that will most effectively organize your data. Modifying table structure is an important part of creating your table. For example, if you want the title of a table to be a single cell at the top of the table, you can join two or more adjacent cells to form a single cell. Or, if you need to include subtotals, you can split the current cell or selected cell into multiple rows or columns to accommodate this need. After reviewing your table, you decide that the title should be centered in a single cell in the first row. You will join cells A1 and B1 to form a single cell. You also decide to show the cost of each book purchased, so you split cell B6.

Trouble?

Move the insertion point so it is almost touching the left cell border.

1. Click **cell B1**, move the insertion point to display the row select pointer ⇦, then double-click
   Cells A1 and B1, the first row, are selected.
2. Right-click in **cell B1**
   The Table QuickMenu appears on the screen.
3. Click **Join Cells** on the QuickMenu
   Cells A1 and B1 are joined into a single cell as shown in Figure F-8. Notice that the cell address is A1. This cell contains the title of your table. Next, you will split cell B6 so that you can show the cost of each of the books that you purchased.
4. Click **cell B6**, right-click in **cell B6**, then click **Split Cell**
   The Split Cell dialog box appears.
5. If necessary, click the **Columns option button**, type **4** in the Columns text box, then click **OK**
   The Split Cell dialog box closes and cell B6 is now four cells, as shown in Figure F-9. Notice the cell address in the status bar for the insertion point is cell B6. You want to check the cell addresses for the new cells.
6. Press **[Tab]** three times
   The insertion point moves one cell to the right each time. As you tab to each new cell, you notice the cell address in the status bar for each cell changes from cell B6 to cell C6 to cell D6 to cell E6.
7. Click **cell B6**, select **62.75**, then press **[Delete]**
   The total is deleted from cell B6. In a later lesson, you will enter a formula in cell E6 to calculate the total amount spent on books.
8. If necessary, click **cell B6**, type **15.25**, then press **[Tab]**
   Continue to enter the following data:

In cell	Type
C6	**27**
D6	**20.50**

The amount of each of the books you purchased is now entered in the table. These amounts are important because they help clarify the total amount spent on books.

Time To

✔ Save

FIGURE F-8: Cells joined

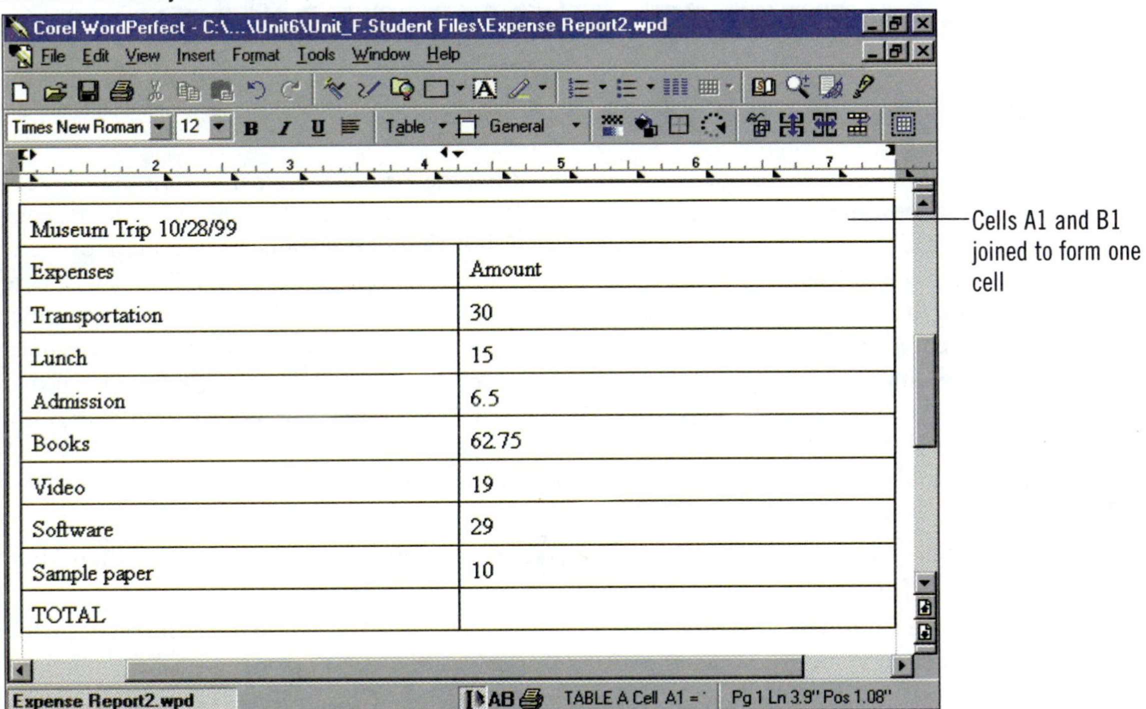

Museum Trip 10/28/99	
Expenses	Amount
Transportation	30
Lunch	15
Admission	6.5
Books	62.75
Video	19
Software	29
Sample paper	10
TOTAL	

FIGURE F-9: Cell split

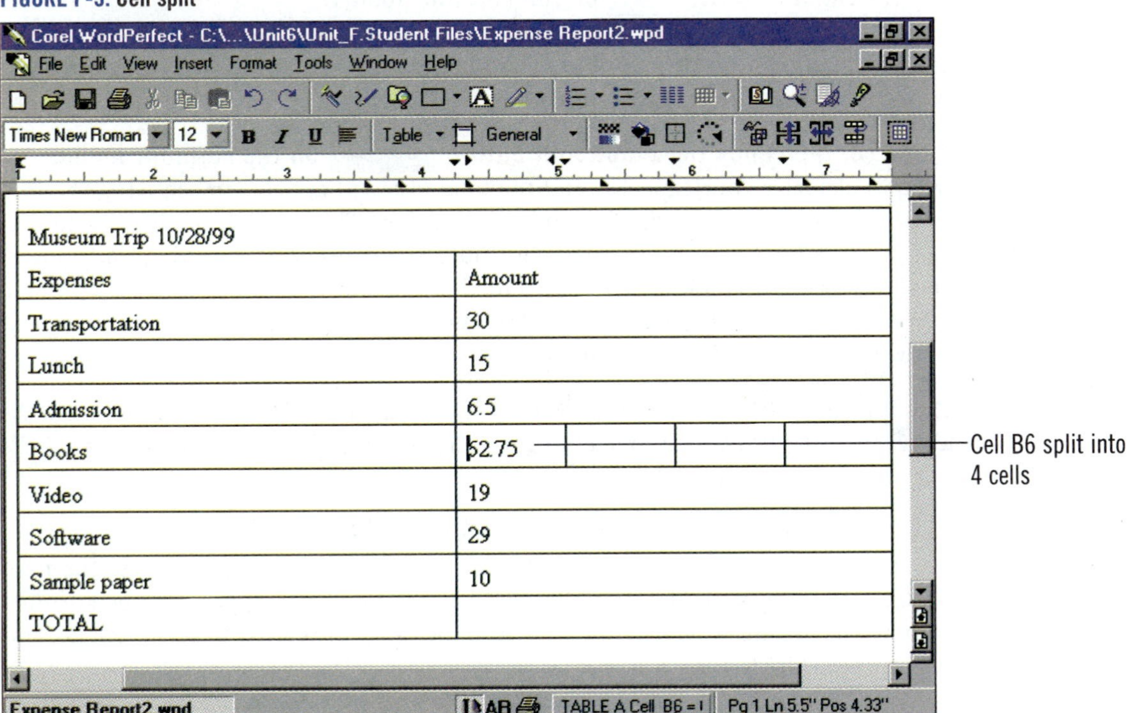

Museum Trip 10/28/99				
Expenses	Amount			
Transportation	30			
Lunch	15			
Admission	6.5			
Books	62.75			
Video	19			
Software	29			
Sample paper	10			
TOTAL				

Deleting a table

There are times when you need to delete an entire table or reuse the structure or contents of the table. To accomplish this, select the entire table, keep the cursor inside the table, click Table on the Tables Property Bar, then click Delete. The Delete Table dialog box opens. You can choose to delete an Entire Table, the Table Contents, the Formulas Only, or the Table Structure (leaving the text in the document). Specify the part of the table to delete, then click OK.

Entering Formulas in a Table

You can create and enter formulas in your table using the Formula Toolbar. A **formula** uses cell addresses and numbers to perform calculations, such as adding the contents of cell B2 to the contents of cell C2 (B2+C2). Formulas are very powerful. If you need the total for a column of numbers, you can add the numbers yourself and simply type the number in the Total cell, or you can use a formula in the table. If the total is just a number, it has to be recalculated manually and retyped in the document if any numbers in the column change. If the total is calculated based on a formula, the total will automatically change to reflect any new numbers in the column. You need to calculate the total cost of the books purchased and you need to calculate your total expenses. You enter a formula in cell E6 to show the total amount spent on books. Next, you use QuickSum to enter a formula in cell B10 to show the total expense amount.

1. Click **cell E6**, click the **Table button** Table on the Tables Property Bar, then click **Formula Toolbar**
   The Formula Toolbar appears as shown in Figure F-10. You will enter a formula in the Formula Edit text box to calculate the total spent on books.
2. If necessary, click **cell E6**, click the **Formula Edit text box**, type **B6+C6+D6**, then click the **Check Mark button** on the Formula Toolbar
   The formula adds the values in cells B6, C6, and D6. The total (62.75) appears in cell E6. You could follow the same procedure to find your total expenses. However, WordPerfect has a QuickSum feature that automatically totals adjacent cells.
3. Click **cell B10**, then click the **QuickSum button** QuickSum on the Formula Toolbar
   The formula calculates your expenses and the total (124.75) appears in cell B10. The formula +SUM(B3:B9) appears in the Formula Edit text box. This formula totals the values in the range of cells B3 to B9. In reviewing the formula, you realize that the cost of only one of the books (the value in cell B6) has been included in the total amount. You will not be able to use QuickSum after all. Instead, you need to enter the formula for the cells you want to total. You will edit the SUM formula in the Formula Edit text box.
4. Click to the right of **B9)** in the Formula Edit text box, then press **[Backspace]** twice
   This deletes the text "9)". You are ready to continue entering the cell addresses of the cells you want included in the formula.
5. Type **5,E6,B7:B9)**, then click on the Formula Toolbar
   Compare your screen to Figure F-11. The formula calculates your expenses and the total (172.25) appears in cell B10. The formula +SUM(B3:B5,E6,B7:B9) appears in the Formula Edit text box. The formula calculates the values in the range of cells B3 to B5, in cell E6, and in the range of cells B7 to B9.
6. Click the **Close button** on the Formula Toolbar
7. Save your work

Trouble?

You must click the Check Mark button to accept the formula and insert it in the current cell.

QuickTip

In a formula, a range is a series of adjacent cells, such as B3:B9. A range is identified by typing the cell address of the first cell in the range, a colon, and the cell address of the last cell in the range.

FIGURE F-10: Formula Toolbar

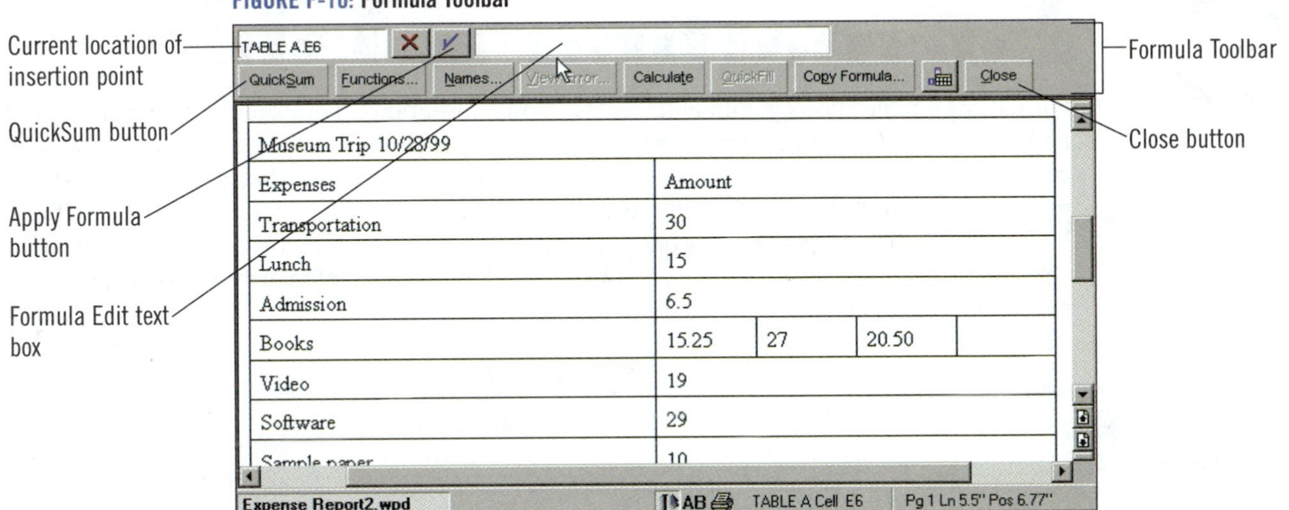

FIGURE F-11: Table with formula

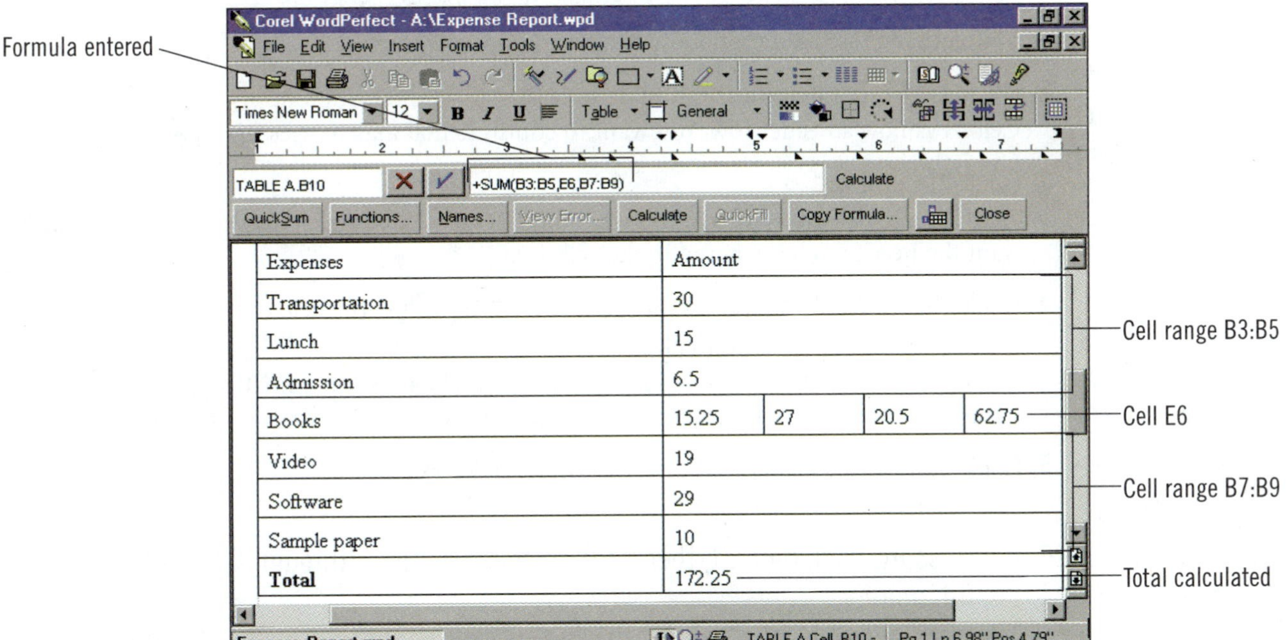

WordPerfect 8

Formatting a Table

Formatting a table allows you to enhance its overall appearance. For example, you can create a table header, select a numerical format such as showing numbers as decimals, percentages, or currency, and specify how numbers should be aligned. These are all formatting options that make the content of the table easier to read and understand. You can use the Properties for Table Format dialog box to change the characteristics of a cell, a column, a row, or an entire table. Now that you have entered and calculated all of the data into your Expense Report, you can enhance your table so that it is more legible.

Steps

1. **Click cell A1, right-click, then click Format on the QuickMenu**
   The Properties for Table Format dialog box opens. You want to make cell A1, the cell with the table title, a header row. A header row always appears as the first row of a table if the table spans more than a single page. The Properties for Table Format dialog box has an option that allows you to identify header rows. See Figure F-12.
2. **Click Row tab, click the Header row check box, then Click Apply**
   Cell A1 is now a header row. You want to continue making changes to cell A1.
3. **Click the Cell tab**
   The Cell tab dialog box opens. You want the title to be centered across the columns and you want the header to be centered in the cell itself.
4. **Click the Horizontal list arrow, click Center, click the Vertical list arrow, click Center, click Apply, then click OK**
   The Properties for Table Format dialog box closes. The title, Museum Trip 10/28/99, is now a header row. It is also centered in cell A1. You are now ready to format the numbers in your table.
5. **Click cell B3, right-click in cell B3, then click Table Tools**
   The Tools Palette appears.
6. **If necessary, click cell B3, then drag to select cells B3 through B10 including cells C6, D6, and E6**
   The numbers are highlighted and the Tools Palette is open as shown in Figure F-13. You want to display the numbers with a dollar sign and two decimal places.
7. **Click the Numeric format list arrow in the Tools Palette, then click Currency**
   The values in your table appear with decimal points and dollar signs. You decide you want the numbers to align on the decimal point.
8. **If necessary, click cell B3 and drag to select cells B3 through B10 including cells C6, D6, and E6, click Format on the Tools Palette, click Column tab, click Horizontal list arrow, click Decimal Align, click Apply, then click OK**
   The Properties for Table Format dialog box closes. The numbers are displayed as currency and they align on the decimal point as shown in Figure F-14.
9. **Click the Tools Palette Close button**
   The Tools Palette closes.

The Tools Palette is a floating palette. Click the title bar to drag the palette anywhere on the screen.

Save

FIGURE F-12: Properties for Table Format dialog box

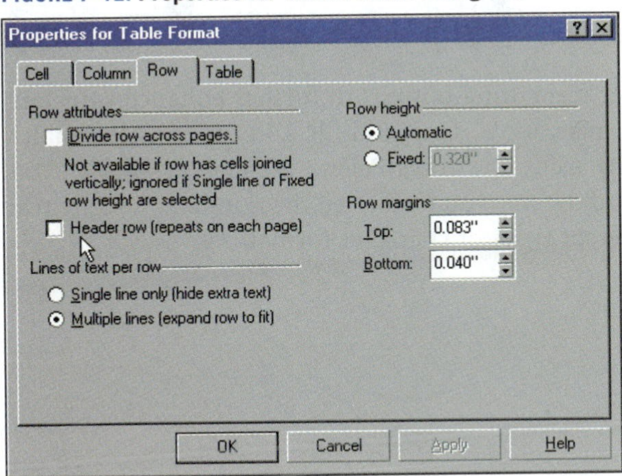

FIGURE F-13: Tools Palette

Numeric format list arrow

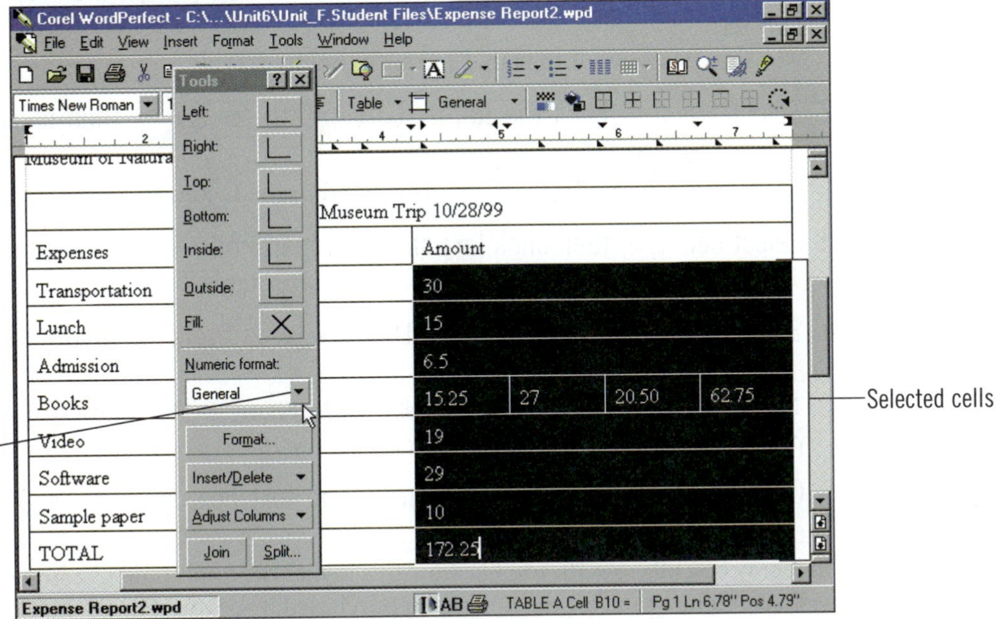

FIGURE F-14: Table with numbers formatted and aligned

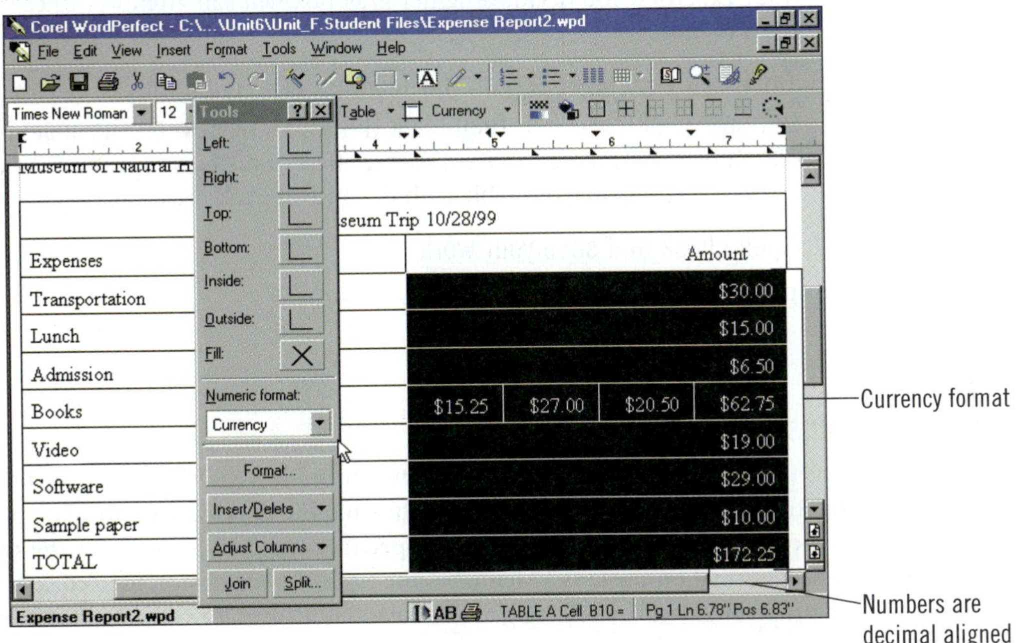

Enhancing a Table

WordPerfect offers other formatting options to further enhance your tables. For example, you can adjust character formats, fonts, sizes, and fill. You can format a table while working in the document window or by using the Tools Palette for tables. You like the change you made to the table title and the way you formatted the numbers. You are ready to further enhance your table by using different types of character formatting.

1. Select cells **A1** through **B2**, click the **Bold button** on the Property bar, then click cell **B3**
   The first two rows of the table appear in boldface type.
2. Select **Amount**, click the **Justify Left button** Left, then click the **Justify Right button** Right
   The word "Amount" appears right-justified in the B column.
3. Select cell **A10**, then click on the Property bar
   The word Total appears in boldface type in your table.
4. Select **row 10**, right-click in row 10, click **Table Tools** on the QuickMenu, click the **Fill button** on the Tools Palette
   The Fill pop-up menu appears as shown in Figure F-15. A variety of fill options are displayed. You want a 30% gray screen to fill row 10.
5. Click the **list arrow** in the pop-up menu text box, scroll through the options, then click **30% Fill**
   A gray box fills row 10. You like how this makes the total stand out. You decide that since cell E6 contains a total for the books you purchased, you would like that cell to stand out as well. However, you do not want this subtotal to display with the same fill as the total amount of your expenses. You decide a lighter gray box will call attention to cell E6 without creating a distraction.
6. Click cell **E6**, click on the Tools Palette, click the **list arrow**, scroll through the options, click **10% Fill**, then click the **Close button** on the Tools Palette
   The Tools Palette closes. You can see the effect of the fill you applied. A light gray box appears in cell E6. Compare your table with Figure F-16. You are pleased with your expense report.
7. Spell check and save your work
8. Print your document and exit WordPerfect

Trouble?

Move the insertion point so it is almost touching the left cell margin, then double-click to select the row.

CLUES TO USE

Using Table SpeedFormat

WordPerfect has a variety of predefined table formats from which to choose. To open the Table SpeedFormat dialog box, click in any cell in the table, right-click in the table, then click SpeedFormat on the QuickMenu. You can preview each predefined style by selecting a style from the Available Styles list box. A sample table showing the selected style format appears in the Table SpeedFormat dialog box. Click the style name to select the style of your choice, then click Apply. The predefined table format will be applied to the table.

FIGURE F-15: Fill pop-up menu

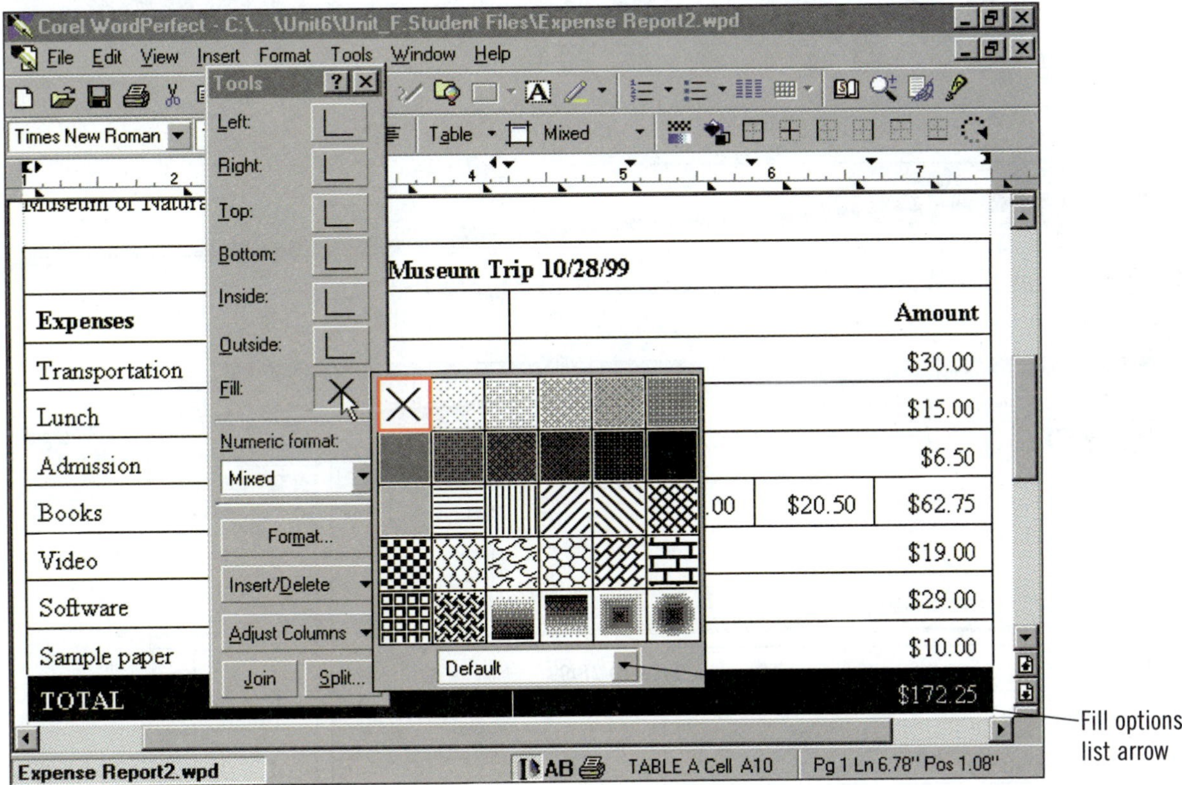

FIGURE F-16: Table with enhancements

EXPENSE REPORT

TO: Emily Caitlin
FROM: *John Christopher*

PROJECT: The American Museum of Natural History, New York City
JOB #: 1978
DATE: November 5, 1999

Expenses incurred while researching and developing the promotional brochure for The American Museum of Natural History:

Museum Trip 10/28/99				
Expenses				**Amount**
Transportation				$30.00
Lunch				$15.00
Admission				$6.50
Books	$15.25	$27.00	$20.50	$62.75
Video				$19.00
Software				$29.00
Sample paper				$10.00
TOTAL				$172.25

Practice

Concepts Review

Label each element of the WordPerfect window shown in Figure F-17.

FIGURE F-17

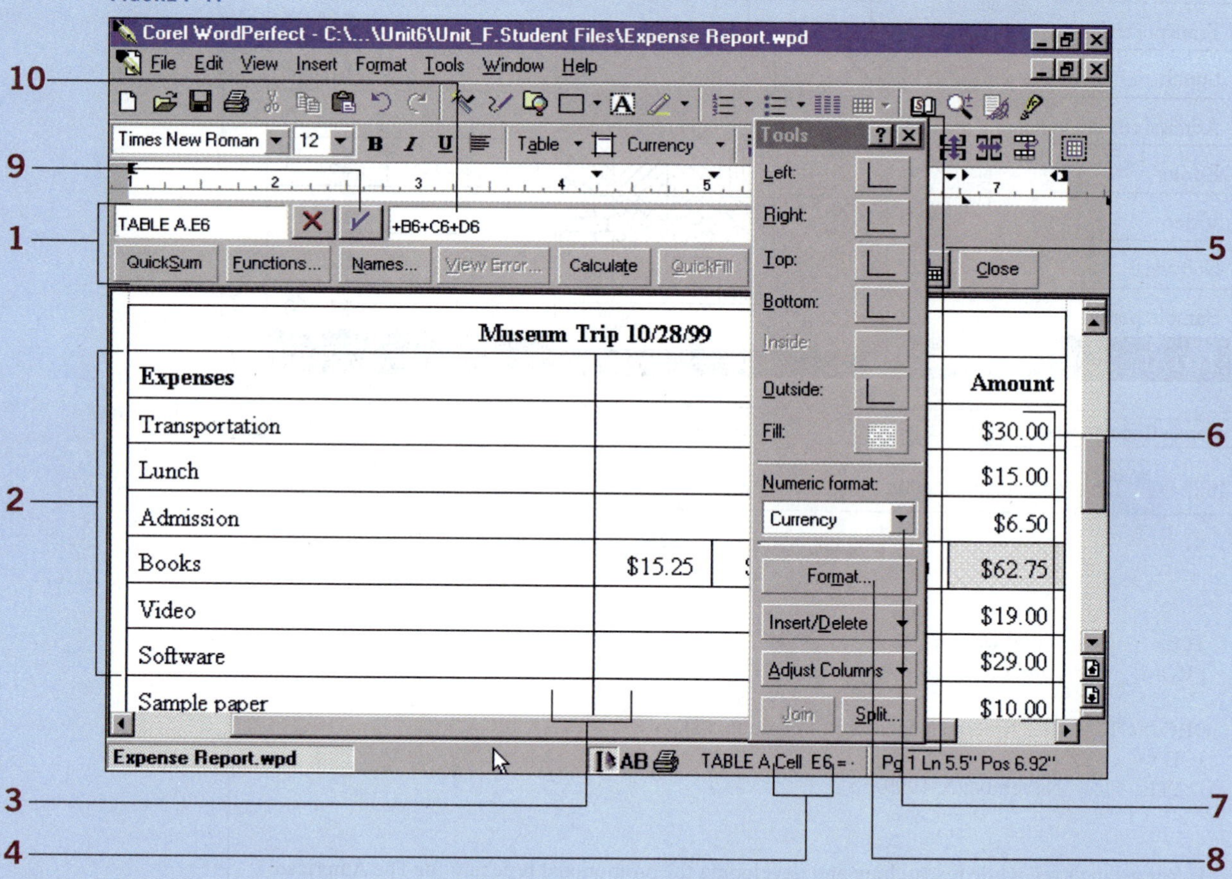

Match each of the following:

11. Moves the insertion point one cell to the left
12. Moves the insertion point one cell to the right
13. Double-click to select a row
14. Applies formula
15. Drag to create a table
16. Cell address

a. ⇦
b. [Shift] [Tab]
c. [Tab]
d. [table button]
e. A8
f. ✓

Select the best answer from the list of choices.

17. Tables consist of
- **a.** Rows and headers.
- **b.** Rows and columns.
- **c.** Columns and footers.
- **d.** Cells and menus.

18. In every table, the cell labeled A1
- **a.** Contains a graphics figure.
- **b.** Cannot be used as part of a formula.
- **c.** Is 2.49" wide.
- **d.** Is the upper-left cell in the table.

19. In the cell address D6, the letter D indicates the
- **a.** Column.
- **b.** Row.
- **c.** Intersection of a row and column.
- **d.** Cell name.

20. The location of a new row inserted in a table is
- **a.** Based on the cell address you type.
- **b.** Determined when you press [Enter].
- **c.** Determined when you press [Tab].
- **d.** Based on the location of the insertion point.

21. When you use QuickSum,
- **a.** The formula appears in the Formula Edit text box.
- **b.** The formula appears in the cell next to TOTAL.
- **c.** Only the sum appears in the table.
- **d.** You select if you want the formula or the sum to appear in the table.

22. If you want numbers to show as dollars and cents, use the Numeric format
- **a.** General.
- **b.** Decimal.
- **c.** Dollar.
- **d.** Currency.

23. If you have two cells that you want to make into one cell,
- **a.** Delete the right-most cell.
- **b.** Delete both cells and make a new cell.
- **c.** Use Join Cells.
- **d.** Use Split Cells.

24. The formula A1+B2+C3
- **a.** Is not an acceptable table formula.
- **b.** Adds the contents of cells in the first row.
- **c.** Adds the contents of cells along a diagonal.
- **d.** Adds the contents of cells in the first column.

► Skills Review

1. Plan a table.
- **a.** On a notepad, write notes that will help you create a table for the information that follows:

State	Total Sales
New Mexico	4724.34
Nevada	3911.27
Texas	11086.67
Colorado	9413.09
TOTAL	

- **b.** State the purpose of the table.
- **c.** Determine how many rows and columns are needed for the table.
- **d.** Make a sketch of how the table should look.
- **e.** Make note of any calculations that will be needed.
- **f.** Hand in the notes with your name on them.

2. Create a table and enter data into it.
- **a.** Start WordPerfect.
- **b.** Use the Table grid and create a table with 2 columns and 6 rows.
- **c.** Type "State" in cell A1, press [Tab], then type "Total Yearly Sales" in cell B1.
- **d.** Continue to enter the text from Skills Review 1 into the table.
- **e.** Practice moving around the table using the keyboard.

3. Insert rows and columns.
- **a.** Insert one row above the row for Nevada.
- **b.** Type "New Jersey" in the new cell in column A.
- **c.** Type "7653.86" in the new cell in column B.
- **d.** Insert another row after Colorado.
- **e.** Type "California" in the new cell in column A.
- **f.** Type "9802.33" in the new cell in column B.
- **g.** Insert a row before cell A1.
- **h.** Type "Acme Sales: Selected States" in the cell in column A.

4. Join and split cells.
- **a.** Select Row A.
- **b.** Right-click A2, then click Join Cells.
- **c.** Verify the new cell's address as cell A1.
- **d.** Select cell B2, right-click cell B2, select Split Cell, type "3" in the Columns text box, then click OK.
- **e.** Type "Jan – June" in cell C2, then type "July – Dec" in cell D2.
- **f.** Continue to split the remaining cells in column B into three cells.

g. Enter "2397.20" in cell C3, then enter "2327.14" in Cell D3. [Note: These amounts total the amount in Cell B3.]
h. Delete the total in cell B3.
i. Continue to enter subtotal amounts for each state in their respective C and D cells, then delete the totals that currently appear in the B cells.

5. Enter formulas in a table.
a. Click cell B3, right-click cell B3, then click Formula Toolbar.
b. Enter the formula C3+D3 in the Formula Edit text box, then click ✓.
c. Verify the total. It should match the total shown in Step 1.
d. Continue to enter formulas to find the yearly total for each state.
e. Verify each total by referring to Steps 1 and 2.
f. Use QuickSum to total the yearly sales, which should be $46,591.56.

6. Format the table.
a. Make the title of the table a row header, then center it in cell A1.
b. Adjust the column widths as necessary to accommodate the column heads.
c. Center the column heads.
d. Use the Tools Palette for tables to show all numbers with dollar signs and decimal points.
e. Align all numbers on the decimal point.

7. Enhance the table.
a. Make the table title and the column heads bold.
b. Make the word "TOTAL" bold.
c. Make the last row of the table 30% Fill.
d. Make the state totals in column B 10% Fill.
e. Spell check and save the document to your Student Disk as "Acme state sales."
f. Print the document, then exit WordPerfect.

Independent Challenges

1. You are the movie critic for the *Daily Times*, a local newspaper. Your managing editor has asked you to write a feature article on the top-grossing domestic movies of all time. You decide to use a table to rank the top ten movies in order of box office receipts.

To complete this independent challenge:

1. Start WordPerfect, create a table and type in the following information:

Movie	Year	Income in Millions
Star Wars	1977	460
E.T.	1982	407
Jurassic Park	1993	357
Forrest Gump	1994	327
The Lion King	1994	313
Return of the Jedi	1983	307
Independence Day	1996	306
The Empire Strikes Back	1980	290
Home Alone	1990	285
Jaws	1975	260

2. Center the headings for each column, then make them bold.
3. Insert a row after Independence Day and type this information in the appropriate cells: "Men in Black" "1997" "299"
4. Show the income figures with dollar signs and decimal points.
5. Align the income figures on the decimal points.
6. Use the Fill option to enhance your table.
7. Use SpeedFormat to select the table format you prefer.
8. Spellcheck your work, then save it to your Student Disk as "Film Study".
9. Preview and print the completed table.
10. Close the document and exit WordPerfect.

2. After weeks of wondering about your food budget, you've decided to keep track of certain grocery items and the prices you are paying for them. Your "study" will be based on three trips to the store. You want to see if the cost of some key food purchases in your grocery bill is staying steady, rising, or falling over a period of three shopping trips. Select five key items that you always purchase (milk, coffee, orange juice, apples, soda, whatever). Keep the receipts for these items so you know what you've paid.

To complete this independent challenge:

1. Plan your table. Decide how you want to organize the information. You will have to make a table with five columns, one column for the item name, one column for each shopping trip, and one column for each row total. You'll probably need seven rows. You might want more columns or rows, either to include notes about these items as part of the table or to include more items. Submit a sketch of your plan.
2. Create the table in WordPerfect. Give the table a title in the document.
3. Include the headings for each column and labels for each row. Use a fill option to separate the headings from the data in the column. Center the headings for each column, and make them bold and italic.
4. Create the last row as a total row to show the total spent on the groceries for each visit. Label this row "Visit Total" and format it in a way to make it stand out.
5. Enter all the data from your receipts into the table.
6. The last column should be another total column to show the total spent on each food item category. Call this "Food Item Total". You can use these totals to quickly compare the total amount spent on each food category. Format the "Food Item Total" label so it stands out.
7. Use QuickSum to enter formulas to determine the total for each shopping visit. Edit the formula so the first cell in each range does not include row 1.
8. Enter formulas to calculate the food item totals.
9. Split cell E7 into two cells.
10. In cell E7, use a formula to calculate the total for the three visits. In cell F7, use a formula to calculate the total for the food items. (Note: If all the other formulas are correct, then the total that appears in E7 should match the total that appears in F7.)
11. Choose Currency for the number format and decimal-align the numbers.
12. Save the document to your Student Disk as "Shopping Study".
13. Preview and print the completed table then exit WordPerfect.

3. It's the start of another semester and you need to adjust to a new schedule. You find the printed schedule provided by the school hard to read. Since you refer to your schedule frequently the first few weeks, you want it to be quick and easy to read. You decide to create a table for the classes you are currently enrolled in.

To complete this independent challenge:

1. Create a table using WordPerfect. Label the column headings as follows: Class name, Class number, Professor, Class days, Class time, Class location, Notes.
2. Enter the applicable data for each class.
3. Create a title for the table.
4. Format the title and column headings with Fills, and if you'd like, with Borders.
5. Join or split cells, as appropriate.
6. Use a font in the title and column headings that is different from the other text in the table.
7. Center the column headings and table title.
8. Align any numeric data in the table.
9. Adjust the width of the columns to best accommodate the data within each column. For instance, if some columns are much wider than necessary, reduce the width. Conversely, if other columns have text that goes to a second line, expand the width.
10. Use SpeedFormat to style the table, then preview the table.
11. Save your work, print the table, then exit WordPerfect.

4. Tables are a useful tool. We encounter tables on a regular basis in our daily lives. Usually tables included in articles enhance or bring meaning to the written word. Find examples of tables in some of your reading material, such as textbooks or magazines. Select one table that you want to analyze and then re-create. First, you will comment on how the table is set up and what formatting was applied to the table. Then you will re-create the table using WordPerfect, writing a summary about each of the features you used.

To complete this independent challenge:

1. Start WordPerfect, and in a new document window answer the following questions about the table.
   a. What is the purpose of the table?
   b. What information is included in the table?
   c. How many rows and columns does the table have?
   d. What formatting features were used to enhance the appearance of the table?
   e. What calculations were used?
2. Re-create the table either below your responses or on a new page.
3. Following the table, write a summary to explain how you replicated the table. Be sure to comment on any special features you used.
4. Spell check, then save your work to your Student Disk.
5. Print your table, then exit WordPerfect.

Visual Workshop

Create the table shown in Figure F-18. Click the Table QuickCreate button on the WordPerfect Toolbar to create the table. Use the Join/Split feature to modify the table to match the figure. Be sure to format and enhance the table as shown, using the Tools Palette for tables to set the correct justifications and alignments. Save the document to your Student Disk with a name of your choice, then print and submit it.

FIGURE F-18

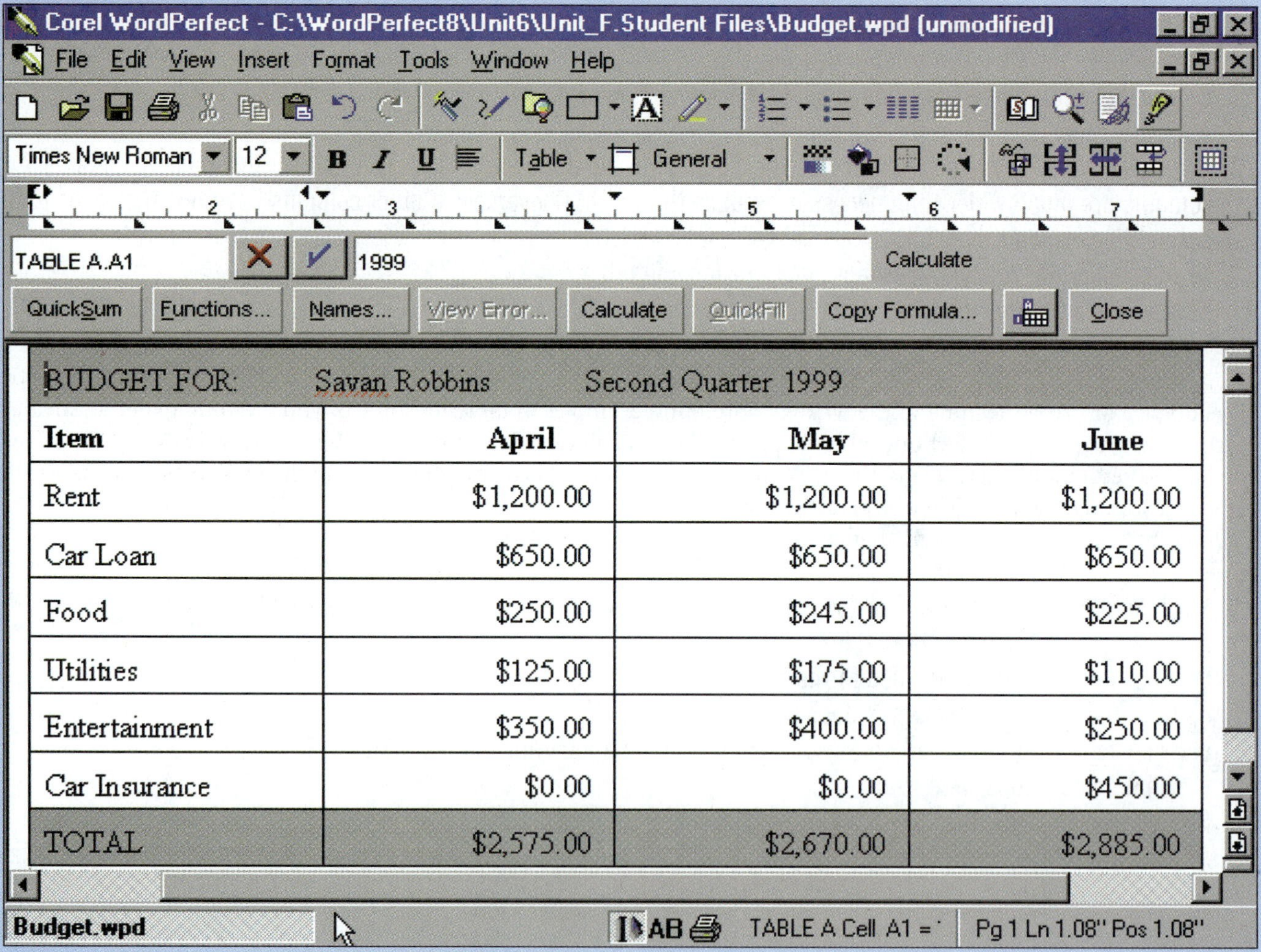

Corel WordPerfect - C:\WordPerfect8\Unit6\Unit_F.Student Files\Budget.wpd (unmodified)

BUDGET FOR: Savan Robbins Second Quarter 1999			
Item	**April**	**May**	**June**
Rent	$1,200.00	$1,200.00	$1,200.00
Car Loan	$650.00	$650.00	$650.00
Food	$250.00	$245.00	$225.00
Utilities	$125.00	$175.00	$110.00
Entertainment	$350.00	$400.00	$250.00
Car Insurance	$0.00	$0.00	$450.00
TOTAL	$2,575.00	$2,670.00	$2,885.00

WordPerfect 8

Creating a Mail Merge

Objectives

- Plan a merge
- Create a data file
- Enter data in a data file
- Create a form document
- Enter fields in a form document
- Merge data files and form documents
- Edit data files and form documents
- Create address labels

When you need to send the same or a similar letter to many recipients, you can use the Merge feature to create professional-looking personalized letters. **Merge** combines one letter in the form document with a name and address list in the data file, to create a single merge file of all the personalized letters that you will print and send out. You can use Merge to mass-produce letters, envelopes, mailing labels, contracts, phone lists, memos, and other documents. Jennifer Laina asks you to send The Write Staff's clients a letter reminding them that the catalog season is just around the corner.

WordPerfect 8

Planning a Merge

Merging is a three-step process that requires careful planning. First, you create a **data source**, such as a **data file**, which contains the names, addresses, and any relevant and unique information for each person to whom you want to send the letter. Next you create a **form document**, which is a form letter containing all the information that you want included in each recipient's letter. Finally, you merge the data file and the form document to create a third file, the **merge file**, which contains all the personalized letters. Figure G-1 illustrates this process. In the past, a job like this would have taken hours. You would have had to write a personalized letter to each client. Now you have the power of WordPerfect's Merge feature to complete this project in a timely manner. You use the following steps to plan the merged letters Jennifer asked you to create.

Steps

1. **Determine the purpose of the merge**
   Jennifer wants you to send a reminder letter to each of your clients.

2. **Make a list of the information that should be in the data file**
   The data file should include the clients' names and the companies' names and addresses. This data will personalize each letter for the recipient.

3. **Decide what the form document will say**
   You will include each client's name, company name, and address. You will ask the client to contact The Write Staff with any new product information they might have so it can be included in the catalog.

4. **Write a rough draft of the letter**
   Determine the form document content. You write a letter that will apply to all recipients, and you decide where the information will go to make each letter personalized. A rough draft of the letter is shown in Figure G-2.

FIGURE G-1: Merging process

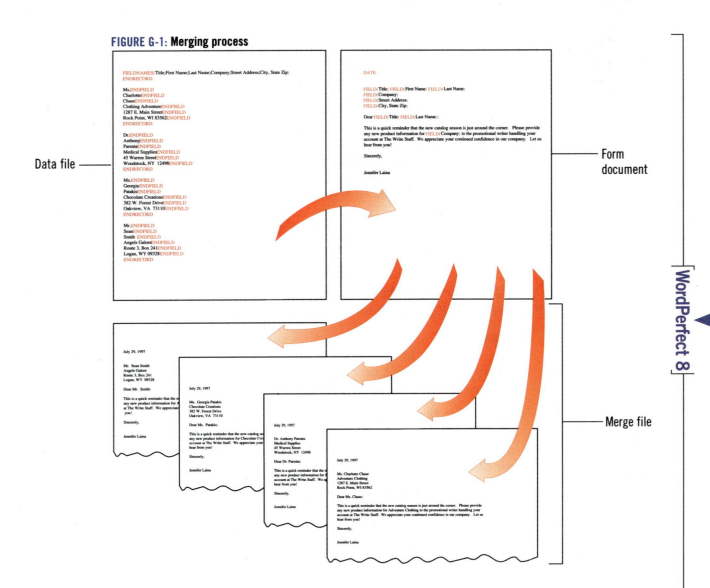

Data file

FIELDNAMES(Title;First Name;Last Name;Company;Street Address;City, State Zip)
ENDRECORD

Ms.ENDFIELD
CharlotteENDFIELD
ChaseENDFIELD
Clothing AdventureENDFIELD
1287 E. Main StreetENDFIELD
Rock Point, WI 83562ENDFIELD
ENDRECORD

Dr.ENDFIELD
AnthonyENDFIELD
ParentaENDFIELD
Medical SuppliesENDFIELD
45 Warren StreetENDFIELD
Woodstock, NY 12498ENDFIELD
ENDRECORD

Ms.ENDFIELD
GeorgiaENDFIELD
PatakisENDFIELD
Chocolate CreationsENDFIELD
382 W. Forest DriveENDFIELD
Oakview, VA 73110ENDFIELD
ENDRECORD

Mr.ENDFIELD
SeanENDFIELD
Smith ENDFIELD
Angels GaloreENDFIELD
Route 3, Box 241ENDFIELD
Logan, WY 09328ENDFIELD
ENDRECORD

Form document

DATE

FIELD(Title) FIELD(First Name) FIELD(Last Name)
FIELD(Company)
FIELD(Street Address)
FIELD(City, State Zip)

Dear FIELD(Title) FIELD(Last Name):

This is a quick reminder that the new catalog season is just around the corner. Please provide any new product information for FIELD(Company) to the promotional writer handling your account at The Write Staff. We appreciate your continued confidence in our company. Let us hear from you!

Sincerely,

Jennifer Laina

Merge file

July 29, 1997

Ms. Charlotte Chase
Adventure Clothing
1287 E. Main Street
Rock Point, WI 83562

Dear Ms. Chase:

This is a quick reminder that the new catalog season is just around the corner. Please provide any new product information for Adventure Clothing to the promotional writer handling your account at The Write Staff. We appreciate your continued confidence in our company. Let us hear from you!

Sincerely,

Jennifer Laina

FIGURE G-2: Draft of letter for merge

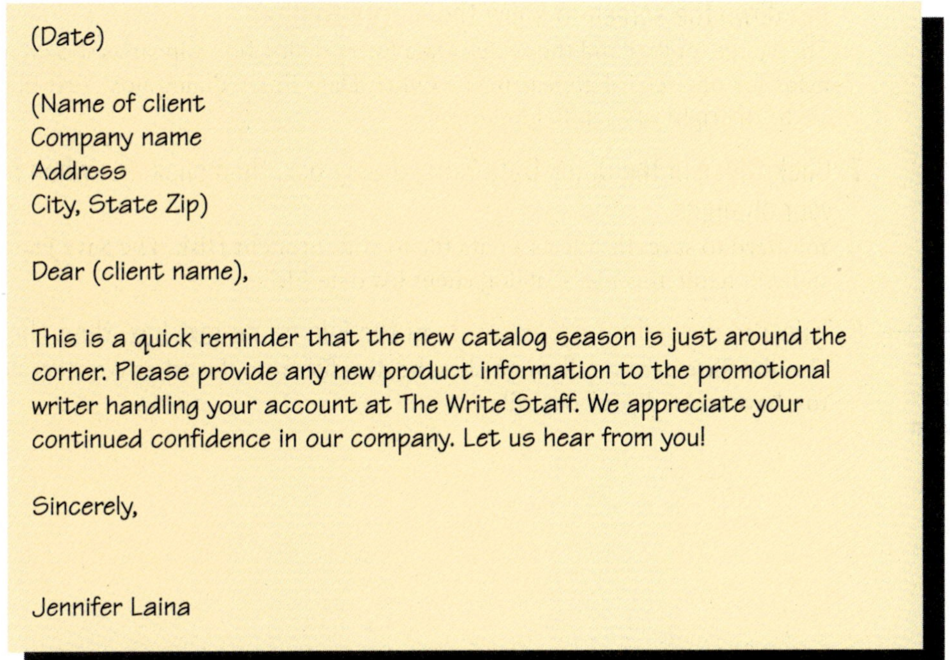

(Date)

(Name of client
Company name
Address
City, State Zip)

Dear (client name),

This is a quick reminder that the new catalog season is just around the corner. Please provide any new product information to the promotional writer handling your account at The Write Staff. We appreciate your continued confidence in our company. Let us hear from you!

Sincerely,

Jennifer Laina

WordPerfect 8

Creating a Data File

Data files contain information, such as names and addresses, that is merged with a form document; this information is arranged into fields and records. A **field** is the smallest amount of information you can specify in a data file. For example, one field might contain a person's last name and another field might contain a zip code. A **record** is a collection of fields, such as a person's first name, last name, company, title, company address, and zip code. You need to create a data file that contains records for The Write Staff's catalog clients. You will merge this file with the form document. First, you set up your data file to include all the necessary fields.

Steps

1. **Start WordPerfect, click Tools on the menu bar, then click Merge**
   The Merge dialog box opens, as shown in Figure G-3.
2. **Click Create Data**
   The Create Data File dialog box appears. You want your data file to include fields for a client's title, first name, last name, company name, street address, city, state, and zip code. You type and add each of these categories as a field.
3. **Type Title in the Name a field text box, then click Add**
   "Title" is added in the Fields used in merge list box, and your insertion point is in the Name a field text box. You continue to add field names. You can press [Enter] instead of clicking the Add button to add each field name that you type.
4. **Type First Name, click Add, type Last Name, click Add, type Company, click Add, type Street Address, then click Add**
   Each field name appears in the Field name list box as shown in Figure G-4.
5. **Type City, State, Zip as one field name, click Add, then click OK**
   The Quick Data Entry dialog box opens.
6. **Click the Quick Data Entry dialog box title bar, then drag the Quick Data Entry dialog box down the screen to show the Merge toolbar**
   The Merge toolbar and the Quick Data Entry dialog box appear as shown in Figure G-5. The fields for one record appear in the Quick Data Entry dialog box. Text boxes for data entry are to the right of each field name.
7. **Click Close in the Quick Data Entry dialog box, then click Yes when prompted to save your changes**
   You need to save this file as a data file to your Student Disk. The Save File dialog box opens, and you name this file "Catalog client list data file".
8. **Type Catalog client list data file in the File name text box, then click Save**
   The .dat file extension distinguishes the data file from the other WordPerfect document files. You have created your data file.

QuickTip

The more fields you have in a record, the more flexibility you have. For example, having both first and last name fields gives you the option of addressing your client informally by using the first name field, or formally by using the title and last name fields.

QuickTip

Be sure that your Student Disk is listed in the Save in folder and that the File name text box shows *.dat.

FIGURE G-3: Merge dialog box

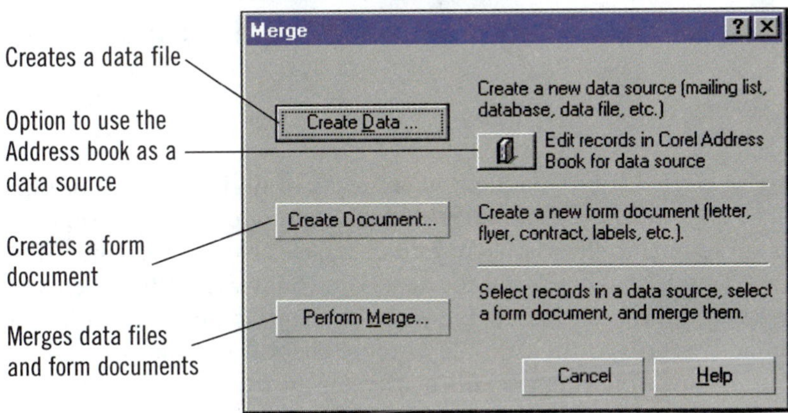

FIGURE G-4: Create Data File dialog box

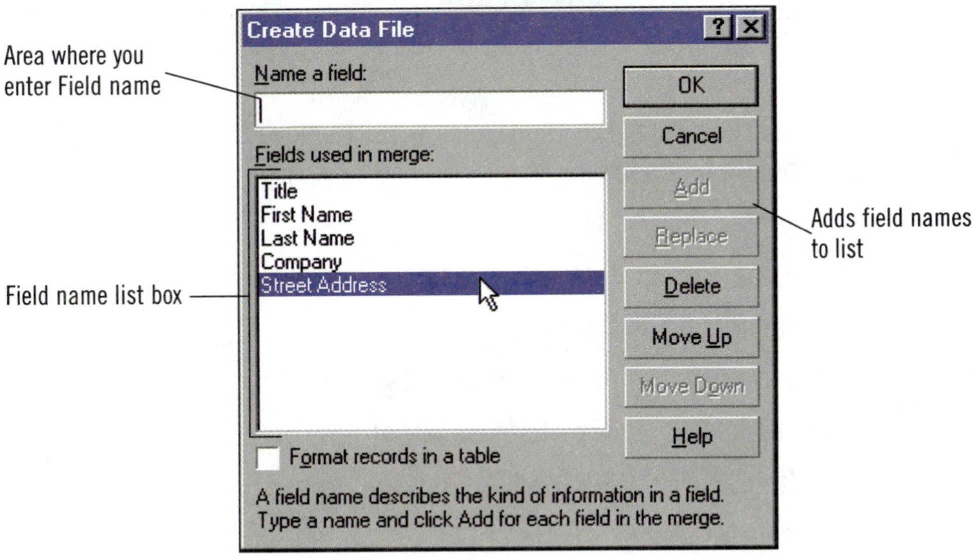

FIGURE G-5: Merge toolbar and Quick Data Entry dialog box

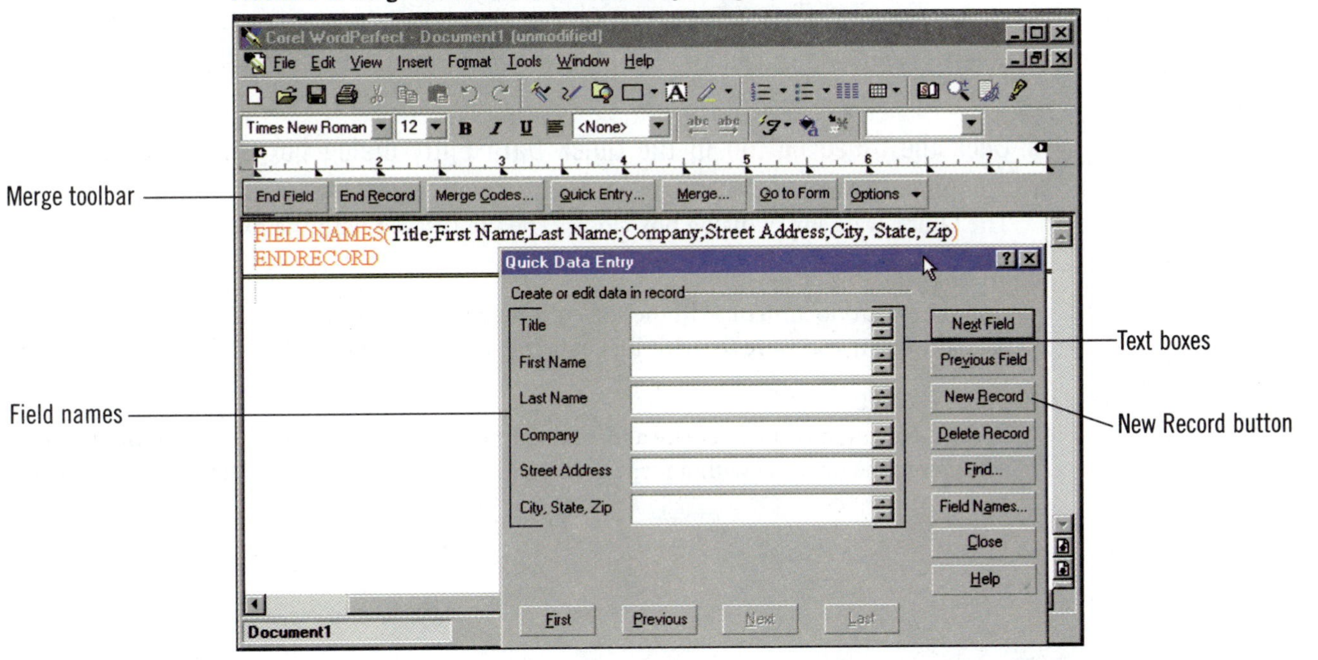

WordPerfect 8

Entering Data in a Data File

Now that you've created your data file, you are ready to fill in the fields using the Quick Data Entry dialog box. WordPerfect uses **merge codes** to separate each field and to end each record. Merge codes are automatically inserted in your data file. Table G-1 lists some WordPerfect merge codes. Jennifer has given you the names and addresses of five clients to include in the mailing. She asks you to create a data file with the clients' names and addresses. She explains that you can add records to the data file as more clients are identified and include any new clients in your mailing. You enter the information for the five clients that Jennifer has given you.

Steps

1. Click **Quick Entry** on the Merge toolbar
   The Quick Data Entry dialog box appears and shows all the fields you entered in the Create Data File dialog box. You are ready to create a record for each client by entering information in each field.
2. Enter the following text, then press **[Tab]** to move to the next field after completing each field name text box:

Title	**Ms.**
First Name	**Charlotte**
Last Name	**Chase**
Company	**Adventure Clothing**
Street Address	**1287 E. Main Street**
City, State, Zip	**Rock Point, WI 83562**

3. Click **New Record**
   You entered the information for each of the fields in one record. Behind the Quick Data Entry dialog box, you can see the record in the data file and the appropriate merge codes that WordPerfect automatically inserted. You continue to create records for the remaining clients.
4. Follow the procedure in steps 2 and 3 to enter the four records shown in Figure G-6
   You have entered the data for your five clients in the data file. The data file has five records, one record for each client.
5. Click the **Close button** in the Quick Data Entry dialog box, then click **Yes** when prompted to save your changes
   The Quick Data Entry dialog box closes. The file is saved with the five records you created.
6. Press **[Ctrl][Home]**
   Compare your document with the screen shown in Figure G-7. The records are separated by page breaks. If you were to print this data file, each record would print on a separate page.
7. Close the file
   In the next lesson you will create a form document in this new document window. Later you will merge the data file with a form document to create personalized letters for each client.

QuickTip

After you complete the last field in the record, you can also press [Enter] rather than the New Record button.

FIGURE G-6: Catalog client list

Dr. Anthony Parenta Medical Supplies 45 Warren Street Woodstock, NY 12498	Mr. Sean Smith Woodlawn Creatures Route 3, Box 241 Logan, WY 09328
Ms. Georgia Patakis Chocolate Creations 382 W. Forest Drive Oaktree, VA 73110	Ms. Rita Louie Desert Designs 376 Pueblo Court Santa Fe, NM 87502

FIGURE G-7: Data file with merge codes

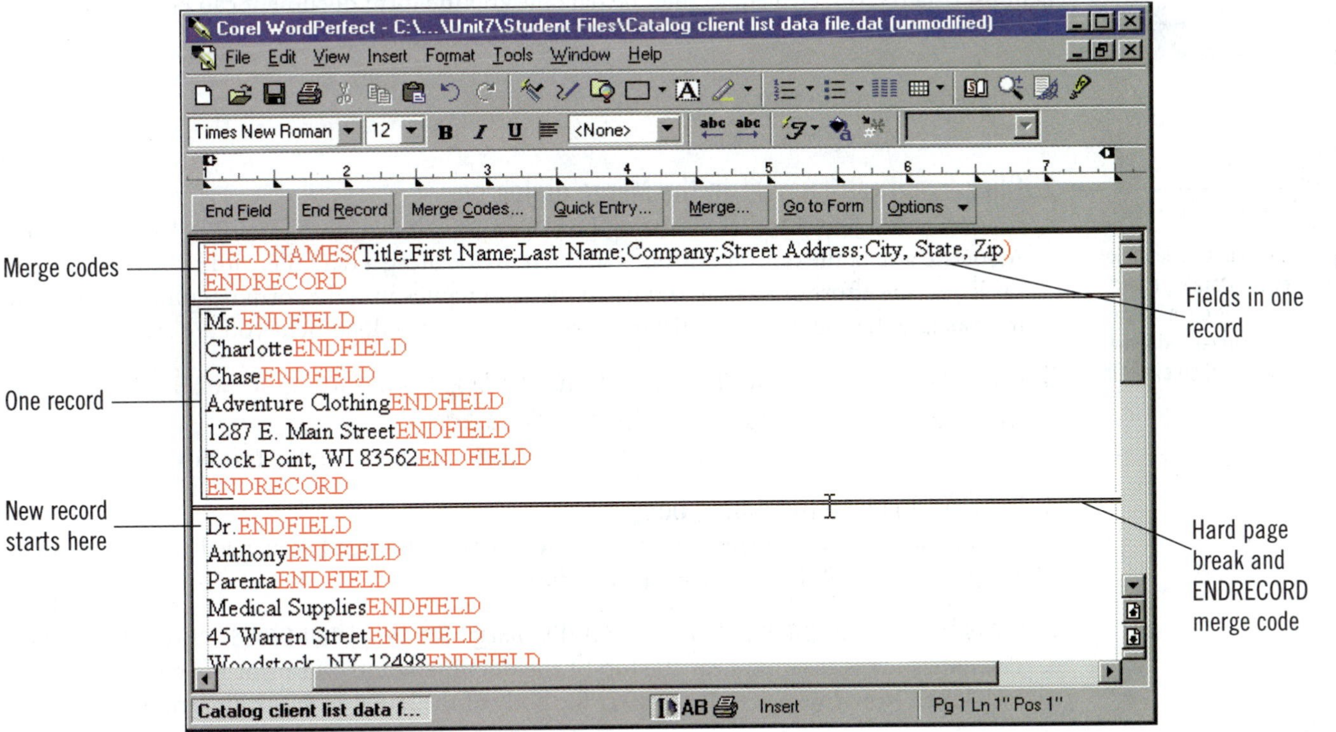

TABLE G-1: Merge codes in a data file

code	use
ENDFIELD	Indicates end of current field in a data file
ENDRECORD	Indicates end of current record in a data file
FIELDNAMES	Lists all fields defined for this data file

Adding records and adding/editing field names

Sometimes after creating a data file, you want to add records or add/edit field names. To add records, be sure the data file is in the current document window, click Quick Entry on the Merge toolbar, click New Record, then complete the record information. To add/edit field names, be sure the data file is in the current document window, click Quick Entry on the Merge toolbar, click Field Names, then add or edit the field names in the Edit Field Names dialog box.

Creating a Form Document

The second step when merging is to create the form document. A **form document** is the base document that contains the text of your final document and the merge codes. The merge codes tell the program where to insert the field information from the data file. You associate the data file with the form document so that the two files are linked; then, anytime you want to merge these files, the form document will automatically locate the correct data file. You create the form document as a new document. You associate the form document you create with the Catalog client list data file you created, so that the data file and the form document can be merged.

Steps

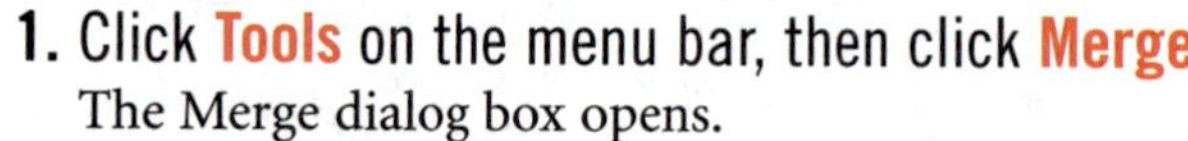

1. Click **Tools** on the menu bar, then click **Merge**
   The Merge dialog box opens.

Trouble?

The Create Merge File dialog box opens if Catalog client list data file is open. Click the New document window option button, then click OK.

2. Click **Create Document** in the Merge dialog box
   The Associate Form and Data dialog box opens, as shown in Figure G-8. Notice that the Associate a data file option button is selected. Associating a data file with a form document saves you the effort of having to type all the field names into the form document. You want to associate the Catalog client list data file with the form document you are creating.
3. Click the **Folder icon** to the right of the text box, click **Catalog client list data file** in the Select Data File dialog box, then click **Select**
   The Catalog client list data file is entered in the Associate a data file text box.
4. Click **OK** to close the dialog box
   Jennifer wants you to print this letter on company letterhead. You need to leave enough room at the top of the letter for the letterhead.
5. Press **[Enter]** ten times, click **Date** on the Merge toolbar, then press **[Enter]** four times
   The date code is inserted near the top of the document and will print the current date on each letter. Now you are ready to insert the body of the letter from the file Jennifer gave you.

Trouble?

Be sure to click Insert on the menu bar and not Insert Field on the Merge toolbar.

6. Click **Insert** on the menu bar, click **File**, click **WP G-1**, click **Insert**, then scroll down the screen to see the letter
   The letter is inserted into your form document. Notice that the letter now consists of the date, the body of the letter, and the closing lines, as shown in Figure G-9. You save this file to your Student Disk as a form document, which will have a .frm file extension.
7. Click **File** on the menu bar, click **Save as**, type **Catalog reminder form document** in the File name text box, then click **Save**

FIGURE G-8: Associate Form and Data dialog box

FIGURE G-9: Form file

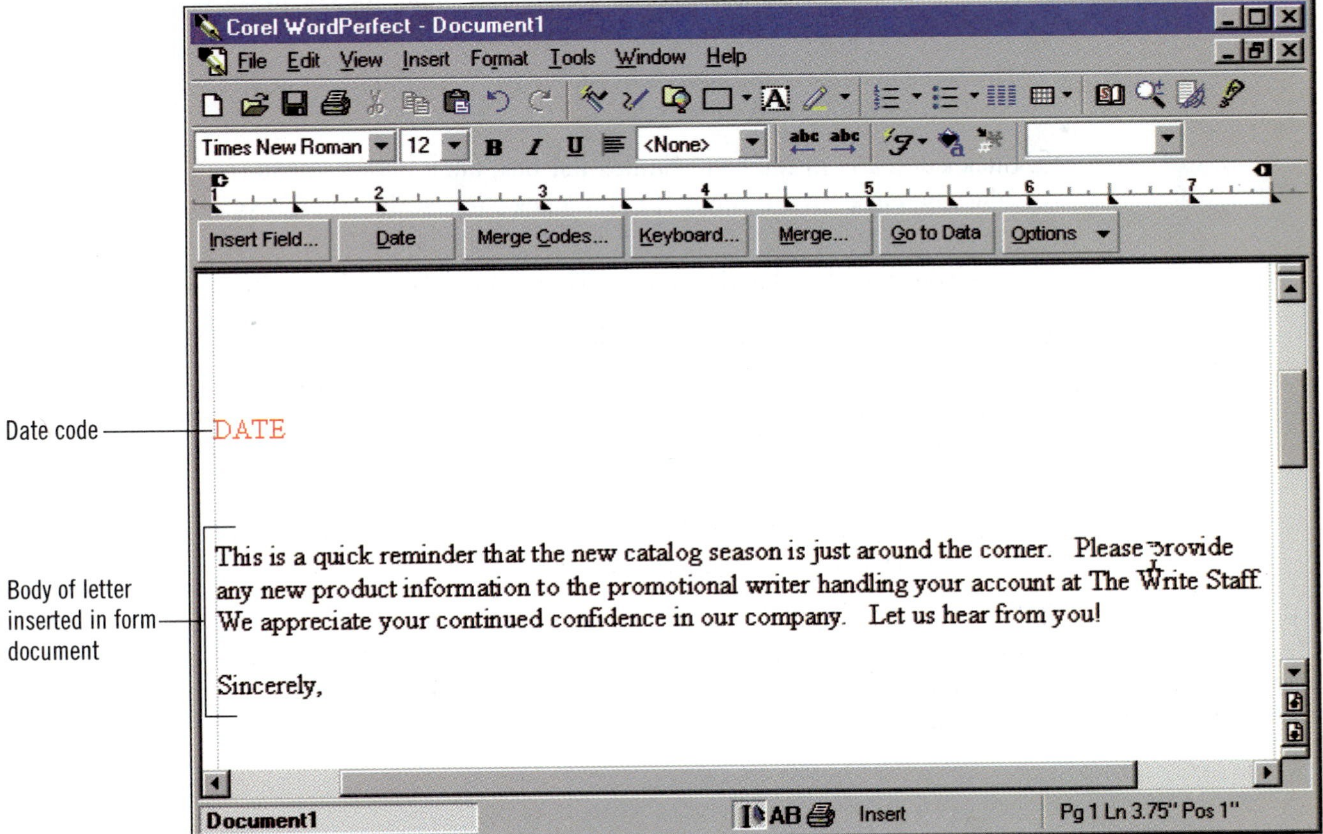

WordPerfect 8

WordPerfect 8

Entering Fields in a Form Document

To complete the form document so that each letter is personalized for each client, you need to specify where the merge codes for the fields from the data file should be placed in the letter. To identify where you want the information from the data file to go in the form document, you use the Insert Field button on the Merge toolbar. Now you are ready to insert the merge codes for the fields into the form document.

Steps

1. **Position the insertion point on the line above the first line of the body of the letter**
   This is where you are going to start inserting the fields for the address.
2. **Click Insert Field on the Merge toolbar**
   The Insert Field Name or Number dialog box opens, as shown in Figure G-10. The fields that you created in the Catalog client list data file are listed in this dialog box.
3. **Click Title in the Field Names list box if necessary, click Insert, then press [Spacebar]**
   Pressing [Spacebar] inserts a space between this field name and the next field name.
4. **Click First Name in the Field Names list box, click Insert, press [Spacebar], click Last Name, click Insert, then press [Enter]**
   This is the first line of the address in your letter. You continue to insert field names to complete the remaining lines of the address.
5. **Click Company in the Field Names list box, click Insert, press [Enter], click Street Address, click Insert, press [Enter], click City, State, Zip, press Insert, then press [Enter] twice**
   Next, you enter the salutation and the Title and Last Name fields for the greeting.
6. **Type Dear, press [Spacebar], click Title in the Field Names list box, click Insert, press [Spacebar], click Last Name, click Insert, then type a colon (:)**
   Make sure you don't type a comma after "Dear" and that you include a space between title and last name. Move the dialog box as needed to view the greeting "Dear FIELD(Title) FIELD(Last Name):"
7. **Click Close in the Insert Field Name or Number dialog box, then press [Enter]**
   This adds a blank line between the greeting and the body of the letter.
8. **Save your document**
   Compare the document on your screen with Figure G-11. You want to show the document to Jennifer so she can review and make any changes to the form document before you perform the merge.

QuickTip

To insert the field, you can also press [Enter] instead of Insert.

QuickTip

It is important to save your document before performing the merge.

FIGURE G-10: Insert Field Name or Number dialog box

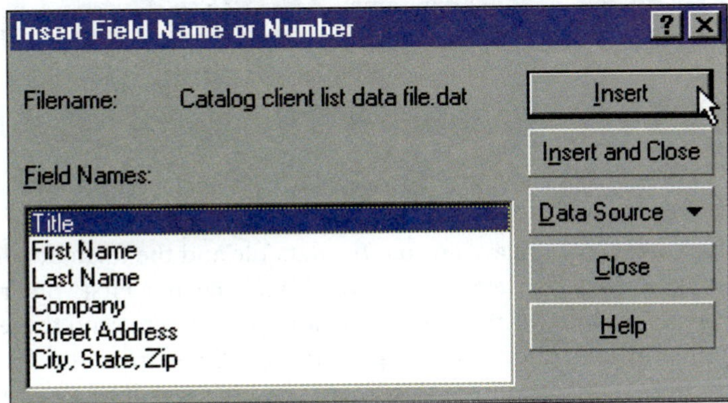

FIGURE G-11: Printed form document

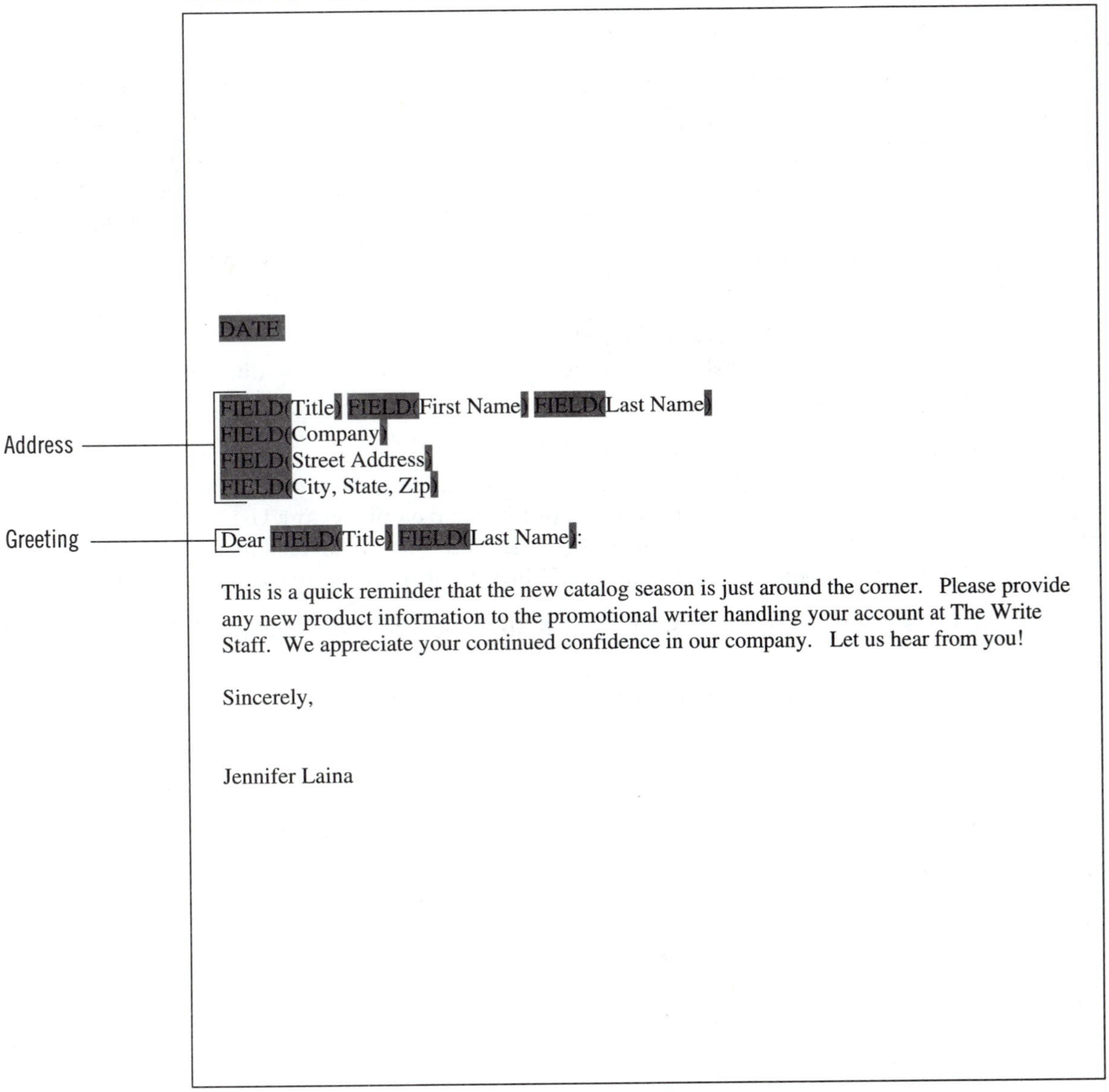

DATE

Address — FIELD(Title) FIELD(First Name) FIELD(Last Name)
FIELD(Company)
FIELD(Street Address)
FIELD(City, State, Zip)

Greeting — Dear FIELD(Title) FIELD(Last Name):

This is a quick reminder that the new catalog season is just around the corner. Please provide any new product information to the promotional writer handling your account at The Write Staff. We appreciate your continued confidence in our company. Let us hear from you!

Sincerely,

Jennifer Laina

WordPerfect 8

Merging Data Files and Form Documents

Once the data file and form document are created, you are ready to merge them. You will use the Merge button on the Merge toolbar. Table G-2 provides more information about the Merge toolbar. You have created the data file and the form document. You will merge these to create personalized letters for The Write Staff's clients. First you created a data file that includes all the information for the clients to whom you want to send the letter. Then you created a form document that includes the merge codes for fields from the data file. Now, you are ready to merge the data file and form document. The merge will result in a personalized letter to each of the clients in your data file.

1. Open **Catalog client list data file**, click **Window** on the menu bar, then click **Catalog reminder form document**
   The Catalog reminder form document is in the current window.
2. Click **Merge** on the Merge toolbar
   The Perform Merge dialog box opens, as shown in Figure G-12.
3. Be sure that **Current Document** appears to the right of the Form Document list arrow, the filename **A:\Catalog client list data file** appears in the text box to the right of the Data Source list arrow, and **New Document** appears to the right of the Output list arrow
   The form document is the current document. Catalog client list data file is the data file from which the client address information will be extracted. The merge will appear in a new document window. If any of these settings are not specified correctly, click the appropriate button in the Perform Merge dialog box and select the correct setting.
4. Click **Merge** in the Perform Merge dialog box
   The Perform Merge dialog box closes. The data file and the form document are merged in a new document window.
5. Scroll through all five letters in the document
   The document in the current window, which is the merged file, contains five letters separated by page breaks, one letter for each record in the data file. Figure G-13 shows the letter for Charlotte Chase, which is the first merged letter in this file. Merged files take up a lot of disk space, so you don't save the merged file. However, it is easy to merge these again if necessary.
6. Close the Merge document, then click **No** to close your document without saving your changes
   Next, you review and edit the data file and the form document.

QuickTip

Your drive information may be different depending on the location of your data file.

FIGURE G-12: Perform Merge dialog box

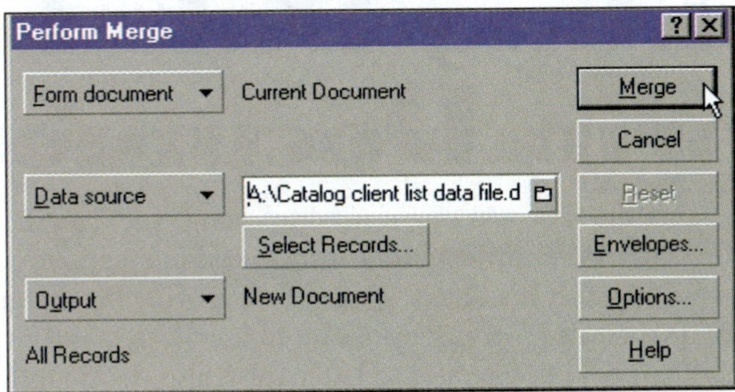

FIGURE G-13: Page 1 of the merged document

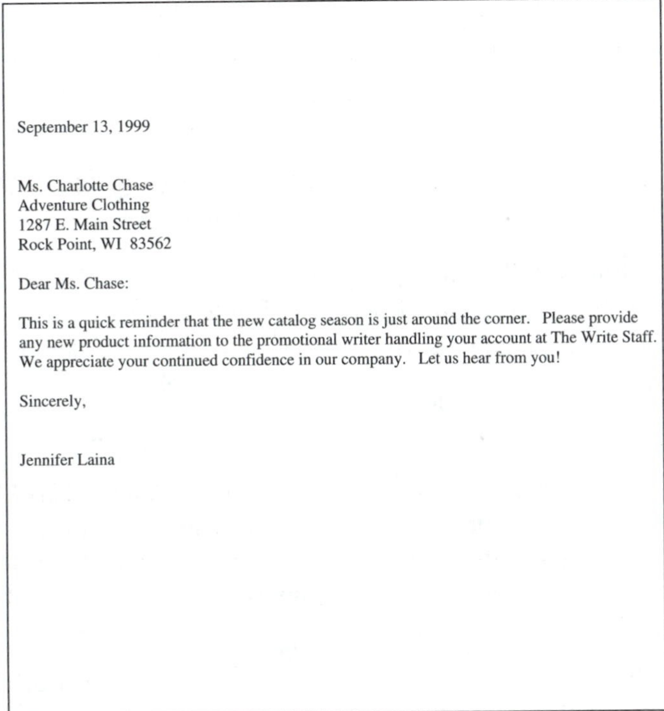

September 13, 1999

Ms. Charlotte Chase
Adventure Clothing
1287 E. Main Street
Rock Point, WI 83562

Dear Ms. Chase:

This is a quick reminder that the new catalog season is just around the corner. Please provide any new product information to the promotional writer handling your account at The Write Staff. We appreciate your continued confidence in our company. Let us hear from you!

Sincerely,

Jennifer Laina

TABLE G-2: The Merge toolbar

option	use to
Insert Field	Insert a field from the data source into the form document
Date	Insert a date code that changes to reflect the current date when merged
Merge Codes	Insert merge codes into the document
Keyboard	Insert a Keyboard command with its prompt
Merge	Combine data file with a form document
Go to Data	Go to the associated data source
Options	Display codes; Display as markers; Hide codes; Remove Merge Bar

WordPerfect 8

Editing Data Files and Form Documents

After merging the files, you might need to change the data file, form document, or both. Client lists, address books, or any data files always need to be updated. You can also modify form documents to use for other mailings. In reviewing the merged letters, you find a spelling error that must be corrected. Because you want to use the data file for future mailings, you edit the data file rather than editing the merged letters. You also decide to make the letter more personalized by including the company name in the body of the document. You edit the form document to do this. Once both changes are made and saved, you perform the merge again to reflect the changes.

Steps

1. Click **Window** on the menu bar, then click **Catalog client list data file.dat**
   The data file appears in the document window. There is an error in Ms. Georgia Patakis' address. The city should be Oakview.
2. Scroll to Ms. Patakis' record, position the insertion point to the left of **Oaktree**, double-click **Oaktree**, type **Oakview**, then save the data file
   The change you made to the data file is saved. Next, you want to add a field to the form document.
3. Click **Window**, then click **Catalog reminder form document.frm**
   The form document appears in the document window.
4. Position the insertion point immediately after **information** in the second line, press **[Spacebar]**, type **for**, then press **[Spacebar]**
   The insertion point is where you want to insert the Company field.
5. Click **Insert Field** on the Merge toolbar
   The Insert Field Name or Number dialog box opens.
6. Click **Company** in the Field Names list box, click **Insert and Close**, then save your work
   The merge code for the field Company is inserted in the text as shown in Figure G-14 and the changes to the form document are saved. When the data file and form document are merged, the company name will appear in this location in each letter.
7. Click **Merge** on the Merge toolbar
   Current Document appears to the right of the Form document list arrow, the filename Catalog client list data file.dat appears in the text box to the right of the Data source list arrow, and New Document appears to the right of the Output list arrow.
8. Click **Merge** in the Perform Merge dialog box
   The data file and the form document are merged for a second time in the current document window.
9. Print the merged document, close all files, save only the form document and data file if prompted
   Compare your letters with those shown in Figure G-15. Notice that each printed letter contains the current date and a different name, company name, and address.

FIGURE G-14: Field inserted in form document

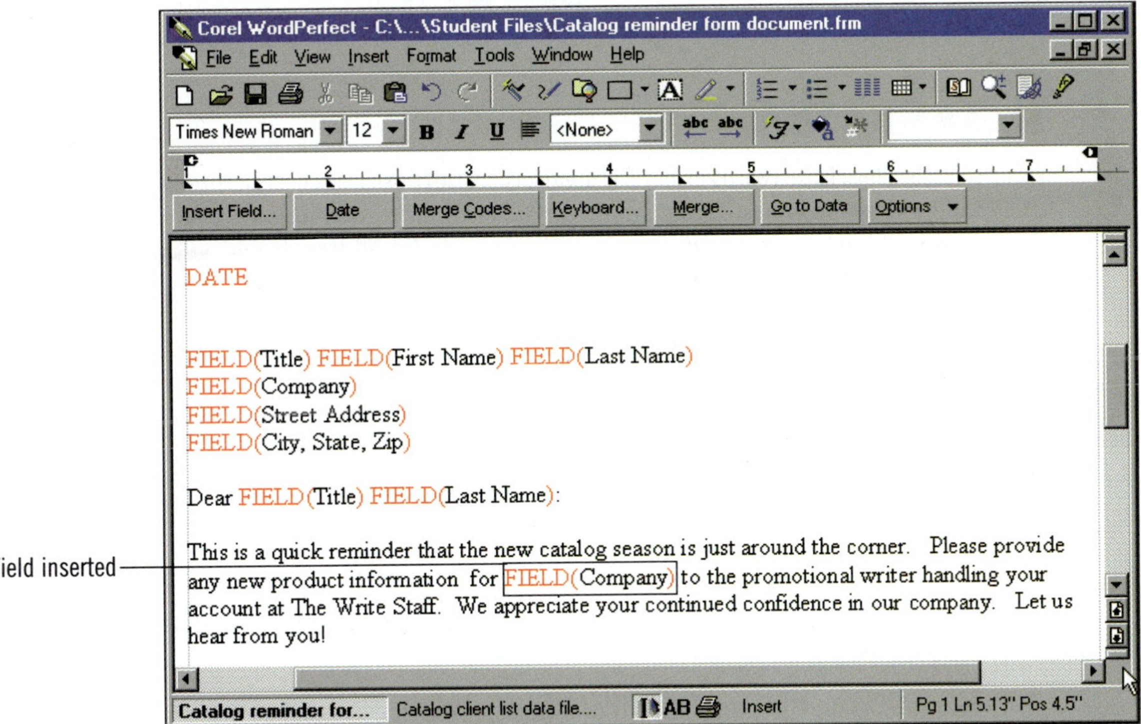

FIGURE G-15: Merged documents

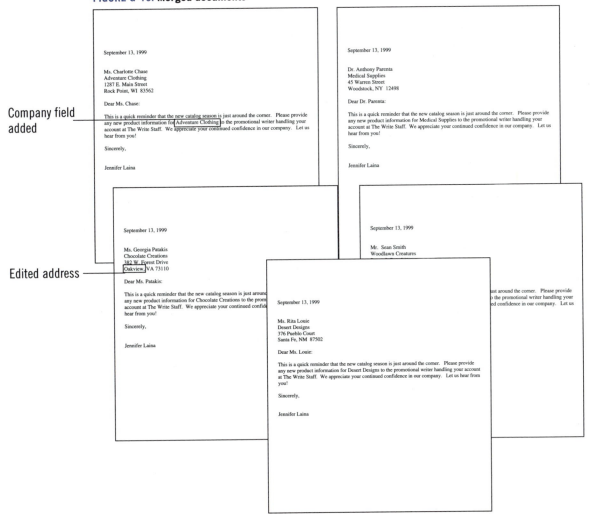

Company field added

Edited address

September 13, 1999

Ms. Charlotte Chase
Adventure Clothing
1287 E. Main Street
Rock Point, WI 83562

Dear Ms. Chase:

This is a quick reminder that the new catalog season is just around the corner. Please provide any new product information for Adventure Clothing to the promotional writer handling your account at The Write Staff. We appreciate your continued confidence in our company. Let us hear from you!

Sincerely,

Jennifer Laina

September 13, 1999

Dr. Anthony Parenta
Medical Supplies
45 Warren Street
Woodstock, NY 12498

Dear Dr. Parenta:

This is a quick reminder that the new catalog season is just around the corner. Please provide any new product information for Medical Supplies to the promotional writer handling your account at The Write Staff. We appreciate your continued confidence in our company. Let us hear from you!

Sincerely,

Jennifer Laina

September 13, 1999

Ms. Georgia Patakis
Chocolate Creations
382 W. Forest Drive
Oakview, VA 73110

Dear Ms. Patakis:

This is a quick reminder that the new catalog season is just around ... any new product information for Chocolate Creations to the prom... account at The Write Staff. We appreciate your continued confid... hear from you!

Sincerely,

Jennifer Laina

September 13, 1999

Mr. Sean Smith
Woodlawn Creatures

...ust around the corner. Please provide ...o the promotional writer handling your ...ed confidence in our company. Let us

September 13, 1999

Ms. Rita Louie
Desert Designs
376 Pueblo Court
Santa Fe, NM 87502

Dear Ms. Louie:

This is a quick reminder that the new catalog season is just around the corner. Please provide any new product information for Desert Designs to the promotional writer handling your account at The Write Staff. We appreciate your continued confidence in our company. Let us hear from you!

Sincerely,

Jennifer Laina

Creating Address Labels

You can create labels in WordPerfect for a variety of purposes, such as mailing labels, file folder labels, and videotape labels. While you can type each label individually, you can save yourself time by using Merge to create labels from a data file or the Address Book. Jennifer has asked you to create mailing labels for the same clients who will be receiving the Catalog reminder letter. You use the Catalog client list data file to create the labels. You create a form document for the labels, then you merge the data file and the form document to print the labels.

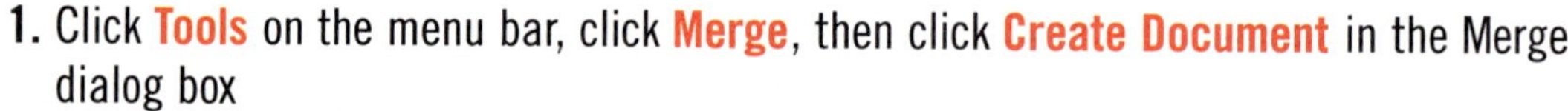

Steps

1. Click **Tools** on the menu bar, click **Merge**, then click **Create Document** in the Merge dialog box
2. Click the **File icon**, click the **Catalog client list data file**, click **Select**, then click **OK**
   You identified the data source file and are ready to create the label form document. First, select the type of label to use.
3. Click **Format** on the menu bar, then click **Labels**
   The Labels dialog box opens. The predefined labels are listed in the Labels list box in ascending numerical order.
4. Click the **Laser printed option button**, then scroll down the list box and click **Avery 5663 Clear Address** in the Labels list box
   Only the labels available for printing on laser printers appear in the list box. A preview of the Avery 5663 Clear Address label appears in the Preview window as shown in Figure G-16.
5. Click **Select**
   You enter the merge codes in the label, save the label form document, then merge the data file and the form document to create the labels.
6. Press **[Enter]** twice, click **Insert Field** on the Merge toolbar, click **Title** in the Field Names list box if necessary, click **Insert**, press **[Spacebar]**, continue entering the merge codes as shown in Figure G-17, click **Close** on the Insert Field Name or Number dialog box, then save the file as **Client Labels.frm**
   You have created the label form document and are ready to merge the form document and the data file to create a new merged file for printing labels. The file Client Labels.frm is the current document.
7. Click **Merge** on the Merge toolbar
   You check to be sure the Form Document, Data Source, and Output information is correct.
8. Click **Merge** in the Perform Merge dialog box
   The results of the merge appear in a new document window. Compare your screen to Figure G-18 to see how the labels print.
9. Close all the files, save only the form document and the data file if prompted, then exit WordPerfect

Trouble?

To create the labels form document, you will follow the same steps you followed in the preceding lessons.

FIGURE G-16: Labels dialog box

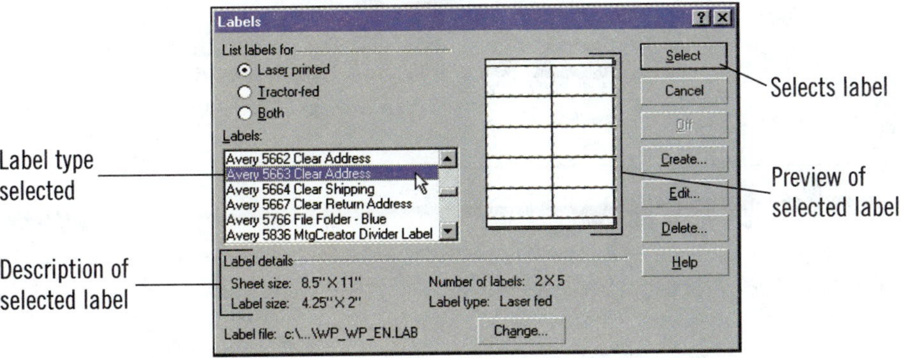

FIGURE G-17: Label form document with merge codes

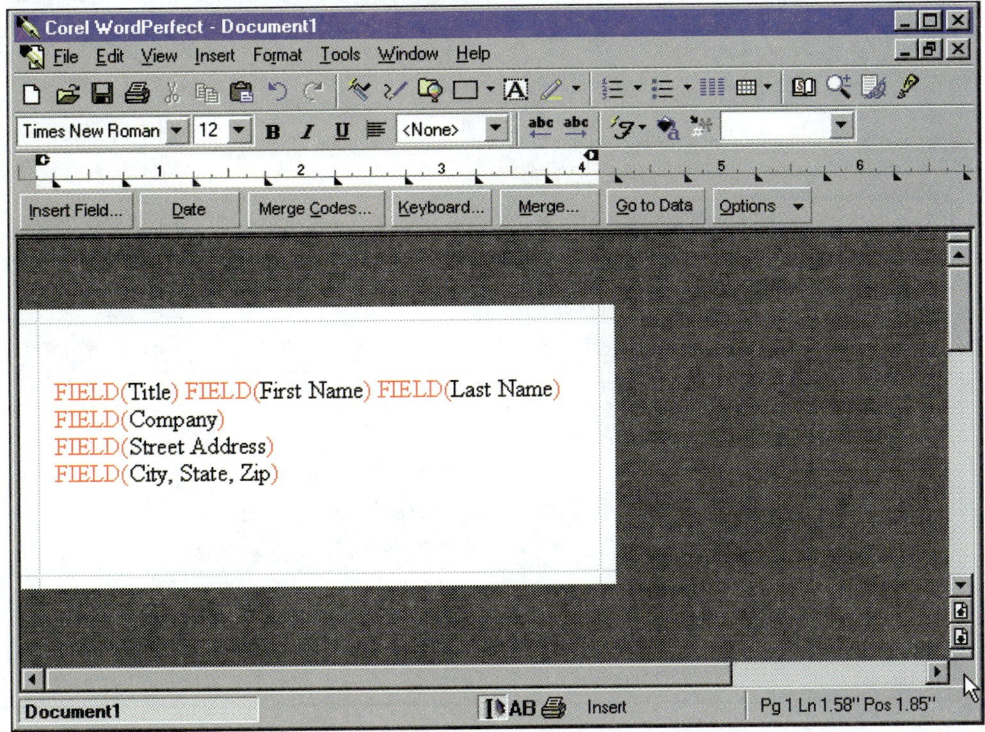

FIGURE G-18: Paper printout of labels

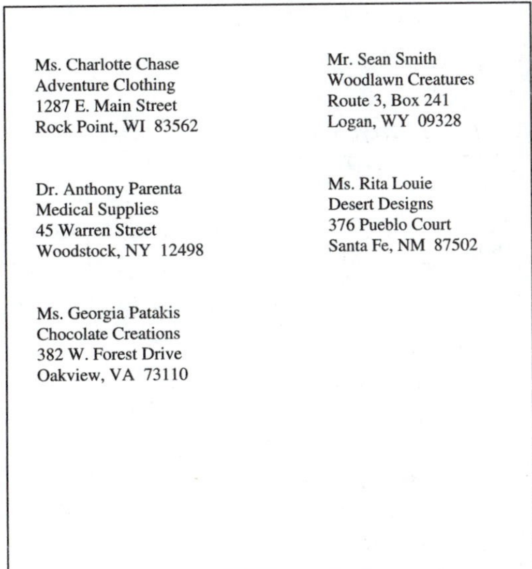

Practice

► Concepts Review

Label each element of the WordPerfect window and the Quick Data Entry dialog box shown in Figure G-19.

FIGURE G-19

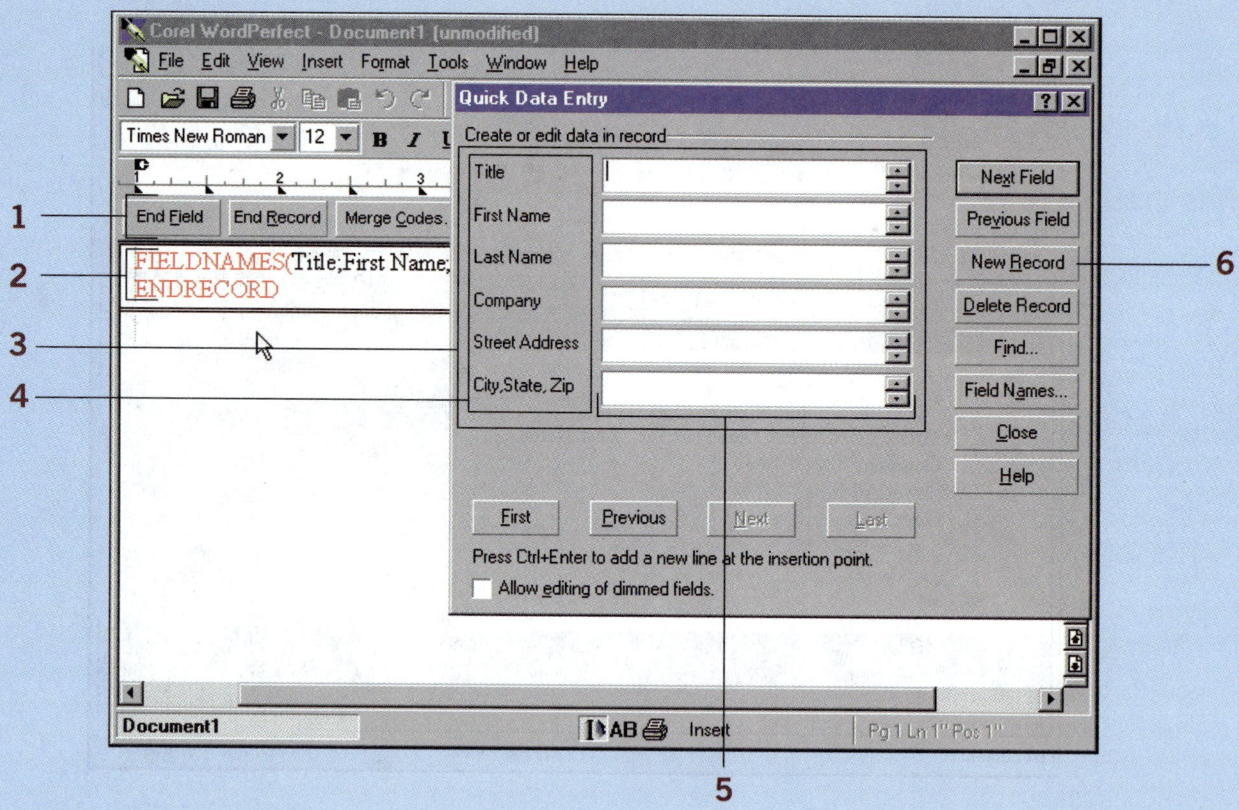

Match each of the following items with the phrase that best describes it.

7. Field
8. Record
9. Data file
10. Form document

a. The data source in a merged document
b. The text and graphic source in a merged document
c. Contains a group of related items in a data file
d. Each piece of information that you provide in a data file

Select the best answer from the list of choices.

11. Which of the following is the best reason to use the Merge feature?
- **a.** To make several exact copies of a file
- **b.** To send the same letter to several people, using each person's name and address
- **c.** To combine two memos into one long letter
- **d.** To copy several paragraphs from one letter to another

12. When you use the Merge feature, the resulting letters are in
- **a.** The data file.
- **b.** The form document.
- **c.** The merged document.
- **d.** A merge code.

13. To create the data file, you click Merge,
- **a.** Then click Merge again.
- **b.** Then click Create Document.
- **c.** Then click Create Data.
- **d.** Then click Quick Data Entry.

14. In the Quick Data Entry dialog box, to begin a new record you can click New Record or press
- **a.** [Tab].
- **b.** [Enter].
- **c.** [Ctrl].
- **d.** [Spacebar].

15. When you create a form document, you must associate the form document with
- **a.** The Quick Data Entry dialog box.
- **b.** A merge file.
- **c.** A second form document.
- **d.** A data file.

16. When you create a form document, the field names you insert are
- **a.** Inserted with data from the data file.
- **b.** Always printed when you print the merge document.
- **c.** Inserted with merge codes.
- **d.** Listed in alphabetical order at the end of the form document.

17. It is not important to save the merged document because
- **a.** It is saved in the data file.
- **b.** It is saved as part of the form document.
- **c.** You can always re-create it using the form document and data file.
- **d.** You can print it and reenter all the personal data.

18. If you want changes that you make to be reflected in future merge documents, you
- **a.** Edit the data file.
- **b.** Edit the form document.
- **c.** Edit the merge document.
- **d.** Both a and b.

19. To create a merge document for labels, you need
- **a.** A data file and a form document.
- **b.** A data file only.
- **c.** A form document only.
- **d.** A predefined label file.

► Skills Review

1. Plan a merge document.
- **a.** State the purpose of the merge document, based on this information: You own an office supply company. You offer a yearly service agreement to customers who purchase their copiers through your store. It is time to send out a reminder to those customers.
- **b.** Create a list of people to whom you want to send the document.
- **c.** Make a list of the fields you want to include in the data file.
- **d.** Decide what the form document will say.
- **e.** Write a rough draft of the letter.
- **f.** Design the mailing labels.

2. Create and enter records in a data file.
- **a.** Start WordPerfect.
- **b.** Click Tools on the menu bar, then click Merge.
- **c.** Click Create Data.
- **d.** Enter the following field names: Title, First Name, Last Name, Company, Street Address.
- **e.** Enter City, State, Zip as one field name, then click OK.
- **f.** Create three records in the data file using the Quick Data Entry dialog box. You can make these up or use your friends' data.
- **g.** Close the Quick Data Entry dialog box, then save the file as "Copier client list data file".

3. Create a form document.
- **a.** Click Tools on the menu bar, then click Merge.
- **b.** Click Create Document, if necessary, click the New document window option button, then click OK.
- **c.** If necessary, click Associate a data file option button, click the File folder icon, click "Copier client list data file", click Select, then click OK.
- **d.** Press [Enter] four times, then insert the date into your form document.
- **e.** Enter four spaces between the date and the inside address.
- **f.** Insert file WP G-2 from your Student Disk.
- **g.** Save your document as "Copier Service Request form document".

4. **Enter fields in a form document.**
   a. Click Insert Field on the Merge toolbar, then select field names so that the inside address appears three lines below the DATE merge code as follows:
   FIELD(Title) FIELD(First Name) FIELD(Last Name)
   FIELD(Company)
   FIELD(Street Address)
   FIELD(City, State, Zip)
   b. Press [Enter] twice to insert a blank line below the inside address.
   c. Create the greeting so that it appears as: Dear [Title] [Last Name]:
   d. Press [Enter] once to insert a blank line between the greeting and the body of the letter.
   e. Spell Check the document, scroll down the page and make editing changes as appropriate, then save the file to your Student Disk.

5. **Merge the data file and the form document.**
   a. Click Window on the menu bar to be sure both the data file "Copier client list data file" and the form document "Copier Service Request form document" are open.
   b. Click Merge on the Merge toolbar; be sure the form document, data source, and output information is correct.
   c. Click the Merge button in the Perform Merge dialog box.
   d. Scroll through the document to make sure that it is formatted correctly, then close but do not save the merge.

6. **Edit the data file and the form document.**
   a. Make sure that "Copier Service Request form document" is the current document.
   b. Edit the form document to personalize the letter by replacing the second "you" in the last sentence with the Company field so the company name appears in the text of the form letter, then save the file.
   c. Click Window on the menu bar, click "Copier client list data file" so that the data file becomes the current document.
   d. Edit the data file by changing one street name.
   e. Add one new record.
   f. Merge, then close and save the form document.

7. **Create address labels.**
   a. Click Tools on the menu bar, click Merge, click Create Document, if necessary, click the New document window option button, then click OK.
   b. If necessary, click the Associate a data file option button, click the Folder icon, click "Copier client list data file", then click OK.
   c. Click Format on the menu bar, then click Labels.
   d. Choose Avery 12-294/295 Laser Tags, then click Select.
   e. Insert three blank spaces, click Insert Field on the Merge toolbar, then insert field names so the label address appears as follows:
   FIELD(Title) FIELD(First Name) FIELD(Last Name)
   FIELD(Company)
   FIELD(Street Address)
   FIELD(City, State, Zip)
   f. Save the form document as "Copier Labels".
   g. Merge the "Copier client list data file" and the "Copier Labels" form document into a new document.
   h. Print the merged document, close all files but do not save the merge document when prompted, then exit WordPerfect.

Independent Challenges

1. You are the publicity chairperson for your upcoming high school class reunion. Use the WordPerfect Merge feature to create personalized form letters to your classmates informing them of the reunion.

1. Create the data file.
   - Include field names: First Name, Last Name, Class of, Street Address, City, State, Zip, Phone Number.
   - Enter information for five classmates into the data file, then save the file as "Class data file".
2. Create the form document.
   - Date your letter so that the current date will be on the letter when it is printed.
   - Insert the field names to create an inside address and a greeting.
   - Insert the file WP G-3 to create the body of the letter. Scroll through the document and make adjustments as needed. After the closing, leave three blank lines for your signature, type your name, then type "Class Reunion Chairperson".
   - Save the file as "Class Reunion Letter form document".
3. Merge, then print the merge document.
   - Use Merge on the Merge toolbar to merge the form document and the data file.
   - Print two letters, one from each class. Save the data file and the form document, but do not save the merge.

2. Each year, just before the start of the New Year, you find yourself wishing you could contact your family and friends to tell them how you spent the past year. You decide to use the merge capability of WordPerfect to create one general letter and personalize it for each of your friends and family members.

1. Create the data file.
   - Include the following field names: First Name, Last Name, Street Address, City, State, Zip, Phone number, Family.
   - Enter information for five friends. For the Field Family, list members of their immediate family.
   - Save the file as "Family List Data File".
2. Create the form document.
   - Type a letter with information about how you spent the last year or insert WP G-4 and add one paragraph.
   - Include an inside address, a greeting, and a closing. Insert the Field Family name in the body of the letter.
   - Save the file as "Family Holiday Letter form document".
3. Merge the files.
   - Merge the form document and the data file to create the personalized form letters.
   - Print and submit two of the letters. Close but do not save the merge, then close the form document.
   - Create address labels.
   - Use the file called "Family List data file" as your data source.
   - Select a label style. Create the labels so they look like the inside address of your form document.
   - Save your file as "Family & Friends Labels". Merge the form document and the data file.
   - Print the merged document on regular paper, not labels. Close the files, then exit WordPerfect.

3. You are interested in pursuing advanced studies. You would like to compare programs at different colleges or institutions that have been recommended to you. You decide to use WordPerfect's Merge command to send a personalized letter to each of the institutions. Use Figure G-20 as your guide.

1. Create a data file that includes the following fields: Title, First Name, Last Name, Degree, Position, Institution, Street Address, City, State, Zip, Phone number, then enter data for three or more records. Save the data file as "College List data file".
2. Create a form document that includes an inside address and formal salutation. Type a letter requesting information or insert WP G-5. Make adjustments as needed. Include a formal closing which includes your address and phone number. Save the file as "College Request form document".

3. Merge the data file and the form document. Make changes to the form document and data file as needed. Print two of the merged document letters.
4. Create address labels using the file "College List data file" as your data source. Save the file as "College Labels", then print the labels on paper. Close the files, then exit WordPerfect.

FIGURE G-20

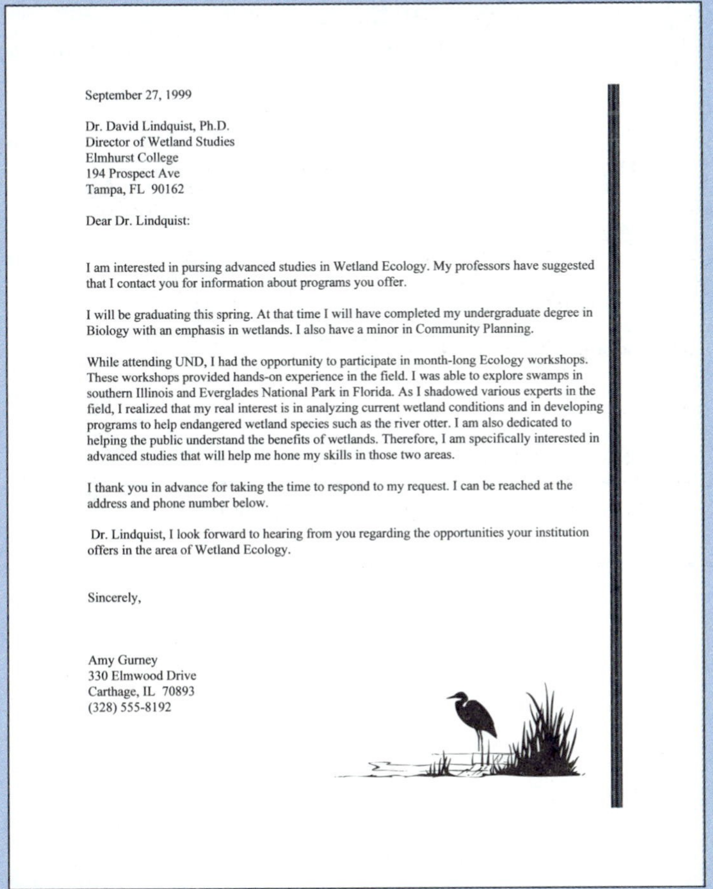

September 27, 1999

Dr. David Lindquist, Ph.D.
Director of Wetland Studies
Elmhurst College
194 Prospect Ave
Tampa, FL 90162

Dear Dr. Lindquist:

I am interested in pursing advanced studies in Wetland Ecology. My professors have suggested that I contact you for information about programs you offer.

I will be graduating this spring. At that time I will have completed my undergraduate degree in Biology with an emphasis in wetlands. I also have a minor in Community Planning.

While attending UND, I had the opportunity to participate in month-long Ecology workshops. These workshops provided hands-on experience in the field. I was able to explore swamps in southern Illinois and Everglades National Park in Florida. As I shadowed various experts in the field, I realized that my real interest is in analyzing current wetland conditions and in developing programs to help endangered wetland species such as the river otter. I am also dedicated to helping the public understand the benefits of wetlands. Therefore, I am specifically interested in advanced studies that will help me hone my skills in those two areas.

I thank you in advance for taking the time to respond to my request. I can be reached at the address and phone number below.

Dr. Lindquist, I look forward to hearing from you regarding the opportunities your institution offers in the area of Wetland Ecology.

Sincerely,

Amy Gurney
330 Elmwood Drive
Carthage, IL 70893
(328) 555-8192

4. As the owner of an electronics store, you created a stereo client list data file and a stereo service request form document. After reviewing the merge, you realize you need a similar letter for other products you sell, such as VCRs. You make changes to the data file and the form document to create a new merged document.

1. Open the document "Stereo client list data file" from the Student Disk and save it as "Customer List data file".
2. Add the field names: "Equipment purchased," "Customer since". For the existing records, add the word "stereo" in the field named Equipment purchased and add a date in the field named Customer since.
3. Add four new records to the file. Use your family or friends' names and information as needed. Type "VCR" in the field named Equipment purchased for these new records.
4. Open the form document "Stereo Service Request form document" from your Student Disk and save the file as "Service reminder form document". Insert the field name "Equipment purchased" in the body of the letter to replace the word "stereo"; personalize the letter by including the "Customer since" field in the last paragraph of the letter. Spell Check and save the form document.
5. Change the data source to "Customer List data file", save the document, then perform the merge.
6. Save the form document and the data file. Print one letter.
7. Create address labels for the Customer list data file. Save the label form document as "Customer labels".
8. Close the files, save the appropriate files, then exit WordPerfect.

Visual Workshop

Create the data file as shown in Figure G-21, then enter five records using the names and information of your friends or relatives. Then create a form document. Write a letter asking for help on your next research project. Be sure to include the name and address fields in the address portion of the letter, and use the first name field at least once in the body of the letter. Perform the merge and print the five letters. Save the data file and the form document. Create address labels. Save the label form document. Merge and print the address labels on paper. Close the documents, save the data and form files, then exit WordPerfect.

FIGURE G-21

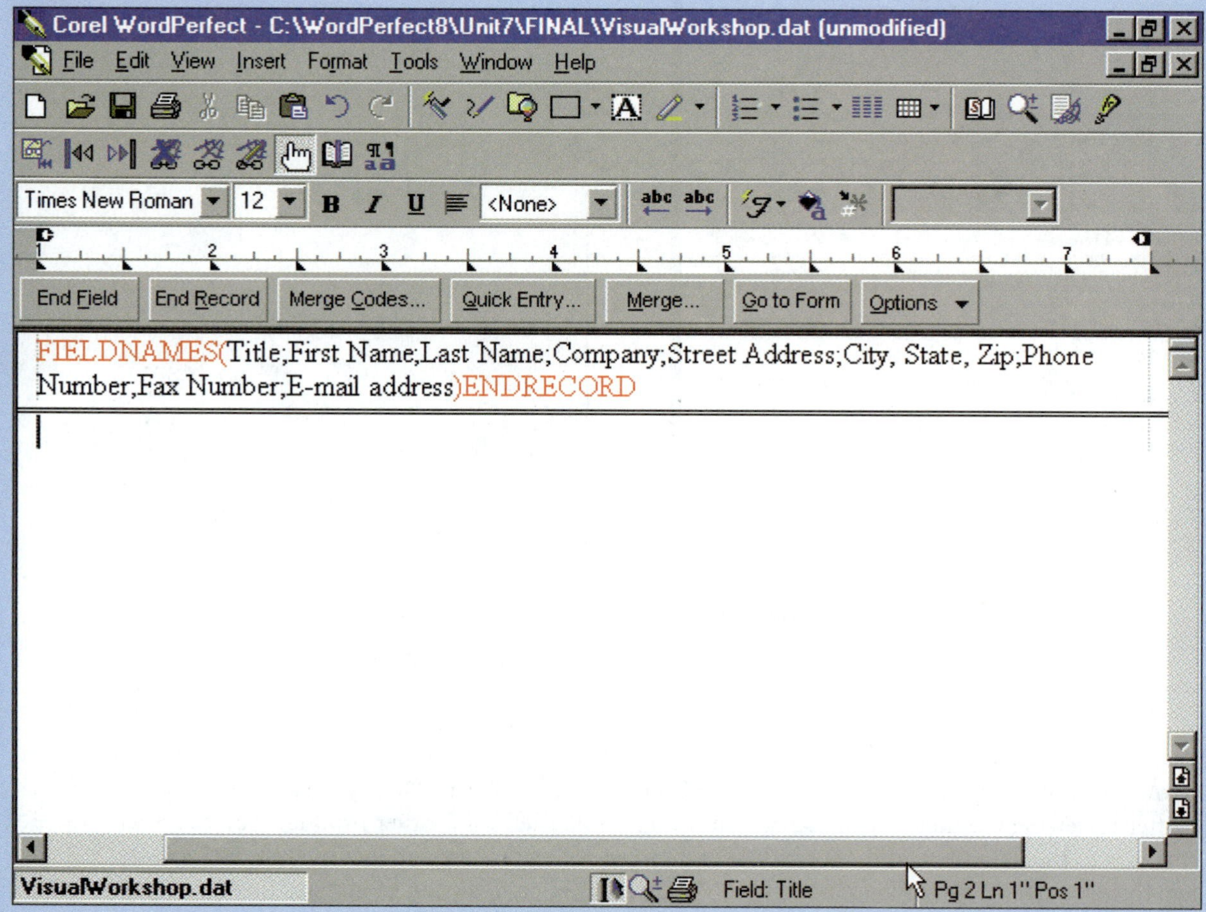

WordPerfect 8

Creating an HTML Document

Objectives

- Plan an HTML document
- Switch between documents
- Move text from one document to another
- Edit the Application Bar
- Create hyperlinks
- Edit hyperlinks
- Convert your document to HTML format
- Edit a document in HTML format

Publishing on the World Wide Web introduces potential clients to company services and products. Many companies, small businesses, and individuals have created **home pages**, which are electronically published documents on the Internet. Most home pages are written in **HyperText Markup Language (HTML)**. **Internet browsers**, such as Netscape Navigator or Microsoft Internet Explorer, can read and display HTML. Anyone with Internet access and an Internet browser can view these home pages. WordPerfect's **Internet Publisher** allows you to convert WordPerfect documents to HTML. Jennifer Laina, the president of The Write Staff, has asked you to finalize The Write Staff home page and several documents that will be linked to the home page. She has also asked you to convert The Write Staff home page from WordPerfect to HTML using the Internet Publisher.

Planning an HTML Document

To make creating a home page easier, you should plan it ahead of time. Table H-1 lists some terms that you need to know when working with home pages. When you plan a home page, you determine its content, the number of hyperlinks it will have to other documents, and the graphics that you want to include. **Hyperlinks** are key words or phrases that are linked to other documents. Jennifer has developed several WordPerfect documents that she wants you to use as you develop The Write Staff home page. She gives you the following guidelines to acquaint you with electronic publishing. You read the guidelines and refer to them as you work with The Write Staff home page.

Steps

1. **Determine the purpose of the home page**
   You need to provide pertinent information about The Write Staff to current and prospective clients.

2. **Present content that is clear and concise**
   You want to provide a statement that provides a quick overview of the company. You also want to provide information about the history of The Write Staff, access to the company catalog, and other topics that will be of interest to your clients. John Williams, head of Customer Service, reminds you that The Write Staff recently won the prestigious Five-Star Award from Writers International, Inc. You want visitors to your home page to know about this award.

3. **Identify graphic images that will enhance your home page**
   You know that graphic images can greatly enhance a document. Indeed, as the old saying goes, sometimes a picture is worth a thousand words. However, too many graphic images on a home page can slow down the time it takes visitors to access your home page. You decide to use graphics sparingly. You want to show The Write Staff office building, as this is a new facility that the company moved into recently. You will also use some spot art to make your page lively and exciting.

4. **Allow visitor feedback**
   John Williams is hoping to add many new clients to the Client List data file based on inquiries from visitors to the home page. In addition to providing the toll-free phone number, you plan to provide a hyperlink that allows visitors to send e-mail messages.

5. **List credits**
   Like any printed document, your home page should contain publishing information. You will note who helped create the home page and who maintains the home page. This will assure visitors that the information they are reading is accurate and up-to-date.

6. **Make a rough sketch on paper of how you want the home page to look**
   In order to use time most efficiently, Jennifer designed the home page on paper. Figure H-1 shows the sketch of The Write Staff home page that Jennifer designed.

7. **Create a concept map on paper to show hyperlinks between the home page and other documents**
   In order to keep the message on the home page clear and concise, you will create hyperlinks, which are keywords or phrases on the home page that will link to other documents. Figure H-2 shows the sketch of the concept map you will use to keep track of the documents and how they link to one another.

FIGURE H-1: **Sketch of home page**

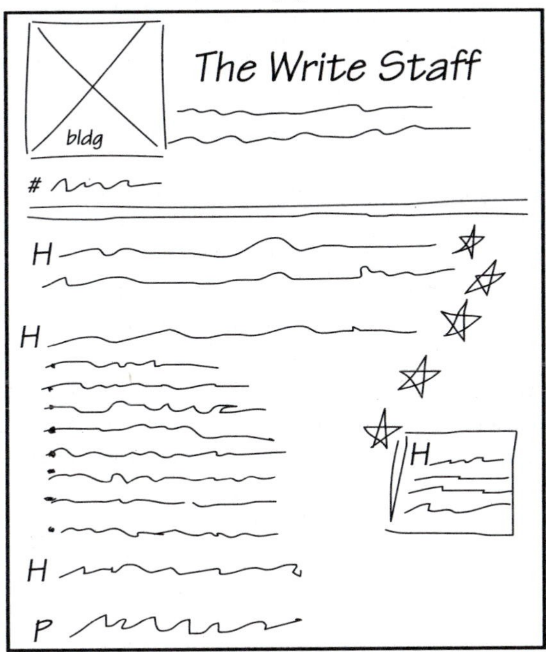

FIGURE H-2: **Sketch of concept map**

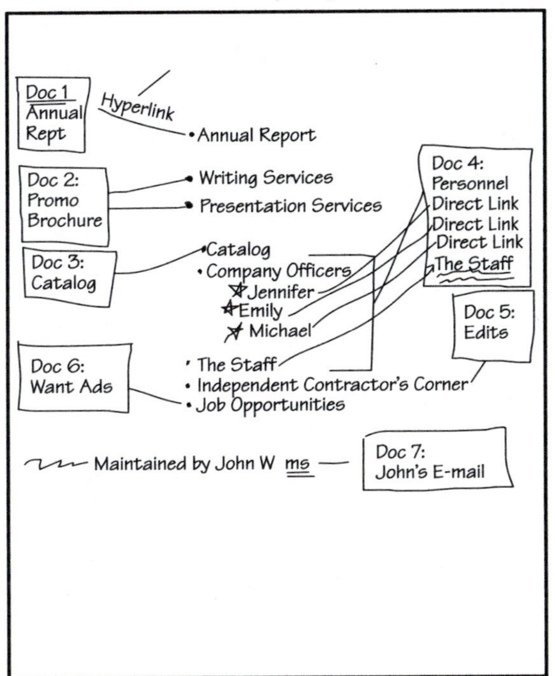

TABLE H-1: **Internet terms**

term	description
Home page	A welcome document on the WWW, usually the first place visitors go to find out about a company
HyperText Markup Language (HTML)	The language in which most documents published on the Internet are written
Hyperlink	Allows you to "jump" or provides a "link" from one part of an Internet document to another or to an entirely different document
Internet	A worldwide network of computers
Uniform Resource Locator (URL)	A unique address assigned to each document on the WWW
World Wide Web (WWW or the Web)	A service that provides organized information on the Internet in an easy-to-access format

Switching Between Documents

An effective home page provides enough information to attract a visitor's attention. Too much information on the home page, however, can overwhelm the visitor or increase the time it takes to access the home page. As mentioned earlier, home pages often include hyperlinks, which allow visitors to "jump" or "link" to other parts of the home page or to other documents. You will learn more about creating hyperlinks in a later lesson. In order to create hyperlinks, you often need to work with multiple documents. WordPerfect's **Application Bar**, which displays information about open documents, helps you move back and forth among these documents easily and efficiently. Jennifer has provided several documents that she wants you to use as part of The Write Staff home page. You want to review and become familiar with these documents. You use the Application Bar to quickly switch between open documents, to go to specific locations within the same document, and to access other features such as Go To and Shadow Cursor.

1. Start WordPerfect, click **View**, click **Toolbars**, make sure the check box next to Application Bar is checked, click **Hyperlink Tools**, then click **OK**
   The Application Bar appears at the bottom of the blank document window. The Hyperlink Toolbar appears at the top of the screen. You will learn more about this in a later lesson.

Trouble?

The information on your Application Bar may be different from the information in Figure H-3.

2. Open **WP H-1** from your Student Disk, save it as **WS Home**, open **WP H-2** from your Student Disk, then save it as **WS Edit Updates**
   Each open document has its own button on the Application Bar, as shown in Figure H-3. You want to look at the document WS Home.
3. Click the **WS Home button** on the Application Bar, then scroll through the document
   As you familiarize yourself with its contents, you notice a few changes that need to be made before converting it to HTML format. You want to see if any changes need to be made to WS Edit Updates as well.
4. Click the **WS Edit Updates button** on the Application Bar
   The WS Edit Updates document appears in the current document window.
5. Click the **Combined Position button** on the Application Bar
   The Go To dialog box opens as shown in Figure H-4.
6. Type **2** in the Page number text box, then click **OK**
   The Go To dialog box closes and the insertion point appears at the beginning of page 2. You verify the exact location by looking at the information that appears in the Combined Position button.
7. Click before the word **Revisions** in paragraph 2, line 1
   Notice how the information that appears in the Combined Position button changes to show the exact location of the insertion point. In the lessons that follow, you will continue to use the Application Bar as you work with multiple open documents.
8. Press **[Ctrl][Home]**

FIGURE H-3: Application Bar

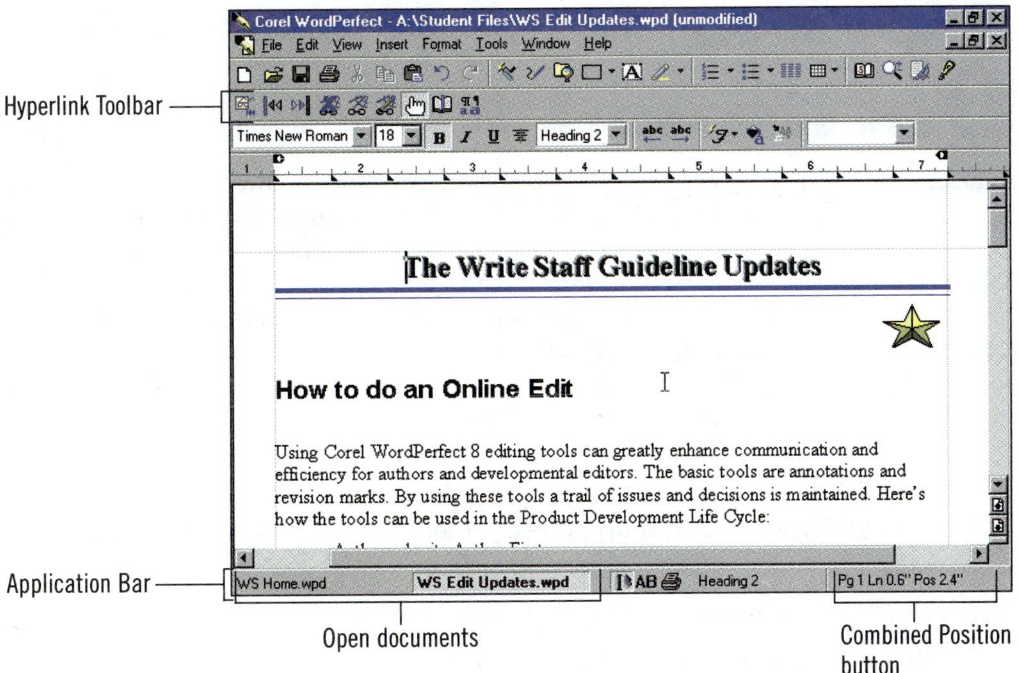

FIGURE H-4: Go To dialog box

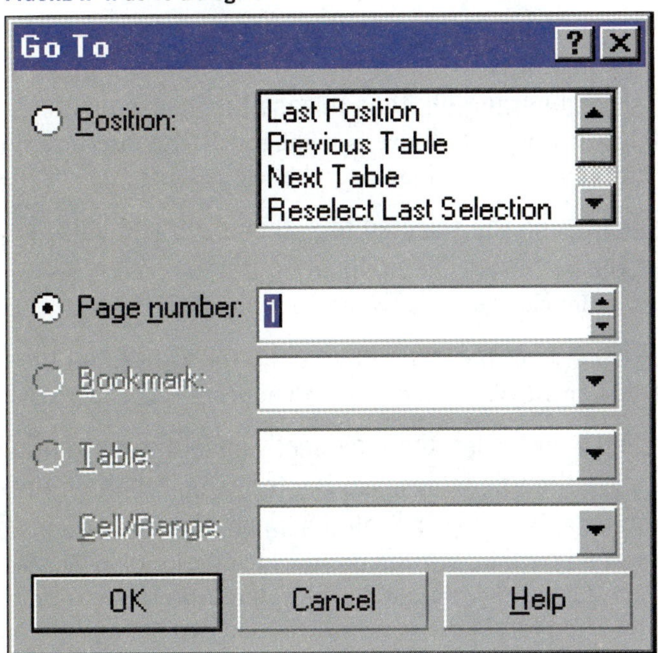

Working with multiple open documents

Today, even books are published on the Web. Frequently the Table of Contents is provided on the home page and each chapter title is a hyperlink to that chapter. In the past, books would be typed as one long document in order to keep page numbers and other features consistent across chapters. Today, WordPerfect master documents and subdocuments allow you to maintain several smaller documents rather than one large document and still have consistency. A **master document** contains information such as the Table of Contents, author information, page numbering format, and so on. It also contains links to other documents called subdocuments. The **subdocuments** can be opened, edited, and saved from the master document. The master document ensures a consistent look across all subdocuments.

WordPerfect 8

Moving Text from One Document to Another

Sometimes when working with multiple documents, you want to move text from one document to another. You can do that using WordPerfect's Application Bar and the drag and drop feature. You simply select the text you want to move, drag it to the document button on the Application Bar, and drop it in the document you selected when it becomes the current document. So far, you are pleased with the design of the home page. However, after reviewing it more closely, you realize you want to move the explanatory information listed with some of the bullets to other documents. You believe this change will help make the home page message clearer and more concise. You use the drag and drop feature and the Application Bar to move text between open documents.

Steps 1 2 3 4

1. Click the **WS Home button** on the Application Bar, then scroll to the Annual Report bullet
   The paragraphs under Annual Report really belong in the Financial Report document. You want to move those paragraphs to that document.
2. Open **WP H-3** from your Student Disk, save it as **WS Financial Report**, then scroll through the document to become familiar with it
3. Press **[Ctrl][Home]**
4. Click **WS Home** on the Application Bar, click immediately after the phrase **Annual Report** and drag to select the text through **help you meet that need.** at the end of the second paragraph, then release the mouse pointer
   The text you want to move is highlighted. The insertion pointer changes from I to I↖ when you move the pointer over the selected text.
5. Position I↖ on the selected text, then click and hold the mouse button down as you drag the I↖ toward the Application Bar
   The pointer changes to ↖ as shown in Figure H-5.
6. Position ↖ over the **WS Financial Report button** on the Application Bar
   The document WS Financial Report appears as the current document.
7. Position ↖ at the left margin directly under the horizontal line, release the mouse button, click the title to deselect the text, scroll through the document and adjust paragraph indents so they are all the same, then save your work
   The text is placed in the open document at the location you specified, as shown in Figure H-6. If you want to move the text again, you must select it again before you can drag it to a new location. You follow the same process outlined in Step 4 to move other text.
8. Click **WS Home**, save the document, select the text from **Here is the latest update** to **The Write Staff Products**, use drag and drop to place the text in **WS Edit Updates** just under the horizontal line, click the title to deselect the text, then save your work
9. Click **WS Home**, delete the blank line between the bulleted text Independent Contractors' Corner and the bulleted text Job Opportunities, make any other improvements you feel are necessary, then save all documents

QuickTip

The blinking vertical bar up and to the left of the pointer indicates where the text will be inserted.

FIGURE H-5: Selected text being dragged

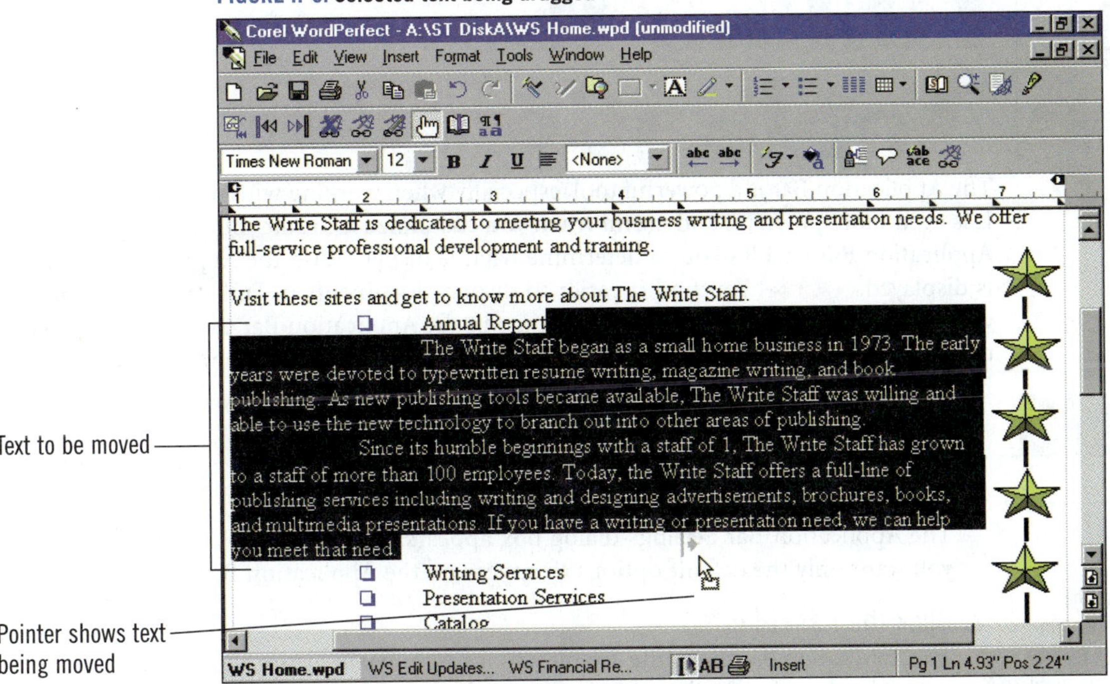

FIGURE H-6: Text placed in new document

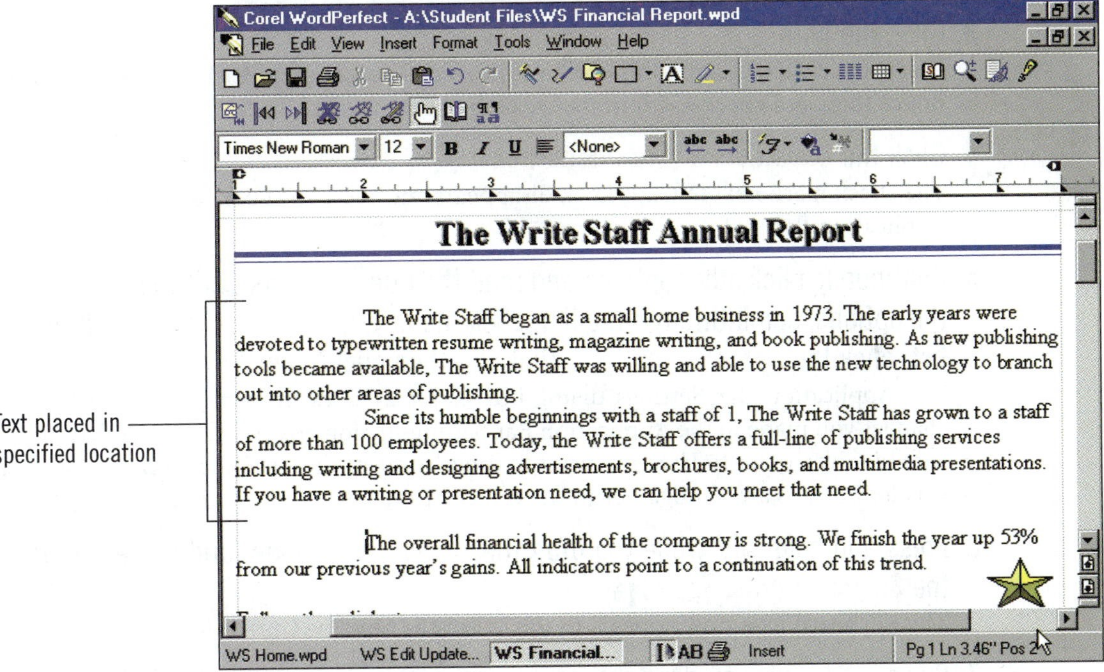

Other ways to move text from one document to another

In addition to using the Application Bar to move text from one document to another, there are several other ways to move text between documents. You can always use Copy and Paste from the Edit menu. This is an effective method when you want text to remain in the original document as well as to be copied to a new document. You use Cut and Paste when you want to delete text from the original document and insert it in a new document. You can also tile windows, which means to arrange two or more documents on your screen so you can see them at the same time. To use this method, click Window, then click Tile Side by Side. Select the text you want to move, then drag it to the other document without changing document windows.

Editing the Application Bar

The Application Bar is a powerful tool, especially when working with multiple open documents. It is even more powerful and useful when you customize it to suit your needs. Customizing the Application Bar enables you to determine what is displayed on the Application Bar and how it is displayed. You find it easier to display documents in Full Page view when working with documents that include graphics. You edit the Application Bar to add the Zoom option to the Application Bar. You decide to read about other options that can be added to the Application Bar and to make other adjustments to the Application Bar.

Trouble?

If you cannot see the Application Bar when the Application Bar Settings dialog box appears, click the title bar and drag the box up until the Application Bar is visible.

1. Click **Tools**, click **Settings**, then double-click **Application Bar**
   The Application Bar Settings dialog box appears. Before customizing the Application Bar, you want only the default options to appear on the Application Bar.
2. Click the **Reset button**
   The Application Bar shows the default settings as shown in Figure H-7. A check mark means the option is selected and will appear on the Application Bar. You notice a number of options available in the Select items to appear on the bar list box, but you are unsure what some of them do.
3. Click the phrase **Alignment Character**
   An explanation regarding this option appears on the screen under Item description. You also notice there is a check mark in the check box next to Caps Lock State.
4. Click the **Caps Lock State check box**
   The check mark next to Caps Lock disappears and the Caps Lock icon is removed from the Application Bar.
5. Continue to click other options and read their descriptions until you are familiar with the options, scroll through the list, click the **Keyboard check box**, scroll through the list, click the **Zoom check box**, click **OK**, then click **Close**
   The Application Bar Settings dialog box closes as does the Settings menu list box. The changes you made in the Application Bar Settings dialog box have been applied. Your screen should look similar to H-8. You want to move some of the Application Bar icons so that the smaller buttons are all together in the center of the bar.
6. Press and hold **[Alt]** while you drag the **Keyboard icon** and place it to the left of the **Shadow Cursor icon**
   The Keyboard icon now appears to the left of the Shadow Cursor icon.
7. Press **[Alt]** while you drag the **Zoom icon** and place it to the left of
   The smaller icons are now centrally located on the Application Bar. You want to resize the General Status button to make it smaller.
8. Press **[Alt]** while you drag the right side of the **General Status button** Insert to resize it
   The General Status button is resized. While looking over the Application Bar, you decide you do not need the Keyboard icon for this project.
9. Press **[Alt]** while you drag off the Application Bar, then save your work
   The Keyboard icon is gone and that option is no longer available. If you want that option to appear on the Application Bar again, you must select it in the Application Bar Settings dialog box. Each time you open a WordPerfect document, this is how the Application Bar will appear until you change the Application Bar settings.

FIGURE H-7: Application Bar Settings dialog box

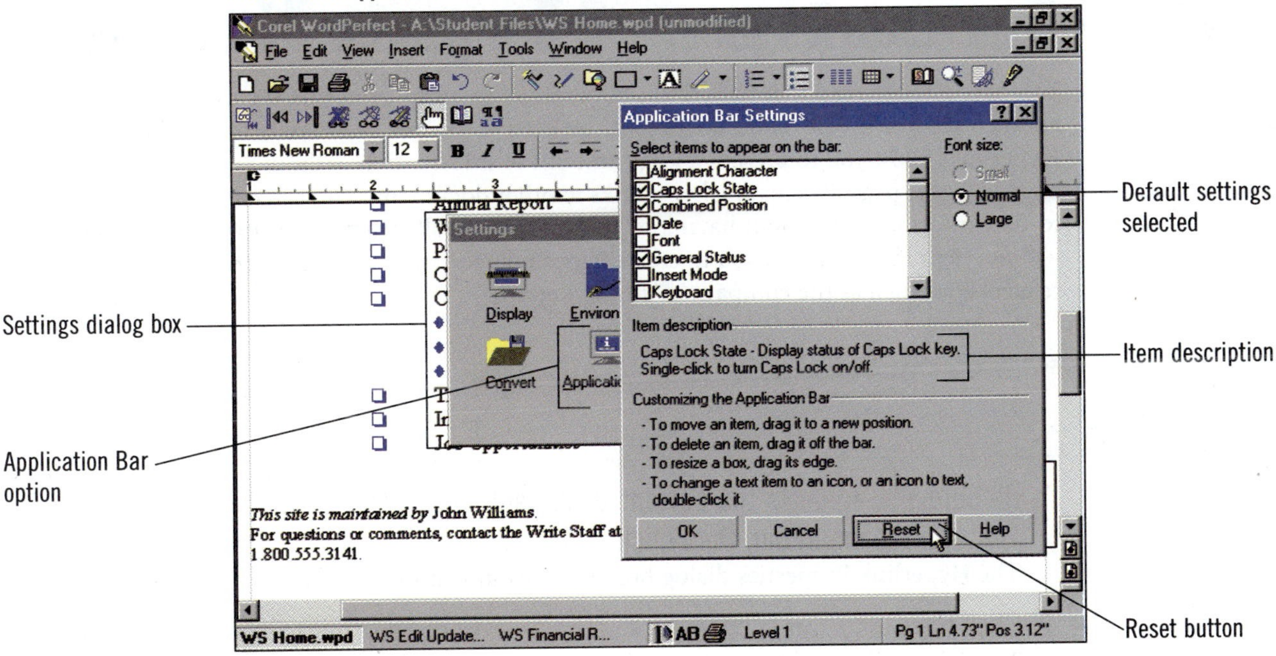

Settings dialog box

Application Bar option

Default settings selected

Item description

Reset button

FIGURE H-8: Customized Application Bar

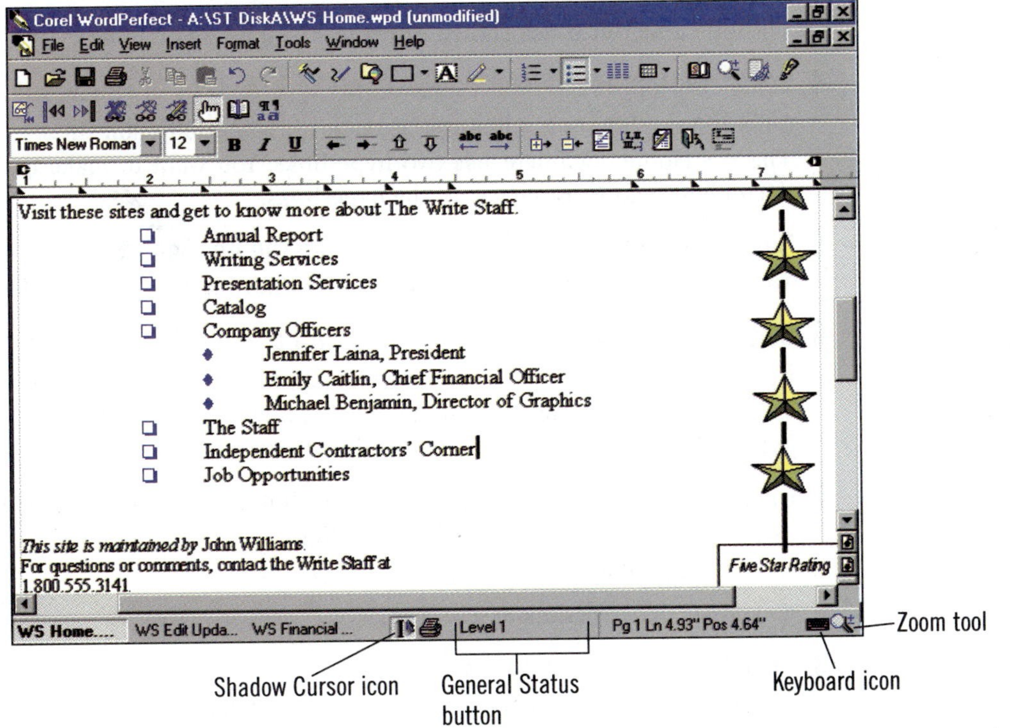

WordPerfect 8

Creating Hyperlinks

You have already read that hyperlinks allow users to jump from one section of a document to another section of the same document, or even from one document to another document. Hyperlinks allow you to present a large amount of information without taking up a lot of space on your home page. By creating hyperlinks to other documents, you can continually provide up-to-date information without having to rework the overall structure or text of your home page. Jennifer has asked you to create hyperlinks so visitors can jump from the home page to related sites, such as the company's Annual Report.

1. Be sure **WS Home** is the current document, select the words **Annual Report**, click **Tools** on the menu bar, then click **Hyperlink**
   The Hyperlink Properties dialog box opens as shown in Figure H-9.
2. Click the **Folder icon**, click **WS Financial Report**, then click **Select**
   The Select File - Student Files dialog box closes and the Hyperlink Properties dialog box opens. The file name WS Financial Report is in the Document/Macro text box. The file name in the text box identifies the file that will be linked to the selected phrase, Annual Report, in the WS Home document. A check mark in the check box next to Activate hyperlinks means this option is selected.
3. Click **OK**
   The blue underlined text shown in Figure H-10 is a hyperlink.
4. Select the phrase **Independent Contractors' Corner**, click **Tools**, click **Hyperlink**, click the **Folder icon**, click **Edits**, click **Select**, then click **OK**
   The WS Home document has two hyperlinks. You want to make hyperlinks in the other documents before testing any of the hyperlinks.
5. Save your work, click **WS Edit Updates** on the Application Bar, then press **[Ctrl][End]**
   You make the last line of text a hyperlink, connecting WS Edit Updates to WS Home.
6. Select the phrase **The Write Staff Home Page**, click **Tools**, click **Hyperlink**, click the **Folder icon**, click **WS Home**, click **Select**, click **OK**, then save your work
   The phrase "The Write Staff Home Page" is now a hyperlink. You want to create a similar hyperlink in the WS Financial Report document.
7. Click **WS Financial Report** on the Application Bar, scroll to and select the phrase **The Write Staff Home Page**, click **Tools**, click **Hyperlink**, click the **Folder icon**, click **WS Home**, then click **Select**
   You create this hyperlink as a button.
8. Click the **Make text appear as button check box**, click **OK**, then save your work
   The selected text, which appears as a button, is a hyperlink. You want to test all the hyperlinks.
9. Click the **Write Staff Home Page button**, then click the **Annual Report** hyperlink to jump to WS Financial Report
   When a hyperlink is active, the pointer changes to a hand. As you click each hyperlink, the screen seems to "jump" to the new document. If you click the Independent Contractors' link, you will discover that you have created an incorrect link. You will learn to edit and correct this hyperlink in the next lesson.

Trouble?

Be sure the name of the disk or folder where you have your student files is the name in the Look in text box.

QuickTip

Always save your work before trying out a hyperlink.

FIGURE H-9: Hyperlink Properties dialog box

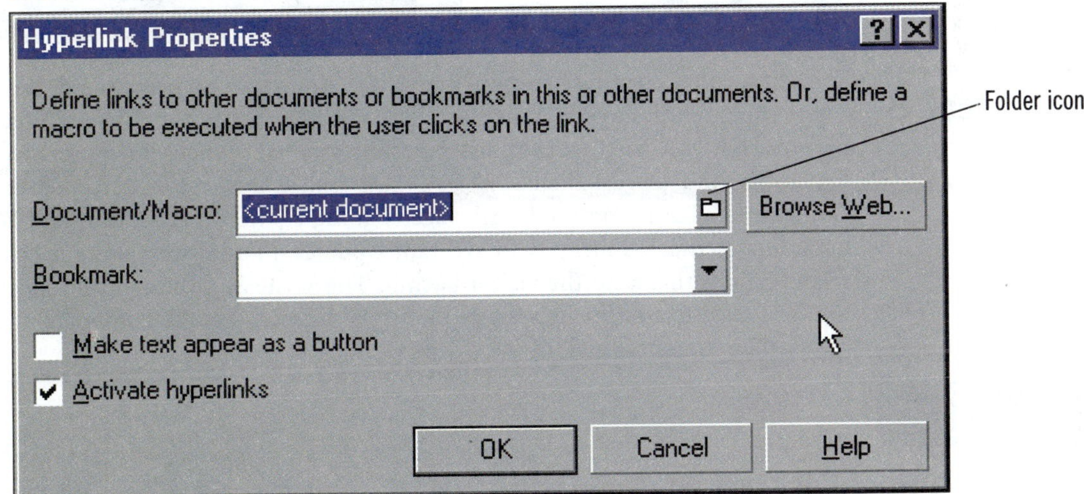

FIGURE H-10: Hyperlink text

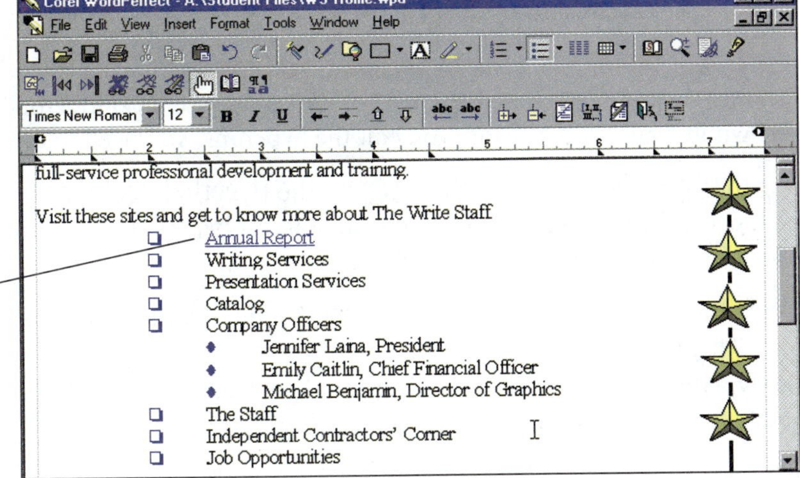

Using QuickLinks

WordPerfect's QuickLinks option allows you to set up links that you use frequently. For example, to create a hyperlink from all pages back to The Write Staff home page, use QuickLinks to specify that typing @WSHP automatically sets up a link to the document WS Home. To create QuickLinks to WordPerfect documents, click Tools, click QuickCorrect, click the QuickLinks tab, type the word you want converted to a QuickLink, then specify the associated document.

Creating a hyperlink to an Internet document

You can create hyperlinks between Internet documents. To create a hyperlink between your document and an Internet document, first select the text you want created as a hyperlink, click Tools, then click Hyperlink. When the Hyperlink Properties dialog box appears, click Browse Web and open the document with which you want the link to be associated. The document you want to link to can be on the Internet or on a local server, but you must be connected to use the Browse Web option. Press [Alt][Tab] to return to WordPerfect. The address of the document appears in the Document/macro text box. Click OK. The text you selected is a hyperlink to the Internet document you identified.

WordPerfect 8

Editing Hyperlinks

Sometimes after creating hyperlinks, you may find that you need to edit them. You cannot click a hyperlink in order to edit it, because that will activate the hyperlink and send you to the linked file. Instead, you need to use the Hyperlink toolbar, which allows you to move through the hyperlinks and to edit them. You realize that the hyperlink from the Independent Contractors' Corner on the home page is going to the wrong document. You need to edit the hyperlink so that it links you to WS Edit Updates. In addition, Jennifer has informed you that all hyperlinks that send the visitor back to The Write Staff home page should appear as a button. You need to edit the hyperlink on the WS Edit Updates document so it appears as a button rather than as underlined text.

Steps

Trouble?

If the Hyperlink toolbar does not appear at the top of the screen, click View on the menu bar, click Toolbars, click Hyperlink Tools, then click OK.

1. Be sure **WS Home** is the current document, click **View** on the menu bar, click **Toolbars**, then click **Hyperlink Tools**, then click **OK**
   You will use the Hyperlink toolbar shown in Figure H-11. You need to move to the hyperlink that you want to edit.
2. Press **[Ctrl][Home]**, click the **Hyperlink Next icon** on the Hyperlink toolbar twice
   The insertion pointer is at the beginning of the Independent Contractors' Corner hyperlink, as shown in Figure H-12. Before you edit the hyperlink, you need to deactivate it.
3. Click the **Hyperlink Remove icon** on the Hyperlink toolbar
   The text is no longer underlined and is no longer a hyperlink. You need to make it hyperlink with the correct associated file.
4. Select **Independent Contractors' Corner**, then click the **Hyperlink Create icon** on the Hyperlink toolbar
   The Hyperlink Properties dialog box appears. You need to identify the file that you want this hyperlink associated with.
5. Click the **Folder icon**, click **WS Edit Updates**, click **Select**, then click **OK**
   The text is again underlined and the pointer changes to a hand when you move the pointer over the text. You have edited the hyperlink to create a new hyperlink. You also want to edit a hyperlink in the WS Edit Updates document.

Trouble?

If WS Edit Updates is not on the Application Bar, open it from your Student Disk.

6. Save your work, click **WS Edit Updates** on the Application Bar, then press **[Ctrl][Home]**
   You are at the beginning of the WS Edit Update document in the current document window.
7. Press on the **Hyperlink toolbar**, press , select the text **The Write Staff Home Page**, click , click the **Folder icon**, select **WS Home**, click **Select**, click the **check box** next to Make text appear as a button, then click **OK**
   The hyperlink appears as a button. You test the hyperlinks to be sure they are working properly.
8. Save your work, then click **The Write Staff Home Page button**
   The WS Home appears on the screen.
9. Click the **Independent Contractors' Corner hyperlink**, then save your work
   The Write Staff Edit Updates appear. Your hyperlinks are all working as you expect them to work.

FIGURE H-11: Hyperlink toolbar

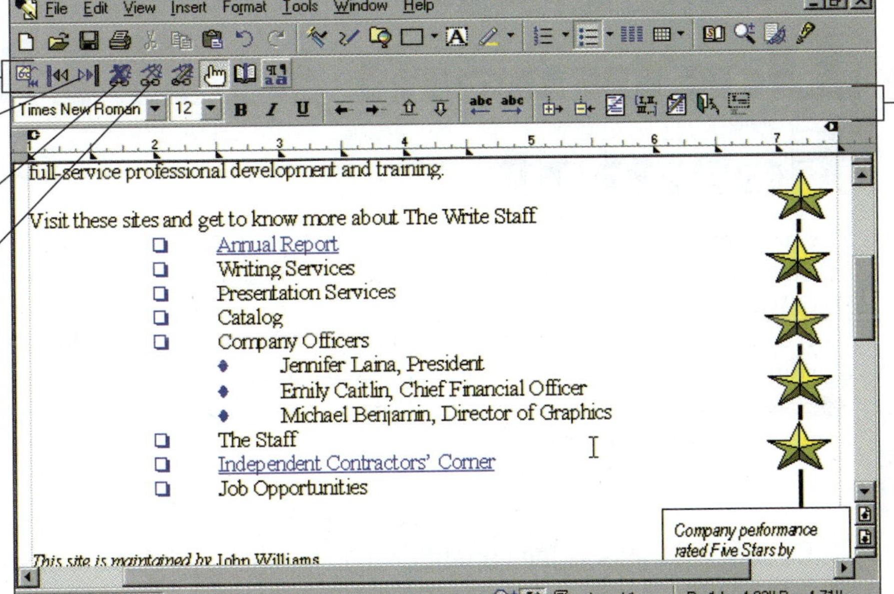
Hyperlink Toolbar
Hyperlink Next
Hyperlink Remove
Hyperlink Create
Property Bar
Corel WordPerfect - A:\Student Files\WS Home.wpd (unmodified)
full-service professional development and training.
Visit these sites and get to know more about The Write Staff
Annual Report
Writing Services
Presentation Services
Catalog
Company Officers
Jennifer Laina, President
Emily Caitlin, Chief Financial Officer
Michael Benjamin, Director of Graphics
The Staff
Independent Contractors' Corner
Job Opportunities
Company performance rated Five Stars by
This site is maintained by John Williams

FIGURE H-12: Hyperlink selected for edit

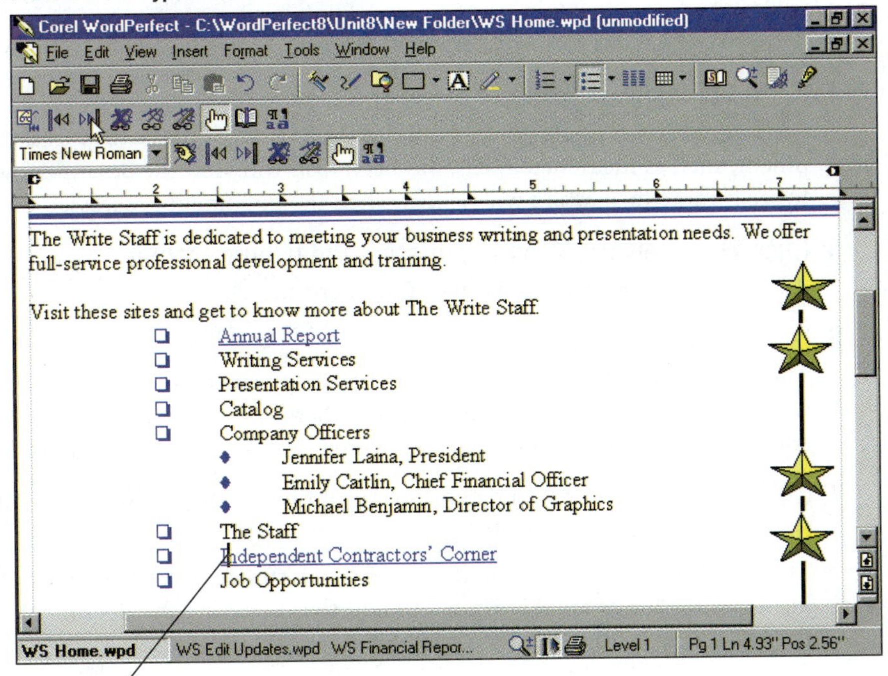
Corel WordPerfect - C:\WordPerfect8\Unit8\New Folder\WS Home.wpd (unmodified)
The Write Staff is dedicated to meeting your business writing and presentation needs. We offer full-service professional development and training.
Visit these sites and get to know more about The Write Staff.
Annual Report
Writing Services
Presentation Services
Catalog
Company Officers
Jennifer Laina, President
Emily Caitlin, Chief Financial Officer
Michael Benjamin, Director of Graphics
The Staff
Independent Contractors' Corner
Job Opportunities
Insertion point

WordPerfect 8

Converting Your Document to HTML Format

The Internet Publisher allows you to create a Web page using a new document or to convert an existing WordPerfect document. Either way, when you publish a WordPerfect document to the Web, WordPerfect codes that do not have HTML equivalents are deleted from the document. (See Table H-2 for features that do and do not convert to HTML.) This means the appearance of your WordPerfect document might change when you convert it to the HTML format. You are ready to convert The Write Staff home page to HTML format and to view the home page with a web browser.

Steps

1. **Be sure WS Home is the current document, click File, then click Internet Publisher**
   The Internet Publisher dialog box appears as shown in Figure H-13. You want to use the WordPerfect document that you have been working on.
2. **Click Format as Web Document**
   The Web View warning box appears. You know that some of the formatting in your current document will be lost during the conversion to HTML format.
3. **Click OK**
   A copy of the file is converted from WordPerfect format to HTML format.
4. **Click [zoom button], then click 50%**
   See Figure H-14. The gray background is the default. Some of the formatting from your document, such as the bulleted lists, has been lost. You view the document with a Web browser to see if more formatting will be lost when the document is accessed on the Web.
5. **Click Web Viewer [button] on the Internet Publishing toolbar**
   A conversion message box flashes on the screen.
6. **Scroll down the page**
   The Write Staff home page in HTML format appears on the screen. Overall you are pleased with The Write Staff home page; however, there are some changes you want to make. Before editing the document, you publish it, which saves the file as an HTML file.
7. **Click the Close button to close the web browser, click File, click Internet Publisher, then click Publish to HTML**
   The Publish to HTML dialog box appears as shown in Figure H-15. An .html extension identifies the file as an HTML file. In addition to saving the document, you must also save the images in the same folder as the document.
8. **Be sure the same path information is indicated in both text boxes, such as A:\Student Disk\, then click OK**
   A conversion message box flashes on the screen during the conversion process. When the conversion is complete, there are two WS Home files on your Student Disk: one is a WordPerfect file and has the .wpd extension, and the other is an HTML file and has an .htm extension.
9. **Save your work, click the HTML option button in the Save Format dialog box, click OK, print your document, then close the file**

QuickTip

The hyperlinks in your document are still active, but they are linked to WordPerfect documents, not HTML documents. Do not use hyperlinks at this time because the link will take you out of the Internet Publisher and will result in additional format changes.

QuickTip

Be sure the path information matches the drive, disk, and folder where you have your Student Files.

FIGURE H-13: Internet Publisher dialog box

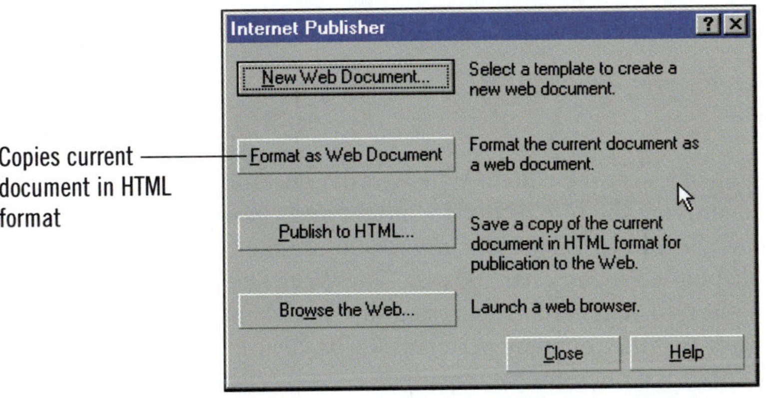

FIGURE H-14: The Write Staff home page in HTML format

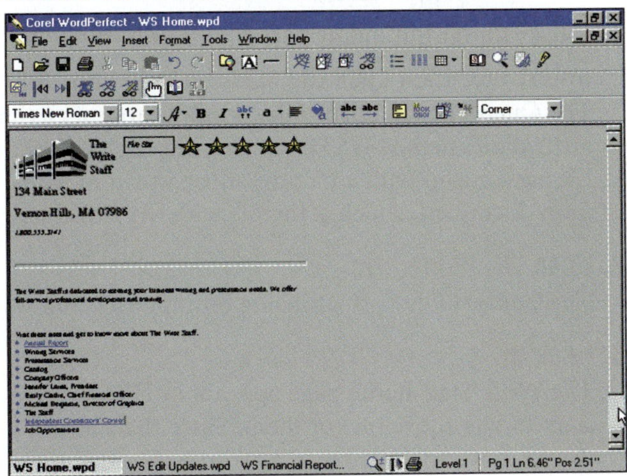

FIGURE H-15: Publish to HTML dialog box

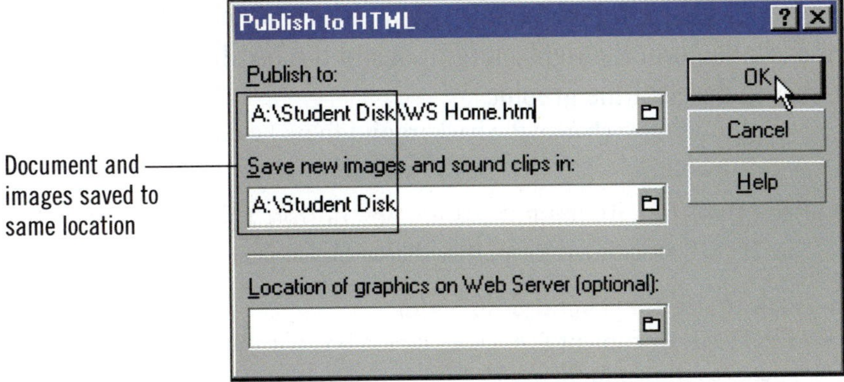

TABLE H-2: Publishing to the Web and WordPerfect features

features not supported in HTML	features modified to convert to HTML	features converted to another code in HTML
Drop caps	Bullet and numbered lists	Columns are converted to hard pages
Fill (shading)	Fonts	Footnotes are converted to endnotes
Headers and footers	Hyperlinks	
Margins (left or right)	Images and sound clips	
Page numbering	Paragraph styles	
Tabs and indents	Table of contents	

Editing a Document in HTML Format

HTML properties can be edited. With WordPerfect's Web Editor, you can make adjustments such as identifying the title of the document and changing the color of the hyperlinks or the background. To edit an HTML document you use the HTML property dialog box. This option is available on the Property bar. The Write Staff home page is almost ready to be published on the Web. Jennifer has suggested that you change the background so that it reflects the type of work that the company performs for its customers and draws attention to the fact that The Write Staff is a publishing company.

Steps

1. **Click File on the menu bar, click Open, make sure Student Files appears in the Look in text box, then click the scroll bar to view all the files**
   The Open File - Student Files window appears as shown in Figure H-16. You notice there are two files named WS Home. One file has the WordPerfect icon in front of it, and the other file has an icon with a picture of the world in front of it. You want to make changes to the .htm document, which is the file with the world icon.
2. **Open WS Home.htm**
   The Convert File Format dialog box appears. You want the file format to stay HTML.
3. **Click OK**
   The Write Staff home page appears in HTML format. You don't like the placement of the stars so you move one of them. Since the star is a graphic, you move it the same way you would move any graphic in a WordPerfect document.
4. **Click one Star, use ✥ to drag and drop the star at the right margin opposite the Annual Report hyperlink bullet item, continue to move the rest of the stars so they cascade down the right margin, delete the text box, then click outside the graphics box to deselect the graphic**
   Now you want to change the background to make the appearance of The Write Staff home page unique.
5. **Click the HTML Document Properties button on the Property toolbar**
   The HTML Document Properties dialog box appears.
6. **Click Text/Background Colors tab**
   The HTML Document Properties dialog box with the Text/Background Colors tab selected appears as shown in Figure H-17.
7. **Click the Folder icon next to the Background wallpaper text box, double-click Paper, click Light Texture, click Select, then click OK**
   The HTML Document Properties dialog box closes and the Write Staff home page appears with the new background. You continue to edit the home page just as you would any WordPerfect document. You move graphics and change text colors.
8. **Make other changes, such as changing the color of the opening paragraph text from blue to black**
   Compare your screen with Figure H-18. You are pleased with the results and you are sure that Jennifer will be as well.
9. **Save your work, click the HTML option button in the Save Format dialog box, click OK, print your document, then exit WordPerfect**

QuickTip

Right-click outside the graphic, then click Properties on the QuickMenu.

Click the Preview Button to initialize the viewer and see graphics as you select them.

FIGURE H-16: Open File - Student Files window

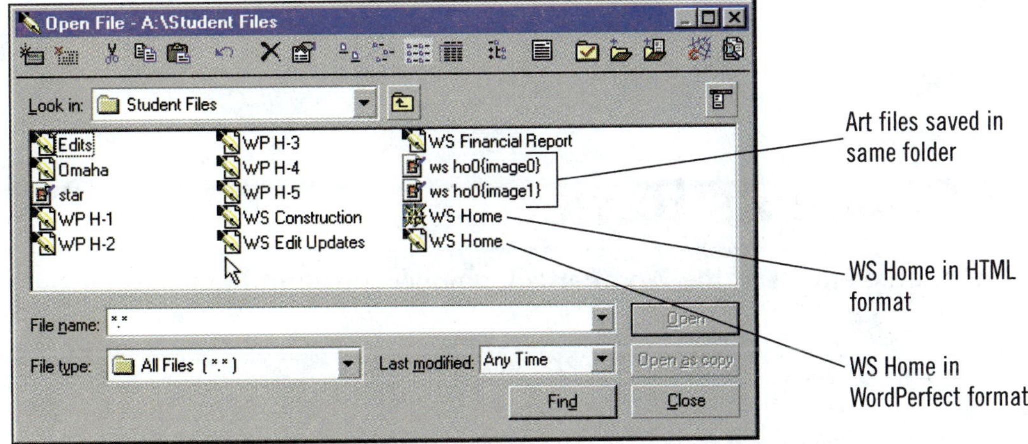

FIGURE H-17: HTML Document Properties dialog box

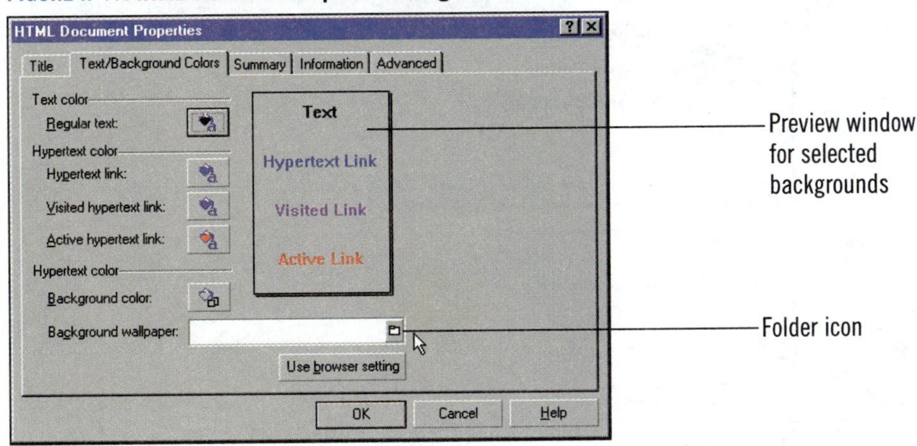

FIGURE H-18: Print version of The Write Staff home page

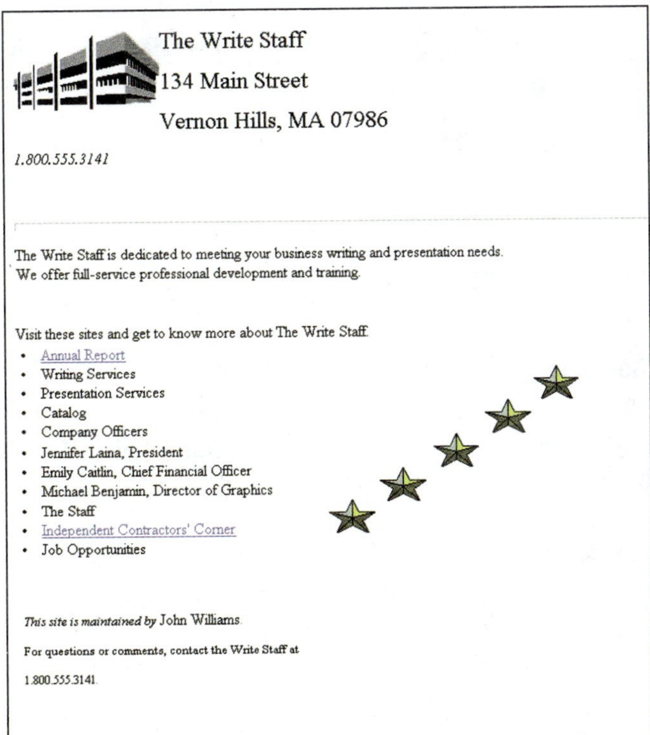

The Write Staff
134 Main Street
Vernon Hills, MA 07986
1.800.555.3141
The Write Staff is dedicated to meeting your business writing and presentation needs.
We offer full-service professional development and training.
Visit these sites and get to know more about The Write Staff
• Annual Report
• Writing Services
• Presentation Services
• Catalog
• Company Officers
• Jennifer Laina, President
• Emily Caitlin, Chief Financial Officer
• Michael Benjamin, Director of Graphics
• The Staff
• Independent Contractors' Corner
• Job Opportunities
This site is maintained by John Williams
For questions or comments, contact the Write Staff at
1.800.555.3141

WordPerfect 8

Practice

► Concepts Review

Label each element of the WordPerfect window shown in Figure H-19

FIGURE H-19

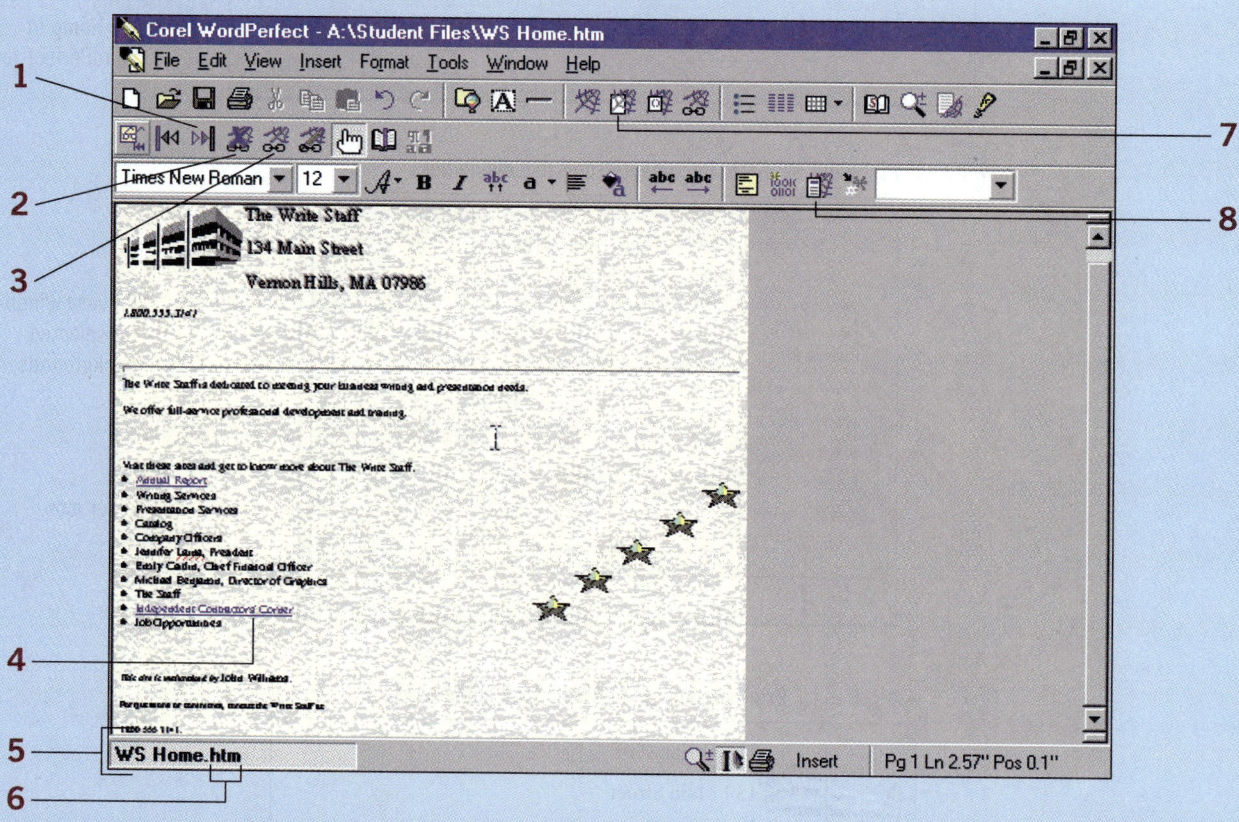

Match each term with the statement that describes it.

9. Hyperlink Create button
10. Language in which most home pages published on the Internet are written
11. Indicates text is being dragged
12. Helps you work efficiently while multiple documents are open
13. Hyperlink Remove button

a. HTML
b. [pointer icon]
c. [button icon]
d. Application Bar
e. [button icon]

Select the best answer from the list of choices.

14. When designing a home page for electronic publishing,
- **a.** Plan the page on paper first.
- **b.** Develop a concept map to show hyperlinks.
- **c.** Present the information in a clear, concise manner.
- **d.** All of the above.

15. The Application Bar is a handy tool because it allows you to
- **a.** Apply changes you make to a document by pressing the Apply button.
- **b.** Switch between open documents.
- **c.** Open more than one application at a time.
- **d.** Preview the effect of changes you are making to open documents.

16. To move text from one document to another,
- **a.** Select the text to be moved, then drop it on the Application Bar.
- **b.** Select Edit on the menu bar, then click Move.
- **c.** Select the text to be moved, then drag and drop it in the other document.
- **d.** Select File on the menu bar, then click Paste.

17. In the Application Bar Settings dialog box, you can
- **a.** Reset the settings so the Application Bar displays the original settings.
- **b.** Read descriptions of the Application Bar Settings.
- **c.** Select items to customize the Application Bar.
- **d.** All of the above.

18. To remove an item from the Application Bar,
- **a.** Press [Alt], select the item, then drag it off the Application Bar.
- **b.** Select the item, then press [Delete].
- **c.** Click the check box next to the item name in the Application Bar Settings dialog box until a check mark appears.
- **d.** Select the item, click Edit on the menu bar, then select Undo.

19. To create text that lets you "jump" from one section of a document to another, use
- **a.** HTML.
- **b.** Hyperlinks.
- **c.** The Application Bar.
- **d.** QuickCorrect.

20. To edit a hyperlink,
- **a.** Click on it, then make your changes.
- **b.** Delete it, then create a new one.
- **c.** Click the Hyperlink Next button to select it, then click the Hyperlink Remove button to deactivate it.
- **d.** Click Tools, click Hyperlink, then make the changes in the Hyperlink Edit text box.

21. When you convert a WordPerfect document to an HTML document,
- **a.** Some of the WordPerfect formats will be lost or modified.
- **b.** The HTML document will look exactly the same as the WordPerfect document.
- **c.** The HTML document can only be viewed online using an Internet connection.
- **d.** The HTML document will appear with a blue background, which is the default browser setting.

22. **To edit the background color of an HTML document,**
    a. Click Edit on the menu, then select HTML.
    b. Right-click the background, then select Edit Background from the QuickMenu.
    c. Click the HTML Properties button on the Property Bar.
    d. Right-click the background and select a new color from the Colors palette.

Skills Review

1. **Plan a home page.**
   a. Start WordPerfect, open WP H-4 from your Student Disk and save it as CityCenter.
   b. Review the home page and write a brief answer to each of these questions:
      - What is the purpose of the home page?
      - Is the content presented in a clear, concise manner?
      - What graphic was used and why do you think that was chosen?
      - Has visitor feedback been provided for on the home page?
      - Are the home page credits listed?
   c. Based on the screen image, make a sketch of the home page on paper.
   d. Make a concept map to show links that will be created for this home page.
   e. Update the home page by including a line for visitor feedback.
   f. Provide credits for the home page. Under the feedback line, type "Web Design: [enter Your Name]. Last updated: [enter today's date]"

2. **Switch between documents and move text from one document to another.**
   a. Open WP H-5 from your Student Disk and save it as WeekendMovies, then scroll through the document to become familiar with its contents.
   b. Click the CityCenter button on the Application Bar, then scroll through the document so that the section titled "Check out these Coming Attractions" appears.
   c. Click the WeekendMovies button on the Application Bar, then click under the horizontal line and press [Enter].
   d. Click the CityCenter button, select the sentence "The Village Public Library presents a weekend at the movies.", drag the text to the WeekendMovies button on the Application Bar, then drop the text under the horizontal line on the WeekendMovies page.
   e. Use the Application Bar to review both files, make adjustments as needed to fine-tune the documents, such as eliminating blank lines between bullet items or moving graphics.
   f. Save both files.

3. **Edit the Application Bar.**
   a. Click Tools, click Settings, double-click Application Bar, then click the Reset button.
   b. Scroll down the Select items to appear on the bar list box, select three unchecked items to add to the Application Bar, click OK, then click Close.
   c. Move the items on the Application Bar so that all the small icons are centrally located.
   d. Resize the General Status button.
   e. Remove at least one item from the Application Bar, then make other adjustments to customize the Application Bar to meet your needs.
   f. Save your changes.

4. Create hyperlinks.

a. Be sure CityCenter is the current document.
b. Select the bullet item "Weekend at the Movies".
c. Click Tools, then click Hyperlink.
d. Click the Folder icon, select WeekendMovies, click Select, then click OK.
e. Save your work.
f. Click the WeekendMovies button on the Application Bar, scroll to the bottom of the page, type "Return to Deer Grove Village Home Page" several lines under the movie list.
g. Select "Return to Deer Grove Village Home Page" and make this a hyperlink using the Hyperlink Create button on the Hyperlink toolbar.
h. Click the Folder icon, select CityCenter, then accept it.
i. Save your work.
j. Test your hyperlinks: click the hyperlink "Return to Deer Grove Village Home Page", click the hyperlink "Weekend at the Movies".

5. Edit hyperlinks.

a. Use the Application Bar to be sure WeekendMovies is the current document.
b. Press [Ctrl][Home], then click the Hyperlink Next button on the Hyperlink Toolbar.
c. Press the Hyperlink Remove button on the Hyperlink toolbar, select "Return to Deer Grove Village home page", click the Hyperlink Create button on the Hyperlink Toolbar.
d. Click the Folder icon, select and accept CityCenter, click the check box next to Make text appear as a button, then click OK.
e. Save your work, then test the hyperlink by clicking the button.

6. Convert your document to HTML format.

a. Use the Application Bar to be sure CityCenter is the current document, click File, then click Internet Publisher.
b. Click Format as a Web Document, then click OK.
c. Scroll down the page to review the page and note any formatting changes that will need to be corrected, then click Web Viewer on the Internet Publishing toolbar.
d. Scroll down to view the page, then close the Web browser.
e. Click File, click Internet Publisher, then click Publish to HTML. (*Note:* Before accepting the settings, be sure the information in both text boxes in the dialog box identifies the student folder as the place to save.)
f. Close the file.

7. Edit a document in HTML format.

a. Open the CityCenter file that is in HTML format.
b. Be sure HTML is the file format in the text box, then click OK when the Convert File Format dialog box appears.
c. Click the HTML Properties button on the Property toolbar.
d. Click Text/Background Colors, select a background of your choice, then click OK.
e. Review the page and make other changes as needed, such as changing text or moving graphics.
f. Save your work as an HTML document in the Save Format dialog box.
g. Print a copy of the home page, then exit WordPerfect.

Independent Challenges

1. The United Investors Group has asked you, as their newly hired marketing consultant, to finish their home page. They want their home page to have a hyperlink to an explanation of their investment choices. As the key person in charge of overseeing the production of their home page, you will see it through from beginning to end.

To complete this independent challenge:

1. Start WordPerfect, open WP H-6 and save it as UIG HomePage, then open WP H-7 and save it as Investments.
2. Use the Application Bar to switch between documents. Review the UIG HomePage document against the guidelines for home page design presented in the first lesson, and make appropriate adjustments—such as adding a line for visitor feedback and a line to give Web design credit.
3. Use the Application Bar to drop and drag the sentence under the bullet Investment Choices: Explained which reads "The United Investors Group currently offers four investment choices to help you meet your financial goal." from the UIG HomePage document to the Investment document. Place the sentence so it becomes the first sentence in the copy under the heading "Investment Choices" in the Investment document.
4. Create the following hyperlinks: on UIG HomePage, create "Investment Choices: Explained" as a hyperlink to the file Investments; on Investments, create the title of the page "United Investors Group" as a hyperlink to the file UIG HomePage. Be sure to save each file after you create each hyperlink.
5. Test the hyperlink in the Investment document, then test your hyperlink in the UIG HomePage.
6. Save, print the document UIG HomePage, then exit WordPerfect.

2. You have been helping design the home page for your high school alma mater. Mary Fran Houlihan, the Class Reunion Chairperson, has sent you the invitation to the 10-year reunion. She would like you to create hyperlinks between the Central High School home page and the Class Reunion letter. She knows many former students are online and feels this will be one more way of getting the word out about the reunion.

To complete this independent challenge:

1. Start WordPerfect, open WP H-8 and save it as CentralHS, then open WP-9 and save it as HS Reunion.
2. Use the Application Bar to review both documents.
3. Customize the Application Bar to meet your needs. Add Fonts to the Application Bar, then move the Application Bar features to a place on the bar where they are easily accessible.
4. Delete any items on the Application Bar that you won't be using.
5. Add copy to both documents that can be used by visitors to provide feedback, such as "Call Central High at 604-555-2991 for additional information.", then add copy to give design credit and last updated information.
6. Create the following hyperlinks between the two documents: In the Central HS document, create a hyperlink for the bullet, "Homecoming" so that it links to the HS Reunion document. In the HS Reunion document, in the line that begins "Where:", create a hyperlink for the words "Central High School" so that it links to Central HS. Save your work as you create the hyperlinks.
7. Test the hyperlinks.
8. Save both documents, print them, then exit WordPerfect.

3. It's that time of year again. People are busy in their gardens, getting everything in order. Fields of Flowers, a mail order garden supply store, has asked you to design a home page for them and to link the home page to their catalog. They also want their customers to be able to order Fields of Flowers products online. You create a rough draft of the home page to present to your client, Fields of Flowers.

To complete this independent challenge:

1. Design the Fields of Flowers home page on paper; include a concept map to show the links.
2. Start WordPerfect. Use your design to create two new documents: one that will become the Fields of Flowers home page, and the other that will be an order form within the catalog. Or open WP H-10 and save the file as Flowers, then open WP H-11 and save the file as FlowersCat.
3. Use the Application Bar to switch between documents and to move copy as needed.
4. Create at least three links: one from the home page to the Catalog page, one from the Catalog page to the home page, and one from the information about the online order form on the Catalog page to the WP Construction file on your Student Disk. Save your work.
5. Edit at least one link so the words appear as a button.
6. Convert the home page to HTML format.
7. Edit the HTML file by changing the background, using a floral or back-to-nature motif.
8. Save your work, then print the home page and exit WordPerfect.

4. Home pages are a useful tool. If you have access to the Internet, you encounter home pages on a regular basis. Companies often capitalize on the "selling power" of their home pages by including pictures of their home pages in printed materials such as magazines, newspapers, or brochures. So even if you do not have access to the Internet, you can still find pictures of home pages in magazines and other print materials. Find examples of home pages on the Internet or in reading materials. Select one home page that you want to analyze, either online or in print, and then re-create it. First, you will comment on how the home page is set up. Then you will re-create the home page using WordPerfect Internet Publisher, altering it in a way that you believe will add value to its clients.

To complete this independent challenge:

1. Start WordPerfect, and in a new document window answer the following questions about the home page.
   - What is the purpose of the home page?
   - What information is included in the home page?
   - How many hyperlinks are included in the home page?
   - How effective are the graphics? Why do you think the graphics that were used on the home page were chosen? If you accessed the home page on the Internet, how did the graphics impact your ability to access the page?
   - What publishing information was listed on the home page, such as Web page designer and date that the home page was last modified?
   - Is there a way to provide feedback?
   - Save your work as "Home Page Analysis".
2. Re-create a portion of the home page as a new document. Save your work as "Home Page Re-creation".
3. Save your document as an HTML document.
4. Edit the background of the document to something you would choose, as opposed to what the creators of the original document have chosen.
5. After re-creating a portion of the home page, write a summary to explain how you made the home page, then how you altered it.
6. Spell check both documents, then save your work to your Student Disk.
7. Print your work, then exit WordPerfect. Include a photocopy of the original home page with the printout of your re-creation of the home page.

Visual Workshop

Create the home page shown in Figure H-20. Create a hyperlink to the file Omaha. Create the feedback information as a hyperlink to the file WS Construction. Show the feedback hyperlink as a button. Select a background pattern. List yourself as the Web page designer and use today's date as the date last updated. Save your work, print, then exit WordPerfect.

FIGURE H-20

Omaha International Investment Planners

International Headquarters

1952 Francis Lane

Freeport, MN 02871

1.800.555.1950

Omaha International Investment Planners has been established in the business since 1952. Since that time the company has become world leaders in developing international portfolio investments. Any investor, who is seriously considering expanding his/her portfolio, should contact Omaha International Investment Planners for information about potential investments. Visit the following sites to find out how easy it is to make your future golden.

- Omaha International Investment Planners: Company History
- International Portfolios
- Diamonds: now and in the future
- Shareholders' Letter
- Shareholders' Meeting
- Direct Link to your Personal Portfolio Manager
- Frequently Asked Questions
- Daily Quotes

Click here to be added to our email list.

Web Design: Clare

Last Updated: 6/5/1999

Glossary

Antonyms Words with opposite meanings.

Application Bar Bar that displays information about all open WordPerfect documents, such as identifying the active document, the current pointer, the current printer, date and time, and general status of the current selection.

Border Frames an image on a page.

Caption The text that describes a graphic image in a document.

Cell Intersection of a row and a column in WordPerfect tables.

Cell name or cell address A column letter and row number that identifies a cell's position in the table.

Charts Graphs, including bar charts, line charts, or pie charts, to represent numerical data.

Clipart Images or symbols stored on disk.

Clipboard A temporary storage place in computer memory that holds a text or graphics selection so that it can be moved or copied from one location to another.

Columns In a table, columns run vertically and are identified by letters.

Data Information that is entered into the cells of a WordPerfect table or the fields and records in a data file.

Data file Contains records to be merged with a form document.

Data source Contains the names, addresses, and any relevant and unique information for each person such as a data file or the address book. Form documents must be associated with a data source to create a merge.

Date code Inserts current date in the document.

Document Text and graphics entered in a word processor file.

Document window Area of the WordPerfect program window where you enter text and work with a document.

Drag and drop A method of moving or copying text without first storing it in the Clipboard.

Edit To modify a document in order to improve it by inserting, deleting, cutting, pasting, or moving text.

ENDFIELD A merge code that indicates the end of the current field in a data file.

ENDRECORD A merge code that indicates the end of the current record in a data file.

Equations Mathematical, scientific, or business formulas and expressions.

Field The smallest amount of information you can specify in a data file. One field might contain a person's last name and another field might contain a zip code.

FIELDNAMES A merge code that lists all the fields defined for a particular data file.

Fill pattern Fills empty spaces in an image with a pattern.

Find and replace Feature that identifies each occurrence of a word or phrase in a document, and replaces it with a new word or phrase.

Font The style and size of computer-generated letters and numbers.

Footer Information that appears at the bottom of each page in a document.

Form document Contains the text that remains the same in each letter when merged with a data file; also includes the field names that correspond to the fields in the data file.

Format To modify a document by changing the appearance of text in a document, including changing font size and style, adding attributes such as bold or italics, changing margins, setting tabs, indenting paragraphs, and changing line spacing.

Formula Calculates data in a WordPerfect table.

Formula Toolbar Contains buttons used to create formulas for data calculations.

Grammatik Feature that checks a document for grammatical errors.

Graphics Pictures or borders that can be inserted into a document to provide clarity, interest, or visual appeal.

Graphics box A box that can contain a figure, an equation, or text.

Hard page break Generates a new page at the insertion point no matter how much text is on the page. By contrast, a soft page break is determined by the margins and often changes depending on the amount of text on the page. *See also* soft page break.

Header Information that appears at the top of each page in a document.

Header row Information that is repeated in multiple-page tables. If a table spans more than one page, this row will always appear as the first row on each page.

Help system Online system that provides definitions and explanations of WordPerfect features, and step-by-step guidance to many WordPerfect tasks.

Home pages Electronically published documents on the Internet; usually the first place Web visitors look to find out about a company.

Hyperlinks Provide a "link" from one part of a document to another part of the same document—or to an entirely different document—so that the user seems to "jump" to the new location.

HyperText Markup Language (HTML) The language in which most documents published on the Internet (such as home pages) are written.

Images Charts, logos, and drawings created in WordPerfect graphic format or another graphic format.

Import Insert clipart images, logos, drawings, or other files into your document.

Indent Moves all text in the current paragraph to the next tab stop.

Insertion point Blinking vertical bar that indicates the position on the screen where text or graphics will be inserted.

Internet A world-wide network of computers.

Internet Browsers Used to view home pages on the Internet because they can read and display documents written in HTML; Netscape Navigator and Microsoft Internet Explorer are two examples of Internet browsers.

Internet Publisher Allows you to convert documents in WordPerfect format to HTML format.

Join cells Create one cell in a table from two cells.

Justification The alignment of text within the right and left margins of a document.

Line spacing The amount of space between lines of text in a document.

Mailing address Name and address of the recipient of a letter.

Make It Fit Feature that adjusts a WordPerfect document's margins, font size, and other elements automatically to fit a specified number of pages.

Margins Boundaries in a document that determine the amount of white space along the edges of a document.

Master document Contains information such as the Table of Contents, author information, or page numbering format; it also contains links to other documents called subdocuments. The master document ensures a consistent look across all subdocuments. *See also* subdocument.

Merge codes Used to separate each field from the others and to end each record in your data file; when inserted in your form document, they tell WordPerfect where to insert the field information from the associated data file.

Merge file Combines the information and text from the data file and the form document into one file.

Mouse pointer Indicates the position of the mouse on the screen.

Orphan A single line of text that appears alone at the bottom of a page.

Page break The next page of your document begins below this point; the previous page ends above this point.

Page/Zoom Full View that provides a full "What You See Is What You Get" (WYSIWYG) environment in which to work on documents.

Point size The size of a particular font, such as 10 or 12; one point equals 1/72 of an inch.

Printing Provides a paper copy of a document.

Property Bar Provides easy access to the most frequently-used features in the current activity, such as editing and formatting or working with a table.

QuickCorrect Feature that automatically corrects misspelled words as you enter them.

QuickCreate Feature that quickly creates and formats tables.

QuickFormat Feature that lets you copy fonts and alignment styles from one text selection to another.

QuickMenu Lists a set of options for a particular feature.

Random access memory (RAM) Area of computer memory that holds all currently open documents so that they can be edited.

Read-only Refers to a file that can be viewed but not changed under its current filename.

Record A collection of related fields, such as a person's first name, last name, company, title, company address, and zip code.

Relative reference A page number included directly in a document that always adjusts to represent the desired page as the document length changes.

Return address Name and address of the person sending a letter.

Reveal Codes bar Bar you can drag to open and size the Reveal Code window.

Reveal Codes window Displays the codes within a document that determine how text is formatted and displayed.

Rows In a table, rows run horizontally and are identified by numbers.

Rules The lines separating columns in a table.

Scrapbook A collection of clipart images.

Scroll bars Bars that allow you to move vertically and horizontally through a document that is larger than the document window.

Select To highlight text in order to work with it.

Sizing handles Small black squares on the graphics box that indicate that the graphics box is selected and ready to be edited, sized, or moved.

Soft page break Generates a new page. *See also* hard page break.

Spell Checker Feature that checks for misspelled words (words not contained in the main dictionary), duplicate words, words containing numbers, and irregular capitalization.

Split cells Create two or more cells in a table from one cell.

Subdocument Parts of a Master document; they can be opened, edited, and saved. *See also* Master document.

Suite Group of programs, such as Corel WordPerfect Suite 8, designed to run independently but work together as needed to increase productivity.

Suppress Option that allows you to skip the header, footer, page number, or watermark on a particular page without deleting it from any other pages.

Synonyms Words with similar meanings.

Tab Designated location in a line where text from the insertion point forward is aligned when you press [Tab]. Also known as a tab stop.

Tables Organize information into columns and rows without using tabs.

Thesaurus List of alternative words to enhance the vocabulary in a document.

Title bar Identifies the program name and the drive, directory path, and name of the current document.

Toggle button A button that turns a feature on or off each time it is clicked.

Toolbar Provides buttons for frequently-used commands.

Uniform Resource Locator (URL) A unique address assigned to each document on the World Wide Web.

User word list Supplemental dictionary in Spell Checker that contains words and phrases not contained in the main dictionary.

Watermark A drawing, logo, clipart image, or headline-sized text located behind the text in a document.

Web editor Allows you to make adjustments to your HTML documents such as identifying the title of the HTML document or changing the color of its hyperlinks or background.

Widow A single line of text at the top of the page.

Word processor Type of application software used to enter, organize, and present text on a page.

Word wrap The way text wraps around a graphic image in a document. Also refers to the way text continues from the end of one line to the beginning of the next line as you keep typing.

World Wide Web (Web) A service that provides organized information on the Internet in an easy-to-access format; also called the Web, W3, or WWW.

Index

Index

Index

►U

►V

►W

►Z